D1736208

Cold Days in Hell

NUMBER 141

**Williams-Ford
Texas A&M University
Military History Series**

William Clark Latham Jr.

Cold Days in Hell

AMERICAN POWs IN KOREA

Texas A&M University Press COLLEGE STATION

Library of Congress Cataloging-in-Publication Data

Latham, William C. (William Clark), 1961–
Cold days in hell : American POWs in Korea / William C. Latham Jr.—1st ed.
p. cm.—(Williams-Ford Texas A&M University military history series ; no. 141)
Includes bibliographical references and index.
ISBN-13: 978-1-60344-073-8 (book/cloth : alk. paper)
ISBN-10: 1-60344-073-9 (book/cloth : alk. paper)
ISBN-13: 978-1-60344-751-5 (ebook)
ISBN-10: 1-60344-751-2 (ebook)
1. Korean War, 1950–53—Prisoners and prisons, North Korean. 2. Prisoners of war—
Korea (North) 3. Prisoners of war—United States. I. Title. II. Series: Williams-Ford
Texas A&M University military history series ; no. 141.
DS921.L36 2013
951.904′927—dc23
2012016998

For those Americans
who died in captivity

Contents

Maps

Acknowledgments

In September 2000 I met Ralph Dixon and Bernie Gaeling at the Camp Two Survivors' POW reunion at West Point, where I was a member of the English Department faculty. I was familiar with the Korean War, but the two men told me harrowing stories of suffering, endurance, and heroism that I had never heard before. A colleague of mine, Col. Lee Wyatt, was also at the reunion that evening, and he and I reached the same conclusion: We needed to record these stories while there was still time. With the permission of Harry Hedlund, president of the Camp Two Survivors' group, Lee and I began contacting and interviewing former POWs. Lee retired to Florida in 2002.

I continued to gather materials, expanding the scope of my research to include American POWs held at other camps. With the help of generous grants from the US Military Academy and the US Army Command and General Staff College, I attended reunions around the country and made research trips to the Pentagon, the Truman Presidential Library in Independence, MO, the National Archives in College Park, MD, the US Army Military History Institute at Carlisle, PA, the National POW Museum in Andersonville, GA, the British National Archives in Kew Gardens, UK, and the Imperial War Museum in London.

Along the way I received encouragement and assistance from an enormous number of librarians, archivists, historians, colleagues, supervisors, former POWs, and their families. The following is a brief catalog of the many people whose help made this book possible:

West Point, NY: Col. Lee Wyatt, Col. Peter Stromberg, Col. Anthony Hartle, Col. James R. Kerrin, Jen Koch, Col. Tom Weafer, Col. Barney Forsythe, Brig. Gen. Dan Kauffman, Stephen Landowne, PhD

National Archives, College Park, MD: Dave Giordano, Tim Nenninger, PhD, Richard Boylan

Department of Defense POW/MIA Office (DPMO): Phillip O'Brien, Herb Artola, Dan Baufman

US Army Military History Institute, Carlisle, PA: Richard Baker, David Keough, PhD, Conrad Crane, PhD, Jiyul Kim, PhD, Sheila Jager, PhD

US Army Center of Military History, Washington, DC: Charles Hendricks, PhD, Bryan Hockensmith

Camp Two Survivors: Ralph Dixon, Bernie Gaeling, Florence Gaeling, Harry Hedlund, Bette Hedlund, Marvin King, Dan Oldewage, Jim Kiser, Ernest "Curly" Reid, Paul Roach, Fred Pelser, Marcia Pelser, Mike Dowe, Sidney Esensten, MD, Jack Doerty, Phil Peterson, Barney Dobbs, William Funchess, Filmore MacAbee, Robert Wood

Combined Arms Research Library, Fort Leavenworth, KS: Theresa Taylor, Michael Browne, Heather Turner, Rusty Rafferty, Kathy Buker, Tammy Garrison

Center for the Study of the Korean War, Independence, MO: Greg Edwards, Paul Edwards, PhD

National POW Museum, Andersonville, GA: Bridget Beers, Alan Marsh, PhD

National Korean War Ex-POW Association: Jack Chapman, Arden Rowley, Harold Addington, Chik Chikami

Wichita Eagle: Roy Wenzl, Travis Heying, Tom Shine

Tiger Survivors: Tim Casey, Wilbert "Shorty" Estabrook, Raymond Mellin

US Army Command and General Staff College (CGSC), Fort Leavenworth, KS: Dennis Barba, Pam Barba, Ann Barbuto, Robert Baumann, PhD, Stephen Bourque, PhD, Alan Boyce, Maj. Gen. Edward Cardone, Carolyn Conway, John House, PhD, Ed Kennedy, Wendell King, PhD, Zoltan Krompecher, John Kuehn, PhD, Gerald Leonard, Christina McReynolds, Bud Meador, James Martin, PhD, Scott Stephenson, PhD, Michael Weaver

I am particularly grateful to Raymond Lech, Phillip Chinnery, Robert Doyle, PhD, and Lewis Carlson, PhD, for their support and encouragement during my research. All four of these scholars have published significant studies on the same topic that I was studying, yet each of them generously gave me more time and attention than I deserved.

I owe a special debt of thanks to Lt. Col. (Ret.) John Wheatley, who challenged me long ago to make something of the gifts that God gave me, and to a series of supervisors, including Rick Kerin, Tom Weafer, Joyce DiMarco, Dave Cotter, and Mike Minyard, who gave me the time, funding, and support necessary to pursue this project. Willis Jackson, deputy director of the Department of Logistics and Resource Operations at CGSC, was especially patient and supportive of my efforts.

I also wish to thank Albert Makkay and Maureen Makkay of Centerville, MA, and the Rev. John Hotze of the Diocese of Wichita, KS, for their insights about Father Emil Kapaun.

I owe an immense debt to my good friends Paula Novash-Leahy, Michael Pearlman, PhD, and Steven Grove, PhD, who volunteered to edit the cumbersome and often confusing early drafts of this manuscript.

Finally, I am eternally gratefully to my wife and best friend, Cindy, and our children, Andrew and Olivia, who have supported my work on this manuscript throughout ten years of travel, research, and writer's block.

No work of history is perfect, and I am confident that other scholars will continue to study and reveal more about this unique chapter in US history. The following account relies on the most reliable witnesses and documents I could find, and I take full responsibility for any errors. This work represents my own opinions and does not reflect the official position of the United States Army or the Department of Defense.

Cold Days in Hell

Prologue

Private First Class Ray Mellin was playing pool in Kumamoto, Japan, when he learned about the Korean War. A radio announcer interrupted the Sunday-afternoon broadcast of a New York Yankees baseball game to report that North Korean forces had invaded the Republic of Korea (ROK). Mellin, a tall, twenty-two-year-old laboratory technician, had just stepped off the boat from the United States only days earlier, having survived a northern Pacific storm off the coast of Alaska. Mellin's previous assignment had been in the Pentagon's medical clinic. Shortly before shipping out for Japan, he remembered his hand shaking while taking a blood sample from Gen. Omar Bradley, then chairman of the Joint Chiefs. Bradley struck the young private as a "very nice man," but friends later teased Mellin about being sent to Japan as punishment.[1]

In fact, many troops agreed with Pfc. Leonard Korgie that occupation duty in Japan was "heaven." Korgie's infantry company was assigned to guard war criminals at Sugamo Prison and thus spent little time on military training, at least according to Korgie: "Life away from the prison consisted mostly of athletics, clubs, nightly dances, theater, and Japanese girls. . . . GI money and cigarettes went a long way on the black market."[2]

Mellin and Korgie were assigned to the 24th Infantry Division, one of four US Army divisions left in Japan after World War II. The American military's postwar drawdown had left these units with only two-thirds of their authorized strength. In addition, poor discipline, high turnover, and "shabby" equipment, left over from World War II and too often unserviceable, further eroded combat readiness. Whether five years of occupation duty had made American soldiers soft, as many historians later claimed, remains a topic for debate.[3]

Under the command of Gen. Douglas MacArthur, these US forces had helped rebuild Japan's shattered infrastructure and develop its consumer economy, creating a constitutional monarchy and a strong regional ally. The American presence and comparative wealth also fueled a booming trade in

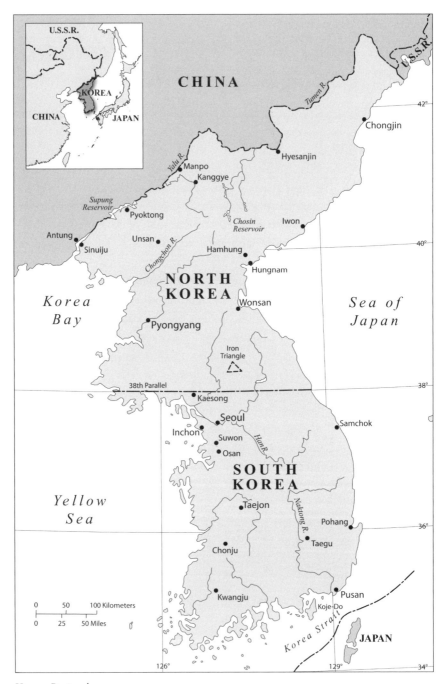

Korean Peninsula

prostitution and black-market profiteering. Nevertheless, MacArthur's success in rebuilding postwar Japan remains one of his greatest achievements.[4]

In the process, however, MacArthur had ignored his obligations as the senior military commander. He had paid little attention to training his units for combat and even less attention to the possibility of a war on the Korean peninsula. In fairness, official responsibility for Korea shifted from MacArthur's Far Eastern Command (FECOM) to the State Department when Truman withdrew US forces in 1949. Furthermore, several US officials, including MacArthur, had publicly indicated on several occasions that the American global "line of defense" did not include Korea.[5]

Still, Korea's strategic position made it a likely place for confrontation, and the four American divisions in Japan represented the region's most significant military deterrent to communist adventurism. Eighth Army commander Walton J. Walker had spent the previous year trying to whip these divisions into shape. His training program was still in progress, and US forces in Japan focused on defending the Japanese islands against a Soviet attack. They had no plans for defending their South Korean allies; they didn't even have maps of the peninsula.[6]

Introduction

An old axiom claims that truth is the first casualty in war. This principle seems particularly applicable to American service members captured during the Korean conflict. Although their fate played a crucial role in the war's outcome, historians tend to overlook both their ordeal in captivity and their subsequent mistreatment after repatriation.

On the other hand, the prisoners of Korea have repeatedly served as scapegoats. Citing their appalling death rate and exaggerated claims of widespread misconduct, critics pointed to this group of prisoners as proof that the US Army had lost its way, that American society had gone soft, and that the prisoners themselves were somehow complicit in their own demise. Those who survived captivity were subsequently branded as traitors and potential spies, thanks to anticommunist fervor and the Pentagon's own hamfisted efforts to prosecute alleged collaborators.

Meanwhile, communist success in persuading twenty-one Americans to refuse repatriation—while employing starvation and torture to coerce radio broadcasts and germ-warfare confessions from others—fed rumors that the enemy had somehow managed to brainwash their prisoners. Although scholars later demonstrated that the rate of prisoner misconduct in Korea was similar to that in other wars, the subsequent cloud of suspicion cast a long shadow over the survivors, obscuring the horrific details of their ordeal while unfairly tarnishing their honor.

Sadly, their suffering does not make the experience of Korean War prisoners of war (POWs) unique. True, their captors generally treated them with casual brutality while providing no clothing, shelter, or medical care, especially during the first deadly winter of 1950–1951. These depredations, however, parallel the mistreatment of American POWs by the Japanese in World War II, as well as the abuse of prisoners by both sides during the American Civil War and by British forces during the American Revolution.

Two important issues, however, separate Korean War POWs from those Americans captured in previous wars. First, Korea marked the first American experience with systemic enemy manipulation of POWs for propaganda purposes. The limited success that communist captors enjoyed from this manipulation is due, at least in part, to the fact that American service members had never before endured such determined efforts to control their behavior. Second, the publicity surrounding this manipulation, whose success was exaggerated in media reports and by the prisoners themselves upon repatriation, caused Pentagon leaders, particularly in the army, to react hastily and unwisely.

The most important work in this field is that of Dr. Albert Biderman, whose 1963 book, *March to Calumny,* thoroughly and convincingly refuted claims that the American POWs in Korea had betrayed their country. More recently, several other distinguished authors have sought to explain what really happened to American prisoners in Korea. Australian scholar Jeffrey Grey has also contributed greatly to this field of study through his analysis of Commonwealth POWs, whose experience paralleled that of American prisoners in many ways. In recent years, Robert Doyle's *Voices of Captivity,* Phillip Chinnery's *Atrocity!,* Raymond Lech's *Broken Soldiers,* and Lewis Carlson's *Remembered Prisoners of a Forgotten War* have examined specific elements of the Korean War POW experience in great detail. Although my own research follows in their footsteps, each of these four gentlemen has been remarkably generous with his time, assistance, and encouragement.

Americans were hardly the only prisoners captured (and mistreated) by communist forces. Service members from nearly every member of the United Nations task force, most notably the British and Turkish forces, endured communist captivity. The overwhelming majority of prisoners captured by the enemy were soldiers of the Republic of Korea. Communist forces repatriated more than eight thousand South Koreans during prisoner exchanges, but countless thousands more either died in captivity or remained behind in North Korea. While this account mentions these prisoners only in passing, their story merits significantly more attention than it has received to date.

This manuscript focuses primarily on the ordeal of American POWs before, during, and after their captivity. Based on memoirs, trial transcripts, debriefings, declassified government reports, published analyses, and media coverage, as well as conversations, interviews, and correspondence with several dozen former prisoners, this work seeks to correct misperceptions that linger six decades after the American prisoners of war came home. In short, it seeks to capture that most vulnerable and elusive of fugitives, the truth.

Note: The historiography of the Korean War offers a multitude of different spellings and punctuations for the Chinese and Korean names and places that are central to the conflict. For the sake of consistency with previous accounts, this work uses the same spelling found in US military documents of the time.

1   The Summer Soldiers

It would be good for someone among the prisoners to make a statement on the radio that the treatment of prisoners by the Koreans is very good.
Joseph Stalin

At 0330 hours on the morning of June 25, 1950, the North Korean People's Army (NKPA) fired a short, heavy bombardment at key targets south of the 38th Parallel. At precisely 0400, armored columns crossed the border along six major attack routes, the most important of which was the corridor through Uijonbu toward the South Korean capital of Seoul. Accustomed to sporadic gunfire along the border, many civilians, including Larry Zellers, an American missionary in Kaesong, assumed the predawn ruckus was merely another "rice raid." He would regret that mistake for the next three years. He and his fellow missionaries spent them in North Korean prison camps.[1]

At Kaesong, the attackers were opposed by a single regiment of South Korean infantry, dispersed along a fifteen-kilometer front. The North Koreans had concealed their attack preparations so successfully that on the morning of the invasion, many South Korean soldiers were absent on weekend passes, leaving only eleven thousand troops along the 38th Parallel to man the border defenses.[2] Behind the armored columns came agents of the North Korean Home Affairs Department. Their mission was to identify and arrest enemies of the people, including land owners, government officials, North Korean refugees, and Western "spies," such as Zellers and his fellow missionaries.[3]

The NKPA invaded with more than one hundred thousand soldiers, many of whom were veterans of the Chinese civil war. North Korean premier Kim Il Sung had planned the invasion for more than a year, hoping to crush the newborn Republic of Korea's pro-American regime and reunify the peninsula under his rule. With generous Soviet support, Kim had built a modern, mechanized juggernaut armed with high-performance aircraft, self-propelled artillery, and T-34 tanks. In addition, Soviet advisors trained the

The epigraph that opens this chapter is from a ciphered cable sent by Stalin to the Soviet ambassador in Pyongyang, North Korea, on July 13, 1950.

General of the Army Douglas MacArthur (l.) and Dr. Syngman Rhee, Korea's first President (r.). (Courtesy Defense Imagery Management Operations Center [NARA file # 111-SC-306875])

NKPA and provided battle plans for the invasion. North Korean spies and infiltrators had been gathering intelligence for months.[4]

Koreans had endured the first four decades of the twentieth century under the harsh colonial rule of the Japanese Empire. When that empire collapsed in 1945, American and Soviet diplomats agreed to divide Korea into "zones of influence," separated by the 38th Parallel, until national elections could be held (see map 1). In the north, the Soviets sealed the border, rejected the proposed elections, and installed a "people's government" led by a young Stalin protégé, Kim Il Sung. In the south, the US Army reluctantly provided combat units to administer the southern zone, guard the border, and assist in the creation of a competent indigenous constabulary force. In 1948, South Koreans elected a representative parliament and their first president, right-wing nationalist Syngman Rhee. President Truman withdrew the combat units in 1949, leaving behind a skeleton crew of advisors—the Korean Military Advisors' Group (KMAG)—to continue training South Korean forces.[5]

On paper, these forces seemed capable of repulsing the northern invaders. The army of the Republic of Korea (ROK), whom Westerners commonly referred to as "ROKs," fielded ninety-eight thousand soldiers, trained and equipped by their American sponsors. Unlike their northern cousins, however, ROK units were armed only with light artillery, antiquated anti-tank weapons, and no armored units. In addition, the ROK Army suffered from desultory training and often inept leadership. Syngman Rhee was both a staunch anticommunist and a corrupt and brutal dictator. The ROK Army included courageous, professional officers, but promotion within its ranks depended more on political patronage than competence. As David Halberstam would later write, it was "the most marginal kind of army fighting to defend the most marginal kind of country, a nation that did not yet really exist."[6]

The US Embassy in Seoul had realized the threat of an invasion, but American officials initially misread both the North Koreans' strength and the South Koreans' weakness. At midnight on the evening of the attack, US ambassador John Muccio belatedly directed the evacuation of American civilians from the peninsula. While the Americans fled, 1.5 million residents of Seoul waited for news from the front. Several dozen diplomats and missionaries from other Western nations ignored Muccio's directive and were subsequently imprisoned by the North Koreans.[7]

The South Koreans fought heroically in places, but even suicide bombers could not stop the North Korean tanks. As the enemy advanced, battered ROK units flooded into the capital, spreading panic among both residents and government leaders. At 0215 on June 28, ROK engineers destroyed the Han River bridges, killing hundreds of their own soldiers and refugees and stranding more than forty-four thousand ROK troops north of the Han. In less than seventy-two hours, the South Korean retreat had become a full-scale rout.[8]

America Responds

When word of the attack reached MacArthur's headquarters that Sunday morning, the general shrugged off the report as "a border incident." Later that day, a still-confident MacArthur reassured Assistant Secretary of State John Foster Dulles that the ROKs could fend for themselves.[9] Back in Washington, Truman's secretary of state, Dean Acheson, took the initial reports far more seriously. Acheson received Ambassador Muccio's initial cable at 2200 hours on the evening of Saturday, June 24 (Washington is thirteen hours behind Seoul). He immediately notified the president, who was spending the weekend at home in Independence, Missouri.[10]

After flying back to Washington on Sunday, Truman met with his cabinet. Earlier the same day, with the Soviet delegation absent (protesting the United Nations' refusal to seat Communist China), the UN Security Council voted 9–0 to renounce the "armed attack" and demand an immediate North Korean withdrawal.[11] Heavily influenced by Acheson's advice and fearing a broader Soviet offensive, Truman made several decisions that would soon commit US forces to combat on the Korean peninsula. These included orders for MacArthur to assume command of all US forces in Asia, protect the evacuation of American citizens, support the Republic of Korea with air and naval assets, and provide arms and equipment to the ROK Army.[12]

It was already Monday morning in northeast Asia when the Pentagon forwarded Truman's message. North of Seoul, the ROK Army was retreating toward its capital. In Tokyo, MacArthur alerted all combat units in the Far East for potential deployment to Korea. On Tuesday, MacArthur sent Brig. Gen. John Church to better assess the situation on the ground. Church landed at Suwon, twenty miles south of Seoul, in the midst of the panic. North Korean tanks had entered Seoul's northern suburbs, three ROK divisions had disintegrated, and many KMAG advisers were trapped north of the Han. Church sent back a grim report: Only American ground troops could salvage the situation and push back the attackers.[13]

Back in Washington, Truman briefed congressional leaders on the crisis; both the House and the Senate quickly approved a one-year extension to the draft and authorized Truman to call up the reserves. In New York, the UN Security Council (with the Soviets still absent) voted to provide aid to South Korea. The resolution embarrassed the Soviets and, in principle, committed all UN members to defend South Korea by force of arms. For the United States, the resolution provided political support for a military response, but it also linked American military forces to an often problematic coalition.[14]

On Thursday morning, MacArthur landed at Church's headquarters. Together with President Rhee and a motorcade of American and South Korean officials, MacArthur drove north to the Han River to view the situation for himself.[15] After watching the ROK forces withdraw south from the Han River, MacArthur sent a message to the Pentagon, echoing Church's initial sentiment: "The only assurance for holding the present line, and the ability to regain later the lost ground, is through the introduction of US ground combat forces into the Korean battle area."[16]

MacArthur sought permission to send a regimental combat team to

Korea immediately, followed later by two infantry divisions. American aircraft were already fully engaged, having bombed North Korean airfields and downed several North Korean fighters. Deployment of US ground forces, however, would mean a far larger commitment to the conflict. Truman approved without delay, thus committing the nation to a slippery slope. The initial mission to repel the invaders later became a crusade to "liberate" the entire peninsula. MacArthur, meanwhile, soon began asking for more men and matériel on the premise that northeast Asia was as good a place as any to confront and destroy communism once and for all.

Task Force Smith

At 2230 hours that Friday evening, Lt. Col. Charles "Brad" Smith was awakened in his quarters in Japan and summoned to an emergency meeting at regimental headquarters.[17] There, Smith received orders to immediately deploy part of his battalion to Korea. Due to limited air transport, Smith could take only half of his battalion: two rifle companies, part of the headquarters, and attached heavy weapons and communications squads.[18]

A combat veteran of the Pacific campaign, Smith had commanded an infantry company in Hawaii when the Japanese attacked Pearl Harbor. Now he commanded a battalion in the 24th Infantry Division. Smith was an exceptional leader, but he faced the same obstacles as other American commanders in Japan: inexperienced soldiers, limited training opportunities, personnel and supply shortages, and worn-out equipment, especially the radios and antitank weapons. Still, his battalion was the best trained outfit in the 21st Regiment, which was stationed on Kyushu, Japan's southernmost island and the end of the American supply line. The regiment's location also made it the American combat unit closest to Korea.[19]

Private First Class Bob Roy remembers that evening beginning like most other Friday nights in Japan:

> As usual, the whole camp cleared out except for the guys who had duty. Everybody else went into town and stayed until midnight curfew. At midnight, we all came in to the barracks pretty well feeling our oats. We'd just gotten to bed when one of our lieutenants came in, threw on the lights and said "Pack your gear. We're headed for Korea."[20]

Despite the rude awakening, Roy and his fellow soldiers quickly gathered their equipment and loaded vehicles for the seventy-five-mile ride through pouring rain to Itazuke Air Base. Among them was Private First Class Mellin, reassigned as a medic in the battalion's aid station. From Itazuke, Smith's troops flew to Pusan, with orders to head north immediately, make contact with Church, and "block the main road as far north as possible."[21]

At Pusan, poor weather further delayed the off-loading of equipment. At 2000 hours, Smith's tiny contingent finally made its way past cheering crowds to the rail station at Pusan, loaded its equipment on flat cars, and began moving toward the sound of the guns. Over the next seventy-two hours, the Americans moved north and west along Highway 1, the main corridor between Pusan and Seoul. On July 2 General Church greeted Smith in Taejon and told him, "We're going to move you up to support the ROKs and give them moral support." That evening the Americans resumed their movement to the northwest.[22]

Bob Roy's recollections of the movement were more prosaic:

> I had no idea where we were going. All I knew was we were headed for the front, wherever the hell that was. I was only a Pfc., and when they tell you to go somewhere, you go. You don't ask questions.
>
> What I remember most about those four days was not getting any sleep. And the flies. The flies would carry you away. We were in this little Korean village, before we went up to our final position, and Marguerite Higgins showed up and started interviewing us, and the flies . . . we were spitting them out of our mouths as we talked.
>
> And the stench. The Koreans put human excrement in their rice paddies, and God did it smell.[23]

On Tuesday, July 4, Smith's task force was joined by an American battery of six 105-millimeter howitzers from the 58th Field Artillery Battalion, which had sailed from Japan immediately behind Smith's troops. With the artillery, Smith's outfit now numbered approximately 540 men, but there were no ROK units to link up with, and there were no friendly units on either flank. The only ROK soldiers that Smith's men saw were retreating or planting explosive charges along the bridges. The closest American combat unit was the 34th Infantry Regiment, which had arrived that morning at Pusan, one hundred miles to the southeast. Amid a cold drizzle on the evening of July 4, Smith's infantrymen dug in along a ridgeline on both sides of Highway 1 at Juk-Mi Pass. The two rifle companies occupied a one-mile front that dominated both the highway and a parallel rail line to the east.[24]

From the muddy ridge, Smith could see northward to Suwon, where the NKPA's 4th Division was preparing to resume its advance down Highway 1. Each of Smith's soldiers carried 120 rounds of ammunition, and Smith also had two 75-millimeter recoilless rifles, two 4.2-inch mortars, four 60-millimeter mortars, and six 2.36-inch rocket launchers (bazookas). He positioned most of his artillery a mile south along the highway, with a string of communication wire linking Smith's command post to the guns.[25]

Unfortunately, Smith had no barrier material, no antitank mines, and worst of all, no air support. America boasted the most advanced air force in the world, but Task Force Smith would receive no help on that gray morning. During the previous week, American and Australian fighters had quickly established air superiority over the peninsula, but costly and embarrassing friendly fire attacks against retreating ROK columns had forced Tokyo to restrict air attacks to targets north of the Han. Even had close air support been available, Smith still lacked a tactical control party with which to direct fire.[26]

At dawn on July 5, the rain-soaked Americans spotted movement out of Suwon. By 0730, Smith could hear and see eight T-34 tanks moving through a steady rain toward his position. At 0800, high explosive shells from Smith's howitzers landed on and around the tanks, 2,000 meters from the American line. The tanks continued forward, unfazed by the exploding shells. When they were 700 meters away, Smith's recoilless rocket crews began firing from the flanks. The Americans scored several direct hits, but the 75-millimeter rounds bounced off, and the tanks kept coming.[27]

As the T-34s climbed toward the pass, Lieutenant Ollie Connor grabbed a bazooka and fired several rounds point blank into the rear of the tanks, where their armor was most vulnerable. Again, the rounds had no effect.[28] Finally, an American howitzer managed to stop two of the tanks as they approached the southern exit from the pass, but the gun crew fired all six of its antitank rounds in the process. The remaining six tanks moved past the two disabled vehicles, destroyed the American howitzer, and continued along the highway toward the rest of the artillery battery.[29]

Ten minutes behind the first wave came a second group of tanks. Traveling in small groups of two and three, these ignored the artillery and small-arms fire, and rolled south through the pass toward the American artillery battery and beyond it, the village of Osan. In the space of an hour, thirty-three tanks rolled through the American roadblock.[30] After an hour's lull, Smith observed another enemy column approaching from Suwon, with trucks, dismounted infantry, and three more tanks in the lead. Despite the futility of their first two engagements and the overwhelming force advancing upon them, Smith's two infantry companies held fast in their positions.[31]

Communications between North Korean units was remarkably poor, and the two infantry regiments moving slowly toward the pass evidently did not realize American infantry were waiting. Smith also had communications problems. With better luck, the American howitzers could have decimated the approaching infantry with well-placed artillery fire, but enemy tanks had severed the communications wire between Smith and his artillery. Instead, the Americans surprised the approaching column with a hail of small-arms and mortar fire. As trucks exploded on the road, North Korean infantrymen scrambled for cover.[32]

The enemy tanks, however, closed to within 200 meters and began spraying the American positions with machine-gun fire. Meanwhile, North Korean infantry advanced through rice paddies on both flanks of Smith's position, and enemy shells began exploding near the American lines. Smith's infantrymen repelled several direct assaults, but by early afternoon their ammunition was running low, casualties were mounting, and North Korean units were outflanking their position. Smith ordered his units to begin withdrawing south toward Osan. Under punishing enemy machine-gun fire, the American withdrawal turned into chaos. Remnants of Smith's task force dissolved into small groups and scrambled through the mud toward safety.[33]

Bob Roy was among the Americans who narrowly escaped:

> I went over a railroad embankment, running like a bastard, because the North Koreans were still firing at us from the hills. Everybody was with me when I went over the embankment, but after running three or four hundred yards I turned around and, Jesus, I'm all alone.
>
> I'm in the middle of all these rice paddies, and I'm thinking, "Where the hell is everybody?"
>
> I found out, forty years later, that everybody else went down the right side of the railroad tracks. They went due south, where the North Korean tanks were, and they got captured. Most of them spent the war as POWs. I went down the left side, kind of southeast, because I wasn't about to go where those tanks were.[34]

Ray Mellin wasn't so lucky. The lab technician from Connecticut had deployed with the battalion headquarters as a combat medic. When word came to fall back, he and a small band of wounded soldiers crawled to safety through a drainage ditch southeast of the ridgeline. Moving south, they avoided enemy infantry and made their way back over the next three hours toward Osan:

We had this young officer with us . . . and out in front of us, some Korean soldiers came out. And he said, "It's okay, they're South Koreans." And then I looked and I saw a red star on their helmets and on their caps and I said "I don't think we're alright; I think they are North Koreans." I knew that represented communism. I was always interested in history, but we heard so little news about communism. I heard a lot more afterwards.

But they lined us up on the road there, and a friend of mine standing next to me had a hand grenade behind him. He said, "Should I throw this?"

And I said, "Wait a little bit," because they had lined up a machine gun and we thought they were going to wipe us out.

And this colonel came up on a big white stallion, and he jumped off. And he came up to a fellow next to me, Tomeo Tadaki, and he took his pistol out and held it at Tomeo's head, and he said, I'll never forget the words, "No ponji wak a doo." He asked him in Japanese, "Do you understand Japanese?"

And Tomeo, in perfect Japanese, said "Witashi wakanai," which means "I don't understand anything."

And he smacked him across the face with the pistol. We thought he was going to shoot him, but then he took him and used him as a translator. And then they said they were going to take us north to Seoul, which they did.[35]

While Mellin's group was being captured, enemy soldiers committed the first of many war crimes to come against defenseless American prisoners. Back at Juk-Mi Pass, the Americans had left behind more than thirty severely wounded comrades at the battalion command post. When the North Koreans arrived, they shot and stabbed the helpless Americans.[36]

Captain Ambrose Nugent, the senior artillery liaison officer in Smith's headquarters, was one of the many who failed to hear the withdrawal order. Seeing that the American positions were abandoned, he initially headed south toward the artillery battery. When he found the route deserted, however, he returned to the command post—just in time to witness the massacre.[37]

Nugent hid in the underbrush as the North Koreans moved south, but less than two hours later he was discovered by a follow-on unit:

Immediately upon being captured, I was severely beaten with fists and rifle butts. All my personal possessions and M43 jacket were confiscated. With hands wired behind my back, I was forced to march about ten miles south toward Pyontek [sic] with a fifty caliber machine gun balanced on my left shoulder . . . I met three American soldiers recently captured . . . We were arraigned and tried before a people's court and told we were to be shot. We were bound with more wire about the biceps.

A Korean officer entered and suddenly we were started on a march northward toward Suwon, the four being tied together. During this march, five

American soldiers were observed lying beside the road, hands bound behind their backs, and shot through the head. We arrived at the outskirts of Suwon about 0200, 6 July 1950. Here I was again beaten by a Korean lieutenant colonel. We were then moved into the city through a warehouse-type building where I observed one human suspended from a rafter by a rope or cable. The body did not move. The light was rather dim and the body could not be identified. We were moved through a few short streets after which we were taken into a rather large well-lighted building where we found a long line of Korean civilians. One stated that this was a people's court and many were being sentenced to death by shooting, some by hanging. Once more a Korean interfered and we were placed in a jail cell in the same building. The cell contained several Korean civilians that were in serious condition from severe beatings.

After daylight on 6 July, we were removed from the jail cell and told we were going to Seoul by truck. A bus appeared and also about 35 more American prisoners. All were loaded into the bus and we started for Seoul. One mile up the road, the bus turned off the highway, became mired, and we were marched back to the highway and started north. Three miles north of Suwon on the road bed we saw another American, hands wired behind his back and shot through the head from behind his right ear . . . Water and crackers was the food given us for the day . . . We were taken to the capitol building in Seoul. The number of prisoners at this time amounted to about forty, all Americans. There were no deaths in this group up to this time and although there were several wounded, it was impossible to obtain medical treatment.[38]

For Nugent, Mellin, and the other prisoners, the ordeal was just beginning.

Hasty Retreat

As North Koreans drove Smith's infantrymen from Juk-Mi Pass on July 5, a second unit from the 24th Infantry Division, the 34th Infantry Regiment, began digging in at the villages of Pyongtaek and Ansong, ten miles to the south. The division commander, Maj. Gen. William F. Dean, knew Korea as well any senior officer in Japan, having served there during the postwar occupation. He ordered the regiment's two understrength battalions to delay the enemy here because these positions represented the narrowest and most defensible point along the corridor from Seoul to Taejon.[39]

The regiment had sailed from Kyushu with two thousand men—including sixty soldiers released from the stockade—and had moved north a day behind Smith's soldiers in search of the enemy.[40] Dean did not yet appreciate the enemy's strength, and without close air support, effective antitank weapons, or supporting artillery, Dean's decision to commit this relatively weak force on such short notice was another gamble. With the ROK Army in disarray, however, and with the rest of his own division still en route from Japan, Dean badly needed more time and space to organize his forces.[41]

On the afternoon of July 5, South Korean refugees and ROK stragglers trudging through Pyongtaek warned the Americans of enemy tanks approaching from Osan. With several reporters in tow, an American reconnaissance platoon boldly sped north to delay them, but their 2.34-inch bazookas again proved useless against T-34s, and the Americans quickly withdrew. That evening, survivors from Smith's task force reached Pyongtaek and reported the defeat at Juk-Mi Pass. The 1st Battalion destroyed a small bridge where the highway crossed a stream about 600 yards north of its defensive line.[42]

At dawn on July 6, a North Korean column rolled into view and halted at the blown bridge. The American defenders opened sporadic fire with small arms and mortars. Enemy tanks returned fire, while infantry dispersed to both flanks, crossed the shallow stream, and began enveloping the American positions. American officers and noncommissioned officers fought bravely, but many junior enlisted soldiers seemed stunned by the North Korean attack and failed to fire their weapons. Commanders later determined that many of the American rifles were either jammed with dirt or improperly reassembled by the soldiers carrying them.[43]

As enemy infantry closed on their positions, the Americans abandoned much of their equipment and fled toward Pyongtaek in disorder. Officers tried to regain control of their dispirited men, but now rumors spread that North Korean troops had executed four surrendering Americans.[44] With permission from the regimental commander, Col. Jay Lovless, the entire battalion withdrew six miles farther to the south to a blocking position south of Ch'onan.[45] As discipline evaporated, the retreating soldiers discarded helmets, ponchos, web gear, rifles, and even their shoes. Fortunately, the North Koreans did not pursue.[46]

On the regiment's right flank, meanwhile, the 3rd Battalion withdrew from Andong without firing a shot. Lovless had ordered the withdrawal at the direction of Brig. Gen. Bittman Barth, who was temporarily acting as Dean's second-in-command. Barth ordered Lovless to consolidate his two battalions at Ch'onan. Dean was furious when he learned of the hasty withdrawal that afternoon. Arriving at the regimental command post, he sent Barth to the rear and ordered Lovless to send units north the next morning to delay the enemy's southern advance. Meanwhile, he replaced Lovless with Col. Robert Martin, whom Dean had personally requested from Japan.[47]

The next day produced more confusion and more tragedy. In compliance with Dean's orders, the 3rd Battalion moved north at dawn to occupy defensive positions along Highway 1. When Maj. John Dunn, the regimental operations officer, drove forward a few hours later, he found the positions abandoned and the battalion marching back to the south. Unable to locate the battalion commander, Dunn raced back to Ch'onan to report the withdrawal.[48]

Colonel Martin ordered Dunn to take command of the battalion and turn it around.[49] Speeding back up the highway, Dunn intercepted a retreating mob of American soldiers and persuaded them to return to their defensive positions. Dunn and a small group of officers moved ahead of the column in two jeeps but drove into a North Korean ambush, in which he and several others were wounded. Crawling from the disabled jeep, Dunn saw an American column approaching from the south. Again, the North Koreans opened fire. After only a few minutes, however, the Americans withdrew; enemy soldiers captured Dunn and his wounded comrades several hours later.[50]

Leaving the 1st Battalion in place to the south, Martin took personal command of the 3rd Battalion and ordered its companies to dig in north and west of Ch'onan.[51] That night, North Korean infiltrators made their way into town, prompting several firefights. At dawn, the T-34s followed. In an effort to rally his troops, Martin led a squad of soldiers through the streets hunting for the tanks but was killed by an enemy tank round. The 3rd Battalion collapsed, and most of its soldiers were killed or captured.[52] Dean ordered the survivors to withdraw toward the Kum River, the last natural obstacle before the Naktong River and the port of Pusan. He also warned MacArthur of a disaster in the making: "[T]he North Korean Army, the North Korean soldier, and his status of training and the quality of his equipment have been underestimated."[53]

Political Pawns

In Seoul, Ambrose Nugent was learning more about North Korean capabilities. By July 10, Nugent found himself the senior officer among seventy-two American prisoners crowded into a single room in the South Korean capitol building. That morning, guards took Nugent and five other Americans to a vacant office and ordered them to sign blank sheets of paper. When they refused, a North Korean officer threatened to execute all of them. Having seen enough dead prisoners already, Nugent took the threat seriously. He and the others signed the blank sheets.[54]

Nugent was then driven to a radio station and ordered to read a prepared speech on the air. Guards beat him with rifle butts and pistol-whipped him in the mouth, breaking several teeth. Finally, an officer with pliers began prying off the finger nails on Nugent's right hand.[55] Nugent capitulated, reading a brief script that condemned the "intervention of the capital monopolists of the US" and calling on his fellow Americans to "come over to the People's Army of Korea." In Okinawa, American radio operators monitored the speech, the first of more than 250 such broadcasts made by American prisoners during the war. Regardless of the circumstances, the fact that American prisoners cooperated with their communist captors would later have an enormous impact on American society, especially within the military.[56]

That same afternoon, Major Dunn and forty other POWs arrived in Seoul. The North Koreans organized a large demonstration against American imperialism, formed the exhausted Americans into columns, and marched them through the streets. Those at the head of the column carried banners with anti-American slogans written in Korean characters, while the surviving residents of Seoul jeered and pelted the soldiers with stones and other objects.[57] When the column reached the rail station, a North Korean officer lectured the men on the crimes committed by American and South Korean soldiers. Finally, the men boarded the train and rattled north toward Pyongyang, arriving the next afternoon.[58]

Upon their arrival in the North Korean capital, the prisoners stood in 100-degree heat while a Security Police colonel, dubbed "Frog Eyes," delivered a second harangue. The men finally received food and water and were forced to conduct another propaganda march, complete with banners and angry protesters. "Frog Eyes" led the column in a jeep. As communist photographers and film crews recorded the scene, Korean guards used bayonets to prod the stragglers, many of whom were already suffering from battlefield wounds. The North Koreans had provided no medical assistance to this point. One enlisted man died of heat exhaustion during the march, and other seriously wounded men were carried by their comrades.[59]

After several miles, the Americans reached a schoolhouse in northcentral Pyongyang. Dunn and several other severely injured men were removed to the city hospital. "We received special kindness from the old ladies who cleaned the building," reported Dunn. "These women also brought us our food and washed our clothes. The people in charge were not friendly, but they treated us well and did the best they could with limited facilities."[60]

Now, the POWs had to worry about their own forces. As Ray Mellin recalls:

> Shortly after we were in the school building—I think the next day—our planes came over and strafed the school building, which was pretty horrendous because I think there was 10 or 12 guys killed. But just having those, I guess, .50 caliber shells bouncing around the cement floors was really horrendous. Another time, the bombers were coming over and they were bombing. The concussion was so great that you would actually lift off the floor, and of course, the windows were blown out.
>
> So, that was pretty scary. But we were able to cook. They had these huge pots out in back, and one of the guys was bright enough, he took ashes and spelled out "P-O-W" around the pots. And so, after that, when the planes came over, they didn't strafe us anymore. . . . We watched the bombing all around us. In fact, there was a tunnel there, and every time the planes came over, there was a locomotive that would run into the tunnel so they couldn't get him, and I guess one weekend, Saturday or Sunday, some Navy planes came in, and they actually dive bombed, or skip-bombed, into both ends of the tunnel and sealed off the tunnel.[61]

Mellin and the other Americans were relocated a few days after their arrival in Pyongyang. The new location, known as the "brick schoolhouse," would be their home for the next six weeks. During that period, American POWs continued to arrive from the south, and by September, the number of Americans at the brick schoolhouse had risen to 725. Compared to captivity in the south, life at the schoolhouse proved relatively civilized. The prisoners cooked their own meals and had access to water, latrines, and rudimentary medical care. There was even a sympathetic Korean doctor in residence, who claimed that his father had once served as an interpreter for General Hap Arnold.[62] Medical supplies proved scarce, however, and nearly two dozen Americans died during this period, many of them from the accumulated effects of battlefield wounds.[63]

Chochiwon

While the first group of American prisoners moved north to Pyongyang, their comrades in the 24th Infantry Division continued to fight and die along Highway 1. On the foggy morning of July 10, North Korean troops attacked the forward positions of the 21st Regiment at Chochiwon, a couple of miles north of the Kum River. American artillery and heavy weapons punished the first wave of enemy soldiers, but North Korean tanks soon punched through the American line, while North Korean infantry gradually maneuvered around both flanks. Outflanked and unable to communicate with their supporting artillery, the Americans withdrew, only to discover enemy roadblocks to their rear. Unable to force the roadblocks, the soldiers abandoned their vehicles and set out on foot. According to historian Allan Millett, in battle after battle during these first weeks, the North Koreans employed the same basic tactics, overran a series of American defensive positions, and captured hundreds of lost and exhausted American stragglers wandering in the Korean countryside.[64]

Charles Kinnard was one of the many Americans captured at Chochiwon. North Korean guards quickly took both his boots and his other belongings and then bound his hands with his leather bootlaces. During the three-day march toward Seoul, the guards entertained themselves by twisting Kinnard's GI can opener into a bullet wound in his shoulder and forcing him to walk barefoot over jagged rocks. On his fourth night of captivity, Kinnard encountered a large mob of American and Korean POWs waiting to cross the Han River. Amid the darkness and confusion, Kinnard ducked his captors and jumped off a ledge into the river. With his hands still bound, the exhausted fugitive had to tread water to stay afloat, while bullets splashed around him. Several days later, Kinnard finally made it back to American lines.[65]

Many of the North Koreans' captives were less fortunate. At dusk on July 10, an American counterattack temporarily recaptured a forward position near Chonui, where six American soldiers from the 1st Battalion, 21st Regiment lay dead. The men had been bound and executed with gunshots to the head. Despite official warnings from Pyongyang and Tokyo, combatants on both sides committed atrocities as the savagery of the fighting increased.[66]

The 21st Regiment delayed the North Koreans for three days but suffered grievous casualties in the process. By the evening of July 12, survivors had withdrawn to the south bank of the Kum, having lost more than half of the regiment in the first week of combat. Meanwhile, the 34th Infantry Regiment delayed the NKPA's 4th Division along the left flank and managed a successful withdrawal across the river with minimal losses. American heavy artillery, light tanks, and combat engineers were slowly reaching the front, and US air power was finally beginning to take a toll on the vulnerable columns of North Korean tanks and trucks that jammed Highway 1 south of Seoul. The North Koreans quickly learned to hide their vehicles during the day, but the adjustments further delayed a blitzkrieg that was already behind schedule.[67]

Trading Space for Time

While two North Korean divisions pushed south along Highway 1, other columns encountered stiff resistance from the remnants of the ROK Army. To newly arrived Americans, the ROKs were a demoralized stream of fleeing soldiers who seemed unwilling to stand and fight for their own country. These, however, were the survivors of hard-fought battles for Seoul and the Han River, where North Korean tanks and artillery had shattered their poorly equipped units. In the rugged T'aebaek Mountains east of Highway 1, the NKPA's technological advantages proved far less important. Steep ridges and narrow valleys provided ideal terrain for South Korean ambushes. The ROK Capital Division, for example, inflicted a series of devastating losses on NPKA columns, including eight hundred casualties at Chonju on July 8. During the first three weeks of July, outnumbered ROK units delayed six North Korean divisions in the eastern mountains, protecting the right flank of the US 24th Infantry Division.[68]

Meanwhile, other American units trickled slowly into South Korea: two understrength divisions from Japan and a regimental combat team from Okinawa. However, until these units could assemble and move forward, Dean's crippled and exhausted division remained the only barrier blocking the North Koreans' advance down Highway 1. With what was left of the 21st Regiment in reserve, Dean now ordered the remainder of the battered 34th Regiment and the newly arrived 19th Regiment to defend the Kum River along a wide semicircle outside the city of Taejon.

Help on the Way

As the crisis deepened, MacArthur's authority expanded. On July 10, Truman appointed him commander of all UN forces. MacArthur, in turn, appointed Lt. Gen. Walton H. Walker to command all of the ground forces in Korea. As Eighth Army commander, Walker had been responsible for the army's occupation forces in Japan. A protégé of George Patton, Walker had struggled to develop his poorly disciplined and inadequately equipped units into combat-ready forces—with limited success. Until more help arrived, he would now have to rely on those same units to save the Republic of Korea.[69]

From his headquarters in Tokyo, meanwhile, MacArthur was gaining new appreciation for his North Korean foes. In response, he steadily increased his demands for more artillery, more tanks, more planes, more ships, but most of all, more men. In the first ten days of the war, MacArthur's troop requirements quadrupled from two divisions to eight, accompanied by comparable demands for additional air power. In response, the Joint Chiefs mobilized whatever available forces they could find, including a provisional marine brigade that embarked from San Diego on July 12.[70]

Elsewhere, however, the cupboard was nearly bare. In the years since World War II, the Truman administration, with enthusiastic congressional support, had cut military spending to the bone. As a result, very few American military units were ready for war. Three of the five active army divisions stationed in the United States were unfit for combat, and the army's eleven separate regimental combat teams were in the same poor condition as those in Japan. The Marine Corps was in better shape but had only two full divisions on active duty, plus smaller units scattered around the world.[71]

With so few active-duty forces available, Washington had to rely on military reservists, many of whom had not worn uniforms since 1945. Over the next three weeks, Truman authorized the recall of thousands of individual army and air force reservists, mobilized ninety-two National Guard and Army Reserve units, and recalled the entire organized Marine Corps Reserve. Truman took these actions without asking Congress for a declaration of war, a controversial decision that paved the way for future commitments of US forces to combat operations.[72]

Another Collapse

On July 14, North Korean forces crossed the Kum River. Enemy infantry easily outflanked the 34th Infantry's weak defenses and overran the 63rd Field Artillery Battalion, capturing eighty-six POWs and most of the ammunition, vehicles, and howitzers. In an effort to rescue these men, the regiment counterattacked with its reserve battalion late in the afternoon. When this attack failed, Dean committed the 21st Regiment to containing the penetration on his southern flank, while repositioning most of the 19th Regiment's reserves to fortify the remainder of the Kum River defenses.[73]

The 19th Regiment's troops were as raw and ill equipped as the rest of Dean's division. The regiment now found itself defending a thirty-mile front, its right flank unprotected.[74] On July 15, probing attacks by the North Koreans located several gaps in the line, prompting a major assault late that evening. The defenders directed withering artillery fire against the massed infantry crossing the river. At a critical point, however, the illumination flares stopped firing, and the forward observers could not adjust their rounds. Hundreds of North Koreans crossed safely in the dark and swarmed over the outnumbered Americans. By sunrise, North Korean infantry threatened the regimental command post, while infiltrators moved south on both flanks.[75]

The regimental commander, Col. Guy Meloy, personally led a successful counterattack with a hastily assembled force of staff officers and support personnel. Although this attack reestablished the center of his line, North Korean infiltrators penetrated to the rear area, where they established roadblocks. Meloy was severely wounded by enemy fire, and his replacement died trying to organize a breakout. At 1300 hours, Dean authorized the regiment to withdraw, but the enemy had established a well-fortified roadblock along Highway 1. Several American attacks failed to open the road. At dusk, the survivors set more than a hundred vehicles on fire to escape on foot.[76] The Americans initially carried their wounded with them, but the exhausted litter bearers eventually left their helpless comrades to the mercy of the NKPA. A short while later, enemy soldiers executed the wounded Americans, including Chaplain Herman G. Felhoelter, who had volunteered to stay with them.[77]

Taejon

With the collapse at the Kum River, the 24th Infantry Division was nearly spent. More than half of its men were dead, wounded, missing, or captured. Over the next two days, stragglers from the battle stumbled into Taejon, ten miles farther south. The city was a major road and rail junction and the last major obstacle before the Naktong River, seventy-five miles to the southwest. General Walker asked Dean to hold Taejon for two more days, while US reinforcements arrived from Japan. Dean's units were battered and unreliable, and the division commander himself was, according to Clay Blair, "a walking zombie." In a decision he later described as "a big error," Dean agreed to Walker's request.[78]

The subsequent battle followed a familiar, tragic pattern. Dean's undermanned battalions established a thin defensive perimeter to north and west of the city, but earlier battles had cost him much of his artillery and tank support. On July 19, the North Koreans launched air strikes against bridges and rail lines. The planes also dropped leaflets—signed by Nugent and five other POWs from Task Force Smith—calling on US troops to surrender. The air strikes were followed by artillery and tank fire against the American forward positions west of Taejon. At noon, American pilots reported enemy tanks and artillery crossing a repaired bridge over the Kum River, ten miles to the north.[79]

On the morning of July 20, the NKPA attacked the center of Dean's line, while infantry moved around both flanks to cut off the Americans' retreat. Poor communications limited the Americans' ability to coordinate fire support and blinded Dean and his subordinate commanders to developments on the battlefield. Infiltrators and guerillas were already sniping at the Americans' command posts and supply points in Taejon, while terrified refugees tried to escape the mayhem. Meanwhile, North Korean tanks rolled into the heart of the city, adding to the havoc. That afternoon, Dean himself led a bazooka team in hunting and destroying one of these tanks.[80]

At 1700 hours, Dean ordered his men to withdraw, but the American convoys ran into enemy roadblocks. More Americans died, more units disintegrated, and more vehicles and equipment were destroyed or captured. Remnants of the 24th Infantry Division limped south, having suffered 30 percent losses at Taejon. Dean himself became one of those statistics. Traveling with a small group of Americans, the general stumbled over a cliff in the dark and fell into a ravine, unconscious. The rest of his party waited for him, without luck. Alone and injured, Dean spent the next thirty-six days trying to survive behind enemy lines. He was finally captured on August 26 and spent the next three years as the North Koreans' highest-ranking prisoner of war.[81]

Flank Attacks

Despite this latest catastrophe, the Americans' situation finally began to improve during the final days of July. On July 22, the 24th Infantry Division's survivors were finally relieved by the 1st Cavalry Division. Like their predecessors, the 1st Cavalry troopers were poorly trained and equipped, but they were fresh, and they provided additional fire support. To the east, Walker deployed the 25th Infantry Division in support of the ROK Army. North

Korean forces continued to push toward the Naktong, but the invaders experienced considerable casualties, and their lengthening supply lines now suffered from daily UN air attacks.[82]

Meanwhile, the North Koreans attacked both flanks to seize Pusan and "cut the windpipe of the enemy," as one division commander described it. These divisions, however, moved slowly and cautiously. The 5th NKPA Division, attacking along the east-coast road, wasted several days and much of its manpower scouting its right flank, giving the ROK Army time to fortify its defenses. Meanwhile, UN airpower and naval gunfire decimated the North Koreans.[83]

In the south, the 6th NKPA Division enjoyed more initial success, moving undetected through southwestern Korea and turning Walker's left flank against sporadic local resistance. When he finally realized the threat in the south, Walker sent the 24th Infantry Division's battered 19th and 34th Regiments, along with two newly arrived battalions from Okinawa, to protect his flank. In hard fighting at Chinju between July 28 and July 31, the North Koreans forced the Americans back toward the port of Masan, only twenty-five miles from Pusan.[84]

The Pusan Perimeter

By August 3, the Eighth Army finally managed to establish a consolidated defensive front behind the Naktong River. This natural barrier was deep and wide in some locations but shallow enough to ford in others. Later known as the Pusan perimeter, this front was centered on Highway 1 above the city of Taegu. The remnants of the ROK Army held the line extending east from Taegu to the coast, while American units defended south from Taegu to the southern coast, with the Naktong River and the southern mountains providing additional obstacles. Over the next six weeks, North Korean commanders, under increasing pressure from Pyongyang, would press the attack on every front and suffer horrendous casualties in the process (see map 2).[85]

Meanwhile, the men and matériel that MacArthur had demanded finally began arriving, including more aircraft, more tanks and artillery, and more and better antitank weapons, most notably the 3.5-inch bazooka. In addition, the Eighth Army's logisticians assumed control of the South Korean rail system within the perimeter, enabling Walker to quickly shift reserve units and supplies, especially artillery ammunition. Most important, more than eleven thousand troops poured into Pusan during August, in-

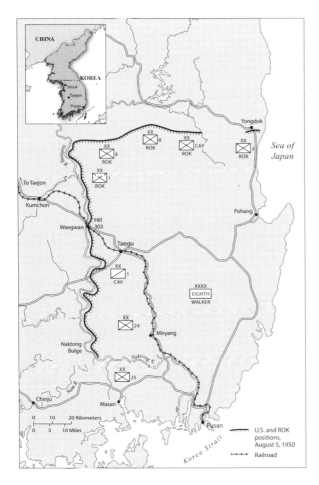

Pusan Perimeter

cluding the provisional marine brigade from San Diego, the US Army's 5th Regimental Combat Team (RCT) from Hawaii and its 2nd Infantry Division from Fort Lewis, Washington, and a British brigade from Hong Kong. MacArthur held the US 7th Infantry Division in reserve to defend the Japanese islands.[86]

These reinforcements did not deter the North Koreans, who launched a series of reckless assaults. The most significant of these commenced on August 5 at a place known as the "Naktong Bulge," where the river flows west for several miles before curving back to the east. The luckless 34th Regiment of the 24th Infantry Division, which had already endured grievous losses, now found itself defending this exposed position. American airpower and artillery pounded the attackers, who built underwater bridges to ford their tanks and artillery. By August 11, an entire North Korean division had crossed the river, and infiltrators were establishing roadblocks and disrupting the American rear area. With available combat power growing daily, however, Walker launched a series of powerful counterattacks against the North Korean bridgehead. By August 19, these attacks, along with devastating American artillery and air support, had all but destroyed one of the enemy's best divisions.[87]

Racing against time, the North Koreans hurled more troops into the battle. While fighting raged inside the Naktong Bulge, the North Koreans mounted attacks along the entire perimeter. In the north, three NKPA divisions advanced to within fifteen miles of Eighth Army headquarters at Taegu. On August 18, North Korean artillery began shelling the city, causing panic among its four hundred thousand refugees. Walker committed his reserve brigade, the 27th Infantry Regiment, to halt the NKPA advance. That evening, the Americans dug in along the southern mouth of a narrow valley, nicknamed the Bowling Alley, and waited for the enemy. Over the next six nights, American firepower defeated a series of North Korean assaults and littered the valley floor with corpses.[88]

The Hill 303 Massacre

On the night of August 14, North Korean forces crossed the Naktong near Waegwan, in the 1st Cavalry Division sector, and outflanked an American infantry company defending Hill 303. The North Koreans easily overran US mortar positions on the reverse slope. Surrounded by enemy troops, the rest of the company withdrew to the hillcrest, where it held out for two days before fighting its way to safety.[89]

The Americans in the mortar platoon were less fortunate. One of them, Pvt. Roy Paul Manring Jr., later described the platoon's fate for a congressional committee:

> They come up and shook hands with us and come right around and grabbed our weapons out of our hands . . . Then they knocked our helmets off. Then they marched us up the road to an apple orchard and they motioned for us to take our boots off. After we took our boots off, they tied up our hands behind our back and first they tied us with the shoestrings out of the boots and they went through our pockets and took everything out of our pockets and the fellows that had wristwatches, they just ripped them right off the wrist.

The next morning, the North Koreans provided a small quantity of cigarettes and apples to the famished prisoners. That afternoon, however, one of the prisoners worked his hands free of his shoestring bonds. Before he could escape, North Korean guards caught him and beat him to death with an entrenching tool, decapitating him in the process.[90]

American artillery fire intensified on the second night, and the North Koreans moved their captives again, adding several more American prisoners to the group. Bound together in groups of ten, the Americans stumbled barefoot through the darkness, while their captors used rifle butts to keep the men quiet. At dawn, the North Koreans again concealed their prisoners in a ravine. In midafternoon, the guards roused the exhausted Americans. As Manring later described it,

> That's when I started hearing shots. I looked around and I saw my buddies was falling, getting murdered with their hands tied behind their back . . . The first time they hit me I got hit in the leg and the upper part of the arm. What caused me to fall was a fellow in front of me. When he fell then I fell and as he fell the wire that they had broke loose and left me by myself. My hands were still tied behind my back . . . I guess they thought we was dead. As they left, a couple of minutes later I heard a sound like somebody was coming back, so I managed to wiggle my body underneath the fellow that was next to me—was dead—and they come by and they started kicking and you could hear the fellows hollering, grunting, groaning, and praying, and when they kicked me they kicked my leg and I made a grunting sound and that's when I caught it in the gut, got shot in the gut at the time.

Fortunately, the North Koreans were retreating back across the Naktong, and a US reconnaissance platoon soon arrived on the scene. Manring and four others survived.[91]

The image of twenty-six dead American soldiers, lying bound and barefoot, shoulder to shoulder in the sun, left an indelible mark on Pfc. Floyd Akins:

> They were lying in a ditch and they had their hands tied behind their backs. They'd all been shot in the back of the head. What made it so bad for me was finding my old company commander from back at Camp Drake, Japan. Right then and there, my heart made a change. . . . Since that day, I don't think I've ever been the same.[92]

Akins was not the only soldier shaken by the brutality of this particular act. As various stories of enemy atrocities spread along the Naktong, American units became less inclined to take prisoners.[93]

The Hill 303 massacre was hardly the first report of North Koreans executing captured Americans, but it became, for a while, the most notorious. Evidence of North Korean atrocities had been mounting throughout the bitter fighting in July and August. Some Americans were burned, others castrated, and others had their tongues cut out before a North Korean bullet put them out of their misery.[94] The Eighth Army's judge advocate general later reported several thousand cases of suspected North Korean and Chinese atrocities but found no substantive evidence that senior North Korean commanders had directed the summary execution of prisoners. In fact, the NKPA's high command had issued orders against such conduct. Still, North Korean mistreatment of POWs was so widespread that Mao's senior field commander, Gen. Peng Dehuai, saw fit to chide Kim Il Sung ten weeks later at their first meeting. Two days after the Hill 303 massacre, MacArthur issued a stern, public warning to the North Korean premier: "I shall hold you and your commanders criminally accountable under the rules and precedents of war." MacArthur's warning, however, was the least of Kim's problems.[95]

Last Chance

The North Korean attacks of early August failed in every sector. Walker's superior mobility and firepower now enabled him to pin down enemy infiltrators while he rapidly shifted reserves to destroy these incursions. In addition, the North Koreans failed to coordinate the timing of their August attacks, thereby enabling Walker and his forces to defeat each assault in turn.

By late August, US air attacks had reduced the flow of North Korean supplies to a trickle. Ammunition, fuel, and especially food were in short supply. Despite heavy losses, the NKPA managed to replenish its ranks, although it now relied heavily on South Korean farm boys drafted at gunpoint. Still, the North Korean forces stood only a few dozen tantalizing miles from capturing Pusan. Under heavy pressure from political leaders in Pyongyang, the NKPA's generals launched a final, desperate effort to finish their conquest of the peninsula.[96]

The assault began almost accidentally on August 27, when a North Korean probe on the northeastern front overran an ROK infantry company. The NKPA's tentative advance soon inspired a panicky retreat by two ROK infantry regiments, creating an immediate crisis on Walker's right flank.[97] As Walker reinforced the east coast, the starving and outgunned North Korean troops launched coordinated attacks along three other main corridors. These synchronized attacks forced back the defenders in every sector and threatened to collapse the Eighth Army's fragile toe hold on the peninsula.[98]

By September 1, North Korean infantry and tanks had advanced to Yong-san, forty miles from Pusan. There they were stopped cold by an ad-hoc task force of American riflemen, combat engineers, and several tanks from the 2nd Infantry Division. When the North Koreans resumed their attack, concentrated American firepower decimated the advancing infantry. The 9th Infantry Regiment recaptured Yongsan that afternoon, destroying several enemy tanks in the process. Over the next two wet and miserable days, the 9th Infantry and the reinforcing marines pushed the faltering North Koreans back.[99]

This counterattack defused the greatest threat to the perimeter, but successful North Korean attacks elsewhere forced Walker to consider a general withdrawal.[100] On the Eighth Army's left flank, enemy assaults scattered two battalions of the all-black 24th Regiment. Like several other American regiments, the 24th had performed poorly during its first weeks in Korea and had suffered five hundred casualties since early August. Counterattacks by the 25th Infantry Division managed to restore the line, but the 24th Regiment's collapse, followed by a similar incident several days later, led the division commander to petition Walker—unsuccessfully—to disband the regiment. While many American units performed disappointingly in the war's early stages, the army's subsequent official history of the 24th Regiment's combat performance proved especially scathing and controversial. Veterans and scholars still debate whether the regiment performed any worse in Korea than several all-white regiments.[101]

In the center of Walker's line, the final North Korean assault forced the 1st Cavalry Division to bend—but not break. By late August, the division had been reinforced by a British infantry brigade and now held a broad swath of terrain north and west of Taegu. The North Koreans outflanked all four of the division's infantry regiments. Several American units disintegrated under pressure, abandoning ammunition and equipment to the enemy. By September 5, the 1st Cavalry Division had withdrawn toward Taegu, terrifying the city's refugees.[102]

While ordering a partial evacuation, Walker gambled on holding the city. Over the next week, the 1st Cavalry Division fought a series of bloody, small-unit battles for anonymous hilltops. On September 11, the North Koreans drew close enough to begin shelling Taegu, only seven miles to the south.[103] This achievement, however, proved to be the NKPA's high-water mark. On September 12, a well-coordinated counterattack recaptured the hill, killing two hundred North Koreans and capturing large quantities of enemy equipment. First Cavalry troopers also discovered the bodies of five Americans tortured and executed by the enemy.[104]

As the second week of September progressed, the North Korean advance faltered, and American morale improved.[105] Elsewhere, enemy forces slowly withdrew, as Eighth Army units reestablished a coherent perimeter. On September 13, Walker visited the 8th Cavalry Regiment's command post. Ignoring sporadic enemy artillery fire, Walker told the assembled staff that their "days of defense were numbered" and that "United Nations forces were now in a position to take the initiative."[106]

Earlier that morning, General MacArthur, his senior staff officers, and the requisite press entourage set sail from Sasebo, Japan, aboard the USS *Mount McKinley*. Once at sea, the *Mount McKinley* would lead an armada of more than two hundred ships that carried the invasion force of soldiers, marines, and Koreans. Their destination was an inhospitable and unlikely target for an amphibious assault: Inchon.[107]

2   **The Tide Turns**

Douglas MacArthur later claimed to have envisioned the Inchon landing while watching the ROK withdrawal from the Han River, ten weeks earlier.[1] His plan required Pentagon support, including a marine division. While the Joint Chiefs of Staff approved the concept of an amphibious assault, they were gravely concerned about risking a landing at Inchon. The port features a swift, narrow channel, thirty-two-foot tides that rank among the world's highest, and, at low tide, several thousand yards of impassable mud-flats. General Omar Bradley later described it as "probably the worst possible place ever selected for an amphibious landing."[2]

For MacArthur, however, Inchon was the only objective worth the risk. South Korea's western coast offered several other suitable landing sites, but these did not support his vision of a deep flanking attack. Instead, he persuaded most doubters that Inchon's proximity to Seoul, the hub of North Korean supplies and communications, made it the only suitable target for such an operation and the only option for crushing the NKPA and avoiding a winter campaign.[3]

The Joint Chiefs, however, still had reservations. As the date drew near, MacArthur first ignored their inquiries and finally sent a junior staff officer to brief them at the last moment, six hours before the landings commenced. Historian Joe Goulden would later conclude that by stonewalling the Joint Chiefs about Inchon, MacArthur gained their unanimous condemnation when Truman fired him eight months later.[4]

In the end, MacArthur's good fortune rendered concerns about Inchon moot. The North Koreans had obligingly committed most of their combat forces to their Pusan offensive, and the combat units near Inchon were poorly trained and equipped.[5] Both the Soviets and the Chinese warned Kim Il Sung of a landing at Inchon, but he had dismissed their concerns. Kim belatedly agreed to mine the narrow channel leading to Inchon, but the shipment of modern, "magnetic" mines was delayed. The North Koreans emplaced only a small field of obsolete "contact" mines, which the invasion fleet avoided. When the fleet arrived off Inchon, its overwhelming firepower stunned the few hundred North Korean defenders. The landings themselves proved relatively easy.[6]

Over the next week, the 1st Marine Division advanced toward Seoul, while the undermanned 7th Division moved south and east to join forces with Walker's Eighth Army. In seizing Seoul, MacArthur would cut the North Korean supply lines, starve the NKPA's divisions along the Naktong, and destroy Kim Il Sung's dreams of conquest. Unfortunately for MacArthur and the men under his command, that was not enough to end the war.

"Better than Any Other Camp"

By September, the North Koreans had captured hundreds of American prisoners, and most of these had been moved north to the schoolhouse in Pyongyang.[7] As UN air strikes grew in intensity, however, the North Koreans decided to evacuate these prisoners to the relative safety of the Yalu River, across from Manchuria. On September 11, more than seven hundred captured American soldiers arrived at the rail station in Manpo, having survived UN air attacks during a slow trip through the North Korean mountains in crowded, open-air coal cars. They were joined by Larry Zellers and the other missionaries from Kaesong, along with several dozen other Western civilians rounded up in the opening weeks of the war.[8]

These civilians, eventually numbering about seventy-four, included missionaries, diplomats, and businessmen from various nations, as well as a small group of South Korean politicians.[9] When Seoul fell, the North Koreans had ignored diplomatic immunity, ransacked consulates, and arrested the foreigners who sought sanctuary therein. Other foreigners had simply been executed.[10] After security forces found a rifle in Zellers's house at Kaesong, interrogators spent a week trying to force him to confess that he was an American spy. Eventually returned to the other prisoners, the young missionary considered himself lucky to be alive.[11]

Zellers's fellow civilians varied in age from infants to octogenarians. They had been poorly fed in Pyongyang, and many had dysentery, but their treatment en route to Manpo compared favorably with that of the captured American soldiers.[12] Most of these men were survivors of the 24th Infantry Division, who had been captured in mid-July during the chaotic American withdrawal. They had survived the initial hours of captivity, when too many of their comrades had been gunned down by North Korean troops after surrendering, and had endured grueling propaganda marches through Seoul and Pyongyang. They suffered from a variety of wounds and diseases, and their personal possessions had been stolen by their captors, who took identification tags, watches, wedding rings, socks, shoes, and even underwear.[13]

Upon reaching Pyongyang, however, these men found conditions to be spartan but tolerable, with warm weather, better food, and rudimentary medical care. Still, after two months of imprisonment, many of the American soldiers, especially those with battlefield wounds, were in poor shape. As Philip Deane, a captured British journalist, observed:

> [T]hey had not been able to wash, and were crawling with lice. A large proportion of them had no shoes. They wore lightweight summer fatigues. . . . Some had been given old cotton quilts, but even they were bitterly cold during the journey through the North Korean September days.
>
> Then the sick appeared. Thinner even than their "healthy companions," they walked like figures in a slow-motion film, helped along by their own medical orderlies and by Korean nurses.[14]

For these men, arrival at Manpo provided a temporary reprieve. After the cold, wet conditions on the move from Pyongyang, they welcomed the warm sunshine of late summer along the Yalu, where they were finally allowed to bathe. Nights were cold, but the civilian prisoners moved into houses in the village, while the military prisoners occupied an abandoned Japanese military camp on a bluff east of town.[15]

Perhaps because of UN advances, the NKPA officials guarding the camp proved surprisingly reasonable. Prisoners received a tobacco issue and three meals a day, usually rice and a soup made of cabbage, potatoes, and daikons (a variety of radish). These meals were supplemented with dried fish, soybeans, pork, beef, and, on two occasions, cookies baked by Manpo's civilians.[16] Guards remained outside the camp, and the Americans ran their own affairs under the capable leadership of Major Dunn. As marine pilot Jesse Booker later observed, "Conditions in the Manpo prison camp were better than any other camp we were interned in while under North Korean control."[17]

Despite Manpo's relative comforts, the prisoners on the Yalu remained in peril. Ambrose Nugent later recalled that "food was fair for about two weeks and then became very bad."[18] The days were getting shorter and colder, and the North Koreans provided a few blankets to their prisoners, whose barracks were unheated.[19] On October 1, the guards issued padded coats and pants to approximately half of the men in the military camp. The other half, however, remained ill clad in the summer fatigues they had been wearing when captured.[20] Worse, many of the American soldiers still had no shoes. Disease also took a deadly toll. Captain Alexander Boysen, the only physician among the prisoners at this time, recorded twenty-eight deaths at Manpo, due primarily to malnutrition, complicated by dysentery and pneumonia.[21]

Still, there was cause for hope. Sympathetic North Korean villagers in Manpo relayed news of MacArthur's landing at Inchon, the recapture of Seoul, and the collapse of the NKPA south of the 38th parallel.[22] Civilian prisoners began a sweepstakes on the date of their imminent release. In early October, two military prisoners escaped but were recaptured within three days. The camp commander beat them with his fists and suspended their tobacco ration, but compared with the North Koreans' earlier conduct, these punishments seemed relatively light. Perhaps the prisoners were not the only ones anticipating the war's end.[23]

The Breakout

Along the Pusan perimeter, however, the war seemed far from over. MacArthur expected Inchon's success to devastate the NKPA: "It will be like an electric fan. You go to the wall and pull the plug out, and the fan will stop. When we get well ashore at Inchon, the North Koreans will have no choice but to pull out, or surrender." MacArthur's analysis, however, was slow in reaching the North Korean infantry, many of whom still held positions well east of the Naktong.[24]

The Inchon landing was supposed to coincide with the Eighth Army's breakout from the Pusan perimeter. MacArthur expected Walker to achieve a swift and dramatic breakthrough, but initial progress proved slow and bloody. News of the landings improved morale in the Eighth Army ranks but had no immediate impact on the enemy. Whether because of deliberate calculation by senior commanders or the chaos in Seoul, the enemy along the Naktong knew nothing of Inchon and continued to fight as persistently as ever.[25]

The combat was particularly brutal north of Taegu, where the 1st Cavalry Division and the 1st ROK Division had struggled to defend the hills overlooking the city. In support of the breakout, the 8th Cavalry Regiment attacked toward Tabu-Dong. The regiment's main effort was the 3rd Battalion, 8th Cavalry Regiment, commanded by Lt. Col. Harold K. "Johnny" Johnson. A survivor of the Bataan Death March and forty months in Japanese POW camps, he eventually became chief of staff of the army. Upon its arrival at Pusan in mid-August, Johnson's battalion was rushed to the front, where it engaged in heavy fighting for three straight weeks. By mid-September, the battalion had lost 400 of its 700 men, an alarming number.[26]

Enemy defenses at Tabu Dong were anchored by Hill 312, from which the North Koreans directed withering fire against any movement toward their lines. The 3rd Battalion launched its first attack on September 17. Captain Filmore McAbee's Love Company gained a foothold on Hill 312 but failed to reach the summit.[27] The battalion's senior company commander, McAbee had earned a Silver Star in Italy during World War II; his previous combat experience soon proved critical.[28]

With division headquarters asking about the delays, McAbee's company captured two more knobs on September 18, but enemy resistance on Hill 312 continued. So did pressure from division headquarters. On the morning of September 19, the division attached an additional battalion to the regiment, with instructions that the "8th Cav would take Tabu-Dong today."[29]

On Hill 312, Love Company were watching American airplanes blasting the North Korean positions when McAbee noticed something: Enemy fire stopped completely during the air attacks. "They were down in their holes," McAbee later said: "So I arranged . . . that we were going to have the fifth pass come in and there would be no fire. They won't fire. And we'll jump 'em. So that was what happened and we took the whole mountain. We caught them with their heads down."[30]

A prisoner later reported that enemy forces lost 275 casualties in this engagement. Other 8th Cavalry units now reported enemy troops withdrawing from their positions, and a supporting artillery battalion reported firing on two thousand enemy soldiers who were heading north.[31]

Resistance was also crumbling elsewhere. The day Hill 312 fell, the 1st ROK Division, operating on the regiment's right flank, advanced thirteen miles, threatening to encircle Tabu-Dong from the north. On the regiment's left flank, the 5th Cavalry Regiment seized the hills east of Waegwan, enabling Tabu-Dong's capture from the southeast. More than two thousand North Koreans surrendered, including the 13th NKPA Division's chief of staff, who obligingly revealed the strength, disposition, and low morale of the division's remaining forces.[32]

Starving, exhausted North Korean units finally began retreating toward Seoul. As a result, Walker's forces now encountered little or no resistance. On September 20, for example, ROK forces recaptured Pohang.[33] That night, the 5th Regimental Combat Team crossed the Naktong. Behind them came the Eighth Army's engineers, racing to bridge the river so that combat forces could catch the retreating North Koreans.[34]

Determined rear-guard efforts by the enemy still threatened the advancing UN forces, but the NKPA's withdrawal soon became a rout. Under heavy air attack and steady pressure from advancing armored spearheads, North Korean units began to disintegrate. Many NKPA conscripts, impressed from South Korean villages, surrendered at the first chance, while some North Korean troops struck out cross-country, trying to escape northward through the mountains.[35]

The 1st Cavalry Division, meanwhile, launched an armored spearhead, dubbed Task Force Lynch, to clear the road and achieve the long-awaited linkup with X Corps in the vicinity of Seoul. On September 22, the task force advanced thirty-five miles northwest to the Naktong River, where they surprised and decimated an enemy battalion crossing the river on an underwater bridge. Lynch's soldiers used the bridge to make their own river crossing.

On September 24, the task force pushed another thirty miles north. After a day's halt, Lynch resumed his advance on September 26. Stopping only to refuel, the Americans drove all afternoon past cheering South Koreans and awestruck enemy soldiers. At dusk, the Americans turned on their headlights and kept going. Lynch's lead tanks finally made contact with elements of the 7th Infantry Division that evening, having advanced 106 miles in eleven hours.[36]

Meanwhile, the 8th Cavalry Regiment launched its own spearhead, using secondary roads north and east of Lynch's route. With Johnson's battalion in the lead, the regiment struck out across the countryside, with two hundred jeeps and cargo trucks driving through the night, their headlights blazing. At dawn on September 28, the battalion rolled into Ansong, southeast of Osan, where it surprised and captured a group of NKPA officers, possibly members of the NKPA I Corps headquarters, which had disbanded during the retreat. Johnson's men established an ambush that captured several dozen prisoners that day, along with twenty-two enemy motorcycles.[37]

Mass Executions

As UN forces advanced, withdrawing North Korean units took out their wrath on thousands of helpless captives who had been imprisoned during their initial conquest. Victims of this killing spree included captured

ROK soldiers, police, and government officials, and South Koreans who had worked for the Americans, refused to join the NKPA, or were merely suspected of anticommunist sympathies. The massacre at Inchon's police station was typical. On the evening of September 15, as marines landed at Red and Blue beaches, three North Korean security police reportedly ordered inmates at Inchon's city jail to sit in two rows on the floor of their cells, then opened fire with carbines, killing or wounding most of the 195 inmates.[38]

Unfortunately, the Inchon massacre was only the first of many such incidents. American war-crimes investigators later accused North Korean forces of murdering more than 14,000 South Koreans during the final days of September. At Yongchong, NKPA soldiers allegedly herded 500 South Korean prisoners into an apple orchard and opened fire, then bludgeoned any survivors and set fire to the corpses. At Hamhung, 300 corpses, their hands bound, were found in caves outside the city. At Sach'on, North Koreans reportedly burned the jail, murdering the 280 political prisoners trapped in the flames.[39] At Tong Tang-Ni, twenty of the young men who refused to join the NKPA were shot at the edge of an open pit, while others were marched to the river and executed there. At Chonju, the number of massacre victims was unclear, but estimates ranged from 600 to 2,000.[40]

The Taejon Massacre

The Taejon massacre, with an estimated 5,000 to 7,500 victims, proved the worst. The US Army's official history later condemned this incident as "one of the greatest mass killings of the entire Korean War." As in other South Korean towns, North Korean security police in Taejon arrested hundreds of suspected anticommunists shortly after they occupied the city. Because of its central location, the police jail and the Catholic mission in Taejon became collecting points for captured American and ROK soldiers and for South Korean political prisoners.[41]

As US forces crossed the Naktong on September 23, the security police began executing their captives. Their hands tied, the prisoners were wired to each other, led to freshly dug trenches in groups of one hundred and two hundred, and shot. The pace of these executions increased as the Americans approached from the southeast, and the executioners finished their work shortly before the 24th Infantry Division recaptured the city on September 28.[42]

American soldiers of the 19th Infantry Regiment discovered rows of dead prisoners stacked on top of each other under a thin layer of soil. Other victims were hidden in the mission well, a church basement, and a nearby river bed. The dead included forty American and seventeen ROK POWs.[43] Only six victims survived, including SFC Carey H. Weinel, who later described his ordeal at a Senate hearing:

> There was fire all night long that night from their own forces, down in their headquarters building down below, this fire firing all night long, and a lot of confusion. . . . Along about 4 o'clock in the morning, they came in on the South Korean prisoners and tied them all together and took them away from the building.
>
> Shortly after they left the building we heard a volley of firearms, so we presumed that they were shot. Shortly after that they come into the room where the Americans were. They told us all to get up, that we was going to Seoul. They was always giving us the story we were going to Seoul anyway. So that was nothing new. They got us up and they started tying our men's hands.

At this point in the hearing, Sen. Charles Potter of Michigan asked Weinel how his hands were tied, and the sergeant showed his scars to the subcommittee. Weinel then continued:

> As they tied them and marched them outside, shortly after a group would leave you would hear a volley of fire and they would come back and pick up another group. Myself, I figured what was going on. As they kept tying them up I moved toward the back of the room. As they tied them up I figured if they made just one slip I was going to go, because I would rather be shot trying to escape than just taking out and shooting me . . . I witnessed the group right in front of me shot by—they was civilians, also army personnel.
>
> I witnessed them shot. After they was shot we was taken to the ditch and sat down in the ditch and shot . . .
>
> All at once the firing stopped and I was still alive. I couldn't figure it out, but I thought I better be doing something, so I leaned over against the next man pretending I was done for . . .
>
> After they thought everybody was dead, they started burying us. I heard shovels, working shovels up at the other end. They went shoveling dirt in on all the men. Myself I come close to getting panicky about that time, but somehow or other I figured as long as I had some breath there was some hope . . . As luck would have it, they barely covered my head and that was it, with loose dirt . . .
>
> I stayed in that position approximately an hour. In that hour's time they made another check on them and evidently somebody down the line moved or something and they finished him off. . . .
>
> I made just a movement to get a pencil hole down to my nose, and I stayed in that position until dark. I estimated it was either seven to eight hours . . .

> After that, it come dark and I got my head out. After I got my head out I
> tried to dig my body out. But, as I said, this hand was tied to these other men.[44]

While US troops battled for the town, Weinel waited two days for help.
South Korean villagers finally rescued him from the mass grave and turned
him over to the 24th Infantry Division.[45] Photographs of the stacked corpses
soon appeared in Western newspapers, reinforcing White House efforts to
justify the removal of the barbarous regime in Pyongyang.[46]

Sadly, Pyongyang had no monopoly on cruelty. According to South Korea's Truth and Reconciliation Commission, established in 2002, the South
Korean national police carried out their own reign of terror during the opening weeks of the Korean War, including the massacre of several thousand
civilians in the Sannae valley near Taejon. Some critics have cited this incident as inspiration for North Korean retribution in September. Commission officials estimate that Rhee's regime ordered the execution of at least
one hundred thousand of its own civilians, often with the knowledge, if not
the approval, of US military and diplomatic officials, several of whom took
photographs, submitted reports, or filed protests. The commission is inves-
tigating more than twelve hundred allegations of such incidents, including
215 accusations of US forces killing South Koreans indiscriminately, usually
by air attack.[47]

Victory?

By late September, the war seemed over. In Seoul, the 1st Marine Division, with help from the 7th Infantry Division and the 17th ROK Regiment, waged a costly battle against five thousand North Korean defenders.
The enemy forces built roadblocks throughout the city and waged stubborn
battles for key intersections. Almond's forces responded with air strikes, artillery bombardments, and tanks, further devastating the already pulverized
city. On the evening of September 27, after six days of combat, many of the
remaining North Korean units fled north. On September 29, MacArthur
ceremonially reinstated Syngman Rhee in his capitol.[48]

As enemy resistance collapsed, Truman's cabinet belatedly considered
what to do next. MacArthur's forces had destroyed most of the NKPA, but
several thousand enemy troops had escaped to the north or disappeared into
the hills, where they would pose a dangerous threat to the UN's rear area.
The original UN mandate authorized MacArthur to repel the invaders, but

it made no mention of unifying the peninsula by force of arms, particularly since, as historian Bevin Alexander later observed, the North Koreans had been condemned for attempting the same feat.[49]

Neither Truman nor his advisors opposed the idea of continuing north. Moreover, the administration had already sent MacArthur a personal, "eyes only" telegram authorizing him to continue north of the parallel. In retrospect, this moment was perhaps the best chance to avert the bloody stalemate to come, but Truman faced tremendous political pressure to "roll back communism," and success at Inchon suggested that any further enemy resistance would be easily dealt with. Moreover, with anticommunist sentiment becoming a significant force in domestic American politics, any perception of weakness on communism would influence the midterm elections, which were only six weeks away.[50]

Still, the president wanted the moral sanction of the United Nations and sought a resolution allowing MacArthur's forces to continue north of the 38th parallel. He also wanted to ensure that UN forces, not Syngman Rhee's vengeful security police, would control the reunification process. On September 30, the British delegation introduced an ambiguous resolution in the General Assembly that recommended that "all appropriate steps be taken to ensure conditions of stability throughout Korea," with the ultimate goal of holding national elections. In the United States, the decision to proceed north was met with overwhelming approval by journalists, the public, and politicians on both sides of the aisle.[51]

Meanwhile, MacArthur's forces paused, perhaps, as he later claimed, because of the Eighth Army's logistical problems.[52] On October 7, the UN General Assembly adopted the British resolution by a vote of 47–5.[53] MacArthur and Truman had their mandate, but the delay, whether political or logistical, allowed the North Korean forces to reorganize. When the Eighth Army attacked north across the parallel on October 9, it found itself fighting two thousand well-armed enemy troops.[54]

Almond's X Corps, meanwhile, reembarked for a second amphibious assault. Hoping to create a second double envelopment, MacArthur planned to land X Corps on North Korea's east coast and push these forces west to meet Walker's Eighth Army. These two pincer movements would trap the remnants of the NKPA in the center of the peninsula. In planning the operation, however, MacArthur's staff ignored the limited capacity of his logistical network. Walker's Eighth Army, preparing to attack north from the border, desperately needed supplies, but X Corps' rearward movement now clogged the supply routes and overwhelmed the port facilities at Inchon and Pusan.[55]

In addition, the complicated scheme effectively removed MacArthur's two freshest divisions from the fight for several weeks. After reloading their ships at Inchon, the 1st Marine Division steamed around the peninsula and up the east coast to Wonsan, where the North Koreans, with Soviet supervision, had done a much better job of mining the harbor. In what the marines derisively called "Operation Yo-Yo," UN vessels spent six days clearing three thousand mines from the harbor, while the ground troops sailed back and forth, waiting to land.[56]

The 1st Marine Division finally made it ashore on October 28, more than two weeks after the ROK 3rd and Capital Divisions had captured the city. A day later, the 7th Division landed at Iwon, farther north, which had also been captured by the ROK Capital Division. The 1st Cavalry Division, meanwhile, broke through enemy forces near Kumchon. Both US and ROK forces entered Pyongyang on October 19. With no enemy left to envelop and the conquest of North Korea nearly complete, MacArthur issued new orders. The Eighth Army and X Corps would proceed north—to the Yalu.[57]

The Tunnel

MacArthur's soldiers were not the only ones moving north in October. In addition to their POWs at Manpo, the North Koreans had collected several hundred more American prisoners at Seoul. Like the earlier group of POWs, these men received meager rations and limited medical care and were marched through the city for the benefit of communist news cameras. After the Inchon landing, however, the NKPA hastily evacuated most of these captives from Seoul, less the sick and severely wounded, on the night of September 20. The evacuation began under heavy artillery bombardment, and the prisoners, many of them barefoot or wearing ill-fitting Korean tennis shoes, walked more than twenty-five miles to Kaesong on the first evening.[58]

Moving only at night, the POWs continued north to Pyongyang and arrived there on October 10. During the march, malnutrition, fatigue, and cold weather took a deadly toll on the prisoners, many of whom were wearing only their summer fatigues. Guards beat the men with rifle butts to keep them moving and shot those who could not continue. Private John Martin, who had been captured two months earlier, later estimated that more than one hundred POWs died during the march.[59]

The prisoners were in Pyongyang less than a week. During their stay, sympathetic civilians secretly brought apples, cigarettes, and money to the

POWs, and twenty Americans managed to escape and remain hidden until UN forces liberated them. Others, however, were less fortunate. The death toll continued to rise, as exhausted prisoners succumbed to their cumulative wounds. While serving with a burial detail, Cpl. Lloyd Kreider discovered UN surrender leaflets in a Pyongyang graveyard. They showed pictures of MacArthur appealing to North Korean forces to end the needless bloodshed.[60]

When Kreider and the other prisoners saw flares over the city, they knew UN forces were drawing near. So did their captors.[61] In fact, by October 17, several American, British, and ROK units were racing toward the capital and threatening to cut off all avenues of retreat.[62] That night, the prisoners left Pyongyang. As Kreider later described it: "They moved us out again the same as they did in Seoul, in a hurry. I would say one-third of the men couldn't possibly stand up, they were so weak. So some of them came out, we carried them out, and some we couldn't even get off the floor. The North Korean guards went in there and said 'Let them go,' and they hit them over the head with butts of rifles." After clubbing and stabbing the defenseless men, the guards marched the remaining POWs to a train depot and herded them into overcrowded boxcars and open-air coal cars.[63]

The prisoners received some food their first night of the journey but nothing more for the next three nights. The train moved north in fits and starts, hiding in tunnels from UN aircraft during the daylight hours. Prisoners slept in the fields during the days, and several more died during the exodus, probably due to dysentery, exposure, or starvation.[64]

On the morning of October 20, the train pulled into a tunnel five miles north of Sunchon. The survivors were so hungry that morning, Kreider later said, that they lay down in a field and formed a human "SOS." In response, US aircraft reportedly dropped some rations, which were promptly confiscated by the North Koreans.[65]

That same morning, paratroopers of the US Army's 187th Airborne Regiment loaded into planes near Seoul. Their primary mission was to capture the key road intersections at Suk'chon and Sunchon, thirty miles north of Pyongyang, in order to cut off withdrawing enemy forces. Intelligence also reported a trainload of POWs moving through the target area, and the regiment hoped to liberate them. Shortly after 1400 hours, the paratroopers landed southwest of Sunchon. Encountering no resistance, they occupied the town and linked up with elements of the 6th ROK Division, which had arrived from the southeast. Neither the ROKs nor the Americans discovered any POWs.[66]

Despite the roar of cargo planes overhead, the POWs were unaware of the nearby paratroopers. In the late afternoon, North Korean guards formed the POWs into three groups and promised to feed them in a nearby village. Sergeant Charles Sharpe later recalled that "Most of the men that could walk went outside and lined up and they seemed to be happy because they hadn't [had] anything to eat that day and they had their bowls, and they took my group to a little ravine just left of the tunnel and at this ravine they told us to go in and set down, that the food would be there in a minute."[67] Instead, Sharpe and his fellow prisoners heard the distinctive sound of rifle bolts sliding forward. Sharpe leaped to his feet with his arms raised just as the guards opened fire.

A bullet struck his arm, spinning him to the ground, and another POW fell on top of him. After shooting their prisoners, the executioners kicked and prodded their victims, bayoneting any who groaned. A blow from a rifle butt broke three of Sharpe's ribs, but he managed to stay silent.[68]

The North Koreans murdered sixty-six American POWs at Sunchon, but Sharpe and twenty-two others survived. In their haste to escape, the North Koreans left the bodies where they fell, and many survivors hid in the hills near the tunnel. The following day, a villager approached the paratroopers' command post at Sunchon and reported the mass execution. A group of American and ROK soldiers, led by Brig. Gen. Frank Allen, followed the villager to the train tunnel, where they found the corpses and rescued the survivors. The rescuers also recovered the emaciated remains of seven Americans who had apparently died en route from Pyongyang.[69]

Soldiers from Task Force Smith arrive at Taejon on July 2, 1950. (Courtesy US Army Military History Institute [Ref. #A9R27C1])

North Korean soldiers guard captured Americans outside the Seoul City Hall. Most of the prisoners were members of Task Force Smith. (Courtesy National Archives and Records Administration [Ref. #306 PSD53-8397])

Captain Ambrose Nugent was the senior American POW among those captured with Task Force Smith. (Courtesy National Archives and Records Administration [Ref. #306 PSD53-8393])

A soldier from the 21st Infantry Regiment lies dead in the road, where his North Korean captors executed him. Rumors of enemy brutality quickly spread through the American ranks. (Courtesy Harry S. Truman Library & Museum)

As commander of the 24th Infantry Division, Maj. Gen. William F. Dean waged a difficult battle to delay the North Korean forces. Dean became separated from his headquarters while evacuating from Taejon and was subsequently captured. He became the highest-ranking POW in communist hands. (Courtesy National Archives and Records Administration [Ref. #SC342957])

Forced to carry propaganda banners, prisoners from Task Force Smith trudge through the streets of Seoul. Major Nugent is on the far right of the front rank. (Courtesy National Archives and Records Administration [Ref. #306 PSD53-7237])

Marines use scaling ladders to clamber over the sea wall at Inchon. (Courtesy Marine Corps photograph [NARA file #127-N-A3191])

Men of the 8th Cavalry Regiment roll north through Korean villages on September 28, 1950, as part of the Eighth Army breakout from the Pusan Perimeter. The Eighth Army's attack cut off retreating North Korean units and captured thousands of enemy POWs. (Courtesy Harry S. Truman Library & Museum)

Recently captured American POWs sit through a propaganda lecture during the summer of 1950. The North Koreans made half-hearted efforts to reeducate their POWs. Later the Chinese would make a far more serious effort. (Courtesy National Archives and Records Administration [Ref. #306 PSD53-8398])

Chaplain Emil Kapaun served with the 8th Cavalry Regiment from its arrival in Korea to his capture at Unsan. In captivity, Kapaun fearlessly defied communist propaganda while caring for his fellow prisoners. He died at Camp Five in May 1951. (Courtesy Ray Skeehan)

Lieutenant Bob Wood was captured at Unsan. (Courtesy Bob Wood)

Lieutenant Mike Dowe was captured near Anju and later made several unsuccessful escape attempts. (Courtesy United States Military Academy)

Lieutenant Bill Funchess was captured with Dowe near Anju. (Courtesy William Funchess)

General MacArthur meets with Maj. Gen. John Coulter to observe the commencement of Eighth Army's final offensive. (Courtesy US Army Military History Institute)

Lieutenant Paul Roach was captured north of the Chongchon River and survived the squalor of Death Valley. (Courtesy United States Military Academy)

Marines and soldiers move south along the MSR during the breakout from the Chosin Reservoir. (Courtesy US Army Military History Institute)

POWs march along a frozen trail during the winter of 1950. More than three thousand Americans were captured during the fighting in November and December, and many more were listed as missing in action. Mainly as a result of mistreatment and neglect by their communist captors, only half of the men captured during this period survived captivity. (Courtesy Associated Press)

A Polish journalist interviews senior POWs in Camp 12 during the autumn of 1951. Major Paul Liles and Capt. Ambrose Nugent are the third and fourth individuals, respectively, from the left. (Courtesy National Archives)

B-26s conduct a low-level attack on an enemy rail yard near Wonsan, North Korea. (Courtesy US Army Military History Institute)

Captured B-29 aircrew members at Camp 12, shortly after their transfer from "the caves." Marvin King is the second POW from the left. Dan Oldewage is on the far right. (Courtesy National Archives)

In the spring of 1952, the Chinese permitted Associated Press photographer Frank Noell to take a series of photographs of life in the POW camps. This photograph depicts Lt. Harold E. Stahlman of Nashville, Tenn., Capt. Anthony Pecoraro, South Windham, Me.; Capt. Sidney Esensten, Minneapolis, Minn., Lt. Walter L. Mayo Jr., Watertown, Mass., and Capt. Harry F. Hedlund, Fullerton, Calif. (Courtesy Associated Press)

In November 1952, the Chinese staged a "POW Olympics" at Camp Five to illustrate their humane treatment of prisoners. Raymond Mellin, who survived the Tiger Death March, is the second basketball player from the left. (Courtesy Andersonville National Historic Site)

President-elect Dwight Eisenhower visits troops in Korea after winning the 1952 presidential election. (Courtesy US Army Military History Institute)

Repatriated American POWs wait to be screened by UN medical personnel after their release from captivity. (Courtesy Jack Chapman)

Newly promoted Cpl. Jack Chapman aboard the USNS *Marine Adder,* en route from Korea to San Francisco. (Courtesy Jack Chapman)

Captain Frederick Smith is greeted by his father after arriving at Fort Mason, Calif., aboard the USNS *Phoenix.* (Courtesy US Army Military History Institute)

3   The Death March

On Saturday, October 7, the prisoners at Manpo learned they would be moving again. Mindful of MacArthur's progress after Inchon, the civilian and military captives hoped for the best.[1] After several false starts, the prisoners finally moved through a pouring rain to the village of Kosang Djin, fifteen miles to the southwest along the Yalu. Although food and shelter were readily available at Kosang, six more POWs died of starvation and dysentery. With the arrival of UN forces becoming a daily possibility, the North Koreans began hedging their bets. Shortly after the prisoners' arrival in Kosang, the camp commandant assembled the civilians, lectured them on their benevolent treatment, and asked them to remember their captors' good intentions when they returned home. Hopes of an imminent release grew even greater.[2]

Instead, after thirteen days at Kosang, the prisoners moved again, this time marching south for twelve miles into the mountains and away from the river (see map 3). The new destination was an abandoned mining camp, but the prisoners spent only a few days there before marching back through a snowstorm toward Kosang, (whose residents, meanwhile, had fled), then back to Manpo. During the march, the prisoners noticed large numbers of Chinese troops moving along the roads, armed with rifles and "burp" (submachine) guns, but no heavy weapons. "None of this will bother the United States Army very much," observed one of the civilians. Larry Zellers later concluded that the Korean villagers had fled in fear of these new intruders. At the village of Goson, many of the POWs received winter clothing, including hats, gloves, jackets, and pants. Seven American soldiers, perhaps believing rescue was imminent, refused to continue the march toward Manpo.[3]

In a grim harbinger of the days to come, the seven were executed after the POW column moved on. According to Major Dunn, the senior POW, two other men "were shot en route for straggling." When the column

A modified version of this chapter appeared as an article in the spring 2010 edition of *Army History* magazine.

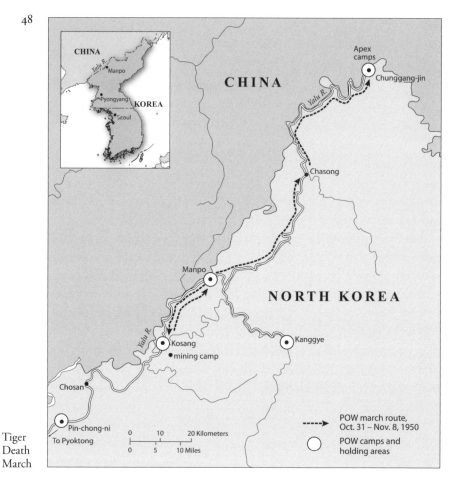

approached Manpo, the prisoners found no billets available, probably due to the influx of Chinese troops. Both military and civilian prisoners spent the week living in a cornfield. The weather grew colder, and the prisoners huddled around small campfires and dug holes to shelter themselves from the bitter Manchurian winds. Rations were increasingly sparse—a handful of corn twice a day—and five more POWs perished. Prisoners traded the last of their tobacco with the residents of Manpo for whatever additional food they could get.[4]

"Let Them March 'til They Die"

On the afternoon of October 31, the NKPA soldiers who had supervised the prisoners since Pyongyang were replaced by a new detail wearing the blue uniforms of the North Korean Security Police. The guards were led by an erratic, ill-tempered major, whom the POWs quickly dubbed "the Tiger." Lean and tall for a Korean, the Tiger announced through an interpreter that the prisoners would be making a long march by foot and that they would conduct the march in military fashion. There were, however, more than forty severely ill prisoners among the group. A British civilian, Commissioner Herbert A. Lord of the Salvation Army, immediately protested that many of these would be incapable of maintaining such a pace. The Tiger responded: "Then let them march 'til they die. That is a military order."[5]

Over the preceding weeks, the prisoners had assembled a rudimentary collection of cooking utensils, including several kitchen knives. Guards now confiscated these "weapons," along with walking sticks and even Zellers's rolled sleeping mat. The prisoners were then divided into groups of forty to fifty individuals, with an American officer given responsibility for each group. Meanwhile, sixteen of the weakest prisoners were left behind in the field. A light snow began falling as the column began shambling toward Manpo, POWs in front, civilians bringing up the rear. The civilians included a Catholic priest from Australia, Fr. Philip Crosbie, who later described the pathetic scene:

> As the men passed by, my gaze went sometimes to their faces, sometimes to their feet. Some of those feet were bare, and some of them were already bleeding. Some feet paced steadily, if wearily, on; but weaker men, dragging on the shoulders of their comrades, put ghastly, shuffling syncopation in the somber rhythm of the march.[6]

Captain Ambrose Nugent, one of the senior POWs, later received word that the sixteen Americans in the cornfield had been executed.[7]

On the outskirts of Manpo, the column halted, and the prisoners waited in another field. After a two-hour delay, the march resumed, now at a faster pace. The Tiger had already announced that they would be marching sixteen miles that night. Father Crosbie later suggested that the delay must have disrupted the timetable, inspiring both the Tiger's rage and the murderous pace. It was now dark, but as the prisoners trudged through Manpo, they were spotted by another POW, Major General Dean, who was moved frequently and kept in solitary confinement by his North Korean captors. Although Dean caught only a glimpse, he was sure the prisoners were Americans.[8]

The shivering prisoners continued along the main road as it left Manpo and headed northeast, paralleling the Yalu River. Columns of Chinese soldiers occasionally passed by, moving through the darkness at a trot. Infants cried, and small children had to trot to keep pace with their mothers. Guards constantly heckled the prisoners with shouts of "Bali! Bali!"—"Hurry! Hurry!"—and Crosbie later blamed the developing tragedy on this merciless prodding:

> Most of the men who died were killed by the grueling pace. The length of the journey, the lack of sleep, the bad and inadequate food, were all contributing causes, but many, perhaps all, could have endured these hardships if they had not been continually hurried along during the hours given to travel. Many who could have walked the distance covered by the party on any one day, if they had been allowed to spread the journey over more hours of the day, were so weakened by the continual hurrying that at last they could not walk at all. This merciless pressure was especially weakening for the many who were suffering from severe dysentery, which seemed to be rife among the POWs. It was pitiful to see poor, emaciated lads who had fallen out, trying to regain their places in the lines, stumbling hurriedly along with a guard at their heels.[9]

About seven miles beyond Manpo, the column finally stopped for the night, and guards ordered the prisoners to get some rest in the frost-covered fields.

At dawn, the guards roused their captives, served a quick breakfast, and resumed the march with such haste that some prisoners went unfed.[10] One American POW died in the night, and according to Nugent, most of the prisoners were already struggling: "Two-thirds of the prisoners were carrying the other third. The order was that no one was to fall out. All men were exhausted and starved. The burden was too much and the pace too rapid."[11] But men did fall out and were left behind at the instruction of the guards. After less than an hour, the guards ordered a halt.[12]

The People's Justice

The Tiger had become enraged by the delays. The officers in charge of sections from which men had fallen out were summoned to the head of the column. The Tiger decided to shoot them as an example for the other prisoners, but Dunn and Commissioner Lord persuaded him to spare their lives. The Tiger relented but announced that he would shoot the section leader who had lost the most men. From the group, Lt. Cordus H. Thornton, of

Longview, Texas, murmured quietly to Commissioner Lord: "Save me if you can, sir," and stepped forward.[13]

As Lord began to plead for Thornton's life, the Tiger wheeled on him in anger, threatening to shoot the commissioner as well. Thornton had been captured in July while leading a platoon in the 34th Infantry Regiment. In the past hour, five soldiers from his section had dropped out by the side of the road. Now the Tiger asked why these men had been allowed to fall out. Thornton answered, "Because, sir, they were dying."

The Tiger now demanded to know why Thornton had not directed other soldiers to carry the dying men. Thornton responded that such an order meant "condemning the carriers to death from exhaustion." The Tiger replied that "In wartime, the penalty for disobedience is death. You disobeyed orders. I will kill you. That is what would happen in the American army also, is it not?"[14]

According to Zellers, who was seated by the road a few yards from this scene, Thornton answered: "In the American army, sir, I would have a trial."

By now, a crowd of North Korean soldiers and villagers had assembled to watch. The Tiger now turned to them and asked what the penalty for disobeying orders should be. They responded unanimously: "Shoot him!"

Turning back to Thornton, the Tiger told him he'd had his trial and had received "the people's justice." Thornton answered: "In Texas, sir, we would call that a lynching."

With tears in his own eyes, Commissioner Lord translated the response, and the Tiger ordered Thornton to turn his back on the column. As Thornton turned away, the Tiger removed his own overcoat and pointed to the rank insignia on his blue epaulettes. As if to convince himself of his own righteousness, he told the prisoners, "You see, I have the authority to do this."[15]

The executioner stepped forward, aimed his pistol, and shot his victim in the back of the head. From the stunned onlookers, SFC Henry Leerkamp, who had served in the same outfit as Thornton, now moved forward and calmly began removing rocks with his bare hands. Seeing his efforts to bury the lieutenant, somebody threw him a shovel, and he began digging into the frozen soil. After several minutes, Leerkamp looked up at the prisoners and asked "Won't some of you come down and help me?"

The question dispelled the state of shock, and several prisoners gently retrieved Thornton's body and moved it toward the grave.[16] When the burial detail finished its task, the prisoners reassembled in their ranks. Perhaps to hide the evidence of any further "justice," the Tiger now ordered the guards to confiscate the soldiers' military identification tags.[17]

The Suffering Continues

The column moved out, resuming its rapid pace. The guards' incessant verbal harassment now turned physical as they used bayonets and rifle butts to punish the slower POWs. The Tiger, meanwhile, strode up and down the column's flanks, exhorting the prisoners to move faster. Even Commissioner Lord was forced to participate in the herding, and Zeller later described the commissioner telling his group in a low voice that "this doesn't mean a thing," then bellowing the order to make haste.[18] The column stopped outside a village in the early afternoon, and the guards requisitioned corn for the prisoners, many of whom had received no food or water during the morning's ordeal. In due time, a detail returned with steaming buckets of boiled corn and began serving the starving prisoners. The serving moved too slowly to suit the Tiger, however, and he barked orders for the march to resume. The prisoners lined up on the road and marched east, leaving much of the food behind.[19]

With the strongest prisoners helping or carrying the remainder, the column made about twenty miles on this day, finally stopping for the evening near a cluster of small farmhouses. There, the North Koreans allowed some of the civilians to sleep indoors. The POWs and the remainder of the civilians, however, spent the night out in the bitter cold, huddling behind the houses to escape the wind. The guards on duty built a small campfire, and the freezing prisoners desperately tried to creep as close as possible to its warmth without irritating the guards.[20]

At dawn, the prisoners were fed another breakfast of boiled corn. On this morning, everyone had adequate time to eat, but Major Dunn found that several more POWs had died of exposure. Several other exhausted POWs had survived the night but were unable to move. The Tiger ordered those who could march no further to drop out, promising that they would be taken to the "People's Hospital." Ray Mellin, the young medic captured with Task Force Smith, recalled begging his comrades to stay with the column: "We were telling them 'Don't go, don't go'—but they went."[21]

They were never seen again. Philip Deane later wrote that Commissioner Lord overheard the Tiger subsequently telling the village head man, "As soon as we are gone, bury them without mounds."[22]

Again the prisoners lined up on the main road, and again the Tiger led them to the northeast, moving at a rapid clip. Exhaustion, malnutrition, and dysentery were taking their toll, and the prisoners grew so weak that many had to be carried by their fellow marchers. Some of these prisoners died while being transported, but the Tiger, perhaps fearing escape attempts, refused to abandon them. Commissioner Lord suggested that the Tiger allow the group's two physicians to examine and verify that these prisoners had died, in which case the bodies would be left behind. The Tiger dismissed the idea of medical examinations and instead directed Lord: "If you think a man is dead, notify one of my guards. He will shoot him through the heart to certify the death. Then you can leave his body by the side of the road." As the day wore on, Zellers passed several POWs sitting by the road, waiting for an oxcart to carry them the rest of the way. Zellers also began hearing shots fired from the rear of the column.[23]

A Night Indoors

The prisoners walked more than twenty miles during this, the second full day of the death march. The column finally halted at a small schoolhouse, where the prisoners received another inadequate meal. During the march, Commissioner Lord had delicately conveyed the danger of forcing prisoners to sleep outdoors, and now the Tiger announced: "You will all sleep inside."[24]

As before, the diplomats and the civilian families were lodged separately. Then the remaining civilians were herded into a larger room, measuring approximately thirty feet by forty feet, followed by the POWs.[25] Father Crosbie described the ensuing melee:

> Exhausted men began pouring in, to sink wearily to the floor. They sat close together, but the room was soon filled to the doors, and there were still hundreds left outside. The guards shouted at the sitting men to crowd closer together, and the shivering men outside added their appeals. Tighter and tighter we were packed, till it was impossible for any more to find sitting space.
> But more kept coming, to find standing room now along the walls. When not another man could be squeezed in, the guards closed the doors.[26]

Under orders from the guards to remain seated, men sat shoulder to shoulder, their knees tucked uncomfortably into their chests.[27]

Muscles began to cramp, while body heat and the smell of dysentery within the darkened room created a stifling atmosphere. As the men shifted, their movement threw entire rows off balance, and so the mass of bodies shifted left and right, from one painful position to another. After thirty minutes, men began to scream. A guard opened the door and warned the prisoners to remain silent. A few minutes later, however, the bedlam resumed and the guard returned, warning that he would fire into the crowd. At this point, Major Dunn warned the men that anyone crying out would be thrown out into the cold and directed the other officers and sergeants to enforce the rule. According to Zellers, two or three of the prisoners were evicted, but the remaining prisoners spent the rest of the arduous night in relative silence. When the door opened at dawn, most of the men were unable to stand and had to crawl from the room in search of fresh air.[28] Four men were found smothered to death.[29]

The Women's Ordeal

The third morning brought news from the Tiger: The women would be provided with transport. Nell Dyer, a Methodist missionary from Arkansas, was placed in charge of this group, and Commissioner Lord stayed behind with them to translate. The women included several elderly nuns. Some of the men in the civilian group now asked to stay behind with the women. The guards angrily refused their request. Shortly after the main column departed, Dyer received word that no transport was available. Left with no assistance, the women set out after the men.[30]

After marching uphill for most of the morning, the main column finally rested at midday. During the break, the men in the civilian group anxiously searched the road for signs of the women. Finally, the exhausted women's party staggered into view, strung out along the road, while guards harried Miss Dyer for her failure to keep her group together. Four members of their party were missing. Two elderly French nuns, Mother Beatrix and Mother Eugenie, had fallen behind almost immediately. Mother Beatrix finally sank down in the road and could continue no further. Mother Eugenie refused to leave her colleague, and the guards finally dragged her away, leaving the seventy-six-year-old Mother Beatrix seated in the road amid hostile guards. With a guard prodding her, Mother Eugenie finally rejoined the main group two hours later.[31]

Behind her came Commissioner Lord and Madame Funderat, an elderly Russian widow. As the two drew nearer, the civilians saw that a rope had been fastened around their two waists and that Lord was pulling the woman along. When the march resumed, the commissioner was ordered to leave the woman behind with a guard. Father Crosbie last saw her hobbling along behind the column with the guard's assistance. Like Mother Beatrix, however, Madame Funderat was never seen again.[32]

After the break, the march resumed. Now the road sloped gently down-hill. Even so, the column began to disintegrate as small groups fell behind. As the afternoon wore on, several of the POWs sat down by the road despite their comrades' pleas. Eventually, the surviving prisoners would hear the crack of rifle shots from somewhere behind them. The column finally reached an abandoned mission. The civilians slept in the chapel, while the POWs slept in an adjoining school. Conditions were marginally less crowded.[33]

Bloody Footprints

Light snow began falling on the morning of the fourth day. To the north-east, the main road rose toward a series of mountains. Guards warned the prisoners that they would be starting early and marching rapidly in order to cross over the pass before snow blocked their path.[34] The Tiger warned that the prisoners would no longer be allowed to help each other and that those who fell out were to be left behind.[35] The roads grew slippery, and the pris-oners feared falling and breaking a leg. Their ill-clad feet left bloody foot-prints in the snow. Despite the Tiger's warning, Zellers continued to assist the struggling members of his party and thus made most of the journey well behind the rest of the column.[36]

Again and again, the horrified missionary encountered young American POWs seated in the middle of the road, accompanied by guards waiting for him to pass by. Several of the victims begged the passersby to knock them senseless with a rock. In one case, a young soldier sang "God Bless America" as tears streamed down his face. In another, a barefoot soldier was forced to abandon his comrade and then, as the guard waited, went back to claim the doomed man's boots. In another case, four exhausted soldiers carried a fifth man until their strength gave out. They dropped him in the road, but as Zellers approached, a senior officer, Maj. Newton Lantron, scooped up the young soldier and carried him along. As before, the North Koreans erased the evidence of their murders by kicking their victims' bodies over the road-side cliff.[37]

The snow had stopped by the time Zellers neared the crest of the moun-tain, and the Tiger, visibly cheerful, had agreed to provide transportation for some of the weakest civilians. As the column moved down the far side of the mountain road, the sun broke through the clouds. The prisoners reached the village of Chasong late in the afternoon, and there the Tiger allowed a pause, apparently pleased to have herded his prisoners through the mountain pass in spite of the snow. The accomplishment cost the lives of twenty-two more POWs.

The prisoners resumed their march on the following afternoon, November 5. The Tiger provided a dilapidated bus to carry a number of the civilians and five of the seriously ill soldiers. The pace slowed considerably, and the guards tempered their abuse. The march continued in this fashion for several more days until November 8, when the column finally arrived at Chunggang-jin, where they were housed in a drafty schoolhouse and nearby civilian homes. The death march had covered more than one hundred miles and had cost the lives of that many prisoners.[38]

The Dying Continues

At Chunggang-jin, however, the dying continued. The same guards who had executed so many prisoners during the death march kept on beating the survivors for the slightest of offenses, and the weary prisoners now began succumbing to a variety of ailments, most notably severe dysentery and pneumonia. Because of the meager rations, which Captain Boysen estimated at four hundred grams of millet per day, malnutrition remained a serious problem. The Tiger, meanwhile, insisted that the prisoners, both soldiers and civilians, undergo physical training each morning. In addition, the schoolhouse was not marked as a POW camp, and on November 11, UN aircraft strafed the compound.[39]

The prisoners subsequently moved to another schoolhouse, four miles farther north. Here, the Tiger's morning exercises resumed. The Koreans provided a medical team, but these doctors and nurses proved brutally inept and by their incompetence lost far more patients than they saved. The POWs' quarters were particularly crowded, filthy, and uncomfortable. Lice and dysentery tormented the prisoners continually, and the guards severely punished the prisoners when their bowels failed prior to reaching the latrines.[40]

As the temperatures dipped well below zero, the guards used the cold as a weapon. They punished misconduct by forcing prisoners outside, where they stood naked or had water poured on them. Boysen later estimated that the group lost as many as eight men a day during the winter. In a particularly brutal incident, five prisoners lit a stove full of wet wood, and the ensuing smoke enraged the guard. He tossed the stove into the courtyard, then locked the Americans inside their hut for the remainder of the night, where they died of hypothermia. In the morning, Captain Boysen recovered their frozen corpses.[41]

In January, another, more reasonable officer relieved the Tiger as camp commandant. Unlike his predecessor, the new commandant wore no side-arm and seemed genuinely concerned about the prisoners' welfare. He conducted inspections of the prisoners' living quarters and restrained some of the guards' worst behavior. Cold weather, as well as shortages of food and medicine, continued taking their toll. In late March, the POWs moved again. This time they were to occupy a former Japanese military compound at An-dong, later designated Camp Seven, which proved more comfortable. As the snows melted and spring returned to the upper Yalu, morale improved.[42]

The two groups saw the last of each other in October of 1951, when the civilians were shipped back to a newly constructed camp at Manpo. The military prisoners were turned over to the Chinese Army, segregated by rank, and sent to established camps along the Yalu River valley.[43] A year earlier, approximately 750 men, women, and children had marched out of the corn-field at Manpo. By October of 1951, the survivors numbered only 330.[44]

4   The Warning

An arrogant enemy is easy to defeat.
Mao Zedong

During the last week of October and the first week of November 1950, Chinese forces attacked and overwhelmed UN forces on both sides of the Korean peninsula, halting their advance and suggesting an important new factor in the war. The 8th Cavalry Regiment's fate at the battle of Unsan, where it was surrounded and nearly destroyed by Chinese forces, provided an especially dramatic warning. The battle illustrated the Chinese ability to defeat American units in combat, and it resulted in several hundred American soldiers being taken as POWs, the largest group captured since the North Korean attacks of July 1950. Unsan represented a significant new chapter in the war for both the UN Command and for several hundred American prisoners, who now trudged north toward internment camps through the frozen mountains of North Korea.[1]

Racing North

By late October, UN forces were advancing north on both sides of the peninsula. Having entered Pyongyang on October 19, Walker's Eighth Army now pushed toward the border at Sinuiju, where intelligence reports indicated that Kim Il Sung's forces were rallying for a last stand. In Pyongyang itself, South Korean security forces executed several hundred alleged spies, traitors, and Communist Party operatives, exacting revenge for the thousands slaughtered by the retreating NKPA. The South Korean brutality evoked a stern protest from the British government. In the east, two ROK divisions raced north along the coastal highway toward the Soviet border. Offshore, the 1st Marine Division was preparing to land at Wonsan, followed by two US Army divisions. Finally, other UN forces were now arriving in Korea, including infantry battalions from Australia, Thailand, and the Netherlands, an infantry brigade from Turkey, and a second brigade of British troops.[2]

With the end of the war in sight, MacArthur issued new orders direct-ing the Eighth Army and X Corps to "drive forward with all speed and full utilization of their forces."[3] Fearing Soviet or Chinese intervention, the Joint Chiefs had earlier prohibited MacArthur from using non-Korean ground forces "in the northeast provinces bordering the Soviet Union or in the area along the Manchurian border."[4] Now, without prior consultation, Mac-Arthur dismissed that guidance. When asked to explain, MacArthur replied that the ROK Army lacked the combat power to adequately secure North Korea by itself, that his orders complied with subsequent guidance from the secretary of defense, George C. Marshall, and that he had discussed the entire matter with the president during the conference at Wake Island.[5]

MacArthur's Confidence

Here, as in several previous incidents, MacArthur demonstrated both a will-ingness to hear what he wanted to hear and a tin ear for the diplomatic issues at stake. Marshall had, in fact, cabled MacArthur on September 29 to "feel unhampered tactically and strategically to proceed north of the 38th Paral-lel," but historian Bevin Alexander argues persuasively that Marshall's inten-tion was to authorize MacArthur "*merely* to cross it with as little noise as possible." As for Truman modifying his instructions at Wake, we have only MacArthur's word to go on. When reporters questioned him, Truman an-swered that he believed only South Korean troops would be advancing to the Yalu. MacArthur's response infuriated Acheson, but with the general's pres-tige greater than ever after the fall of Pyongyang, the Joint Chiefs declined to challenge the new order on the grounds that it was, as Bradley later said, "too late for the JCS to do anything about the matter."[6]

The Wake Island conference had been one of Truman's worst ideas of the war. Truman later claimed that his intent was to meet MacArthur in per-son because "I thought that he ought to know his Commander in Chief and I ought to know the senior field commander in the Far East." In retrospect, Truman appears to have been motivated at least partly by his desire to reap the political benefits of MacArthur's success prior to the midterm elections. Secretary of State Dean Acheson advised against the meeting, and both he and Marshall declined to attend.[7]

On the morning of October 15, the president met MacArthur on the tiny island in the middle of the Pacific. Although MacArthur failed to salute his commander in chief, the two chatted amiably, first in private and then with advisors. There seemed to be no agenda for the group meeting; discussion topics included the impending peace treaty with Japan, the cost of rebuilding South Korea, and North Korean prisoners' attitudes. MacArthur did most of the talking during the group meeting, and both the general and the president seemed to go out of their way to flatter each other. MacArthur downplayed the danger of Chinese intervention and agreed to transfer US forces to Europe once combat operations were finished. The meeting lasted less than three hours and settled nothing.[8]

The Chinese Threat

Truman had no intention of provoking a war with China, but MacArthur repeatedly dismissed the threat of Chinese intervention. In July, the general told visitors that he would destroy any such incursion among the tunnels and bridges of North Korea, perhaps with the use of atomic weapons. In August, he confided to Lt. Gen. Matthew Ridgway that he prayed for a Communist Chinese attack on Taiwan because it would enable him to administer "such a crushing defeat that it would be one of the decisive battles of the world." Others were less confident. Acheson worried about Communist Chinese intervention as early as June 30, when he advised Truman to reject a Nationalist Chinese offer to send troops to Korea.[9]

From Mao's perspective, the US intervention in Korea created both a danger and an opportunity. The failure of Kim's invasion and the subsequent UN advance into North Korea posed an immediate threat to the sovereignty of the nascent People's Republic of China, while also damaging the prestige of "revolutionary forces" in Eastern Asia. On the other hand, a Chinese victory over the invading Americans would solidify Mao's reputation as the leader of Asian communism.[10]

Mao's government responded to the initial US intervention by implementing a "hate America" campaign in early July, thus mobilizing Chinese public opinion in favor of their communist comrades in Pyongyang. In August, Beijing began warning that any UN advance across the 38th parallel would be interpreted as a direct threat. These cautionary notices grew louder in September as the NKPA failure became apparent. Chinese premier Zhou Enlai issued a final alert on the evening of October 2, summoning the Indian ambassador to his residence in Beijing and informing him that China would intervene if US forces crossed the 38th parallel. Truman and his senior advisors were concerned, but they shared MacArthur's view that these cautions were a bluff. Still, concerns about the Chinese threat nagged Truman and his advisors until it was too late.[11]

American intelligence, meanwhile, provided little assistance. Intent on controlling the flow of information back to Washington, MacArthur had kept the Office of Strategic Services (OSS) from operating in his theater during World War II. He continued this policy in Japan and Korea, deliberately marginalizing the influence of the fledgling Central Intelligence Agency (CIA). The agency's representatives had no direct access to the general and were reduced to filing reports based on data gathered by MacArthur's G2 section, run by Brig. Gen. Charles Willoughby. Willoughby's staff did gather accurate data on the Chinese buildup in Manchuria between August and October of 1950, but he refused to believe these forces would dare to intervene south of the Yalu. On September 8, Willoughby's daily intelligence summary presciently speculated that if the North Korean forces failed to expel the UN forces from Korea, "the forces of General Lin Biao's Fourth Army will probably be committed." On September 21, Willoughby's section reported the presence of 450,000 Chinese troops in Manchuria. On October 14, Willoughby identified twenty-four Chinese divisions at crossing points along the Yalu. After noting this development, however, Willoughby categorized the Chinese threats as "diplomatic blackmail." That same evening, Mao's forces began crossing the Yalu.[12]

"Many, Many Chinese"

Still, MacArthur's confidence was infectious. His troops had overcome token resistance in capturing the enemy's capital and were now racing toward the Yalu on several axes. By October 24, Eighth Army engineers had bridged the Chongchon River, the last significant obstacle before Sinuiju, at the mouth of the Yalu. Farther east, the 6th ROK Division captured Huich'on, within fifty miles of the Yalu. As they advanced, the South Koreans entered difficult, mountainous terrain. Still wearing their summer uniforms as the temperatures dropped, the ROK forces pushed up the narrow valleys, the mountains to their north looming ever higher. Still, enemy resistance was minimal, and the advancing ROK forces captured several trainloads of abandoned military equipment.[13] On October 26, a platoon from the 7th ROK Regiment reached the Yalu, becoming the only South Korean unit to accomplish the feat. During their brief stay on the southern bank, the South Koreans fired at North Korean soldiers fleeing across a bridge into Manchuria.[14]

Other ROK units, however, ran into stiff resistance. On the morning of October 25, the 1st ROK Division halted in the face of heavy enemy fire north of Unsan, a market village situated in the broad valley of the Samtan River, forty miles south of the Yalu. During this engagement, South Korean troops captured an enemy soldier wearing a thick, quilted winter uniform. Under interrogation by General Paik, commander of the 1st ROK Division, the prisoner claimed to be a Chinese regular from Kwantung province and reported at least two Chinese divisions situated north and east of Unsan. The Chinese launched a series of attacks that night, and Paik's troops spent the next several days fighting to hold their positions at Unsan. After personally inspecting several enemy corpses, Paik reported that these were not individual volunteers but organized Chinese units. There were, he said, "many, many Chinese."[15]

Northeast of Unsan, the 2nd ROK Regiment encountered similar resistance on the morning of October 25, when its lead battalion stumbled into an ambush near the village of Onjong. A second ROK battalion mounted a rescue expedition, but these troops were unable to relieve their comrades. They did, however, capture two Chinese prisoners, who claimed that Chinese forces had been waiting in the vicinity since October 17. That night, a determined Chinese attack scattered the 2nd Regiment. The South Korean troops fled in panic, leaving their vehicles and heavy weapons. Two more ROK regiments now attacked to retrieve the abandoned gear. Chinese counterattacks overwhelmed both regiments, which lost all three of their artillery batteries in the collapse.[16]

Farther north, meanwhile, the 7th ROK Regiment found itself thirty miles behind enemy lines and low on fuel and ammunition. After aerial resupply, the regiment began fighting its way south to safety. By midday on October 29, the regimental convoy had moved twenty miles south before halting at the inevitable Chinese roadblock. A fierce battle ensued, and the Chinese overran the ROK perimeter that night, killing or capturing most of the thirty-five hundred troops. Word of the Chinese presence panicked the frontline ROK troops, many of whom had an unusual fear of their new opponents. Like the North Koreans, the Chinese preferred night attacks, when their massive assaults, accompanied by bugles and gongs, proved particularly unnerving. By October 31, the ROK II Corps was withdrawing below the Chongchon River and threatening to disintegrate. Both the testimony of Chinese prisoners and the ferocity of the Chinese attacks suggested that Walker's Eighth Army now faced a very serious threat.[17]

"Disbelief and Indifference"

Walker's response, however, was inexplicably muted. The Eighth Army's intelligence report for October 26 dismissed the prisoners as Chinese reinforcements of North Korean units "in order to assist in the defense of the border approaches." In Tokyo, Willoughby's assessments proved even more obtuse, concluding that the information from the Chinese prisoners was "unconfirmed and thereby unaccepted." On October 28, despite his own earlier reports of large Chinese formations at the Yalu, Willoughby insisted that the Chinese forces had already missed their best opportunity to intervene: "[I]t is difficult to believe that such a move, if planned, would have been postponed to a time when remnant North Korean forces have been reduced to a low point of effectiveness."[18]

MacArthur had publicly dismissed any threat of a significant Chinese intervention, and, like that of too many other staff officers in Tokyo, Willoughby's analysis usually protected his commander's reputation regardless of evidence to the contrary. Willoughby had served on MacArthur's staff since 1941, and his obsequious conduct earned him the contempt of many of his colleagues. Lieutenant Colonel Jack Chiles, the X Corps G3, believed Willoughby had intentionally falsified his reports and should have been put in jail. "MacArthur did not *want* the Chinese to enter the war in Korea," said Chiles. "Anything MacArthur wanted, Willoughby produced intelligence for." Another of Willoughby's colleagues later told historian David Halberstam that Willoughby "got everything wrong! *Everything!*"[19]

At Unsan, meanwhile, the situation remained tenuous for the encircled 1st ROK Division. The nearest friendly unit on their left flank was the 24th Infantry Division, fifteen air miles to the west. To the east, the ROK II Corps' collapse left that flank wide open, threatening the Eighth Army's entire position north of Pyongyang. Paik's embattled division enjoyed a brief respite on October 28, and he ordered another attack on the morning of October 29. The assault failed in the face of accurate and heavy enemy mortar fire. The Chinese troops had dug in carefully along the ridges north and west of Unsan, and neither the 1st ROK Division's firepower nor repeated air attacks could dislodge the well-camouflaged enemy.[20]

Influenced by Willoughby's skepticism, Walker and his staff remained dubious of the Chinese threat. Nevertheless, he now ordered the 1st Cavalry Division to attack north through the 1st ROK Division. At dawn on October 29, the 8th Cavalry Regiment led the division north out of Pyongyang.

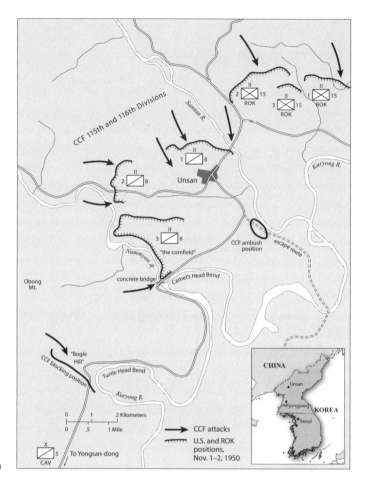

Battle of Unsan

While Eighth Army staffers doubted the reports of Chinese units at Unsan, the I Corps G2, Col. Percy Thompson, was positive that the Chinese posed a formidable threat and had briefed the 1st Cavalry Division's leaders accordingly. Thompson became alarmed, however, when these senior officers, particularly those in the 8th Cavalry, responded with "disbelief and indifference" (see map 4).[21]

"Out on a Limb"

The troopers of the 8th Cavalry Regiment arrived at Unsan on the afternoon of October 30, ill prepared to fight for their lives. Captain Jack Bolt, who commanded an artillery battery in support of the 8th Cavalry, later conceded as much. "We had a false picture of what we were going to do," said

Bolt. "We thought we were going to dash to the Yalu as a regimental combat team."[22]

Their mission was to relieve the South Koreans and "prepare to attack north to the border and destroy all enemy in the vicinity."[23] Still wearing their summerweight uniforms, the Americans welcomed the unseasonably warm weather, but ominous clouds of black smoke floated across the sky overhead: Chinese forces had deliberately set fire to underbrush in order to foil aerial reconnaissance. The 8th Cavalry commander, Col. Raymond Palmer, positioned his battalions in a loose goose egg, with 1st Battalion, under Maj. John Millikin, blocking the road north of town; 2nd Battalion, under Lt. Col. William Walton, defending along a ridgeline northwest of town; and 3rd Battalion, under Maj. Robert Ormond, screening the regiment's east and west flanks to the south. Ormond established a hasty command post in a dugout by the main road, with the infantry companies dispersed around a flat, plowed field four thousand yards southwest of Unsan. "We really didn't establish a CP in a real sense," Captain McAbee later remembered. "We stopped there because we felt we were covering this withdrawal area and then we're out of there."[24]

Ormond, formerly the regimental operations officer, had just replaced Lt. Col. Harold K. Johnson, the 3rd Battalion's commander since its deployment from Fort Devens in August. Widely respected by both peers and subordinates, Johnson was one of the division's senior lieutenant colonels and was thus reassigned to command the 5th Cavalry Regiment when that position came open. Ormond, meanwhile, asked that Maj. Veale Moriarty be reassigned as his battalion executive officer. The two had been staff officers together since the regiment's days in Japan, but they knew little about the 3rd Battalion, which did not join the regiment until late August.[25] McAbee, whom Johnson had earlier promoted to battalion S3 (operations officer), got along well enough with the new commander but found the changes frustrating. "I wasn't impressed with them," said McAbee, "but I didn't have much say in it either."[26]

While the Americans dug hasty defensive positions that afternoon, the 12th ROK Regiment continued fighting against heavy enemy pressure north of town. At the same time, the 15th ROK Regiment clung to its blocking positions northeast of Unsan, on the eastern bank of the Samtan River. The regiment's US advisors had no doubt they were fighting Chinese regulars, but the 8th Cavalry staff seemed indifferent. During its first night in Unsan, Palmer's command post received reports from North Korean civilians "that there are definitely Chinese communist troops this side of the Yalu."[27] That same evening, enemy forces probed the American perimeter but were driven off by artillery fire. Palmer's staff assumed these were North Korean stragglers, and he made no move to tighten the ragged defensive perimeter.[28]

Later that night, a determined enemy attack drove back the 12th ROK Regiment by about four thousand yards. At dawn, the Korean regimental commander insisted his battalion recapture its lost ground before accepting relief from the Americans. Millikin's 1st Battalion moved into positions directly behind the South Koreans, who spent the day preparing for their counterattack.[29] In midafternoon, Palmer's command post received a disturbing intelligence report stating that two communist Chinese corps had crossed into North Korea on October 19 and that at least three Chinese divisions were operating near Unsan.[30] Shortly after this report, Maj. Gen. Hap Gay, the 1st Cavalry Division commander, visited each of the regiment's three battalions. The general was assured that all was well, but Gay worried that his troops "were out on a limb."[31]

Gay was not the only concerned visitor that day. After establishing the 5th Cavalry command post at Yongsan-dong that morning, Lieutenant Colonel Johnson drove nine miles north to visit the 8th Cavalry Regiment. Johnson's regiment was at Yongsan-dong to protect the 8th Cavalry's rear, but Johnson had heard the rumors of large enemy formations in the area and worried that the 8th Cavalry might get cut off. As he drove forward along the rock-strewn main supply route (MSR), the silent, empty landscape made the back of Johnson's neck "prickle": "Anytime you encounter that kind of atmosphere it arouses a feeling of apprehension."[32]

At Unsan, Johnson stopped by to visit his old unit and was dismayed by the battalion's disposition. Service protocol normally restricts former commanders from criticizing their replacements, but 3rd Battalion's vulnerability infuriated Johnson. He found Ormond and privately gave him some blunt advice: "You've got to get these men out of the valley and up on the high ground! They're much too vulnerable where they are! You've got no defense if you're hit!" Johnson later observed that Ormond had "ignored" his advice.[33]

On his way back to his own command post, Johnson stopped to speak with Sgt. Bill Richardson, a section leader in Love Company's weapons platoon. An old hand in the 3rd Battalion, Richardson and his section were guarding a concrete bridge over the Nammyon River, a shallow stream flowing south and west of the 3rd Battalion sector. Johnson warned Richardson that enemy forces might be in the area. Later Richardson recalled his "famous last words" to his old CO: "Colonel, if they come up the river bend, they've had it." Johnson wished him luck, shook his hand, and drove south.[34]

Halloween night proved cold but relatively quiet. While Major Millikin's battalion waited to relieve the ROK battalion north of town, Palmer ordered the other two battalions to patrol aggressively on the regiment's east and west flanks. Shortly before 2100 hours, the 8th Cavalry command post learned that the 15th ROK Regiment was under heavy attack to the east and might not be able to hold.[35] A collapse in the 15th ROK sector would threaten the 8th Cavalry's right flank. During the night, Millikin's battalion captured several enemy infiltrators who had made their way through the ROK lines. Millikin was surprised to learn that "one was definitely Chinese—the first we had ever seen . . . we were being told at the time that only Chinese volunteers were with the North Koreans."[36]

November 1 was All Saints' Day, and Father Emil Kapaun, one of the regiment's three chaplains, moved about the perimeter, celebrating mass for the Catholics in each battalion. Temperatures had dipped overnight, and the day would bring scattered snow flurries. Overhead, black smoke continued to drift south out of the barren hills, limiting visibility on the ground. On his platoon radio, Lt. Bob Wood could hear foreign voices chattering over the radio net. When he asked for a translation, a Korean soldier shrugged and responded, "Chinese." The regiment, meanwhile, received several reports of large enemy movements both north and south of their positions. In one of these, UN airstrikes and artillery fire dispersed an enemy column eight miles southeast of Unsan, killing one hundred horses and a large number of enemy soldiers.[37]

That morning, General Gay visited the 1st ROK Division command post and was alarmed to discover that most of Paik's forces had already withdrawn from Unsan. Gay's own regiments were spread across twenty miles, with the northernmost 8th Cavalry Regiment particularly vulnerable. He phoned the I Corps chief of staff, informed him of the ROK's withdrawal, and strongly recommended the 8th Cavalry's withdrawal and consolidation of his own three regiments at Yongsan-dong (nine miles south of Unsan). Gay was so irate that he demanded the conversation "be made a matter of record." Several years later, Gay recalled the conversation with anger: "The recommendations and the request of the Division Commander were *not* approved."[38]

Meanwhile, one of Lieutenant Colonel Johnson's battalions reported an enemy roadblock six miles south of Unsan, and two infantry companies went north to reopen the road. Despite help from several airstrikes, however, they were unable to dislodge the Chinese, who held strong positions on both sides of the roadblock. Earlier that morning, Palmer's executive officer, Lt. Col. Hal Edson, had gone south to visit division headquarters. Shortly after noon, he relayed an order from division to establish road guards south of Unsan in order to prevent single vehicles from stumbling into the road-block. Edson also conveyed the mood at division: "Situation of whole sector shaky and much concerned."

As Gay monitored the situation from his command post, the position at Unsan grew increasingly dangerous. At 1400 hours, a US spotter plane ob-served another large mass of enemy troops moving seven miles to the west of Unsan and called in artillery. "Our shells are landing right in their col-umns," reported the observer, "and they keep coming. . . . The slaughter is terrific." At about the same time, General Walker phoned General Milburn, the I Corps commander, to inform him that the ROK II Corps had col-lapsed and that Milburn's entire right flank was now dangerously exposed. Apparently unaware of the dangerous salient at Unsan, Milburn turned his immediate attention to the situation of the ROKs.[39]

Gay overheard the spotter plane report and immediately sent a mes-sage forward to the 8th Cavalry command post authorizing Colonel Palmer to "close in" his defensive positions. Gay also contacted corps headquarters again, repeating his earlier request to withdraw the regiment. Once more, corps denied the request. As the afternoon wore on, Johnson's two infantry companies continued to face stiff enemy resistance at the roadblock south of Unsan, and as dusk approached, Johnson dispatched a third rifle company to help break through. When darkness fell, the Chinese counterattacked, drove one of the rifle companies from its positions, and captured the unit's four 81-millimeter mortars. Johnson withdrew his three companies to the south and committed a second battalion to the battle.[40]

At Unsan, the ROK battalion north of town launched its counter-attack at 0800 hours, assisted by a US rifle company and several tanks. By noon, the ROKs had regained two thousand yards along the west bank of the Samtan, but their attack stalled amid an enemy mortar barrage. Several US patrols made contact with enemy forces during the day, capturing five prisoners in the process, but reported no significant enemy threat. To the Americans' east, heavy fighting continued in the 15th ROK sector. Watching this battle on his right flank, Millikin was shocked by the number of enemy troops on the far side of the river: "By 1500, the entire hillside appeared to be alive with ants as watching through my field glasses I could see the waves of enemy moving along the ridge leading into the 15th ROK line."[41]

By midafternoon, Palmer had received Gay's message about "closing in" his defenses but made no move to reposition his battalions. Instead, he forwarded the division commander's warning to them, directing that "all personnel dig in and form close defense." By 1600 hours, the ROK battalion north of Unsan had retreated to Millikin's position. The exhausted South Koreans withdrew along a route that bypassed the roadblock. Millikin now assumed responsibility for the sector by default, with Walton's 2nd Battalion defending a heavily forested ridge a mile west of town. Having earlier detached a rifle company to secure the I Corps command post, Walton's battalion was shorthanded and spread thin. A ridge line separated the two battalions, who tried to maintain contact with patrols.[42]

As darkness settled over the Unsan valley, Sergeant Richardson reported hearing enemy activity in the hills south of his position at the concrete bridge. The 3rd Battalion headquarters finally sent a patrol to investigate, and their half-hearted reconnaissance found an abandoned shovel and several empty fighting positions. Ormond's staff ignored the warning.[43]

"Situation Serious"

Shortly after dark that evening, the warnings became moot when the Chinese launched an assault on the 1st Battalion, north of town. The attack began with enemy mortars and Katyusha rockets exploding near Millikin's command post. American artillery fire drove off the rocket launchers but not before a rocket destroyed an ammunition truck. At the same time, Chinese infantry, supported by mortar fire, attacked Millikin's front. The assault drove the Americans from their forward positions, while approximately two hundred Chinese rushed through a gap between Able and Baker companies. Millikin launched his two reserve platoons to plug the gap and asked regiment for reinforcements. Fifty soldiers from the regiment's heavy mortar company and its engineer platoon arrived in time to help Millikin hold his right flank.[44]

Millikin continued to monitor the battle across the river to the northeast, where heavy fighting continued. By 1900 hours, the American artillery batteries supporting the ROKs began pulling back. By 2200 hours, the 15th ROK Regiment was in full retreat on the 8th Cavalry Regiment's right flank, and South Korean soldiers were wading across the Samtan to reach the relative safety of the western shore. The night was clear, and a full moon provided enough illumination for a US tank crew guarding Millikin's right flank to observe large groups of men heading south.[45]

During these first hours of darkness, Millikin's battalion managed to hold its line north of the village. Walton's 2nd Battalion was less fortunate. Shortly after dark, Chinese scouts began probing the battalion's defenses. At 2000 hours, they launched a full-scale attack on Easy Company's positions, defending the battalion's right flank.[46] The Easy Company commander, Capt. William "Moose" McClain, later described the assault:

> We were hit hard without warning by a large force. They were in and on our positions before we knew what had happened. We were scattered so thin along our defense line that the attackers could not be seen or heard until it was too late. My company was in disarray and retreating. I had momentarily lost control but we got as many together as possible.

Unable to contact either his battalion or regimental headquarters, McClain made his way south toward the 3rd Battalion command post.[47]

By 2100 hours, the Chinese had bypassed Walton's battalion and were advancing toward Unsan. At 2300 hours, Walton reported the collapse of his right flank: "situation serious—men are panicky—some men moving back." Ten minutes later, he reported a separate attack that forced George Company to withdraw from its frontline positions. Walton's command post lost communications with both companies.[48]

As fighting intensified around Unsan, General Milburn belatedly ordered all I Corps units to assume a defensive stance. As part of this transition, he directed Gay to withdraw the 8th Cavalry Regiment immediately. Gay relayed the order through his division command post, and the order reached Palmer at Unsan at 2300 hours. At midnight, Palmer directed the regiment to begin its withdrawal to the southeast, following the route taken by ROK elements that bypassed the Chinese roadblock. Lieutenant Colonel Edson had returned from division headquarters by this time, and Palmer sent him and two squads to a critical road junction south of the village to coordinate movement across the Kuryong River. Palmer also designated Ormond's 3rd Battalion as the rear guard, telling him to "Hold as long as possible. Move infantry out tomorrow during daylight. Use tanks to hold road junction at daylight."[49]

Until Palmer's withdrawal order, many of Ormond's men had literally slept through the battle raging to the north and east. The battalion had manned the perimeter in strength during its evening "stand-to," but the only hint of trouble came from the steady artillery fire of Captain Bolt's howitzer battery, located a few hundred yards north of the 3rd Battalion's command post. At 1930 hours, Captain McAbee sent the battalion's engineer platoon forward to reinforce Millikin's position. Otherwise, the battalion leadership had little inkling of the situation. Ormond's report to regiment at 2100 hours was negative, and many soldiers had already gone to bed, including the battalion executive officer and several members of the battalion staff.[50] Shortly after 2200 hours, the 3rd Battalion lost its wire communications to regiment. When the line was restored thirty minutes later, Ormond asked about Millikin's status north of town and received a brief overview of the regiment's predicament.[51]

The report appears to have alarmed Ormond, who now ordered the battalion's vehicles assembled at the command post in preparation for a possible withdrawal. The convoy would have to wait, however, until the remainder of the regiment completed its evacuation. McAbee, meanwhile, led the Item Company commander and an infantry platoon across the moonlit cornfield to help Edson secure the road junction. Over the next two hours, most of the regimental supply train, along with those of the 1st and 2nd battalions, rolled through the road junction and headed southeast to safety across the Kuryong River. Chinese forces had now occupied Unsan, and withdrawing units fought their way through the village, losing several vehicles in the process.[52]

The Escape Route

After the supply-train vehicles came the regiment's supporting artillery batteries. By 0200 hours, two batteries had passed safely to the east. Behind them, however, one of Captain Bolt's Charlie Battery vehicles took a wrong turn, forcing a halt. When the column resumed its movement, Chinese forces ran forward from the left flank and attacked the vehicles with small-arms fire. Riding in the lead vehicle, Bolt ordered his driver to "Keep rolling!" and the jeep sped forward.[53]

As Bolt rounded a curve, however, he surprised a platoon of Chinese soldiers, who opened fire on the jeep. Bolt returned fire with his submachine gun, scattering the Chinese. Speeding forward, Bolt's vehicle passed two more groups of Chinese before catching up with the Baker Battery column, five hundred yards farther east. Bolt saw none of his vehicles behind him and found his radio disabled by enemy fire. He asked a tank crew to turn back

and assist the remainder of his column, but the tank commander replied that
he was out of ammunition.[54]

Accounts vary as to what happened to the rest of the convoy. The official
army history reports that Chinese fire caused the second vehicle to veer off
the road. The truck was towing a howitzer, and the jackknifed vehicle now
blocked the entire road. As bullets and grenades raked the American trucks,
artillerymen and an attached infantry platoon from King Company poured
out of the vehicles into a ditch on the right side of the column. Several officers, including Edson himself, tried and failed to rally enough men to break
through the roadblock.[55]

At 0300 hours, the 99th Field Artillery battalion commander ordered
Able Battery, still waiting behind Charlie Battery, to destroy its guns and
equipment and evacuate on foot. The survivors fell back in small groups
toward the road junction, and many of them made their way, along with the
remnants of several other units, to the 3rd Battalion command post. Behind
them, Lieutenant Colonel Walton and Major Millikin abandoned the rest
of their vehicles and led portions of their battalions to safety by crossing the
Kuryong River and walking south to Ipsok, guided by the steady fire of an
American artillery battery. Behind them, Chinese forces closed the escape
route.

In the 3rd Battalion sector, meanwhile, Ormond decided the route
toward Ipsok was already too crowded with vehicles. Planning to evacuate
his battalion along a different path, he dispatched an officer to find a ford
across the Nammyon River, bordering his perimeter's southern flank. Meanwhile, Ormond ordered his attached platoon of tanks, under the command
of SSGT Herbert Miller, to protect the battalion's withdrawal. Captain Mc-
Clain, meanwhile, had finally reached 3rd Battalion's command post and
reported to Ormond.[56]

Melee in the Cornfield

As McClain was reporting, disaster struck. At 0100 hours, a group of Chinese infiltrated through the 3rd Battalion checkpoint at the concrete bridge,
where Lieutenant Colonel Johnson had wished Sergeant Richardson good
luck the previous day. According to a published Chinese account, this group
was a specially trained platoon of commandos, the "Sharp Swords," wearing
helmets and gear taken from South Korean corpses. Their commander spoke
enough English to convince the sentries that the group was from the "6th

ROKs." The lone sentry allowed them to pass, and they continued up the road toward the 3rd Battalion command post.[57]

Years later, Bill Richardson dismissed this version. "There was no need for disguise," he told David Halberstam. "They just poured in from the east, which was completely open." Mortar and machine-gun fire drove Richardson's squad from the bridge. As they neared the command post, the enemy assault force blew bugles and opened fire. In conjunction with this attack, the Chinese launched a coordinated strike against the Love Company front, along the river bank.[58]

At the sound of gunfire, Ormond and McAbee went to investigate. McAbee headed left toward the bridge, while Ormond moved right, toward Love's command post. As McAbee neared the bridge, a round struck the left side of his head, knocking off his helmet. A moment later, another round fractured his left shoulder blade. As he stumbled back toward the command post, McAbee met more infiltrators. He ducked for cover behind a jeep, and when they followed, McAbee shot them with his carbine.[59]

Across the field, McAbee now spotted a group of thirty Chinese soldiers trying to set a tank on fire. He emptied his carbine clip at the men, killing several and scattering the remainder. As he continued back toward the command post, three Chinese soldiers stepped out of a ditch and blocked his path with their bayonets but made no effort to disarm him. McAbee finally pointed up the road, and the Chinese soldiers, after some discussion, left. McAbee staggered the other way, toward the command post. There, Moriarty helped him to the dugout, where the battalion surgeon, Capt. Clarence "Doc" Anderson, had established an aid station.[60]

By now, Chinese infiltrators were running amok inside the 3rd Battalion's perimeter, throwing grenades and satchel charges into the line of vehicles. Many Americans had just woken up, and small groups fought back with whatever weapons were available, occasionally their bare hands. Sergeant Miller went to inspect the ford site but rushed back when the shooting started and discovered several Chinese troops climbing onto the deck of his tank. Miller helped clear the enemy soldiers with his pistol; then he and two other tanks directed their fire against the Chinese troops wading across the Namwon River from the south.[61]

Outside the dugout, Moriarty saw one of his staff officers wrestling with a Chinese soldier. Moriarty shot the enemy with his .45-caliber pistol and moved toward Miller's tank, where twenty American soldiers were crouching for cover. Enemy mortars began targeting the tank, so Moriarty led the small group toward the river, where they overcame a squad of Chinese. The soldiers then waded across the waist-deep river and made their way south, un-opposed. Along the way, dozens of other survivors joined Moriarty's group, which numbered more than a hundred men by the time it reached Ipsok two hours after sunrise.[62]

Meanwhile, the melee around the 3rd Battalion command post continued, with clerks, staff officers, and elements of Love and Mike Companies struggling to repel the Chinese attackers. Gradually, the defenders gravitated toward the three US tanks, where they held a small perimeter. Another group of Americans formed another boundary around the dugout. When the Chinese finally withdrew at dawn, only five of these defenders were left unscathed.[63]

Inside the dugout, Anderson continued treating casualties and was ably assisted by Father Kapaun. Dodging tracers and grenades, Kapaun repeatedly risked his life to recover wounded men in the dark and was briefly captured by the Chinese. As they led him away from the fight, another soldier saw Kapaun in enemy hands and yelled, "There goes the chaplain." Several GIs fired at his captors, giving Kapaun time to escape.[64]

King Company's Fate

Amid this chaos, King Company tried to make its way back toward the battalion headquarters. Positioned on a low ridgeline to the north, the unit was initially ordered to assemble at the battalion command post in preparation for the withdrawal. Moving down the hill toward the battalion, King Company walked into an ambush and suffered heavy losses, including its command group.[65] The soldiers scattered, and Lt. Phil Peterson, the company's forward observer, narrowly escaped by diving into an irrigation canal, where he managed to dodge several enemy hand grenades:

> The Chinese finally set up a machine gun on each end, and they started with shooting back and forth at one another, up and down the ravine there. It was the middle of the night, and I couldn't see them . . . They couldn't see either, and probably felt that they had done enough damage and had probably decimated our unit, you know, that we were no longer effective. . . . And all of a sudden I looked up, and there's this guy walking towards me. And I had my .45 out, and I had it pointed right at his bulk, you know, and I'm going to wait until he gets close enough to me that I know that I'm not going to miss him.
>
> And then common sense took over: "Hey Phil, there's only a few of you

here, and there's probably thousands of them, why make a big noise for one guy?" So I held off. I didn't shoot him. I let him go.

Once the enemy soldier had passed, Peterson moved back toward the hill, gathering a dozen King Company survivors en route. There, the small group waited for daylight to assess their situation:

> We had a panoramic view, flat as a pool table, and we see that the guys have dug a circular trench. . . . I turned to the guys and I said, "You know, it would appear to me that we have two choices: one would be to go on around the mountain. We don't know what's there at all. The other would be to try our best to get down to the rest of our guys inside the perimeter."

The group quietly moved to the base of the hill, where they abandoned all of their equipment except weapons and ammunition.

As Peterson prepared to lead the men toward the safety of the perimeter, he worried that their movement might draw the defenders' fire. Suspecting that his friend, Lt. Walt Mayo, was inside the perimeter and that Mayo or the other defenders would recognize his voice, Peterson hollered "Mayo! Mayo!" at the top of his lungs, while he and the others sprinted toward the Americans, tumbling safely into the perimeter: "The battalion headquarters was over by the road, and in between the battalion headquarters, which was all shot to shit and full of dead people, sat our battalion trucks, just sitting there, loaded."[66] Heavy enemy mortar fire continued to harass the survivors for an hour after sunrise, but UN aircraft soon appeared over the valley, and their attacks kept the Chinese at bay until dusk.[67]

The Perimeter

The surrounded Americans used the respite to dig new trenches and scavenge food and ammunition from the few remaining undamaged trucks. Approximately 200 men, including six officers, now held the 200-yard-wide perimeter, with Sergeant Miller's three tanks in the middle. Another 170 wounded Americans, including Major Ormond, lay in and around the perimeter, along with countless Chinese and American dead. Though seriously injured, Ormond insisted that Anderson treat the other wounded soldiers first. Kapaun and several other Americans braved enemy fire to recover injured men from the field between the perimeter and the Chinese positions. Several dozen of the most severely hurt men, including Captain McAbee, remained stranded in the dugout, 150 yards southeast of the perimeter—in no-man's land between the Chinese and the Americans. At dusk, Kapaun dashed back to the dugout to give whatever care and comfort he could provide.[68]

Inside the perimeter, the survivors used a tank radio to relay messages through the aircraft overhead. One observation plane flew low over the field and dropped a mailbag of morphine and bandages. A helicopter also flew into the valley, hoping to evacuate the seriously wounded, but was driven off by enemy fire. Meanwhile, the Americans took hope from the news that a rescue mission was heading their way. Realizing his former battalion's desperate situation, Lieutenant Colonel Johnson was preparing a major assault against the Chinese roadblock in order to reach Unsan. At the same time, a separate battalion would outflank the roadblock to the west.[69]

The rescue attempt proved a bloody failure. The battalion attacking along the road lacked adequate artillery support to reduce the heavily defended roadblock, and dust and smoke along the ridgeline obscured the Chinese positions from the attacking aircraft. The flanking battalion, meanwhile, became bogged down in rough terrain and missed the fight completely. By late afternoon, Johnson's troops had suffered 350 casualties and had not broken through.[70] Gay reluctantly ordered a withdrawal. As dusk approached, a liaison plane flew over the Unsan perimeter and dropped a grim message to the men below, ordering them to withdraw under cover of darkness. Sergeant Miller received a similar message over his tank radio: The survivors were on their own and were to use their own judgment to get out. After a brief council of war, however, the Americans chose to stay put in hopes that they could hold out until dawn.[71]

That evening, the Chinese resumed their attack with a barrage of heavy mortar fire. The shells targeted the three tanks, so Miller moved them outside the perimeter, and the mortar fire followed. The Chinese had earlier destroyed several US tanks with satchel charges, and Miller's tank crews, running low on fuel and ammunition, stood little chance of surviving outside the perimeter. With the approval of the senior officer in the perimeter, Miller's tanks withdrew to the southwest but ran out of fuel at the Kuryong River. The three crews made their way to safety on foot.[72]

Back at the perimeter, meanwhile, the defenders shot bazooka rounds into the remaining vehicles outside their lines, and the resulting fires illuminated the Chinese infantry as they assaulted the American positions. The Chinese launched six attacks during the night but failed to break through. During this battle, about fifty men from 2nd Battalion, most of them survivors of Captain McClain's Easy Company, fought their way into the perimeter, providing welcome reinforcement to the defenders, some of whom were reduced to throwing rocks.[73]

At the dugout, however, the Chinese troops easily overwhelmed the American defenders and captured the position. The dugout was still jammed full of wounded soldiers, including an injured Chinese officer. At Kapaun's request, the officer directed the attackers to cease fire, and the priest persuaded these soldiers to leave the wounded Americans unharmed. The Chinese then evacuated Kapaun, McAbee, and about fifteen other walking wounded. As they left the dugout, Kapaun and the others climbed over corpses piled three high in places about the entrance. Kapaun spotted a Chinese soldier preparing to execute a wounded American lying nearby in the frozen mud. He shoved the surprised Chinese soldier aside, dragged the GI to his feet, and carried him, limping, back to the column of prisoners.[74]

As the sun rose over the corpse-strewn field on November 3, the men inside the small perimeter realized their desperate situation. From their positions, the Americans could hear the scrape of shovels as the Chinese troops began digging their own trench from the river bed toward the American lines. One of the noncommissioned officers collected all of the grenades from the defenders inside the perimeter, then crawled out to the Chinese work party, and launched a one-man attack. The assault worked, and the digging stopped. Still, food, water, ammunition, and medical supplies were all becoming scarce. Worst of all, the perimeter included about two hundred wounded men, most of whom would not get far in any breakout attempt.[75]

That night, the Chinese struck again. The assault force suffered horrific losses in these attacks, but each effort brought them closer to the American lines. The defenders' ammunition was nearly gone, and, between assaults, they crawled out onto the darkened field and recovered enemy weapons and ammunition. Despite a growing number of casualties inside the perimeter, the Americans held.[76]

The Breakout

At dawn on November 4, the surviving officers, most of them injured as well, met to discuss their options. With surrender as the only alternative, they decided to leave the wounded in Chinese hands, while the rest of the party, about sixty men, tried to escape. Captain Anderson insisted on staying with the injured, and a scouting party consisting of Lieutenant Mayo, Lieu-

tenant Peterson, Sergeant Richardson, and a fourth soldier volunteered to locate a safe escape route. As the four moved toward the perimeter, a wounded
soldier from King Company begged Peterson not to abandon him. With
tears in his eyes, the young lieutenant explained, "I'm sorry, but we have to
go and get help."[77]

Outside the perimeter, the group crawled first to the dugout, where they
learned the Chinese had removed some of the prisoners. A lieutenant and
a medic, both of them injured as well, were doing what they could for the
rest of the wounded. Mayo and the others next made their way to the trucks
and salvaged some boxes of cigarettes and candy, which they left with their
injured comrades. From the dugout, the four moved northeast toward Unsan through a series of ditches strewn with corpses. Save for a few wounded
Chinese soldiers, the village itself was now empty. The group crept east and
found an unguarded ford across the river. At 1430 hours, the two lieutenants
sent the other men back to report the escape route.[78]

Richardson and the other soldier returned to the perimeter just before
dusk. As darkness fell, the Chinese launched a barrage of white-phosphorous
mortars, which blanketed the perimeter with smoke. A steady rainfall further limited visibility. Expecting an attack to follow, the Americans dashed
east across an open field, eventually reaching the river, about a half mile
south of the two lieutenants. The entire party crossed and moved southeast
toward Ipsok. The group traveled all night through a rainstorm, then hid
during the following day. They resumed moving south at dusk. At some
point during the night, they stumbled into an outpost and exchanged fire
with the enemy. The officers ordered the men to split up, but it was too late.
Most were subsequently captured by Chinese patrols.[79]

Mayo and Peterson escaped with a third soldier and hid in a cornfield
for a day before deciding it was safe to move south. They got as far as the
first hilltop. But then, as Peterson later described it:

> Up out of the ground came a platoon of Chinese, one as close as you and me.
> He had a 45 caliber submachine gun pointed right at my belly. He pulls the
> bolt, lets it go, and he says, "Well! Well! Well!" I said, "Okay! Okay! Okay!"
> That afternoon they played with us, interrogated us . . . The guys were very
> nonchalant, they pointed with their machine guns, obviously not loaded, and
> one would pull the trigger.

Finally, the Chinese soldiers allowed the three exhausted prisoners to sleep.
The Americans awoke in the dark and started marching north, away from
the American lines.[80]

Back at the perimeter, meanwhile, Captain Anderson surrendered with about two hundred wounded men. They joined several dozen other American prisoners, whom the Chinese had captured elsewhere on the battlefield and in the hills to the southeast. Most of the Americans were injured, and the Chinese did move some of the severely wounded prisoners north in captured American trucks. Many others, however, had to walk or be carried, and the Chinese provided almost no medical supplies or treatment.[81]

At Ipsok, the 8th Cavalry Regiment initially reported more than a thousand soldiers missing in action, but more than four hundred of these made their way back to friendly lines over the next few weeks. In addition, the regiment lost an enormous number of radios, vehicles, and heavy weapons, including twelve howitzers and nine M-26 tanks. Losses were heaviest in 3rd Battalion, which lost six hundred of the eight hundred soldiers who had arrived at Unsan on October 30. The Chinese casualties are harder to calculate, but American firepower, especially artillery and air attacks, took a heavy toll.[82]

The 8th Cavalry's fate and the South Korean collapse prompted General Milburn to halt the 24th Infantry Division's advance along the west coast, only a day's march from Sinuiju and the Yalu. The Americans, along with accompanying British and Australian troops, withdrew to Anju, where they endured a series of heavy attacks from Chinese forces between November 4 and 6. Other Chinese forces simultaneously attacked the 7th ROK Division on Walker's eastern flank, near Kunu-Ri. In the X Corps sector, meanwhile, both the 3rd ROK Division and the 1st Marine Division encountered heavy resistance from Chinese troops north of Hungnam.[83]

On November 6, Chinese forces began an abrupt withdrawal on both sides of the peninsula. In one sector, an Australian battalion witnessed Chinese forces stopping in midattack and withdrawing to the north. During the following days, UN pilots identified large columns of enemy troops retreating, and these formations soon disappeared back into the mountains.[84] MacArthur, having already miscalculated the intentions of the Chinese once, now had a second opportunity to consider the battlefield situation. Unfortunately for the soldiers under his command, it would be an opportunity lost—with tragic consequences.

5   Home by Christmas

If you have a son overseas, write to him. If you have a son in the 2nd Division, pray for him.
Walter Winchell, November 1950

Shortly after dusk on November 4, Capt. Clarence Anderson surrendered what was left of the 3rd Battalion, 8th Cavalry Regiment, at Unsan. Well acquainted with enemy atrocities committed in earlier battles, Anderson and his fellow prisoners anticipated brutal treatment. They soon discovered that Chinese treatment varied dramatically from that of their North Korean allies. During the vicious battles for the Pusan perimeter, the North Koreans had often tortured and killed captured Americans. Air Force researcher Albert D. Biderman later calculated that the North Koreans had conducted approximately one thousand such executions. In other cases, the North Korean soldiers stole watches, rings, and boots from their prisoners and subjected them to petty cruelties. Lieutenant Armando Arias, a platoon leader captured at Unsan, later reported that he and a large group of prisoners were marched north by the Chinese but were briefly placed under the guard of North Korean troops. During this four-hour interlude, the North Koreans "stripped the prisoners of most of their personal belongings."[1]

The Lenient Policy

Chinese soldiers, on the other hand, frequently treated captured opponents with remarkable humanity during the first weeks of combat. On several occasions, the Chinese forces either sent back captured Americans or left severely wounded prisoners for the advancing UN forces to recover. During the 5th Cavalry's battle for the roadblock south of Unsan, for example, Capt. Norm Allen recovered several dozen wounded Americans. According to Allen, these men reported "being carried by the Chinese to the road on stretchers marked 'Donated by the American Red Cross.'"[2]

In other cases, however, Chinese troops showed no hesitation in killing severely injured prisoners and harshly punished those who broke the rules.[3] Lieutenant Mike Dowe of the 24th Infantry Division reported several examples of Chinese brutality while he and his fellow prisoners marched north. In one case, the Americans were forced to spend several hours in an open hole, where they contracted frostbite.[4]

More often, though, the Chinese troops greeted their surprised captives with stunning hospitality. Corporal Claude Batchelor of the 8th Cavalry Regiment described his captors offering him food and cigarettes.[5] Lieutenant Bill Funchess, who was captured with Dowe near Anju, describes a similar experience: A Chinese officer "walked within inches of me, stopped, reached up, and pulled my right arm down and started shaking my hand. Then he spoke in perfect English. 'We are not mad at you. We are mad at Wall Street.'" Dowe and Funchess soon learned that not all Chinese troops were so amiable, however. The night of their capture, a Chinese doctor refused to treat Funchess or the other wounded Americans in his group, and Chinese troops later stole the prisoners' personal items, including Funchess's field jacket.[6]

Many American prisoners also remember Chinese efforts to reorient their political views. An officer, often speaking perfect English, would brief the prisoners on the "lenient policy" of the Chinese. The policy promised food, shelter, and medical treatment, along with an opportunity for the prisoners to learn the errors of capitalism. Once they had completed their reeducation, promised the officer, they would be safely repatriated.[7]

Marching North

The surprising success of the initial Chinese attacks, later dubbed the "first phase offensive," produced an unanticipated problem—hundreds of South Korean and American prisoners of war. Just as the North Koreans had established no permanent holding areas for the prisoners they had captured in the first months of the war, so the Chinese now had to improvise makeshift holding areas for their captives.[8]

Their first step was to evacuate prisoners to the north. At Unsan, Captain Anderson and the wounded men in his care spent their first night of captivity in a barn near the village, then marched north a few miles to a collection point, where they were fed and hastily interrogated. The following evening, Anderson's group made a longer march—sixteen to twenty miles—

before stopping in a small village. Here, they were interrogated a second time, then crowded into huts. Most of the prisoners came from Unsan, but over the next week, they were joined by Americans captured near Anju, and their number grew to about 450. The Chinese allowed Anderson and the few medics in the group to provide care for the wounded, but because no medical supplies were available, several prisoners, including Major Ormond, died during that week.[9]

From here the prisoners again marched north, while some of the most seriously wounded men rode in trucks provided by the Chinese. During rest stops, Father Kapaun, the 8th Cavalry chaplain, moved up and down the column, cheerfully encouraging the men with prayers and exhortations. When trucks were not available, the prisoners had to carry their own seriously wounded on litters, and several Americans refused. Kapaun, already suffering from frostbite, insisted on carrying the litters without missing a turn. At the end of each break, he would stand and call out: "Let's pick 'em up!" Kapaun's selfless example shamed others into service.[10]

Fatigue, however, was the least of the prisoners' problems. The Chinese guards had confiscated most of their water-purification tablets, so the prisoners drank untreated water from the streams. As a result, they developed diarrhea and dysentery, which later proved fatal in many cases. In addition, rations were limited to whatever the Chinese spared or could find in the deserted villages through which they marched, and the prisoners often received no more than a handful of millet or cracked corn. The corn was frequently undercooked, which further aggravated the Americans' intestinal discomfort.[11] Instead of the food, shelter, and medicine promised by their Chinese hosts, the prisoners would soon endure horrific losses due to the combined effects of dysentery, malnutrition, and exposure to the extremely cold weather.

Moving only at night, the first large group of American prisoners reached the village of Pyoktong on November 16, 1950. More soon arrived, but on November 20, American B-26 bombers attacked the village. The Americans survived the airstrike, but half of Pyoktong burned to the ground, along with their intended prison camp. After a day's delay, the prisoners marched a few miles south to a valley near the village of Sombokol.[12]

The prisoners included seventeen litter patients, but finding volunteers to carry the stretchers again proved difficult. The senior officer, Maj. Paul Liles, physically threatened several men in order to enforce discipline. At one point, four men simply put down a man on a stretcher and left him by the roadside in the dark. Unable to compel the soldiers to retrieve the man,

Captain Anderson and three volunteers took up the load. The group finally made it to the valley, but discipline problems grew worse over the next two months.[13]

Baiting the Trap

While the American prisoners struggled for survival in the frozen valleys of North Korea, leaders and policymakers struggled to make sense of the sudden disappearance of the Chinese forces. Why had they attacked in the first place, and why had they subsequently withdrawn?

By early November, the Chinese had already moved three hundred thousand troops across the Yalu, and more were arriving daily. When Beijing radio announced the presence of Chinese troops in Korea on November 2, the broadcast maintained the disingenuous claim, first suggested by Stalin, that the Chinese troops were volunteers sent to protect dams and hydroelectric plants along the Yalu.[14] In fact, there was no evidence that Chinese soldiers were fighting as part of the North Korean units, but the claim provided the Chinese with diplomatic maneuver room, depending on the American response.[15] Some analysts thought these initial attacks, later dubbed the "first offensive," merely signaled a warning to stay clear of the Chinese border. In fact, Mao intended to probe the enemy's weaknesses and then lure the UN forces farther north, where poor weather and rugged terrain favored a massive ambush.[16]

At least one contributing factor in the sudden withdrawal was the rudimentary Chinese supply system. Each Chinese soldier had enough food, water, and ammunition to sustain himself for three to five days. By November 6, however, many Chinese combat units had been engaged for ten days and needed replenishment. Rail- and motor-transport capabilities were limited and vulnerable to UN air attacks south of the Yalu, so the Chinese recruited more than a half million porters to carry supplies on their backs. Like their supplies, Chinese troops traveled on foot, moving cross-country through terrain inaccessible to their road-bound opponents. So did prisoners of war, most of whom walked, limped, or were carried to the Yalu camps.[17]

While Truman's advisors debated the intentions of the Chinese, MacArthur and his senior staff remained unconcerned. Willoughby dismissed the initial Chinese attacks as exaggerations meant to justify the ROK Army's poor performance. The CIA's October 26 report echoed Willoughby's tone, dismissing information from Chinese prisoners as unreliable. At Major

General Almond's X Corps headquarters, Col. William McCaffrey had more leeway than most of the staff, having served with Almond during World War II. When McCaffrey expressed concerns about the Chinese threat, however, Almond issued a stern rebuke: "Bill, you keep on underestimating General MacArthur."[18]

But evidence was mounting. After the Unsan debacle and the collapse of the ROK II Corps, Willoughby abandoned the claims that Chinese volunteers were simply fighting as part of NKPA formations. Acknowledging organized Chinese opposition, Willoughby's November 3 summary estimated their strength at between 16,500 and 34,000 troops. The following day, MacArthur conceded that Chinese forces in the region threatened "the ultimate destruction of my command" but warned against "hasty conclusions," declaring it "impossible at this time to authoritatively appraise the actualities of Chinese Communist intervention in North Korea." On November 5, MacArthur informed the United Nations that his forces were "in hostile contact with Chinese Communist military units."[19]

Neither the White House nor the US delegation to the United Nations registered the significance of this report. Ambassador Warren Austin presented it to the Security Council, but discussion of the contents was then postponed for two days. Perhaps the member nations had embraced MacArthur's earlier message that the war was all but won. MacArthur himself did not seem to give the report much significance and made no effort to notify the Pentagon.

That same day, MacArthur ordered his bombers to destroy every bridge over the Yalu, along with all cities, villages, and lines of communication between his forces and the Yalu. This order violated previous restrictions from the Joint Chiefs, who had limited US bombers from striking targets within five miles of the Yalu. While MacArthur stipulated that aircraft bomb only the North Korean end of the bridges, the proposed attacks constituted a brazen provocation of the Chinese. As with the UN report, MacArthur apparently felt no need to clear the campaign with the Joint Chiefs, who received word of it through US Air Force back channels three hours before takeoff.[20]

Washington Loses Control

Justifiably alarmed by the risk of a confrontation with Mao or Stalin, the nation's senior military leaders finally asserted some authority. With Truman's

approval, they sent a message to Tokyo reaffirming the earlier five-mile re-
striction and postponing the missions until MacArthur could explain his rationale.[21] The cancellation demonstrated Washington's ability to impose its
will, but the moment proved fleeting.

The cancellation message reached MacArthur at 0200 hours, rousing
him from bed. His irate response implied a radically more dangerous threat
from the Chinese:

> Men and materiel in large force are pouring across all bridges over the Yalu
> from Manchuria. This movement not only jeopardizes but threatens the ulti-
> mate destruction of the forces under my command . . . The only way to stop
> the reinforcement of the enemy is the destruction of these bridges and the sub-
> jection of all installations in the north area supporting the enemy advance to
> the maximum of our air destruction. . . . Under the gravest protest I can make,
> I am suspending this strike and carrying out your instructions. . . . I trust that
> the matter [will] be immediately brought to the attention of the President as I
> believe your instructions may well result in a calamity of major proportion for
> which I cannot accept the responsibility without his personal and direct under
> standing of the situation.[22]

In forty-eight hours, MacArthur's ambivalence had vanished. Enemy forces
were suddenly "pouring across," and "the ultimate destruction of my command" was apparently imminent. The message offered no explanation for
the sudden mood swing, but clearly the hour of crisis was at hand. The closing appeal to presidential authority provided a blunt demonstration of Mac-
Arthur's readiness to bypass the chain of command and deal directly with
the White House. His implied threat of resignation, meanwhile, set a new
standard for insubordination.[23]

With Truman's Democratic Party under heavy political pressure for an
increasingly unpopular war and for the "loss" of China, the president could
ill afford to be seen as coddling the communist enemies.[24] MacArthur's apo-
plectic tone—Acheson later characterized it as one of MacArthur's "purple
paragraphs"—forced Truman to approve bombing the North Korean
bridges.[25] The Pentagon lifted the five-mile ban but reiterated earlier restrictions against hitting dams and power plants and limited attacks to the North
Korean half of the bridges. Despite the bombing restrictions, MacArthur
had forced Washington to back down. Worse, neither Truman nor his advisors paid adequate attention to the earlier message about Chinese forces
"pouring across," which seemed to call for a major strategic review. Instead,
they merely asked MacArthur for additional information.[26]

MacArthur's response to this query downplayed his earlier warnings of imminent peril. Instead, he cautioned against "weakening at this crucial moment." Conceding the Chinese presence in North Korea, he maintained that they had not intervened in force but observed that Chinese elements in Korea "could be augmented at will," which might halt the UN advance or perhaps even force "a movement in retrograde." Nevertheless, MacArthur intended to resume his advance to the Yalu "possibly within ten days" if air attacks could disrupt "the flow of enemy reinforcements."[27]

It remains unclear whether MacArthur himself believed that air attacks could keep the Chinese north of the river. To date, MacArthur's air campaign had achieved mixed results. Air attacks in July and August had failed to stop North Korean pressure along the Pusan perimeter, and several costly incidents of fratricide had occurred. In October, two air force jets mistakenly strafed a Soviet airfield near Vladivostok, forcing Washington to apologize. Meanwhile, aerial reconnaissance over North Korea failed to identify massive Chinese formations, which avoided detection primarily by moving only at night. The bridge attacks proved fruitless; the Yalu froze in December, allowing reinforcements to simply walk across the ice.[28]

On November 9, MacArthur notified the Joint Chiefs that Walker's forces would resume their advance to the Yalu on November 15. That same day, the National Security Council (NSC) met to discuss the situation. The British government had proposed halting at the narrowest part of the peninsula (the Pyongyang-Wonsan corridor) and negotiating a settlement. The Joint Chiefs recommended solving the problem "by political means" but did not advocate cancellation of MacArthur's offensive. The CIA estimated Chinese troop strength in Korea at 30,000 to 40,000 but identified 700,000 more troops in Manchuria that were capable of "halting further UN advance" or "forcing UN withdrawal to defensive positions farther south by a powerful assault."[29] The meeting produced no changes in policy, and MacArthur continued planning his final offensive to complete the destruction of the NKPA before Chinese forces or winter weather could intervene decisively (see map 5).

Home by Christmas

MacArthur's final offensive had three major components. First, aircraft would destroy the Yalu bridges and "isolate the battlefield." Second, Walker's Eighth Army in the west would push north along a broad front, with the

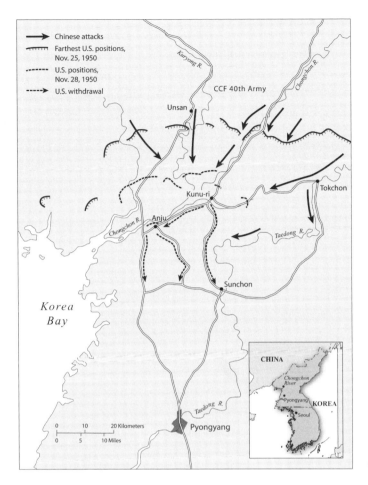

Chongchon River

Chongchon River as a central axis of advance. Finally, Almond's X Corps in the east would advance along both sides of the Chosin Reservoir, protecting Walker's right flank. Supply problems, particularly in ammunition and winter clothing, delayed Walker's advance from November 15 to November 20 and then to November 24. Still, with no sign of the Chinese, an exuberant MacArthur assured reporters that the troops would be home by Christmas, a promise he would later regret.[30]

In the east, Almond's forces enjoyed better logistical support, thanks to the proximity of the all-weather ports at Wonsan and Hungnam. Still operating under MacArthur's October directive to advance to the Yalu, these formations had advanced into North Korea's sparsely populated northeastern provinces. On the X Corps' left flank, Major General Smith's 1st Marine Division moved cautiously up a narrow mountain road toward the Chosin Reservoir. Upon reaching Hagaru-Ri, they paused to construct an airfield.[31]

In the center, the 7th Infantry Division's regiments raced north through the mountains toward the Yalu. Commanded by Maj. Gen. David Barr, the division was woefully inexperienced and undermanned, relying heavily on Korean fillers to round out its formations. Unlike Smith, who was commanding the marines, Barr was an army general and had less ability to resist the considerable pressure from Almond and MacArthur to press forward. On Almond's right flank, ROK forces continued their rapid advance up the coast road toward Siberia. The Chinese apparently dismissed these formations as insignificant and focused on the US forces advancing toward the Yalu. On November 25, the ROK Capital Division captured the city of Chongjin, only sixty-five miles from the Soviet border.[32]

MacArthur had hoped to avoid fighting throughout the winter, but it arrived with a vengeance on November 10. Temperatures plunged across the peninsula, dropping by forty degrees that afternoon in the hills south of the Chosin Reservoir, where fierce winds buffeted the 7th Marine Regiment. For the remainder of the campaign, the nighttime temperatures routinely dropped well below zero. Almond's forces had already drawn cold-weather gear, but the frigid temperatures affected everything. Weapons jammed, vehicles failed to start, medicine and plasma froze, and troops succumbed to frostbite injuries. Despite the formidable weather, a regiment from the 7th Infantry Division reached the Yalu on November 21, prompting Almond to send an effusive congratulatory message.[33]

While Almond celebrated, Walker worried. On paper, he commanded a juggernaut of nearly a quarter of a million soldiers, organized under three corps headquarters, eight divisions, and numerous separate artillery, armor, and infantry brigades.[34] Compared with the enemy, his forces enjoyed significant advantages in communications, transport, heavy artillery, and tanks, and despite the Soviets' recent deployment of MiG-15 aircraft in Manchuria, UN jets dominated the skies over most of the peninsula.[35]

Still, Walker had legitimate cause for concern. Mountains blocked contact with X Corps, and Eighth Army's right flank was exposed, with only the ROK divisions to protect it. Many of Walker's units remained understrength, and his American formations relied on poorly trained Korean conscripts (KATUSAs [Korean Augmentation to the US Army]) to fill manpower shortages. Eighth Army's frontline units were already spread thin, and the terrain to their north would disperse them even more. Finally, Walker knew little about his enemy. He had lost faith in MacArthur's jaunty optimism, on full display when MacArthur flew in to witness the beginning of the assault. Walker never challenged his commander's orders, but when MacArthur left, the Eighth Army commander shocked his aids by muttering

"Bullshit!" Walker then forwarded a message to Col. Richard Stevens, whose regiment was leading the 24th Infantry Division's attack: "You tell Dick the first time he smells Chinese chow to pull back immediately."[36]

On the morning of the attack, Eighth Army's forces straddled the lower Chongchon River, with the ROK II Corps on the right flank, the US IX Corps in the center, and the US I Corps on the left. The Chongchon flowed southwest out of the central Korean mountains, widening as it neared the sea below Anju. The three corps would advance carefully on a broad front into the narrow mountain valleys leading north. Remembering the bloody mistakes of the previous advance, Walker and his staff synchronized each detail to ensure close coordination between advancing units.[37] In case of a setback, Walker could rely on a robust reserve force that included most of the 1st Cavalry Division.[38] Many of Walker's soldiers would be advancing into familiar territory, having abandoned these hills and valleys to the Chinese only three weeks earlier.

To Walker's north, 180,000 Chinese troops waited to launch their own grand offensive, while another 120,000 waited for Almond's X Corps on the eastern side of the peninsula.[39] The Chinese knew their opponents' strengths and weaknesses. A pamphlet widely distributed among the Chinese troops after Unsan warned about the dangers of US firepower: "Their firing instruments are highly powerful. . . . Their artillery is very active. . . . Their infantry rate of fire is great and the long range of fire is still greater." The pamphlet was less complimentary about the qualities of American soldiers:

> Their infantrymen are weak, afraid to die, and haven't the courage to attack or defend. . . . They specialize in day fighting. They are not familiar with night fighting or hand to hand combat. . . . They are afraid when the rear is cut off. When transportation comes to a standstill, the infantry loses the will to fight."[40]

This was a harsh verdict, but the events to come would validate some of these conclusions.

The Chinese enjoyed one other significant advantage. Unlike their UN opponents, the Chinese knew both MacArthur's order of battle and his plan of attack as a result of several communiqués from Tokyo broadcasting the UN's intentions. On November 24, MacArthur announced that the war now approached its "decisive effort":

> The eastern sector of the pincer . . . has steadily advanced in a brilliant tactical movement and has now reached a commanding enveloping position, cutting in two the northern reaches of the enemy's geographical potential. This morning,

the western sector of the pincer moves forward in general assault in an effort to complete the compression and close the vise.

This advance publicity was, observed the *London Times,* "a curious way to fight a war."[41]

The Chinese planned to employ the same tactic that had beaten the Chinese Nationalists, the ROK Army, and the 8th Cavalry at Unsan. The approach, called *hachi-shiki,* deployed troops in a V formation, with the open end nearest the enemy. Using flares and simple bugle calls to coordinate their attacks, lightly armed infantry outflanked their opponents on both sides, while other forces moved swiftly to cut off retreat and destroy any rescue efforts. This tactic proved particularly effective in the Chongchon Valley's broken terrain, where ridges and valleys prevented the American formations from maintaining contact with adjacent units. The North Koreans had employed similar tactics during their summer campaign, with mixed results, but their Chinese allies were more experienced, more organized, and far more numerous. In addition, the Chinese excelled at night fighting, and their troops were highly motivated in the wake of their earlier success. Finally, the Chinese faced an unsuspecting enemy charging blindly into their trap. The farther north MacArthur advanced, the more effective the Chinese tactic became.[42]

On November 23, the day before the attack, most Americans in Korea celebrated Thanksgiving with a lavish dinner that was flown, trucked, and even airdropped to the front lines with enormous logistical effort. In the 5th Cavalry Regiment, PFC James Cardinal enjoyed turkey, sweet potatoes, corn, stuffing, gravy, olives, pie, and candy but was just as thrilled with the opportunity to take a hot shower, his first since September 22.[43] The British, meanwhile, witnessed this feast with mixed feelings. Some were appalled at the expense, yet impressed by the Americans' ability to provide such luxury in so barren a combat zone.[44]

Despite the army's best efforts, many soldiers missed out on the feast. Second Lieutenant Paul Roach, of Las Cruces, New Mexico, spent Thanksgiving Day manning a frigid outpost south of the Chongchon River. Like many of his Academy classmates in the class of 1950, Roach went to Korea a few weeks after graduating from West Point. By August, he was leading an infantry platoon in the 2nd Infantry Division's 9th Regiment. During the desperate fighting along the Naktong River, Roach assumed command of his rifle company after a sniper killed the senior officer. The fatal bullet punctured the windshield of the jeep, reminding the new commander of the job's inherent risks. In late September, Roach was wounded in the leg while trying to lead his company out of an ambush and spent the next six weeks recovering in Japan.[45]

When Roach returned to the 9th Regiment, he was assigned to King Company. The rifle company had only sixty-five soldiers and officers, less than half its authorized strength. Roach's commander, Capt. Benjamin Benton assigned him to lead a rifle platoon of sixteen US soldiers and five Korean augmentees. By Thanksgiving, Roach had been with King Company a week and knew hardly anyone outside his platoon, including the commander, whom he had met only a few times.[46]

The first day of the offensive—November 24—provided a brief warm spell, with temperatures climbing into the fifties. Walker's forces advanced several miles and met little resistance.[47] The biggest news of the day was the Chinese release of one hundred prisoners of war, including twenty-seven Americans, most of them 8th Cavalry soldiers selected from the large group at Pyoktong. This goodwill gesture, however, was a deliberate ruse. In an effort to further undermine MacArthur's confidence, the prisoners had been told the Chinese forces were withdrawing to Manchuria because of supply shortages.[48]

As day one of the offensive drew to a close, Roach's platoon was finally relieved of outpost duty. The undersized platoon moved forward to the banks of the Chongchon, where it spent the night in bivouac. At dawn, Roach and his men located the rest of King Company in time to eat warm leftovers for breakfast. They drew C rations for dinner and moved out to the north, leading the company across the Chongchon and into the hills on the western bank. On their right flank, other units from the 2nd Infantry Division moved carefully into high ground on the eastern side of the valley, where they encountered stiff resistance on several objectives. On this second day of the advance, the 2nd Infantry Division was already farther north and more exposed than any other division in the Eighth Army. By evening, King Company would be the most exposed company in the division.[49]

As the day progressed, King Company advanced about six miles along the western side of the Chongchon Valley and reached its designated objective by early afternoon. Roach's men encountered no enemy troops but found enemy foxholes and Chinese papers that appeared to be payrolls. It was only 1400 hours, so King Company advanced to its next objective, a hill mass approximately two thousand yards farther north. The new position, Objective 35, was a small ridge with a dry creek bordering the western and southern base. From King Company's position, the creek bed led southeast toward the Chongchon River, a thousand yards away. The nearest help would be Love Company, situated twenty-five hundred meters to the south, but King Company had no communications with them. Because of the ridgelines, their SCR-300 radios were useless, so a sergeant returned to battalion headquarters to lay wire for a telephone connection. The sergeant drew the wrong type of wire, however, and the spool ran out before he could make it back to the company position. The only other means of communication was the forward observer's radio, which worked intermittently.[50]

To make matters worse, Benton sent out no patrols and established a weak perimeter. He placed First Platoon on the top of the ridge line, oriented north, while his other two platoons dug in on low ground at the southern base of the ridge. Roach thought it was "a weird deployment." Third Platoon occupied the southwest corner of the hill, and around to their left, Roach's Second Platoon faced south, overlooking the creek bed and a small village. In his detailed study of the campaign, historian S. L. A. Marshall later suggested that Benton had put these two platoons in low ground because it made for easier digging, and Roach agreed, assuming that Benton had put his exhausted men there to give them a break. Unfortunately, the three platoons could not see or hear each other and had no communications with Benton at the company command post. Benton, meanwhile, had only sporadic communication with battalion headquarters and no contact with other American units in the area.[51]

As dusk fell, a runner arrived at Roach's position to report that Item Company (operating to the southwest of King's position) had met some resistance and might be withdrawing through the village to his south. Immediately after sunset, the small valley became exceptionally dark. Roach heard movement along the road and first assumed it was Item Company. When he heard horses, he changed his mind, and his men opened fire:

> Big mistake! [S. L. A.] Marshall says it was at least a regiment but it seemed like more to me. My machine gun jammed. My BAR man had lost most of his ammo. Anyway, we held off small attacks all night. Just before dawn I discovered that Third Platoon had disappeared [they and the rest of the company's survivors withdrew to the north]. I sent a black soldier to contact the company command post. He was gone a long time and it had turned light. He finally returned wearing a Korean hat and a white shirt (disguised) and reported, "Sir, they ain't nobody on that mountain but Chinamen!"
>
> That was when I decided that it was time for us to bug out. I told Sergeant Coleman to take half of what was left of the platoon and we would leapfrog

back to where we left Love Company. Just as they left, the Chinese attacked out of a small ravine. I never got a chance to leave. We held them off until about noon and I was the only one left shooting. The others were killed or wounded. When I ran out of ammo, I told my assistant platoon sergeant that it was time to give up. He said he was going to play dead but I later saw him as a POW. I think he died in captivity.

After I had been captured for about a week, the 3rd Battalion S1 and XO showed up. I asked if they knew if Master Sergeant Coleman and the others had gotten out. They said that they had seen Coleman, so I believed for many years that he made it. I now know that they are still MIA [missing in action] and declared dead. I believe that I am the only survivor of the Second Platoon.[52]

Heavily outnumbered and without communications, the rest of King Company withdrew to the north under enemy pressure. Abandoning the company position, small groups of Americans and Koreans tried to make their way east, but several Chinese units were moving through the area, and most of these men, including Captain Benton, were either killed or captured. Other survivors chose to hide and wait until morning, when they were able to make their way back to the American lines.[53]

The Chinese attack on King Company was part of an offensive that overwhelmed the entire Eighth Army front on the evening of November 25–26. Under cover of darkness, thousands of Chinese infantry poured into the gaps between American positions, and many American units simply disintegrated amid the chaos. Others survived the night without a scratch, bypassed by Chinese troops who did not see them in the dark. In several cases, Chinese columns passed within meters of US units without making contact. In the 2nd Infantry Division sector, Chinese forces had penetrated the front on both sides of the Chongchon, overrunning several battalion command posts, supply bases, and artillery positions in the rear area. At dawn, however, most of the attackers withdrew, giving the survivors a much-needed respite.[54]

That morning, Maj. Gen. "Dutch" Keiser, the division commander, committed most of his reserve—two infantry battalions and the division's combat engineer battalion—to bolster the 9th Regiment's defenses.[55] With his division front crippled by the previous night's battle, Keiser faced an even more serious threat on his right flank. There, South Korean units had again collapsed in the face of a massive Chinese assault, which now threatened to cut the 2nd Infantry Division's line of retreat. Keiser's division remained farther north than any other element in the Eighth Army, and only two unimproved roads were available in case it needed to withdraw. By noon on November 26, the Chinese had captured Tokchon, blocking escape to the east. The only other road led southwest to the crossroads at Kunu-Ri. There the road split. One fork continued southwest toward Anju, while the other led south through the mountains to Sunchon.[56]

The New Surgeon

Chinese night attacks also battered the units on Keiser's left flank. As dawn broke on November 26, Chinese forces threatened to puncture the center of the 25th Infantry Division's front, near Unsan. Reinforcements, including the 2nd Battalion of the 27th Infantry Regiment, rushed forward to fend off the Chinese attack.[57] The battalion's new surgeon, Capt. Sidney Esensten, had just arrived the night before.

Like thousands of other reservists that year, the young doctor had recently been recalled to active duty. He shipped out in October, leaving behind his pregnant wife and two children in Minneapolis. It was hard to say goodbye, but millions of men had endured the same hardship in the previous war. Besides, he was on orders for Japan, where he was slated to fill in as a pediatrician. When he arrived, however, he spent his first ten days at the port of Yokohama, doing triage on wounded soldiers arriving on hospital ships. In early November, he was reassigned as a replacement surgeon in Korea and flew to Kimpo Airfield in Seoul, where he spent several days waiting for his assignment.[58]

On the morning of November 25, Esensten finally received orders and rode two hundred miles north from Seoul in a jeep, arriving at his unit after midnight. At dawn the next morning, his battalion moved forward to reinforce American units near Unsan. Esensten and his medical section convoyed north to their new assembly area, which they reached after dark. The battalion was fiercely engaged throughout the evening, and shortly after midnight, the battalion commander decided to evacuate his wounded to the town of Ipsok, several hundred meters south of the battalion command post.

At 0200 hours, Esensten and a small convoy of ambulances and medical vehicles drove south into the darkness. They had gone six hundred meters when enemy fire struck Esensten's driver in both legs. Their jeep jerked to a halt, blocking the narrow road. Esensten tumbled out of the passenger's side and into a roadside ditch, where he was immediately captured. Most of the Americans were unarmed medical personnel. The Chinese quickly killed or captured all of them.[59]

Collapse

As dawn broke on November 27, General Walker finally realized the scope of the calamity on his right flank, where the Chinese had scattered three South Korean divisions. He committed all available reserves, including the newly arrived brigades from Turkey and Great Britain, in an effort to plug this gap and protect the lifeline to his forward units. The Chinese, perhaps emboldened by their success on the previous two days, continued attacking in broad daylight, ignoring UN air strikes. On the morning of November 28, after another night of heavy fighting in most sectors, Walker ordered a general withdrawal. With the exception of rear-guard units, most of the Eighth Army escaped to the relative safety of the Chongchon River by the evening of November 29.[60]

The 2nd Infantry Division's situation, however, remained perilous. Two of its three regiments had been severely mauled, leaving Col. Paul Freeman's 23rd Infantry as the division's only combat-effective regiment. A poorly co-ordinated attack by the Turkish Brigade had briefly halted the Chinese pressure east of Kunu-Ri, but the ill-trained Turks were quickly surrounded and defeated. Under Chinese pressure, Freeman's battalions leapfrogged back toward the village of Won-ni, where they joined the remnants of the 9th Regiment in a new defensive line. The battered 38th Regiment, meanwhile, dug in east of the village and finally established contact with the Turkish and South Korean remnants that had fought their way out of the encirclement to the east.

Over the next twenty-four hours, Keiser's staff scrambled to coordinate a withdrawal through Kunu-Ri toward Sunchon, where the 1st Cavalry Division was, in effect, holding the door. Near dawn on November 29, however, Keiser received more bad news—Chinese forces now blocked the road below Kunu-Ri. Keiser sent two companies south to break the roadblock, while asking higher headquarters for more information about the enemy situation. The IX Corps staff had no information to share, but it eventually dispatched a British battalion north to open the road. This attack failed, but Keiser's requests to withdraw along the southwestern route were repeatedly denied, so he ordered the 9th Regiment, now reduced to four hundred men, to attack the roadblock in the south.[61]

The attack began at 0730 hours on December 1 and made little progress. Later that morning, Keiser considered making a last stand at Kunu-Ri. At 1330 hours, he sent his remaining forces down the road in hopes of breaking through, leaving Freeman's regiment and the 2nd Engineer Battalion as a rear guard. When the division convoy moved south, Chinese infantry and mortar fire began engaging the slow-moving vehicles from both sides of the narrow valley.[62]

Soon, disabled American trucks blocked the road, forcing others to halt while heavy vehicles came forward to clear the way. Meanwhile, Chinese weapons sprayed the convoy, which soon stretched seven miles toward Sunchon. The retreating Americans loaded the wounded onto any available vehicle but had to abandon their dead, who clogged the roadside ditches. Although UN air strikes pounded the Chinese positions along the ridge lines, they had limited effect. As the afternoon progressed, Keiser's withdrawal became a debacle. His entire division had plunged into a Chinese ambush. Freezing and exhausted, some US troops simply sat down by the road in an apparent state of shock. A few escaped south on foot, but many more did not. The remnants of Keiser's division arrived in Sunchon that night, but he had lost five thousand men, many of whom joined Paul Roach as prisoners of the Chinese.[63]

As the rear guard, Colonel Freeman's 23rd Infantry Regiment held its positions until dusk, then withdrew southwest toward Anju. To cover their withdrawal, Freeman's gunners fired their remaining ammunition in a twenty-two-minute fusillade that convinced the Chinese that a counterattack was impending. While the Chinese began digging fighting positions, Freeman ordered the convoy to "Get the hell out of here, and don't stop!" The 2nd Engineer Battalion was less fortunate—most of its soldiers were killed or captured. The survivors felt that Freeman had abandoned them.[64]

6   The Reservoir

Kill the marines as you would snakes in your homes.
Gen. Sung Shih-lun, commander, Ninth Army, CCF

While Walker's Eighth Army narrowly escaped destruction along the Chongchon River in late November, the Chinese Ninth Army Group waited patiently in the snow-covered mountains surrounding the Chosin Reservoir.[1] Advancing toward them was Maj. Gen. O. P. Smith's well-trained and well-equipped 1st Marine Division, with experienced leaders and a full complement of artillery, armor, and close air support. Despite their robust combat power, the marine position at the reservoir was exceptionally vulnerable. The division's right flank was guarded by two understrength infantry battalions from the 7th Infantry Division. The division's left flank, meanwhile, was completely unprotected. Worst of all, the army and marine units at Chosin relied on a single dirt road for reinforcements and resupply. The Chinese plan called for several divisions to infiltrate south through the eighty-mile gap between the marines and the Eighth Army, cut the marines' supply line, then turn east and complete the destruction of Maj. Gen. Ned Almond's X Corps.[2]

Race to the Yalu

The mission of X Corps had changed significantly since capturing Seoul six weeks earlier. First, the marines and the 7th Infantry Division were directed to land at Wonsan, a major port on North Korea's east coast. After the landing, these forces would drive west toward Pyongyang and cut off the remnants of the North Korean People's Army in the center of the peninsula. Before the landings took place, however, Walker's Eighth Army captured Pyongyang, thereby precluding the need for Almond's assistance.[3]

Fehrenbach, *This Kind of War,* 360.

With the North Korean forces apparently defeated, MacArthur had thrown caution to the wind and directed both Almond and Walker to continue to the Yalu. On the east side of the peninsula, South Korean forces continued their progress north along the coastal road. The marines finally came ashore at Wonsan on October 26, and the 7th Infantry Division landed at Iwon, 170 miles farther north. Both the marines and the 7th Infantry Division began pushing north into the mountains. At Sudong, the 7th Marine Regiment met significant Chinese resistance during the first week of November, but the Chinese forces vanished on November 6 and 7 in concert with a similar disappearance on the Eighth Army front.[4]

Following this withdrawal, Col. Homer Litzenberg's 7th Marine Regiment climbed a narrow trail through the Funchilin Pass to Koto-ri, eleven miles south of the Chosin Reservoir. During their withdrawal, the Chinese had neglected to destroy a bridge spanning a critical portion of this mountain road. Its destruction would have delayed the marines' advance, and the Chinese failure to do so led Smith and his staff to suspect a trap.[5] Litzenberg's regiment reached the nearly abandoned village on November 10 and was greeted by a Siberian cold front. That afternoon, temperatures plunged from 40 degrees to –8 degrees Fahrenheit, while thirty-five-mile-per-hour winds amplified the misery. The arctic conditions temporarily disabled two hundred marines with cold-weather injuries.[6]

Aware that marine pilots had reported convoys of Chinese trucks crossing the Yalu, Smith had already recommended that X Corps postpone offensive operations to the spring.[7] Almond rejected Smith's advice but did acknowledge the importance of consolidating forces, perhaps mindful of the 8th Cavalry's fate at Unsan. Moreover, he agreed with Smith that operations north of the Chosin Reservoir would need an airfield to deliver supplies and evacuate casualties. Airfield construction required bulldozers, but these would not arrive until improvements were made to the mountain road leading to the reservoir. This road quickly became known simply as "the MSR" (main supply route). Its twisting path from the reservoir back down to the sea became a critical battleground.[8]

As November progressed, Almond's support for the consolidation of Smith's division seemed an empty promise. With MacArthur intent on reaching the Yalu before the onset of winter, Almond's forces continued to advance on a wide front. In the 1st Marine Division sector, the 7th Regiment established a forward base at Koto-ri, but the rest of Smith's division guarded the supply lines, manned blocking positions, and conducted patrols across a broad swath of territory to the south and east. Unhappy with the dispersion of his forces, General Smith finally wrote a private letter to the commandant of the Marine Corps and relayed his concerns:

> My mission is still to advance to the border. The Eighth Army, 80 miles to our southwest, will not attack until the 20th [later changed to November 24]. Manifestly, we should not push on without regard to the Eighth Army. We would simply get further out on a limb. . . . I believe a winter campaign in the mountains of North Korea is too much to ask of the American soldier or marine, and I doubt the feasibility of supplying troops in this area during the winter or providing for the evacuation of sick and wounded.

Smith then commended the achievements and morale of the men in his command but closed by questioning the wisdom of "stringing out" his troops "along a single mountain road for 120 air miles from Hamhung to the border."[9]

While engineers improved the MSR, newly arrived units from the US Army's 3rd Infantry Division relieved Smith's marines of various rear-area security missions. On November 14, the 5th Marine Regiment arrived at Koto-ri, enabling the 7th Regiment to advance to Hagaru, at the southern tip of the Chosin Reservoir. By November 19, the road conditions enabled work to begin on the Hagaru airfield. Smith resisted pressure to advance further until the airfield was operable.[10]

Change of Plans

On November 15, however, MacArthur redirected the X Corps a second time. Acknowledging the possibility of a major Chinese presence below the Yalu, he directed Almond to support Walker's Eighth Army by sending forces north to Changjin and then west toward the Huichon-Kanggye-Manpo corridor, one of two main supply routes for Chinese men and matériel traveling south. With the approval of MacArthur's staff, Almond amended the plan by sending the marines due west from the Chosin Reservoir toward Mupyong-ni, while the 7th Division advanced north along the eastern shore of the reservoir. On the 7th Division's right flank, the South Korean I Corps would continue its advance northeast toward the Russian border. In the south, the newly arrived 3rd Infantry Division would attack west into the mountains to protect the marines' left flank.[11]

The new concept made some sense on paper. Assuming they faced no significant enemy threat, the marines, Almond's most capable force, would drive fifty-five miles to the west, cut the Chinese supply line, and threaten enemy defenses from the rear. If it worked, the Chinese would be caught between Walker's hammer and Almond's anvil. In reality, the plan completely ignored the terrain, the weather, and the enemy, oversights that alarmed both the marines and Almond's own staff. If MacArthur's original concept of advancing along widely dispersed routes seemed risky, the new concept appeared delusional. It was, as Almond's chief of staff, Maj. Gen. Nick Ruffner, later wrote, "an insane plan. You couldn't take a picnic lunch in peacetime and go over that terrain in November and December." Hoping that MacArthur might regain his senses, Almond's planners dragged their feet. Loyal to a fault, Almond refused to challenge the new plan, especially after Inchon had made fools of MacArthur's doubters.[12]

Meanwhile, the coldest winter in a decade descended upon the Taebaek Mountains. The frigid weather effected military operations throughout the peninsula and had a particularly devastating impact on the Koto-ri plateau, four thousand feet above sea level, where soldiers and marines were about to fight the coldest campaign in US military history. Thin air, freezing winds, and subzero temperatures made even the most routine tasks difficult for Almond's mechanized forces. The cold disabled engines, weapons, radios, and rations. Frozen plasma bottles exploded, and men had to urinate on the machine guns to thaw the firing mechanisms. Unlike the battles in the Eighth Army's sector, ice, fog, and deep snowdrifts limited visibility, delayed vehicle movements along the mountain roads, and frequently grounded air operations. On November 21, a regiment from the 7th Infantry Division managed to negotiate the icy roads all the way to the Yalu, literally shoveling through snowdrifts in one pass, but there was no way to resupply the regiment once it arrived.[13]

The marines were scheduled to launch their advance on November 27, three days after the Eighth Army launched its attack in the west. In the meantime, Almond finally permitted Smith to consolidate more of his division in and around Hagaru, where the marines had established a divisional command post (see map 6). By the eve of the offensive, Smith had pushed the 5th and 7th regiments fourteen miles up the west side of the reservoir to the village of Yudam-ni. Farther south, the three battalions in Colonel "Chesty" Puller's 1st Regiment provided security at Hagaru, Koto-ri, and the railhead at Chinhung-ni. Puller's battalions, however, were positioned ten miles apart, with no way to help each other. The Chinese could cut the MSR whenever and wherever they wanted.[14]

On November 27, Almond drove forward through a blinding snow-

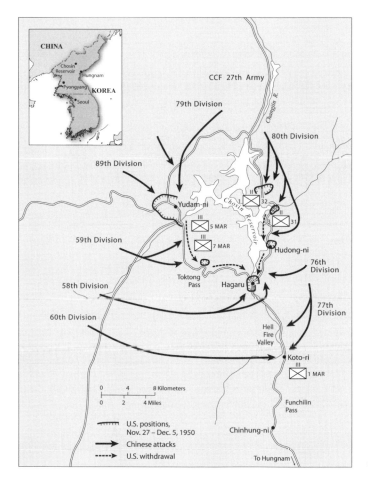

Chosin Reservoir

storm to watch Murray's 5th Marine Regiment launch its westward assault. By this time, Chinese attacks had crushed Walker's offensive in the west, destroying his right flank and threatening to encircle his remaining forces. In Tokyo, however, MacArthur's staff was slow to acknowledge the danger in Eighth Army's sector, much less realize the threat to X Corps. Thus, at 0815 hours, marine infantry moved out in subzero temperatures to seize the initial objectives along the road toward Mupyong-ni.[15]

While the marines advanced cautiously, the Chinese Ninth Army made final preparations for a massive counterattack. In the hills west of Yudam-ni, however, it made a mistake. Advancing marines encountered stiff resistance and spent the next several hours fighting for key terrain west of the village. By midafternoon, the lead companies had progressed less than two miles when they wisely halted and began digging in. Had the Chinese withdrawn farther to the west, the marines might have continued advancing into the enemy's trap.[16]

As it was, the 1st Marine Division's positions on the evening of November 27 remained dangerously exposed, especially at Hagaru. There, a reinforced infantry battalion, two artillery batteries, and assorted combat engineers and support troops protected the division's forward command post, its supply dumps, and the critical, albeit unfinished, airfield. Fortunately for the marines, a planned Chinese attack at Hagaru was delayed by twenty-four hours. On the marines' right flank, a composite force of three thousand troops from the 7th Infantry Division, Task Force Mclean, occupied similarly vulnerable positions along the reservoir's eastern shore.[17]

The temperature plunged to 20 degrees below zero after dark. At 2100 hours, several Chinese divisions slammed into the American defenses around the reservoir. Two Chinese divisions attacked the perimeter at Yudam-ni, one division struck Task Force McLean in the east, and other Chinese forces established roadblocks along the MSR between Yudam-ni, Toktong Pass, Hagaru, and Koto-ri. The Chinese overran a number of platoon and company positions and successfully cut the MSR in several places. Their progress came at a terrible price, especially at Yudam-ni, where American firepower slaughtered successive waves of Chinese attackers. On Hill 1282, for example, a reinforced marine company held its positions while inflicting four hundred casualties on the attacking Chinese battalion.[18]

Fox Hill

The most significant battle on this night took place at Toktong Pass, halfway between Yudam-ni and Hagaru. There, 240 marines of Company F, 7th Regiment, under the command of Capt. William Barber, occupied a commanding hill mass overlooking a sharp curve in the MSR. Another marine company had occupied a hill farther north along the MSR, but Chinese assaults forced it to withdraw toward Yudam-ni. With the nearest friendly units seven miles away, the men of Fox Company were on their own. Lieutenant Lawrence Schmitt later recalled that "Captain Barber acted as if he expected to be attacked. God bless him." After checking his perimeter, Barber established a watch schedule in his command post to monitor the perimeter's status throughout the night. Barber's caution would soon pay dividends.[19]

In the early hours of November 28, Chinese infantry attacked Barber's position from three separate directions. The attack fell heaviest on the north side of the perimeter, killing fifteen men and wounding nine in Lt. Robert

McCarthy's third platoon. In addition, the Chinese grabbed three prisoners in their assault, immediately hustling the captured marines to the rear. Survivors withdrew toward the hilltop, throwing grenades to cover their retreat. When his machine gun jammed, one of McCarthy's men stood and fired his pistol at the attackers, killing six. Elsewhere, Pvt. Hector Caffereta stood in his stockings to fire a steady stream of bullets at the enemy, while a wounded buddy passed loaded rifles to him. Caffereta, who later received the Congressional Medal of Honor, had not had time to don his boots. His courage helped save the second platoon's position on McCarthy's left flank.[20]

By dawn, Fox Company was running dangerously low on ammunition, but they had held their position, decimating the attacking Chinese in the process. Later that day, air strikes pummeled the Chinese positions at Toktong Pass, while cargo planes dropped medicine and ammunition to Barber's men. From Yudam-ni, Colonel Litzenberg sent a battalion to relieve the stranded marines, but the rescue mission stalled in the face of heavy enemy resistance. A reinforced company set forth from Hagaru with the same mission and experienced similar results.[21]

At midday on November 28, Almond arrived by helicopter to visit General Smith at Hagaru and then flew forward to the 1st Battalion, 32nd Infantry, commanded by Lt. Col. Don Faith. Faith's soldiers occupied high ground on the northern bank of the Pungnyuri inlet, four road miles northeast of Task Force MacLean's main body. Faith's battalion had weathered the previous evening's assaults in relatively good shape, but the forces at the inlet, consisting of the 3rd Battalion, 31st Regiment and elements of the 57th Field Artillery Battalion, had fared much worse. Both battalion commanders had been injured, and the Chinese had captured several key positions along the high ground overlooking the American position. Instead of attacking, the 1st Marine Division and Task Force McLean now found themselves trapped in isolated pockets around the Chosin Reservoir. Neither MacLean nor Almond seemed to appreciate the danger. During the meeting, Almond approved MacLean's plan to resume the offensive as soon as reinforcements arrived and dismissed the enemy that had nearly overrun the perimeter as "remnants of Chinese divisions fleeing north."[22]

The majority of the 1st Marine Division's combat power, including two infantry regiments and most of the division's artillery, was located forward, within the perimeter at Yudam-Ni. Dwindling ammunition and mounting casualties meant these forces could not hold out for long. Captain Barber's company still controlled Toktong Pass, but with fifty-four wounded marines on "Fox Hill," their situation looked desperate as well. Hagaru, however, was the lynchpin of the entire American position. As long as Smith controlled this critical road junction, he could support the withdrawal of his own two regiments, as well as that of Task Force MacLean. Based on reports from Korean refugees and their own scouts, the marines at Hagaru expected a major attack on the night of November 28.[23]

Task Force Drysdale

To strengthen Hagaru's defenses, Smith ordered Puller to send reinforcements from Koto-ri, which now contained a hodgepodge of units forced to halt by enemy roadblocks. These included a variety of combat and support units and a contingent of 235 British commandos, led by Lt. Col. Douglas Drysdale. Arriving late on the afternoon of November 28, Drysdale's men assumed a section of the thinly manned defenses inside the perimeter. At 2000 hours, Puller assigned Drysdale to lead a hastily assembled task force of combat and supply units to break through to Hagaru on the following morning. While Drysdale tried to locate and coordinate his attack with various commanders inside Koto-ri's darkened perimeter, two Chinese divisions attacked at Hagaru. Fortunately, neither division committed its full strength to these attacks. Again, the Chinese suffered horrific losses, and Hagaru held.[24]

At 0945 the next morning, Drysdale's task force began its attack from Koto-ri. Following air strikes and an artillery barrage, Drysdale's commandos assaulted the first hill mass east of the MSR. Drysdale planned to use his three combat units—the commandos, an infantry company from the US Army, and a marine rifle company—to seize a series of hill masses along both sides of the road. Meanwhile, the rest of his convoy, including a large number of staff officers and support troops, would push forward to Hagaru, ten miles to the north.[25]

Wearing distinctive green berets instead of helmets, the British commandos brushed aside light opposition to capture the first objective. A mile and a half to the north, the marines overcame entrenched enemy resistance to seize the next ridgeline. Meanwhile, enemy fire slowed Drysdale's progress to a crawl. Ignoring several air strikes, the Chinese continued to fire from multiple positions at both the assault forces and the convoy, inflicting heavy casualties. "We finally came to understand," a British commando later recalled, "that there were a lot of Chinese bastards shooting at us from every conceivable angle and that we were all in the same bloody boat."[26]

After seizing his first two objectives, Drysdale received word that tank reinforcements would soon be available. He chose to wait, but the tanks did not arrive until 1330 hours, and their commander refused Drysdale's request to disperse the tanks throughout his column. Leading the way forward, the buttoned-up tanks halted repeatedly to engage enemy targets, blocking the MSR. Each of these engagements forced Drysdale's column to a halt, exposing vehicles and passengers to enemy small-arms fire.[27] By late afternoon, Drysdale's column had stopped four miles north of Koto-ri, where they were confronted by a heavily fortified roadblock. With dusk rapidly approaching, Drysdale faced a difficult decision. The tankers felt they could make it the rest of the way. Drysdale, however, had already lost several trucks and dozens of men to enemy fire; the rest of his light-skinned vehicles stood little chance of making the journey. Drysdale asked Division Headquarters for guidance, and Smith, desperate for reinforcements, responded: "If it is at all possible, fight your way through."[28]

Hell Fire Valley

While US Marine aircraft plastered the ridgelines, the tanks refueled and resumed their advance, followed by a marine rifle company, the British commandos, an infantry company from the US Army's 31st Regiment, and the marine headquarters and support vehicles. A mile to the north, the column entered a long, narrow stretch of road, later dubbed "Hell Fire Valley." Once again, enemy fire forced the column to stop, and once again the men abandoned their vehicles, took cover, and returned fire. A Chinese mortar ignited one of the abandoned trucks, and the burning vehicle blocked the road, cutting the column in half. Chinese gunners now concentrated on the men south of the blockage. Drysdale, mindful of Smith's urgent need, ordered the remaining vehicles to resume their advance. Unaware of the roadblock, Drysdale and the other commanders assumed the rest of the column would catch up as it had done several times earlier in the day. After another sharp exchange with Chinese forces two thousand yards from his objective, Drysdale's contingent reached the Hagaru perimeter at 1915 hours, with the tanks and four hundred men. The reinforcements significantly bolstered Hagaru's thin defensive line, but that success came with a price.[29]

Back in Hell Fire Valley, isolated groups of soldiers, marines, and commandos returned fire against the Chinese. As darkness fell, marine Corsairs bombed and strafed the enemy positions until they could no longer identify their targets. Enemy fire intensified as mortars and small-arms fire rained down on the column from an elevated plateau east of the road. Lieutenant Colonel Arthur Chidester, the 1st Marine Division's assistant G4, ordered the vehicles back toward Koto-ri, but Chinese mortars hit a second truck, this one carrying ammunition, and the rounds began to "cook off" amid the fire. In addition to blocking the road south, the ammunition truck further splintered the survivors. Chidester and approximately 140 men, including Capt. Charles Peckham and most of Baker Company, 31st Infantry, were trapped north of the blazing truck. Major James Eagen tried to organize a defensive position near the truck but was wounded and captured by Chinese forces during a probing attack. Chidester was also severely wounded early in the fighting and relinquished command to Maj. John McLaughlin, a marine liaison officer to X Corps. McLaughlin organized a hasty defense and was ably assisted by Warrant Officer Lloyd Dirst, who commanded a detachment of marine military police with the convoy. The growing number of wounded men soon overwhelmed the army medics trapped with this group.[30]

Three smaller groups formed hasty perimeters farther south under the leadership of Maj. Henry Seeley, the marine division's transport officer. A column of tanks had been scheduled to join the rear of the column that afternoon, and Seeley hoped these reinforcements would arrive in time to support a breakout. In fact, the tanks made little progress before encountering heavy Chinese resistance. Under withering enemy fire, the reinforcing column broke into smaller groups. The rear element, including a tank platoon and several trucks, returned safely to Koto-ri. The forward element, a tank platoon led by 1st Lt. Herbert Turner, continued forward to within a half mile of Seeley's position, where enemy fire forced it to halt. Turner had no communications with Seeley and did not know either his location or situation. Turner's platoon established a tight defensive perimeter and, with supporting artillery fire from Koto-ri, survived the night, withdrawing the next morning. The middle of the column, however, suffered numerous dead and wounded. Despite losing most of their trucks to enemy fire, the survivors fought their way back to Koto-ri, arriving after midnight.[31]

At Hell Fire Valley, Chinese snipers kept the survivors pinned down for several hours, while bolder Chinese troops looted the American trucks. This interval gave McLaughlin and Seeley an opportunity to assess their plight. Armed with grenades and small arms, the remnants of Task Force Drysdale clung to a mile-long section of the road. Some American trucks were loaded with ammunition, but the flames and enemy small-arms fire prevented all salvage efforts. Two Chinese regiments controlled the high ground to the east, as well as the valley's northern and southern exits. The valley itself was about five hundred meters wide, with snow-covered fields and a mountain stream on the western side of the road. Any escape attempt would expose the men to a deadly crossfire in the open ground. Besides, McLaughlin's group now had several dozen wounded men to consider. McLaughlin sent reconnaissance parties south to link up with other groups, but these efforts failed. Their best chance was to hold out until dawn, when air cover might even the odds.[32]

Shortly after midnight, however, squads of Chinese began probing the positions along the road. For a while, the defenders managed to deter these maneuvers with grenades and small-arms fire. An army gun crew managed to put a 75-millimeter recoilless rifle into action, and the crew destroyed several Chinese mortar crews. The gun also attracted the attention of enemy snipers, who killed three gunners during the battle. Meanwhile, ammunition was becoming scarce within the American perimeter. By 0230 hours, the Chinese had crept to within grenade distance of McLaughlin's positions. McLaughlin's group continued taking casualties, including Warrant Officer Dirst, who moved continuously between fighting positions during the battle until he was seriously wounded by enemy fire. Staff Sergeant James Nash dashed forward to drag the officer to safety.[33]

Surrender and Escape

By 0300 hours, McLaughlin's group had about forty able-bodied men left, with the rest either dead or wounded. Marine captain Ernie Reid was among those injured during the Chinese attacks due to a grenade that peppered his legs with shrapnel. Lying in the makeshift aid station, Reid witnessed the final minutes of the battle in Hell Fire Valley as the defenders spent their last ammunition:

> So we were down to the "fix bayonets" situation, ready to give it the last fight, when two youngsters, they were two PFCs, came to Major McLaughlin and said, "I've got my jeep here. Let me go in the jeep and I can get back to headquarters in Koto-ri and get some ammo." The major said, "Well I don't think you've got much of a chance, son. If you want to do it, then take off."

The two privates and another passenger got the jeep started but made only a hundred yards before the Chinese captured them.[34]

At 0430 hours, the Chinese sent the prisoners back with a demand that McLaughlin surrender his forces. McLaughlin and a British commando agreed to the parley, hoping to stall for time. As McLaughlin later recounted, "Initially, I demanded a Chinese surrender! But it made little impression." McLaughlin next delivered a list of conditions. The Chinese agreed to McLaughlin's demand to send seriously wounded men back to Koto-ri, but they soon lost patience with his delaying tactics. Speaking through an interpreter, the senior Chinese officer gave McLaughlin ten minutes to coordinate the surrender with his officers before the Chinese overran the perimeter.[35]

McLaughlin returned to the perimeter, where he discussed the terms with other officers and confirmed the ammunition shortage. As Captain Reid later recalled, "Somebody said, 'Well, we're not going to surrender. We're not going to do that.' And he [McLaughlin] says, 'Wait a minute. Let's be very clear. I am surrendering and you don't have anything to say about it and we will all remember this.' Finally, McLaughlin and his men disabled their weapons and surrendered."[36]

During his negotiations with the Chinese, McLaughlin had asked to confer with Major Seeley. With forty-four troops, plenty of ammunition, and relatively few injured men, Seeley and his men held a much stronger position to the south. The Chinese allowed the meeting, and Seeley told McLaughlin he would not surrender his position. As Seeley made his way back, the Chinese moved in and disarmed McLaughlin's troops. As this was happening, Seeley met briefly with his officers and decided to break out to the west. Dragging and carrying their wounded, Seeley's group waded through the freezing stream and climbed the ridge line behind it, then turned south. They took five hours to make it back to Koto-ri.[37]

Several other small groups of men escaped on foot, including Lt. Alfred Catania, an army truck platoon leader. Like Seeley's group, Catania and several other men crossed the stream and escaped across the ridge line to the west. Catania had been severely hurt in the initial ambush, but he managed his way up the hill, where he cut the boots from his water-soaked feet. His socks had frozen to the boots, so Catania wrapped one foot in strips of blanket and used his pile-liner cap for the other foot. The other three men with Catania followed his example. At dawn, Catania decided to risk traveling on the MSR, and he and his group limped back to Koto-ri. Watching from the ridge lines, the Chinese troops mercifully allowed the group to proceed without interference.[38]

Empty Promises

In the valley, the Chinese soldiers resumed looting the American trucks as soon as McLaughlin's group laid down their weapons. Others greeted their US and British prisoners with smiles and handshakes. The Chinese commander broke his promise to evacuate McLaughlin's wounded men but did shelter some of the seriously injured in a Korean house, including Warrant Officer Dirst. These men survived for eight days before being rescued by marines withdrawing from Hagaru and Yudam-ni. The rest of the captives marched into the hills east of the road.[39]

Captain Reid was placed in a hut with Lieutenant Colonel Chidester and Major Eagen, both of whom lay on stretchers, severely wounded. Reid vividly recalled their desperate situation:

Lieutenant Colonel Chidester had been gut shot, and he was very pale, a very brave man, a very thoughtful leader. Of course, I knew him from my liaison duties going into the G4 shop. He spoke Chinese; he'd been in China and understood the language of the soldiers there, and he was trying to convince this young Chinese officer that spoke English that he didn't have a chance, he was going to be a dead man, so why didn't they just let him and the major go back to Koto-ri where there was medical aid. And of course the Chinese said, "We're going to take you to our doctor."

Then Colonel Chidester says to me, "How bad are you hurt?" And I said I could walk, but I was in a lot of pain. And he says: "Let me tell you something. You walk. Don't let them put you on a litter. Because you're the junior guy, and if they have to drop somebody, you're a dead man." So he says, "When they move us, don't let them put you on a litter. Gut it out." And here's a man that is dying, but he's thinking about me.

And that's the best advice I think I've gotten. I don't know whether I'd have been shot or not, because this was a pretty good crowd of Chinese, as it turned out. So they took the three of us, the two on the litter, and they had a litter for me and we went cross-corridor for half the night, we went to the west, and then we went north the rest of the way.

A little before first light we ran into this smell. . . . I didn't have anybody to talk to, because both of the officers [Chidester and Eagen], by this time, were out of it, and I couldn't identify what it was. When it got light enough I could see we were walking by—in a column of twos—the Chinese. And these were guys that were wounded, carrying sleds with guys who couldn't walk. And we walked and we walked and it was full light before we got to the aid station, a mud farm house.

They had one doctor and four or five assistants or nurses, and they were doing amputations. It must have been over a mile they had these guys lined up.

So the guard took me into the aid station. He gave the doctor a piece of paper that he had written [on]. It must have said: "Take care of these guys if you're able to." And the doctor looked, and he looked outside and he looked over there and he came back with the equipment, and what I understood was "Yes, I'll take care of it after I take care of these guys."

I would not want to go in front of that line to save me. I'd have been a dead man if I tried, I think, because these guys were watching. I went outside another door and when I did, I could see the bodies that were stacked up were Chinese, and there were limbs that had been amputated.

Reid and the other two officers spent the following day at the Chinese aid station. The Chinese provided no treatment for the wounded marines. Chidester and Eagen perished, and Reid was marched to the northwest, where he rejoined McLaughlin and other prisoners from Hell Fire Valley. Other captives taken at Chosin Reservoir eventually joined them, and the group of approximately three hundred men spent the winter eating meager rations and enduring Chinese indoctrination at a temporary camp north of Kanggye.[40]

Task Force Faith

While the Chinese herded their prisoners away from Hell Fire Valley, another disaster was developing on the east side of the Chosin Reservoir. There, on the morning of November 30, remnants of Task Force MacLean clung to a defensive perimeter at the Pungnyuri inlet, eight miles north of Hagaru along the shore of the frozen reservoir. In three nights of bitter fighting, they had suffered heavy losses, including Colonel MacLean, whom the Chinese had captured. Having withdrawn his battalion to the inlet position, Lieutenant Colonel Faith now assumed command of the task force, renamed Task Force Faith, and ordered his men to fortify their perimeter and wait for rescue. They had been resupplied by air the previous afternoon, and aggressive marine air strikes had discouraged daylight attacks by the Chinese in the surrounding hills.[41]

Well aware of Faith's tenuous position, the Chinese had committed reinforcements to the assault at the inlet. The Americans' plight was further complicated by poor communications with Hagaru and by the presence of five hundred wounded men, many of them litter cases, inside the perimeter. In addition, the antiaircraft vehicles that had provided critical firepower were desperately short of ammunition. November 30 brought more bad news: the withdrawal of the 31st Tank Company from Hudong-ni, four miles south of Faith's perimeter. The tankers had failed in two earlier attempts to break through to Faith's perimeter, but their presence at Hudong-ni had kept the Chinese from blocking Faith's escape route.[42]

When the tankers reached Hagaru, they were immediately assigned to defensive positions along the perimeter, where the marines expected another major assault. Shortly after dark, three Chinese regiments launched a coordinated attack along two sides of the perimeter, and the fighting raged until midnight. The 31st Tank Company and the reinforcements from Task Force Drysdale played a key role in defeating these efforts, while inflicting more heavy losses on the Chinese 58th Division.[43]

In conjunction with these attacks, the Chinese 80th Division assaulted Task Force Faith's fragile perimeter from three sides, overrunning several more positions. The Americans fought back savagely, and the battle raged until after dawn, as scattered enemy units continued to attack in broad daylight. As was often the case at Chosin, Chinese troops suffered horrendous losses to heavy-weapons fire during the battle. An American survivor later thought the attackers had been ordered to seize the position regardless of the cost. Meanwhile, the number of American and South Korean wounded had grown to six hundred, and Faith concluded he could hold no longer. Shortly after dawn on December 1, Faith issued orders to load the wounded on trucks, destroy the heavy weapons, and prepare for a breakout at noon.[44]

The move began badly. Faith's marine air controller had coordinated for a flight of Corsairs to provide air support during the breakout, but the aircraft arrived an hour late, and the lead plane's first bombing run fell short. Napalm engulfed the head of the American column, killing at least one American and seriously injuring others. Faith managed to restore order in his badly shaken men, and the column inched forward in fits and starts under steady Chinese fire. By 1500 hours, the column had advanced two miles south to the base of Hill 1221, where a blown bridge forced it to halt. As daylight faded, Faith's men slowly winched thirty trucks across a semi-frozen creek bed. The process took two hours, during which Chinese machine gunners raked the column and inflicted heavy casualties, particularly among the helpless wounded in the trucks.[45]

A few hundred meters south of the creek bed, the column encountered a heavily defended roadblock at Hill 1221. In this moment of desperation, Faith rallied the survivors, including many of the severely hurt, to mount a series of assaults against the Chinese positions on the hill and at the roadblock. Incredibly, these attacks succeeded, but in the midst of the firefight, a Chinese grenade fragment hit Faith in the chest, mortally wounding him.

Faith was placed in the cab of the lead truck, and the remaining vehicles continued south into the darkness. More obstacles forced the convoy to halt again just south of Hudong. Several trucks flipped over, crushing their occupants. Many of the remaining solders were captured or slaughtered, as Chinese forces attacked the stalled trucks with machine guns and phosphorous grenades. The survivors abandoned the column and stumbled across the frozen reservoir toward Hagaru, unmolested by the Chinese.[46]

Over the next two days, several hundred survivors limped to safety, and the Chinese returned some of their gravely wounded prisoners. Search parties from Hagaru braved enemy fire to rescue several hundred more, but a marine patrol also counted more than three hundred dead in the abandoned American trucks at Hudong. In four days of battle, approximately half of Task Force Faith was killed or captured, but it delayed two Chinese divisions in the process, thus helping to save Hagaru and the 1st Marine Division.[47]

Breakout

Meanwhile, the tide was turning at Yudam-ni. Rescue efforts on November 28 and 29 had failed to reach Fox Company's position at Toktong Pass, but Chinese attacks on the Yudam-ni perimeter slackened. On Fox Hill, daily air drops replenished Captain Barber's men with food, ammunition, and medical supplies. A few hours before dawn on November 30, Barber's men destroyed another Chinese attack. The marines lost five dead and twenty-nine wounded, while killing another 150 Chinese. That day, General Almond finally called off the X Corps' offensive and ordered the forces at Yudam-ni to withdraw to Hagaru.[48]

Borrowing a page from the Chinese, a marine battalion marched cross-country from Yudam-ni toward Toktong Pass on the night of December 1. Despite deep snowdrifts and several firefights, the battalion reached Barber's positions on December 2, scattering the Chinese forces in the area, while a second marine battalion from Yudam-ni fought its way south against heavy resistance on the MSR, arriving the next afternoon. Behind this battalion came the two marine regiments with their supporting artillery, all of their equipment, and fifteen hundred wounded men. As night fell, the marines continued south along the MSR, while Drysdale's British commandos, supported by tanks, launched a supporting attack from Hagaru. The marine column met scattered enemy resistance along the way and lost several casualties and nine 155-millimeter howitzers in the process. Lead elements entered the perimeter at Hagaru shortly before midnight on December 3, and the rear guard finally arrived fourteen hours later.[49]

While the marines fought their way back to Hagaru, General Smith made excellent use of the new airfield. Despite enemy attacks, engineers had worked around the clock to hack a landing strip out of the frozen ground. By December 1, the airfield was less than half the recommended length for twin-engine cargo planes to land and take off. Because of the growing number of casualties, however, Smith allowed a C-47 crew to conduct a trial landing. When this proved successful, aircrews immediately began flying severely wounded men out of the perimeter. Over the next five days, US Marine and Air Force crews evacuated more than forty-three hundred casualties, many of them suffering from severe frostbite. At the same time, these planes delivered 537 replacement marines and several tons of food, ammunition, and medical supplies.[50]

Enemy attacks on the Hagaru perimeter, meanwhile, dwindled to a halt. United Nations firepower and the cumulative effects of the brutal cold had already destroyed four Chinese divisions and badly damaged two others. In response, the Chinese abandoned the previous strategy of frontal assault and focused on destroying Smith's troops as they withdrew, much as Chinese forces had destroyed Keiser's 2nd Infantry Division south of Kunu-ri.[51]

Meanwhile, Smith and his staff coordinated with the X Corps staff for withdrawal to the coast, where Almond planned to establish a fortified enclave. Rejecting the notion of retreat, Smith famously informed a British reporter that his marines were simply attacking in a different direction.[52] While Smith's forces fought their way down out of the mountains, Almond withdrew the rest of his far-flung units into a heavily fortified perimeter around Hungnam. In a superbly coordinated maneuver, the US and South Korean navies evacuated all of X Corps' personnel and equipment, including the two ROK divisions and nearly one hundred thousand North Korean refugees. Tragically, they left at least that many more refugees behind. During the final days of the evacuation, the crowded perimeter at Hungnam offered an inviting target, but UN airstrikes and naval gunfire discouraged any serious Chinese attacks. On Christmas Eve, massive explosions signaled X Corps' departure from North Korea, as explosive charges and naval gunfire flattened the abandoned port.[53]

Official estimates later claimed that the Chinese forces sustained approximately fifty thousand casualties during the campaign. Their losses were particularly heavy during frontal attacks against established defensive positions around the Chosin Reservoir. Cold weather and poor logistics, however, proved equally expensive, as the Chinese commanders endured shortages not only of weapons and ammunition but also of food and winter clothing, especially gloves and boots. One Chinese prisoner, for example, reported that frostbite had rendered his entire battalion combat ineffective.[54]

Losses for the UN forces during the campaign totaled 10,495, including 4,778 men reported as missing in action, many of them soldiers and Korean augmentees killed or captured in the destruction of Task Force Faith. The marines recorded 192 men missing in action and estimated that a third of these were prisoners, most of them captured in Hell Fire Valley. Postwar debriefings of repatriated American prisoners offer only the sketchiest information regarding the percentage of men captured and of those who died on the battlefield. Others died of wounds shortly after their capture, including Colonel McLean, Lieutenant Colonel Chidester, and Major Eagen. Many prisoners perished as a result of injury or illness sustained during movement to prisoner-of-war camps.[55]

Despite the courage and sacrifice of those directly involved, the campaign in northwestern Korea proved a disastrous failure for the UN command. President Truman bears the ultimate responsibility for this calamity. His reluctance to assert control over MacArthur's conduct of the war allowed the general to risk his entire force in a bold but reckless gamble. MacArthur's directive of October 24, which committed all UN forces to an advance to the Yalu, sent Almond's five divisions into restrictive terrain against unknown enemy forces in the midst of ferocious winter weather. Truman's advisors also deserve a share of the blame for their indecisiveness in early November, when a series of contradictory reports from Tokyo indicated a growing disconnect between MacArthur's perceptions and reality on the battlefield. MacArthur's surreal confidence may help to explain Almond's reluctance to challenge the general's dubious judgment. As MacArthur's most trusted confidant, however, he had a clear obligation to make such an effort.[56]

Finally, MacArthur himself bears much of the blame. Despite his disingenuous later statements to the contrary, he received numerous indications that organized Chinese forces were fighting in North Korea as early as October 26. The Chinese government publicly announced its involvement a week later. After Inchon, however, MacArthur became fixated on the conquest of the entire peninsula and repeatedly discounted reports that contradicted his vision of the campaign, particularly those regarding Chinese intervention. His cavalier advance to the Yalu permanently tarnished his reputation as one of America's great soldiers and contributed heavily to Truman's decision to relieve him four months later.

7   **The Deadly Winter**

We have no obligation to keep alive those who do not adhere to the side
of truth and righteousness.
Colonel Han, North Korean People's Army, November 1950

The first week of December 1950 marked a dramatic turning point in the war. This was the week that Chinese forces overwhelmed LTG Walton J. Walker's Eighth Army along the Chongchon River Valley, nearly destroying the 2nd Infantry Division on the road from Kunu-ri. The subsequent withdrawal came to be known derisively as "the big bugout." Walker's forces retreated 120 miles in ten days, all of the way south past the 38th parallel, leaving a trail of abandoned supplies and equipment in their wake. Supply officers, meanwhile, destroyed thousands of tons of supplies and equipment in the Pyongyang rail yards, where they had finally arrived, too late to help those units destroyed by the Chinese. This chaotic retreat in December remains one of the most embarrassing chapters in US military history. Nevertheless, the speed of Walker's withdrawal enabled his forces to break contact and regroup below the Imjin River, thus preventing a UN evacuation of the peninsula.[1]

On the eastern side of the peninsula, this was also the week that isolated marine units finally broke through Chinese resistance to consolidate their forces at Hagaru, while other elements of X Corps began their own withdrawal toward the coast—and safety. In Tokyo, Gen. Douglas MacArthur railed against restrictions that gave the Chinese a "privileged sanctuary." Warning that his forces were now fighting "a new war against an entirely new power of great military strength," MacArthur threatened a complete abandonment of the Korean peninsula if he were not heavily reinforced. In Washington, however, MacArthur's rhetoric fell on dubious ears. His imperious conduct during the previous six weeks had alienated the Joint Chiefs

Testimony of Lt. Col. Paul V. Liles, transcript of court martial of Maj. Ambrose Nugent, Fort Sill, Okla., February 1955.

and permanently destroyed his credibility. When MacArthur claimed that nobody had questioned the wisdom of pushing forward to the Yalu, Undersecretary of Defense Robert Lovett characterized the statement as "false and mendacious." Though reluctant to relieve MacArthur in the moment of crisis, President Truman and his advisors assumed a far more active role in managing the war.[2]

Marching North

Amid North Korea's frozen valleys, hundreds of captured Americans huddled for warmth in temporary internment camps. At least two thousand more trudged north in pathetic columns. The first of these groups, the US soldiers captured in July and August of 1950, had endured the deadly march from Manpo in early November. The survivors of that ordeal now suffered from the Tiger's continuing mistreatment at Chungang-ni, a camp in the "Apex" area, so named for its location at the northern tip of North Korea (see appendix).[3]

As December progressed, three other large groups of American prisoners struggled to stay alive. The second large group—soldiers of the 1st Cavalry and 24th Infantry Divisions captured in early November—had just arrived at the village of Sombakol, where they would spend the next six weeks. The third group consisted of US, British, and South Korean troops captured near the Chosin Reservoir. The Chinese gathered these prisoners at a temporary holding area in the Taebaek Mountains before marching them farther north to Kanggye, a few miles south of the Yalu. The fourth and largest group of American prisoners consisted almost entirely of soldiers from the 2nd and 25th Infantry Divisions captured at the battle of the Chongchon River. In the first week of December, these prisoners were just beginning their march into the northern mountains of Korea.[4]

Other, smaller groups of Americans were being held or transported across North Korea in early December of 1950, but these prisoners eventually made their way to larger compounds—if they survived. The one notable exception to this rule was Maj. Gen. William Dean. Dean was the highest-ranking prisoner captured and thus the North Koreans' prize possession. The North Koreans kept him in solitary confinement throughout the war and refused to transfer him to Chinese control.

Most American prisoners had assumed they would be shot upon capture. Those taken by the Chinese, however, were initially promised food, shelter, medical treatment, and a brief period of political education before repatriation. It is hard to gauge the sincerity of these promises. During the Chinese civil war, hundreds of thousands of captured National Chinese had transferred their allegiance from Chiang Kai-shek to Mao Zedong. In some cases, entire Nationalist divisions had changed sides. Initially, at least, Chinese commanders in Korea seem to have assumed they would have similar success in converting American prisoners once they learned the errors of capitalism.[5]

Regardless of Chinese intentions, the prisoners endured barbaric conditions while marching north. Columns generally moved only at night to avoid airstrikes, and prisoners spent daylight hours sleeping in huts, caves, railroad tunnels, or open fields. As part of their "lenient policy," the Chinese told the prisoners that they were no longer soldiers and thus had no obligation to obey the orders of their officers. According to Capt. Sid Esensten of the 25th Infantry Division, "some men jumped at the opportunity." The night after he was captured, Esensten was challenged by a young private whom the Chinese had appointed as group leader. Esensten responded firmly: "I sent him back to the group, told him I was in charge and didn't care what the Chinese said."[6]

While treatment varied between groups, most prisoners received food twice a day, usually boiled corn, boiled rice, sorghum, or millet. Provisions were usually in short supply and often undercooked, thus debilitating prisoners unused to such primitive rations. Those prisoners with water-purification tablets soon exhausted their supply. Wood was rarely available to boil the water, so thirsty prisoners drank from streams and rice paddies polluted by the human waste. As a result, most of them contracted diarrhea or dysentery, conditions that often proved life threatening.[7]

The Chinese rarely provided their prisoners with medical supplies, much less medical treatment. Guards would routinely prod slow-moving prisoners with their bayonets or rifle butts and abandoned those who could not keep up. Some of these men were left in shelters where they could be rescued by US forces, as happened several times at the Chosin Reservoir. More often, however, the Chinese guards simply executed the badly wounded, either out of mercy or convenience. Without treatment or medicine, many other prisoners died of injuries, including Colonel MacLean, captured at the Chosin Reservoir, and Maj. Robert Ormond, seized at Unsan. The Chinese occasionally provided transport for the wounded, either by truck or oxcart, but these conveyances, too, could be hazardous. Passengers risked freezing to death in the slow-moving oxcarts, while transport in an enemy truck attracted the deadly attention of UN aircraft.[8]

The Temporary Camps

By the time they reached the temporary camps, most of the prisoners were too exhausted to contemplate escape. Both the North Koreans and the Chinese conducted communist-indoctrination classes at these camps and segregated prisoners by rank in order to limit organized resistance to their efforts. In addition, most of the prisoners were initially required to write some sort of autobiography, including apparently harmless details such as prior employment and family history. Later the interrogators would use these details to coax other information from them. The Communists deliberately exploited fatigue, malnourishment, sickness, cold, and occasionally brutal physical torture to persuade the prisoners to make propaganda broadcasts, sign peace appeals, confess to war crimes, and inform on each other.[9]

Although the Chinese appeared to have a coherent plan for the internment and indoctrination of prisoners, the temporary camps were initially operated by the North Koreans, who proved dangerously incompetent. The most basic requirement was shelter, and the North Koreans and the Chinese hastily requisitioned schoolhouses, mining camps, peasant huts, and even empty caves and mine shafts to house prisoners. In some instances, the captors marched their prisoners in circles until accommodations could be found. Men captured at Kunu-ri, for example, walked back and forth for nearly four weeks until they finally reached an abandoned mining camp near Pukchon Taragol, twenty miles northeast of Anju. At Sombakol and Kanggye, the captors evicted the residents from their homes and herded the American prisoners into the vacant huts.[10]

Sombakol

The camp at Sombakol lay in a deep, narrow valley that stretched approximately four miles from east to west. At first, the North Koreans ran this camp, and a few Chinese officers provided "political guidance." There was no wire around the camp, and a small cadre of guards kept a casual watch over their captives. Prisoners lived in abandoned mud huts, with the thirty-three officers in the group crowded into a single three-room house on the eastern end of the valley. About 600 enlisted prisoners, most of them from the 8th Cavalry Regiment and the 24th Infantry Division, occupied the other huts. Another 150 prisoners, including Sid Esensten, arrived in early December, swelling the camp population to more than 750 men.[11] For eight weeks, the

men in the valley survived in unheated huts without blankets, winter clothing, or medicine. In spite of these hardships, only two dozen prisoners died.
Anderson later attributed these deaths to "battle injury improperly cared for
and dysentery."[12]

The North Koreans prohibited any contact between the officers and the
enlisted soldiers at Sombakol. The only exception was Dr. Clarence Anderson, who persuaded the camp commandant to permit the establishment of a
rudimentary hospital in the middle of the valley. Sid Esensten joined Anderson at the hospital once he arrived at the camp. Working with the help of enlisted medics, the two doctors did what they could with dirty bandages and
homemade surgical instruments. All of the prisoners wore the same filthy
uniforms in which they had been captured, and body lice and scabies began
causing significant skin irritation. Because of rampant dysentery and diarrhea, the men frequently soiled themselves before they could reach a latrine,
and the latrines themselves soon became overwhelmed. In response, the men
defecated all over the campground. Malnutrition, extreme cold weather, and
the psychological shock of captivity further weakened the prisoners' will to
survive.[13]

Prisoners in the valley received a daily ration of about four hundred
grams of cracked corn per man, supplemented occasionally by cabbage or
soybeans. Several prisoners, including Emil Kapaun, the 8th Cavalry chaplain, supplemented the food supply by actively robbing both the guards'
food stores, as well as corn bins in the local countryside. Invoking the protection of the biblical "good thief," Kapaun quickly earned the respect of his
fellow prisoners for his bold forays into the enlisted men's compound, where
he provided invaluable spiritual encouragement along with pilfered food and
tobacco. On one occasion, Kapaun managed to steal a sack of potatoes that
weighed nearly a hundred pounds. "He was the best food thief we had in the
camp," recalled Capt. Joe O'Connor.[14]

The senior US officer among the prisoners was Maj. Paul V. Liles, a
young West Pointer captured while serving as an advisor to the ROK Army.
Liles had been wounded in the legs prior to capture, and these injuries became infected; Liles became seriously ill during the prisoners' hiatus at Sombakol and barely survived the winter. With Liles's assent, the duties of the
senior officer were assumed by Maj. Harry Fleming, an older reserve officer
who had also been captured while serving as an ROK advisor. To placate
the Chinese, the prisoners staged a vote and elected Fleming to be their
spokesman.[15]

Although his captors limited Fleming's contact with the enlisted prisoners, he ruled the officers' compound with an iron fist, becoming extremely unpopular in the process. Fleming organized the officers into a staff and directed the prisoners to conduct daily physical exercise, avoid petty arguments, pick lice from their bodies, boil water before drinking, and defecate only in the designated latrine area. Fleming reportedly made several officers clean up after themselves when he caught them violating the latter rule.[16]

Fleming also negotiated with his Korean and Chinese captors in hopes of improving conditions for the other prisoners in the valley. According to Fleming, he spent a great deal of time and energy trying, without success, to persuade his captors to provide more food and medicine or allow the United Nations to airdrop supplies to the prisoners. Fleming did, however, persuade the commandant, a North Korean major named Kim, who insisted upon being addressed as "Colonel," to provide kitchen utensils and allow the prisoners to cook their own food. This concession significantly improved the quality and quantity of the prisoners' rations, which the North Korean guards had been pilfering, and the cooking fires provided some much-needed warmth in the primitive huts. On another occasion, Fleming persuaded the commandant to issue a ration of pork to the prisoners in celebration of Thanksgiving.[17]

The North Koreans, however, expected quid pro quo. In early December, Colonel Kim ordered the officers' group to sign a series of leaflets encouraging the UN forces to surrender. The officers protested violently, and Kim responded by threatening to cut off the prisoners' already meager rations. Fleming had already seen communist brutality in person, having witnessed both the aftermath of the Sunchon tunnel massacre and the execution of his American deputy, Capt. Alfred Roesch, by Chinese troops.[18] Both he and Liles had already agreed to make whatever sacrifices were necessary to save lives. To placate Kim, Fleming and Maj. David MacGhee, a B-29 pilot, rewrote one of the pamphlets as a vague statement of humanitarian principles. As MacGhee later testified, "We again submitted it to the group for their comment. The reaction again was negative, and it was decided then that the three majors—myself, Major Fleming, and Major Liles—would sign the leaflets, and if there was any question with respect to its being a bad decision, the onus would be on us." Kim accepted the new pamphlet, but his willingness to compromise did not go unnoticed by either the communists or the American officers.[19]

As 1950 drew to a close at Sombakol, minor disagreements flared into major feuds inside the overcrowded officers' hut. Resentment toward Major Fleming also grew during this time, and rumors circulated regarding Fleming's frequent visits to the North Korean and Chinese headquarters. One officer later testified that he "often returned from these visits with gifts of cigarettes and tobacco which he did not share with the others" and that Fleming had once suggested the North Koreans establish a disciplinary barracks. Another officer felt that Fleming and Liles were collaborators who had "refused to accept their responsibilities as senior officers." Sidney Esensten, who would have spent most of his time at the valley's makeshift hospital, never met Fleming and assumed the camp was run by Capt. Filmore McAbee. Most of the prisoners remembered several incidents in which North Koreans had massacred prisoners. According to Esensten, McAbee and another officer organized the prisoners into squads, with assigned missions in case a rescue force appeared on the horizon. "This organization kept morale high," said Esensten, "and that's why we had such a low death rate."[20]

The Valley of the Shadow of Death

Prisoners at Pukchin Taragol, on the other hand, experienced a horrific death rate. Survivors would later report that as many as a thousand men perished. Today, Pentagon experts conservatively estimate that 252 American prisoners died there in the short time the camp was in operation, while another 85 prisoners died while marching to the camp.[21] Regardless of the actual death toll, Pukchin Taragol clearly deserved its grim nickname, "Death Valley."

Almost all of the prisoners interned at Death Valley had been captured near the Chongchon River Valley during the Chinese second phase offensive. Most of these men were captured during the 2nd Infantry Division's disastrous withdrawal from Kunu-ri. On the afternoon of December 1, 1950, the encircled division fought its way through a massive Chinese ambush along the narrow road leading south from Kunu-ri to the UN line at Sunchon. Many American troops abandoned their vehicles and fled for the relative safety of the hills. Those left behind were slaughtered by Chinese troops and North Korean guerillas. In one case, Capt. Gene Lam, a battalion surgeon in the 9th Regiment, witnessed Chinese soldiers kill 118 out of 119 defenseless men. The next morning, UN aircraft destroyed the vehicles on the road.[22]

Shortly after capture, several hundred American and South Korean prisoners, including Captain Lam and Lt. Paul Roach, were herded into a cave near Kunu-ri. The cave was crowded, and food and water were scarce. Still, these prisoners briefly escaped the harsh winter weather. A separate group of prisoners, including Maj. Andrew Fedenets of the 38th Field Artillery, were less fortunate. Fedenets later reported that he and a group of approximately sixteen hundred men simply marched at night through the hills around Kunu-ri for two weeks before finally heading north.[23]

In his superb memoir of his captivity, Capt. Bill Shadish recalled the following:

> Sometimes we moved to the east and sometimes to the west, but mostly we moved slowly northwards. I was quite sure we marched over sections of road that we had already been on. Because the permanent camps were not yet ready for prisoners, they evidently did not know where to put us. . . . Sometimes a guard would take away a prisoner's boots and then he had nothing to put on his feet except perhaps an old shirt or some rags. We could never get lost along the trail because there was a trail of blood in the snow from those who had lost their boots. . . . At midnight on Christmas Eve, we reached the top of a mountain. It was a clear night with lots of stars. We looked around, and it was the most beautiful sight imaginable, with snow-covered mountains as far as the eye could see. I thought, "What a place to spend Christmas Eve."

The next morning, Shadish and his group arrived at an abandoned mining camp near Pukchin Taragol, followed shortly by more than a thousand other prisoners from Kunu-ri. There they joined several hundred South Korean and Turkish prisoners.[24]

The prisoners occupied ramshackle huts in a narrow valley stretching three miles from south to north, bisected by a dirt road and a shallow stream. According to Bill Shadish, the valley's sides were so steep that farmers lay on their stomachs to till their crops. The high ridges blocked direct sunlight and cast cold shadows that contributed to the valley's grim atmosphere. The camp itself was divided in half: The North Koreans controlled an upper compound that held Turks and South Koreans, while the Chinese were in charge of all of the American prisoners in a larger, lower compound. As at Sombakol, the prisoners lived on top of each other, twenty and even thirty men huddling for warmth inside tiny adobe houses with no doors and almost no heat. They alternated sitting, standing, and sleeping on dirt floors or lice-infested straw mats inside the cramped rooms. They were allowed to forage for wood, but there was little to be had in the barren, icy canyon. Gene Lam later recalled there being enough wood to heat his building for an hour a day.[25]

Frostbite, malnutrition, and sheer exhaustion had already weakened most of the prisoners before their arrival. In Death Valley, the overcrowded, unsanitary conditions and a rapid collapse in discipline, encouraged by the Chinese, made matters worse. Most prisoners were 2nd Infantry Division soldiers. The division had suffered heavy casualties during the battles along the Naktong, and new recruits had arrived to bolster the unit rosters. Gene Lam observed that these replacements, many of them still teenagers, had far less discipline than the veterans. Bill Shadish vividly recalled giving a direct order and being told to "go to hell." The senior officer at Death Valley was Lieutenant Colonel Campbell, captured with the South Koreans at Tokchon. Within days of his arrival, however, the Chinese sent most of the field-grade officers, including Campbell, to an interrogation center twenty-three miles away. Paul Roach could not remember any chain of command at Pukchin Taragol: "It was practically every man for himself."[26]

The vacuum in leadership would prove deadly. The lower compound included several slit latrines, but these were already filled to the top with frozen waste. Without tools, the Americans could not clean these trenches, and the Chinese refused their requests to dig new latrines outside the compound. Instead, they marked a new latrine area in the middle of the camp. Dysentery and diarrhea afflicted nearly all of the prisoners, and many relieved themselves in the common area. Others were too weak to make it outside and soiled their uniforms. Men tracked human waste back into the huts, further contributing to the stench and spread of disease. Gene Lam later described the mounting health crisis: "We attempted unsuccessfully to keep the area clean but could not do this due to lack of cooperation. The water supply came from the nearby river, but as it ran on a lower level from the latrines, it was contaminated at all times. The men were instructed to boil the water for drinking, but many did not heed this advice." Army medic Lawrence Donovan, captured with the 25th Infantry Division, recalled the stench: "Our quarters reeked of infected wounds and dysentery. Men died every night. Men who could have been saved with just a modicum of civilized treatment." As dysentery, diarrhea, nutritional edema, hepatitis, tuberculosis, and pneumonia spread from hut to hut, prisoners died by the dozens.[27]

The Chinese allowed Bill Shadish and Gene Lam to establish a "hospital" but provided almost no medical supplies. The Chinese did issue some DDT and a few sulfa tablets, and once the two doctors learned where these supplies were kept, they stole more. Two dozen medical corpsmen from the 2nd and 25th Infantry Divisions assisted the doctors by washing soiled bandages, treating infections with heated bricks, and manufacturing crude scalpels from the reinforcing plates in their combat boots. Still, the dying continued. "Unfortunately," said Gene Lam, "few men who went into the hospital came out of it." It was, said Lam, "a place to die."[28]

In late January, the Chinese ordered the consolidation of prisoners of war in Pyoktong, which the Chinese designated as Camp Five. Major Fleming had suggested just such a consolidation to his captors at Sombakol, assuming the Chinese could then feed and care for their captives far more effectively. Whether from indifference or incompetence, however, the facilities at Pyoktong were no better than those at Death Valley and significantly worse than those at Sombakol. Perhaps because of its proximity, the prisoners from Sombakol, now numbering about a thousand, arrived first at the new camp. A few days later, about nine hundred prisoners from Death Valley limped into camp, having marched another seventy miles through the mountains in subzero temperatures. At least another eighteen prisoners died en route.[29]

Shadish, Lam, and most of the medics stayed behind at Pukchin Taragol to care for 250 to 300 prisoners who were too ill to travel. Shadish later described this period as "the worst of times." The doctors pestered their captors for more medicine and bandages without success; when they asked for Red Cross assistance, the Chinese insisted that such help was not necessary. Meanwhile, the pitiful men in the hospital died at a rate of fifteen per day. There were enough sulfa pills to save only a few, and the doctors found themselves making life-and-death decisions. As Shadish recalled, "Men who were sick and dying would cry out 'Help me, Doc.' That really hurt, because all I could say was 'Hang on. We'll be getting help pretty soon.'"[30]

Only 109 of the prisoners left behind survived Death Valley. The dead were stripped of their clothing and stacked like cordwood in caves near the camp. The Chinese promised to bury the corpses in the spring and to provide the names of the dead to the United Nations Command. Shadish, however, had seen enough broken promises to discount their assurances. Like several other prisoners that winter, he began keeping a secret list of the deceased, which he later smuggled out in a ballpoint pen.[31]

After seven weeks of arguments, Shadish finally convinced the Chinese that conditions at Death Valley would get progressively worse in the spring and would kill not only the prisoners but also their captors. On March 12, he, Lam, and the other survivors finally departed for the four-day journey to Pyoktong. Behind them, starving dogs crept down from the hills to feed on the naked, unburied bodies of the dead American soldiers.[32]

Kanggye

Fifty miles northeast of Death Valley, near the village of Kanggye, 290 prisoners captured at the Chosin Reservoir endured a very different kind of ordeal. Like thousands of other American prisoners that winter, the men who reached Kanggye, later designated "Camp Ten," had survived a horrific march from the Chosin Reservoir battlefields and had lost numerous comrades along the trail. Many of these men had suffered multiple battlefield wounds prior to their capture. Private First Class Jack Chapman, for example, was wounded seven times while manning the 75-millimeter recoilless rifle at Hell Fire Valley and barely made it to Kanggye, supported by two other prisoners. As elsewhere, the Chinese and North Koreans executed prisoners who were too weak to keep pace and offered little food, no water, and no medicine or treatment for the rest. The survivors ate snow along the trail to slake their thirst and scavenged a few cans of C rations for food. As a result, most of those who reached Camp Ten suffered from malnutrition, frostbite, and dysentery. In short, they were the perfect control group for a Chinese experiment in psychological warfare.[33]

Most of the prisoners were soldiers captured with Task Force Faith, but the group included soldiers from other units, along with thirty-six US Marines, eighteen British Royal Marine Commandos, and one US Navy corpsman. The senior officer in this group was Maj. John McLaughlin, who had made the difficult decision to surrender at Hell Fire Valley. As usual, the Chinese immediately took steps to subvert the military chain of command by abolishing rank and informing prisoners that they were no longer in the military. The Chinese handpicked squad leaders for the prisoners, usually selecting the youngest ones or those who seemed particularly cooperative, or "progressive." McLaughlin and the other fourteen officers were organized into one squad, and other squads were segregated by race or nationality, including one squad of Puerto Rican soldiers from the 65th Infantry Regiment. The Chinese made no other effort to isolate officers from other ranks, and McLaughlin managed to establish some command and control over the prisoners.[34]

Like other prison quarters that winter, the squad huts at Kanggye were small, crowded, and usually unheated. The Chinese issued insulated comforters to the prisoners and allowed them to wash themselves in cold water. The smaller population may have limited the hygiene problems experienced at other camps. Prisoners reportedly ate the same diet as their captors, a combination of millet, sorghum, and corn, with occasional servings of daikon, rice, and pork. Sympathetic Korean villagers occasionally provided additional food.[35]

The camp also included a rudimentary aid station staffed by Chinese medical personnel, who prescribed aspirin for most illnesses and occasionally amputated frozen limbs without anesthesia. In early January, the Chinese evacuated a group of severely ill prisoners on oxcarts, promising to send them to a hospital. Instead, these men were transferred to the North Korean security police, and many subsequently died of neglect. At Kanggye, only twelve prisoners died during the camp's ten-week existence, the lowest death rate of any temporary camp. The Chinese wanted their subjects alive.[36]

On Christmas Eve, the prisoners were promised that "a big surprise" was in store. The two companies of prisoners formed up outside their huts and then marched to a large barn decorated with pine trees and Christmas greetings, where they received peanuts, candy, and cigarettes from smiling Chinese guards. Next to the signs with Christmas greetings hung other signs bearing slogans such as "Down with the Warmongers!" and "You Are Cannon Fodder." The prisoners were amused by some of the slogans, but the mood soon changed.[37]

Shortly after the prisoners' arrival, they were directed to take seats on the cold, dirt floor, and a cadre of Chinese officials mounted the stage at the far end of the room. One of these officials stepped forward and delivered a lengthy speech in Chinese, which another officer translated for the prisoners. As Jack Chapman later recalled, the speaker addressed the prisoners as comrades and welcomed them to the peace camp of the Chinese People's Volunteers: "You are very lucky to have been liberated by us because we have a lenient policy for all the people we liberate. If it was not for that, all of you would be dead by now." Many of the prisoners were struck by the length of the speech and by the repeated invocation of trite propaganda phrases.[38]

It all seemed relatively harmless. After the Chinese official's remarks, however, the men were dismayed to see several of their fellow prisoners, including SFC William "Pop" Olson, deliver brief, memorized speeches. These speakers promised that the Chinese would issue food, medicine, clothing, and tobacco and urged their fellow prisoners to comply with their captors' "lenient policy." After the war, Olson stated that he had already witnessed his captors' low regard for human life and believed that he "might be tortured or killed" if he did not cooperate. On Christmas morning, the Chinese marched the prisoners back to the barn for another five hours of lectures, followed by a meal of white rice with meat broth. For the next nine weeks, the prisoners at Camp Ten endured an intensive program of coercion, persuasion, and reeducation.[39]

The Chinese strategy later came to be known as "brainwashing." In fact, it was merely the modification of centuries-old interrogation tactics mastered by Soviet intelligence agencies in their treatment of political prisoners and of German and Japanese prisoners of war and then adapted by Chinese communist forces during the Chinese civil war and the Korean War. The Soviet method sought to produce a sincere confession by the prisoner. The Chinese also sought long-lasting changes in the prisoner's attitudes and behavior. Their strategy seemed to have worked well in converting captured Chinese Nationalists to communist ideology; the Kanggye prisoners presented an opportunity to test the same methods on captured Westerners.[40]

The indoctrination sessions at Kanggye were long and rigorous, lasting from dawn until after dark, seven days a week. The Chinese officials combined lectures, readings, student "reflections," and group discussions to instill the proper attitudes in their prisoners. English-speaking monitors, many of them educated in the United States, supervised sessions in the prisoners' cramped squad rooms. Attendance was mandatory, and each man had to read aloud from various articles translated from the *Shanghai News* and other communist newspapers. Prisoners recorded their thoughts about these articles in diaries provided by the Chinese and then discussed the issues presented in the articles. After a couple of weeks of indoctrination, the Chinese directed prisoners to write autobiographies so that they (the Chinese) would have a better understanding of "how to improve camp life." Prisoners were also permitted to write letters home, although there was no guarantee that these letters would ever leave North Korea. In addition, the Chinese interrogated each prisoner repeatedly, focusing on the individual's family background and economic status. Chinese officials carefully reviewed these interrogation records, as well as the prisoners' diaries, letters, and autobiographies, for personal details that would provide leverage.[41]

Discipline at Camp Ten was strict but lacked the deadly brutality evident elsewhere. Monitors rewarded good behavior such as active participation in group discussions and accused nonparticipants of "thinking negatively." Many of the topics, such as Marxist theory and dialectical materialism, proved too esoteric for the American soldiers. "I had only gone to eighth grade," recalled Roy Hardage, "and did not even understand many of the questions they asked, much less anything about communism."[42]

Those who remained silent or denied the virtues of communism received individual attention. Marine M. Sgt. William Pettit, for example, commented that one of the Chinese lectures was "a bunch of lies." His monitor told him "to shut up and listen to the lecture, that I must study hard to find the truth, and that I was stupid." Alternating between polite kindness and punishment, the Chinese officials used every angle to gain cooperation, from rewards of food and tobacco to reminders of the prisoners' worried families. Jack Chapman believed the married prisoners suffered the worst harassment: "The Chinese would say their wives were probably sleeping with their best friends."[43]

With strong encouragement, as well as badgering by their captors, some of the men composed short articles for publication in the weekly camp newspaper, *New Life*. These men received a handful of cigarettes in return for submitting articles like "Truman a Swindler" and "We Were Paid Killers." After the war, investigators would be appalled by how easily these men had shed their loyalty. While some prisoners seemed genuinely interested in the communist message, most participants were simply opportunists. Marine corporal Charles Kaylor, for example, received a Silver Star for heroism, but at Kanggye, he believed Chinese promises that cooperative "students" would be released earlier. "I was interested in only one thing and that was getting home," said Kaylor. "And I thought that if by cooperating I could get home, I'll do it."[44]

Major McLaughlin's efforts to rally the prisoners achieved mixed results. Men lived in separate, well-guarded huts, so he had few chances to communicate with other squads. Prisoners occasionally gathered for group lectures in the barn, however, and these assemblies allowed McLaughlin to send messages and influence his fellow captives. With Chinese permission, McLaughlin used these occasions to address the entire group. Jack Chapman later recalled the major's talent for ambiguous language:

> For example, he would say, "The Chinese have told us why we are in Korea. So now, of course, we know why we are here. When we return to our homes we will have our work cut out for us. There, we must continue our fight for peace." To the Chinese this would show some inclination toward becoming "progressive," since they were hearing what they wanted to hear. But to us, it would clearly tell us to be strong, to persevere; we know exactly why we are in Korea.

Food and medical care seemed to depend on cooperation, so McLaughlin passed the word to appear cooperative but told the men to avoid words or deeds that could hurt their fellow prisoners or their country. Noting the low death rate, many of the prisoners would later credit McLaughlin for both his leadership and his discretion.[45]

In late January, the Chinese assembled the prisoners for a "peace rally," complete with music and dancing. The men were issued cigarettes and then pressured to sign a document known as the Stockholm Peace Appeal. This document had been drafted by the Communist World Peace Committee shortly before the Korean War began and called on the United Nations to outlaw nuclear war. Several prisoners spoke in favor of the appeal. Roy Hardage could not remember exactly what they said, "but the rest of us were so pissed off at a Sergeant Olson that we could have slit his throat." The prisoners objected loudly until the Chinese threatened that those who failed to sign would not go home. Finally, Major McLaughlin rose to speak, and the room fell silent. According to Hardage, McLaughlin argued in favor of signing. The text seemed relatively inoffensive, and "we figured the people in the States would realize we were still soldiers and Americans." All of the prisoners at the rally signed the document, which the Chinese then modified with additional propaganda statements.[46]

Next, the Chinese officials organized a "peace committee" of prisoners at Camp Ten and directed the group to prepare its own appeal for peace. A British postwar study noted that this effort "met with little success." Marine SSGT Charles Harrison, who had been a prisoner of the Japanese during the Second World War, carefully drafted an "innocuous" text that would meet Chinese demands without providing them with a propaganda victory. The Chinese, however, rejected five such efforts and finally drafted a petition of their own and ordered the committee to sign it. The committee refused, as did the remainder of the prisoners. After further threats, some of the committee members agreed to sign on the condition that other signatures would not be required. Several of these signatures were illegible, and others were misspelled.[47]

Shortly thereafter, the Chinese disbanded the committee. The experiment was over, and Camp Ten was closed. The Chinese had not converted as many "students" as they had hoped, but they had learned valuable lessons on how to coerce the desired behavior from their haggard, desperate prisoners. It was time to apply these lessons to a larger audience. On March 3, 1951, all of the remaining prisoners left Camp Ten and marched a few miles to the Kanggye rail platform, where they boarded a southbound train, headed toward what they hoped was repatriation.[48]

Pyoktong

Instead of improving the prisoners' lot, as Major Fleming had hoped, the Chinese effort to consolidate the prisoners at Pyoktong proved a disaster. As at Sombakol, the Pyoktong camp, later designated Camp Five, was jointly administered by North Korean and Chinese officials. To make room, they simply evicted families from the mud huts that had survived the November bombing and replaced the villagers with groups of freezing, exhausted prisoners. The first of these men arrived from Sombakol in mid-January of 1951, followed a week later by the main group of prisoners from Death Valley and thereafter by other, smaller groups of prisoners. Camp Five was conveniently located directly across the Yalu from Manchuria. The Chinese eventually made it their largest camp, their administrative headquarters, and the hub of their prison-camp network. In the winter of 1951, however, American prisoners learned that Pyoktong was a place to suffer and die.[49]

The first challenge was morale. According to Sid Esensten, the prisoners firmly expected the imminent arrival of a US rescue force throughout their eight-week stay at Sombakol. Based on this expectation, the Sombakol prisoners made careful plans to seize control of the prison camp, and Esensten thought that both the sense of purpose and the hope of rescue kept morale high. These expectations disappeared with the transfer to Pyoktong.[50]

The American, British, and Turkish prisoners who arrived a week later from Death Valley had no such hopes. Unlike the earlier arrivals, these men, numbering about a thousand, had endured a second, grueling death march to reach the new camp, and many arrived with severe illnesses. Sid Esensten observed that morale within this group was already at "rock bottom," and another Sombakol prisoner later described this group as "the most weakened and bedraggled and sick and dying prisoners that I had ever seen." The Chinese had led the prisoners to expect a permanent camp with heated barracks and adequate food and medical care, but Camp Five provided none of these basic requirements. The diet actually grew worse for the Sombakol prisoners, who had at least received some cabbage in their rations at the valley.[51]

By the end of January, the camp housed more than two thousand prisoners, and the population would eventually swell to thirty-five hundred men. The officers, again segregated from the rest of the men, had no way to establish or enforce discipline. Some of the prisoners responded heroically by sharing their food and clothing and caring for the sick. Lieutenant Bill Funchess, for example, suffered from severe hepatitis and stopped eating, but his company commander, Capt. Lew Rockwerk, forced him to eat and nursed him back to health. In other prisoners, however, the adversity brought out their worst instincts. Their captors constantly undermined the military chain of command, and some of the squad huts descended into brutal anarchy. With ranking soldiers too sick or too apathetic to enforce discipline, the stronger prisoners preyed on the weak and the dying. In return for food or cigarettes, some of the men informed on their fellow prisoners, while others stole food, money, and clothing from the dying men. In one notorious incident, a military court later convicted Sgt. James Gallagher of murdering two sick prisoners at Camp Five by physically hurling them out into the snow. Amid these barbaric conditions, morale plummeted.[52]

The second challenge at Camp Five was heat. Brisk winds and arctic conditions magnified the suffering and the death toll throughout the winter of 1951. At other camps, details of prisoners foraged for wood in the surrounding hills. At Pyoktong, however, the prisoners initially had to rely on their captors for firewood, which was shipped in and rationed accordingly. Lack of heat magnified the prisoners' cold-weather injuries and illnesses, such as frostbite and pneumonia. The wood shortage also made it hard to boil drinking water, which was often contaminated. Filmore McAbee remembered scavenging for wood the size of matchsticks: "It would take me all day long to get something this big so I could boil water with it at night." McAbee was not the only scrounger. The officers were housed in buildings damaged by the earlier bombing raid, and several of the officers, including Father Kapaun, found enough nails and scrap material to repair their drafty quarters. At night, the prisoners huddled together for warmth in their crowded shacks. By morning, their breath had formed layers of frost on the walls and ceilings.[53]

The third and most frustrating challenge was the lack of medical care. Neither the Chinese nor the North Koreans seemed concerned with the mounting health crisis on their hands and made almost no effort to relieve the situation. By late January, most of the Camp Five population was suffering from one or more diseases. Foul water and meager rations had produced dysentery in most of the prisoners, and many also suffered from anorexia, scabies, frostbite, pneumonia, upper respiratory infections, and an assortment of battlefield wounds.[54]

The North Koreans allowed two American doctors, Sid Esensten and Clarence Anderson, to visit the sick prisoners in their living quarters, and they reserved two poorly heated buildings as a camp hospital. Despite daily requests from the doctors, they provided no fresh bandages and almost no medicine. At Sombakol, Esensten and Anderson had struggled to care for several hundred men. Now, with the help of a few enlisted medics, they tried to care for three times as many prisoners, many of whom were in far worse condition. The passage of time had magnified the combined effects of malnutrition, exposure, exhaustion, and untreated wounds.[55]

Prisoners began dying as soon as the camp opened. Dysentery accounted for many of the early deaths, and men died covered in their own filth. Chaplain Emil Kapaun sneaked out of the officers' quarters each night to feed and care for the dying, often washing their soiled clothes or bringing them food and water. Lieutenant Jeff Erwin later observed that Kapaun "had more damn guts than any man I've ever known. . . . He was always going from room to room comforting the sick. The most unselfish man I've ever seen in my life."[56]

One chaplain, however, could not save three thousand sick and dying men. All too often, Kapaun had to administer last rites. The survivors stripped boots and clothes from the deceased and stacked the naked, emaciated bodies outside, in front of their huts. Some men died with their eyes open, their lifeless corpses staring at the cold, gray sky. "Here were the bodies of America's finest young men," wrote Bill Funchess, "covered with filth and lying in stacks in a hostile country."[57]

Sid Esensten, meanwhile, began noticing a deadly pattern of "psychogenic dysentery": "An individual would start out with an irritative diarrhea, would begin to worry about the fact that he might die, and the more he worried, the worse his diarrhea became. The worse his diarrhea became, the more he worried, and a vicious cycle was set up. The continued severe diarrhea led to a progressive downhill course ending in death." Eventually the Koreans would collect the bodies in an oxcart. In early February, typhus, hepatitis, and pneumonia spread throughout the camp, and the doctors soon found themselves treating more than 350 cases a day, with very limited success.[58]

By late February, the two doctors were counting two dozen deaths per day, with the youngest prisoners dying at the fastest rate. Finally, the Chinese general in charge of the camp summoned the two doctors and asked what could be done. The Americans recommended better food, more wood, warm clothing and blankets, and, especially, medicine. The general promised to comply with these requests but, in return, demanded an end to the dying within two weeks. The Chinese reneged on most of these promises, but the diet did improve to three meals a day, with rice replacing the corn and millet, and the two doctors eventually received a shipment of sulfa tablets and penicillin. The Chinese announced the medicine's arrival in the middle of a snowy night, awakening the two doctors at midnight and ordering them to start giving shots immediately. The dosage was sufficient to provide decent treatment for three men, but the Chinese insisted on dispensing the medicine as widely as possible. Ultimately, ten men received the medicine, to no avail. All ten prisoners died.[59]

February turned to March, but the dying continued. Every morning, the two doctors would travel from hut to hut, recording the name, rank, and service number of the deceased, along with the cause of death, usually dysentery, pneumonia, or starvation. To avoid embarrassment, the Chinese forced the doctors to list "irritable bowel syndrome." Pneumonia replaced dysentery as the leading killer, but a growing number of deaths were attributable to psychological factors. A disturbing number of prisoners, reduced to a primitive existence in Camp Five, simply lost the will to live. Victims would remain curled up on the floor and refuse to move about or engage in conversation with the other prisoners. Initially, these men would not eat food without drinking large quantities of ice water, and they eventually refused to eat anything at all. In their final hours, the men simply turned toward the wall and perished. The majority of deaths occurred overnight, and many prisoners awoke to discover that a neighbor to their left or their right had perished.[60]

At a 2002 reunion, Esensten described his recurring nightmare, in which he saw the faces of the hundreds of deaths he was helpless to prevent. One face in particular haunted him, that of a red-haired, freckle-faced teenager from Kentucky:

> He was not that sick—had dysentery—but I had him in the hospital to protect him from others as he refused to get up to use the latrine. I spent twenty minutes talking to him one day, at first using a sympathetic approach—about the love his parents had for him—ending up scolding. He just looked up at me and said "Doc, you can't make me live." I just turned to talk to another patient for two minutes, looked back, and he was dead.

Sid Esensten noted that the condition was nearly impossible to reverse and that mortality would usually occur within three weeks of the first symptoms. The best way to save men in this condition was to anger them, either with insults or physical blows, until they were mad enough to strike back at their tormentors. Still, the doctors lost far more men than they could save.[61]

In late February, Clarence Anderson became ill with pneumonia, leaving Sid Esensten as the lone American doctor until a British physician, Capt. "Sandy" Ferrie, arrived in the camp. Esensten's angry protests had repeatedly provoked the Chinese officials, and when Ferrie arrived, they confined Esensten to the officers' compound. But Ferrie faced the same obstacles as his predecessors, and the dying continued. Later in the month, Bill Shadish and Gene Lam arrived with other survivors from Death Valley, but men continued to perish. As the death toll climbed, the captors forced the prisoners to bury their own dead. The burial parties did the best they could to dig into the frozen ground and cover the deceased with rocks on the far side of the reservoir. By mid-March, the makeshift cemetery, dubbed "Boot Hill" by the American survivors, held nearly four hundred such graves, with more joining them daily.[62]

In retrospect, the failure of the Chinese to provide adequate food, shelter, or medicine was the single biggest contributor to the horrific death toll among the POWs during the winter of 1951. The Chinese routinely blamed the inadequate supplies on UN air strikes against their supply lines, but these attacks did not prevent the delivery of tons of propaganda material to the camps, nor did they halt the continued Chinese assaults south of the 38th parallel. This excuse proved especially flimsy at Camp Five, located directly across the Yalu from Manchuria, where the Chinese supply lines were safe from such raids. In light of their own, well-advertised "lenient policy," the indifference of the Chinese to the POWs' suffering during the winter of 1951 severely undermined their later efforts to persuade the captives that China was a communist paradise.[63]

8 Spring 1951

American prisoners were not the only ones glad to see spring arrive. The previous year had ended badly for the UN forces. In December, *Time* magazine had characterized the Eighth Army's hasty withdrawal below the 38th Parallel as "the worst defeat the United States had ever suffered," one that could "mean the loss of Asia to communism." Although the UN forces had withdrawn intact, they had lost significant quantities of men and equipment, particularly among the ROK formations.[1]

Shortly before Christmas, the course of the war turned again. With US support, a UN panel proposed a cease-fire, to be followed by negotiation with Beijing on East Asian issues. Mao rejected the proposal, perhaps because he expected his military success to win further concessions. Instead, as historian Bevin Alexander has observed, Mao's stubbornness increased America's resolve to hold Korea, while squandering the chance to isolate the Chinese Nationalist regime on Taiwan and garner worldwide support for Communist China's admission to the United Nations.[2]

That same day, General Walker died in a traffic accident and was replaced by LTG Matthew Ridgway. A highly decorated commander of airborne troops during the Second World War, Ridgway, as a Pentagon insider, was already familiar with the situation in Korea. More important, MacArthur knew and trusted Ridgway from their previous assignment together at West Point. When Ridgway arrived in Tokyo, MacArthur reassured him: "Do what you think best, Matt. The Eighth Army is yours." MacArthur's confidence gave Ridgway a free hand that Walker had never enjoyed.[3]

With Almond's X Corps reorganized under the Eighth Army, Ridgway commanded approximately 365,000 US, South Korean, and allied forces against an enemy force of approximately 600,000 men. From Tokyo, MacArthur requested four more divisions, but Washington had none to send. Besides, Truman worried that further commitments in Korea might invite Soviet aggression in Europe.[4]

At dusk on New Year's Eve, Chinese and North Korean forces attacked along a broad front. Wary of being outflanked, Ridgway abandoned Seoul and withdrew across the Han River. On January 4, 1951, Chinese soldiers occupied the South Korean capital. Farther east, communist forces seized Wonju, a critical road junction in the mountainous central region. The UN command now faced its darkest hour.[5]

In Washington, the Joint Chiefs rejected MacArthur's proposals for widening the war and directed him to defend the peninsula from "successive positions" while "inflicting maximum damage to hostile forces." The message placed the responsibility for any evacuation decision on MacArthur's shoulders, but the general was not satisfied. Warning the Joint Chiefs that his troops were "embittered," MacArthur reiterated his arguments for escalation. In response, General Collins flew to Tokyo, bearing a personal letter from Truman that sought to bolster MacArthur's confidence and clarify national policy.[6]

Truman's encouragement had little effect. MacArthur misread the president's courteous tone as a shift toward his own view and repeated his urgent need for reinforcements. On January 15, Collins flew on from Japan to Korea, where he concluded that MacArthur's fears about tired and demoralized units were misplaced. Ridgway had begun replacing many of his senior commanders in the Eighth Army, and his aggressive leadership restored troop morale. When Collins returned to Washington, his optimistic report contradicted MacArthur's dire warnings. "Henceforth," observed biographer William Manchester, "the Pentagon would see him as a peevish, stubborn old man, pouting in Tokyo, despising politicians while they, supported now by the Joint Chiefs, ignored his sententious forecasts of doom."[7]

Having recaptured Seoul, the communists now seemed reluctant to press their advantage. Instead, they shifted the bulk of their combat power to the mountainous region northeast of the capital. On February 11, communist forces launched another full-scale attack that struck the 8th ROK Division, which quickly collapsed. The breakthrough trapped a Dutch battalion and most of the 38th Regiment, who suffered nearly eighteen hundred casualties while fighting their way south through Chinese roadblocks. Eight miles to the west, Freeman's 23rd Regiment held its ground at the village of Chipyong-ni, its presence blocking the enemy's efforts to outflank X Corps.[8]

Freeman drew his battalions into a tight, well-fortified perimeter and directed devastating artillery fire against the enemy. In two nights of battle, Chinese infantry captured several American positions but suffered more than five thousand casualties in the process. On February 15, the Chinese launched desperate daylight assaults, only to be slaughtered by UN aircraft. At dusk, Col. Marcel Crombez led an armored column from the 5th Cavalry

Regiment to relieve the embattled survivors, but most of his supporting infantry were killed or captured along the way. The latter included Lt. Col. Edgar Treacy, an infantry battalion commander who later died in captivity. After the battle, many infantry officers in the regiment openly criticized Crombez for abandoning these men.[9]

Following their usual pattern, the Chinese withdrew into the central mountains, planning to break contact with Ridgway's forces while they replenished their formations for the next big push. Ridgway pursued, hoping to deny them respite. The communist forces fought a series of delaying actions, but foul weather proved more effective than enemy resistance in slowing the Eighth Army's counterattack. Late-winter rains turned the roads to soup, and mountain streams flooded over their banks. Still, Ridgway's troops pushed slowly north.[10]

In mid-March, Ridgway launched a major attack in the center of the peninsula. The Eighth Army's advance threatened to cut off the communist forces on both flanks. On March 15, Ridgway's troops recaptured Seoul unopposed, and his forces continued to advance, nearing the 38th Parallel by the end of March. The Chinese, meanwhile, consolidated their forces north of the parallel, where mountainous terrain favored the defense. Ridgway's commanders proceeded cautiously, assuming another massive attack would be forthcoming.[11]

The Bean Camp

Communist forces suffered tremendous casualties during their abortive February offensive, but they captured several hundred soldiers from the 23rd Regiment and other 2nd Infantry Division units during the battle. Marching through deep, wet snow, these prisoners moved north for three to four weeks to a temporary camp near Suwan, a few miles south of Pyongyang. As the winter progressed, more prisoners arrived, and the population eventually exceeded seven hundred men. The camp was jointly administered by both the Chinese and the North Koreans, who fed the prisoners a paltry diet of bean balls. The place soon earned the nickname of the "Bean Camp."[12]

Bean Camp prisoners endured the same hazards that afflicted other captives that winter. Inadequate food, shelter, and medicine made the living conditions miserable, while the polluted water system ravaged the men with dysentery and diarrhea. The prisoners included French, British, Australians, Canadians, and Turks, but most of them were American. Their captors forced them to conduct nightly wood runs, requiring the exhausted prisoners to carry up to forty pounds of branches back to camp. Officers were segregated and forced to remove their rank, and the guards prohibited the other prisoners from speaking with them. As at Death Valley and Camp Five, internal discipline among the Bean Camp prisoners soon collapsed—and with it, morale. In addition to intestinal problems, influenza and pneumonia spread through the camp. Sick and starving prisoners lost the will to live, and at least 150 men died. For the survivors, life became a brutal struggle simply to exist. In this staggering effort, the stronger prisoners preyed on the weak.[13]

The most notorious predator was PFC Rothwell "Tiny" Floyd, a large, foul-mouthed soldier who allegedly stole food, watches, and money from dying men, forced sick prisoners to pay him money for their rations, struck a commissioned officer, and beat a fellow prisoner to death. The Chinese made Floyd a squad leader at the Bean Camp, and he used his authority and his physical size to bully those too weak to defend themselves. On one occasion, Floyd allegedly kicked a member of his squad who was too sick to go on a wood detail. The man died the following day. Floyd also insisted on drawing the rations for his squad and allegedly pocketed food meant for the sick and the wounded. Master Sergeant Ray Langfitt later recalled Floyd sitting down one day in front of three severely ill prisoners and eating their rations while the helpless men watched. One of the men protested, "Tiny, please give me my chow." According to Langfitt, Floyd responded, "You son of a bitch, you don't need it. You are going to die anyway and I am going to live."[14]

Throughout the war, Chinese and North Korean authorities ignored the Geneva Conventions requirements to identify prison camps; as a consequence, UN aircraft occasionally targeted the prisoners and their living quarters. By mid-April, aircraft had already strafed the Bean Camp on two occasions, injuring several prisoners. The camp was located near a major supply route, and the senior American officer, Lt. Col. John Keith, repeatedly asked the Chinese to mark the tin rooftops. The officials denied the request, telling Keith that the UN aircraft "would bomb it anyway." On the afternoon of April 22, a pair of F-51 Mustangs made two passes over the unmarked camp, dropping bombs and firing rockets and .50-caliber machine guns on the prisoner barracks. The attack killed eighteen prisoners, wounded dozens more, and destroyed several buildings. A North Korean doctor arrived to treat the wounded, and the prisoners learned that their camp was located near a hospital stocked with medicine and bandages. The Chinese had apparently forbidden any medical assistance. Two days later, Chinese officials announced the evacuation of the prisoners "for their own safety."[15]

On the cold, clear evening of April 24, about six hundred prisoners assembled in columns, ready to leave the Bean Camp. A Chinese officer named Wong stood before them and announced in perfect English that "I will march you American sons of bitches until you all die." Then the group departed, leaving behind another hundred sick and injured men. Moving only at night, the column marched northwest for eleven days through the heavily bombed outskirts of Pyongyang toward the rail junction at Sinanju. Wong forced several prisoners to carry ammunition and TNT on the march, while others carried sacks of beans, their rations for the journey. The guards hustled the prisoners forward with shouts of "Hubba, hubba," beat those who faltered, and shot those too sick to continue. Wong used a four-foot club to personally smack exhausted prisoners in the mouth. Execution squads shot those who did not respond.[16]

At Sinanju, the prisoners crowded into filthy boxcars and continued their journey north, again moving only at night. Each boxcar held between sixty and seventy prisoners, with no room to sit. On the second morning of the trip, the train hid in a tunnel, but the Chinese left the locomotive engine running. A blanket of toxic smoke soon engulfed the prisoners, and thirty-three died before guards evacuated the tunnel. When the train finally reached Sinuiju, at the mouth of the Yalu in northwestern Korea, the death march resumed, this time to the northeast along the bank of the Yalu River. The beatings continued, and more prisoners died. Captain William Shirey later recalled one of these victims "on the verge of death from exhaustion," lying beside a mountain trail: "I was so fatigued myself that I could not help him. A stupid Chinese guard was beating the man with a small branch from a tree, trying to get him to move along. I doubt that anything short of a miracle could have moved the man; in all probability, he died where he lay." On May 17, approximately three hundred survivors finally reached a permanent camp at Chongsong, which the Chinese designated "Camp One." The remaining Bean Camp prisoners either perished or were left for dead.[17]

The Long Walk

As the winter of 1951 finally began to relent, prisoners at Camp Ten at Kanggye hoped for the best. They had endured Chinese indoctrination for two months in the valley north of Kanggye, and now they were headed south, perhaps toward freedom. That, at least, was what their "instructors" had been hinting at for several weeks. On March 5, their train arrived in Anju, and the prisoners marched ten miles to the village of Somidong. After two days spent in crowded farm huts, the men assembled in the village schoolhouse, where the Chinese divided them into two groups. Sixty prisoners, including three junior officers, would continue south and be released. The other 230 prisoners, including Major McLaughlin, would move north for internment at a permanent POW camp. The large group moved north by train, then marched the rest of the way to the Yalu. After three months in captivity, many Kanggye prisoners were in no condition to march a hundred miles over mountain trails. Fortunately, the Chinese took particular care to ensure that their "students" survived, and all of the prisoners eventually arrived at permanent camps. Officers went to Camp Five, and most of the enlisted prisoners continued on to Chongsong, where they became some of the first inhabitants at Camp One.[18]

The group of sixty, meanwhile, began walking south. This group, apparently chosen at random, included three officers, twenty-four marines, and Pfc. Jack Chapman. A few days into their journey, Pfc. Leon Roebuck complained of severe stomach pain. He died two days later, and his fellow prisoners buried him with their bare hands. Jack Chapman, whose feet were frostbitten, inherited the dead marine's combat boots, and these helped him to survive the coming days. A short while later, Pfc. Hans Grahl also became severely ill. Marine Corporal Andy "Chief" Aguirre carried Grahl for several days, but the young private's condition grew worse, and the Chinese finally left him with Korean villagers. Grahl presumably died shortly thereafter.[19]

Now reduced to fifty-eight prisoners, the group continued southeast across the Taebaek Mountains and finally reached Chorwon, near the Iron Triangle region, on April 13. During the march, Charlie Harrison, who had earlier drafted the innocuous peace appeals at Kanggye, emerged as a key leader in the group. The marine staff sergeant had been captured by the Japanese at Wake Island and spent nearly four years as a prisoner of war. He shared survival lessons with his fellow prisoners, and his knowledge of Japanese enabled him to read road signs and gather information from Korean villagers.[20]

At Chorwon, the group further divided in half and continued moving south along separate routes. Within a few days, however, the Chinese marched both groups back to a collection point. There, the Kanggye prisoners received white cloth tags identifying them as "workers" and were assigned to explain the "lenient policy" to newly captured prisoners and to assist them in filling out questionnaires. Now, communist officials informed the two groups that half would be released, but the other half would remain with the Chinese "to fight for peace" in the POW camps. After three weeks, the Chinese finally selected eighteen marines and an army corporal, loaded them on trucks, and sent them south bearing surrender leaflets. On May 24, Chinese guards marched the men toward the front lines near Chunchon but fled when artillery landed nearby. The prisoners ran in the opposite direction and hid overnight. The next morning, the group used wallpaper from an abandoned house to signal an American observation plane. The pilot relayed their position to the nearest ground unit, and a tank platoon from the 7th Infantry Division arrived soon afterward. The rescued prisoners immediately discarded the propaganda.[21]

Chinese officials informed the remaining Kanggye prisoners that they could not be released because of the tactical situation. Jack Chapman and twenty-seven other prisoners in his group began retracing their steps to the north. Chinese guards herded the other eleven soldiers and marines from place to place in the forward battle area, hoping to use them to "explain" the lenient policy to other newly captured prisoners. After several weeks, these prisoners were also marched north, and by the end of the summer, they had rejoined Chapman and the rest of his group at the Mining Camp, another temporary collection point near Pyongyang. From there, the prisoners continued moving north, eventually reaching Camp One in late October 1951.[22]

Easter at Pyoktong

Major McLaughlin and the other officers from Kanggye arrived at Camp Five on Good Friday—March 23, 1951. They were appalled by what they saw. Ice and snow were beginning to melt, and desperate prisoners hunted for dandelions and other weeds that might be edible. Conditions at Kanggye had been difficult, but most of the prisoners had survived. At Pyoktong, however, the new arrivals saw details burying at least a dozen corpses a day. Still wearing their filthy and threadbare uniforms, the men who had survived pneumonia during the coldest months of the winter now succumbed to the combined effects of sickness and malnutrition. The weather had grown milder, but as the ground thawed, runoff from fields fertilized with human excrement further polluted the camp's water system and prompted a second wave of dysentery.[23]

Meanwhile, the prisoners who had been captured in November and December had now survived up to five months on a starvation diet sorely deficient in vitamins, fats, and protein. Many lost more than 40 percent of their body weight, and, as Bill Shadish observed, "Their emaciated bodies began to look like the victims of Buchenwald and Auschwitz." The widespread malnutrition led to a host of other health problems, including scurvy, which causes infections and ulcerations of the gums. Weakened teeth cracked and broke trying to chew the half-cooked rations, and Shadish pulled as many as seventy-five teeth at Camp Five, often without anesthesia. Prisoners that spring also suffered and often died from tuberculosis, fever, bronchitis, pellagra, roundworm, and beriberi.[24]

By late March, Camp Five had several American and British doctors, but aside from Shadish, the others were confined to the officers' compound either because of illness or by order of the Chinese. Shadish himself was initially prohibited from holding any conversations with enlisted soldiers that were not directly related to their medical care. In addition, he had to negotiate with a poorly trained Chinese "doctor" who frequently overruled the American's recommendations about prisoners who were too sick to go on work details. Whether because of incompetence or ideology, the Chinese refused to acknowledge the mounting health crisis in the camp. Like Anderson and Esensten before him, Shadish had to negotiate with the Chinese on health-care matters great and small, from the rare distribution of medicine to the hours for sick call.[25]

Although medical care at Camp Five was primitive, the prisoners received daily encouragement from Father Kapaun, the fearless Catholic chaplain who had played such an important role at the valley camp earlier that winter. Despite suffering from frostbite and beriberi, Kapaun persisted in his ministry once the prisoners arrived at Pyoktong. During the day, he would assist the medical personnel at the camp hospital by feeding and bathing those men who were too weak to care for themselves. Many soldiers in the hospital lay in their own feces, unable even to stagger to the latrines. Kapaun gently removed their soiled clothes and bathed them in hot water, then dressed them again. At night, he sneaked past the guards to visit the enlisted huts, where he shared news and encouragement and said a quick prayer during each visit. He also continued to steal various items from the Chinese, including food, tobacco, and even firewood, which he would share with the other prisoners during his visits.[26]

His fellow captives particularly admired the chaplain's patient defiance of the Chinese, whose ideology renounced religious faith. Though he refrained from deliberate provocation, Kapaun quietly defied restrictions on the practice of religion and reminded his captors that their ideology claimed to incorporate religious tolerance. His determination seemed to earn the grudging respect of his captors, who relaxed their prohibition against religious worship. Some of the Chinese interpreters had learned English in missionary schools. When they claimed that religion "exploited the masses," the priest would shame them by asking whether their missionary teachers were guilty of such crimes. Many prisoners would later attribute their survival to their spiritual faith.[27]

On Easter Sunday, Kapaun openly defied Communist ideology by celebrating an ecumenical sunrise service in the ruins of a burned-out church. Holding a makeshift crucifix, Kapaun wore his priest's stole, as well as the purple ribbon signifying his pastoral office, and recited the Stations of the Cross. Most of the men in the officers' compound attended, including Catholics, Protestants, Jews, and atheists. While the Chinese guards watched nervously, Kapaun ended the service by leading the men in song; "America the Beautiful" echoed from the surrounding mountains, still blanketed by snow. The officers sang at the top of their lungs, hoping the music would reach the other prisoners at Pyoktong. "There was nobody there," recalled Sid Esensten years later, "who did not feel the thrill of the music, the meaning of the words, the solemnity of the occasion, the goose pimples up and down their bodies and the feeling that this brought them much closer to home than they had felt for many, many months."[28]

Learning the "Truth"

A few days later, life changed dramatically for the prisoners along the Yalu River. On April Fool's Day, the Chinese assumed control of the prison-camp system in North Korea. At Camp Five and shortly thereafter at Camp One, a host of Chinese interrogators and political officers implemented a massive indoctrination program nearly identical to the curriculum taught at Kanggye. The tone of this instruction, however, proved significantly more hostile. At Pyoktong, the guards assembled all available prisoners in a large barn (many were too sick to move), and a Chinese officer named Wong addressed them in clear, crisp, English: "You will learn the truth and we don't care if it takes one year, two years, ten years, twenty years; we don't care if you die here because we will bury you and bury you deep so that you won't stink." As at Kanggye, the prisoners began a grueling daily schedule of mass lectures, small-group discussions, and mandatory "cognitions" written in their Chinese-issued diaries.[29]

The new schedule, however, had no effect on the death rate, and the burial details continued their grisly work. Chinese claims about a socialist paradise and the humane treatment of prisoners contrasted starkly with the grim reality of life and death at Pyoktong, a fact not lost on most American prisoners. As Sergeant Archie Edwards later recalled:

> Every day we had to go to school, listen to them tell us how lousy our country was, how hungry the people were in the United States. . . . They talked about your war mongers, your big business men, like DuPont and [the] Rockefellers with plenty of money. That's who they would run down all the time. When you look out and see nothing and remember what you had back here in the United States, you couldn't agree with people like that because they had nothing. They'd try to tell us how good they were treating us when eight and ten people were dying every night in this camp.[30]

Each day of indoctrination started early in the morning with the entire company of "students" assembling to hear a political lecture. Afterward, the prisoners returned to their squad rooms to read and discuss an assigned book or article. Finally, the prisoners wrote a "cognition" that explained how they felt or what they had learned about the day's topic.[31]

Instruction often continued until after dark, with the Chinese instructors collecting reading materials and cognitions at the end of the day. Some of the prisoners listened attentively and participated enthusiastically during the lectures and discussions, thereby earning Chinese favor and the disdain of their fellow prisoners. Other pulled down their earflaps to block the sounds. Many prisoners, however, were simply bored. When the Chinese instructors were present, they would mouth the appropriate concepts, but they daydreamed through the lectures and discussed girls, cars, and especially food whenever the Chinese were absent.

Because the Chinese lacked sufficient staff to supervise the discussions in each squad, they appointed monitors from among the prisoners, often selecting the youngest man in the group. Monitors had to draw the lesson materials for each day's study sessions, ensure that their fellow prisoners read and discussed the assigned readings, and turn in the daily cognitions and assigned materials. The appointees refused these duties at their own peril. Lieutenant Jeff Erwin, for example, stood at attention for several hours while the guards occasionally beat him with rifle butts until he agreed to become a monitor.[32]

Some monitors, however, performed their duties with studied negligence. Like many other prisoners, the officers in Paul Roach's hut tread a thin line between mockery and outright disobedience:

> I would assign a different squad member each day to think up and write down an opinion for the rest of us while we discussed the only subject that was on everyone's mind—*food*. One guy was the lookout. When Comrade Sun came around to check on us we would start talking about the Communist propaganda. I remember one discussion we had when Sun was present. We discussed how the Wall Street big shots were eating meals like big thick steaks, mashed potatoes with brown gravy, carrots, a salad with fresh lettuce, nice red tomatoes, onions, with a nice salad dressing, wine, ice cream and cake while the poor working class in the US was eating millet. We managed to "lose" some of the writing paper and Shanghai newspapers to use as toilet paper and cigarette papers. Not enough to get me in trouble.

Roach and his squad mates were lucky they didn't get caught.[33]

Crime and Punishment

Despite their "lenient policy," punishment by the Chinese could be harsh. Master Sergeant Howard Bostwick observed that the Chinese would severely punish the monitors if squad members made "reactionary" comments during the discussions. In a particularly gruesome incident, Maj. Thomas Hume told a Chinese instructor that a particular speech by Chou En Lai was "not worth the paper it was written on." Already dangerously ill, Hume was charged with "slandering the Chinese Communist Forces." Using ropes, the Chinese tied the major's hands to a ceiling beam so that his feet barely touched the ground, then sent him to solitary confinement for several weeks. By the time he was released, the officer weighed only 65 pounds and could not eat. He died shortly after returning to the officers' compound.[34]

Likewise, the "lenient policy" had no room for escape attempts. After the deadly winter of 1951, most of the survivors lacked the strength to break out of camp, much less to make their way to the coast and possible rescue. Nevertheless, in late April, four junior officers crept furtively out of camp under the cover of darkness, carrying a stolen bag of cooked rice. They made about seven miles that night but were captured the following afternoon. One of the escapees was Capt. Hector Cordero, a young army lawyer from Puerto Rico who would later be appointed as a federal judge. The other three officers, including Capt. "Moose" McLain, had been captured at Unsan. The Chinese hog-tied Cordero and McLain and beat them into submission, forcing them to sign a prepared confession that they had been planning a mass escape of all of the prisoners.[35]

A few nights later, the Chinese arrested Filmore McAbee and took him from the officers' compound at gunpoint. At camp headquarters, the guards bound McAbee's hands behind his back and looped the rope around his neck, forcing his hands and wrists up to the back of his neck. The guards then beat McAbee's shoulders, chest, back, and legs with clubs resembling baseball bats. Each time he collapsed on the floor, they kicked him in the stomach or groin until he got back on his feet. When he passed out, they revived him with cold water. After several hours of this treatment, the Chinese dragged McAbee to another room and stood him on a rock. They tied another rope around his wrists and fastened the other end to a hook above his head. The guards then removed the rock, and McAbee had to extend his toes to support his weight.[36]

He was left in this position all day, the weight of his body slowing tearing the muscle fibers in his shoulders and wrists. That night, the guards released him from the hook, only to inflict another round of physical beatings. In the morning, he was again bound and suspended from the hook. After three days of this treatment, the guards escorted him to use the latrine, where McAbee discovered that he could no longer use his hands or fingers. He finally confessed to planning an escape and was sentenced to three weeks in the "hole," a filthy, rat-infested dugout. After his release, McAbee's wrists and forearms were so badly damaged that for several months, he was unable even to button his own pants. The four escapees suffered from similar injuries. The Chinese had deliberately shattered these men, both physically and psychologically, and their fate provided a brutal example for the others.[37]

During the Chinese crackdown, Father Kapaun began to suffer from the various physical ailments that had accumulated during his five months in captivity. He had already developed frostbite during his first weeks of imprisonment. At the valley, a chip flew up and struck his eye while he was chopping wood, forcing him to wear an eyepatch for several weeks. At Pyoktong, he developed beriberi, probably due to the lack of nutrients in the prisoners' diet. Finally, like most of his fellow prisoners, Kapaun had lost a great deal of weight. His hair was long and scraggly, and he had grown a thick, reddish-brown beard. Unaware of his growing frailty, the soldiers teased Kapaun about his increasing resemblance to Christ, and the normally outgoing priest would turn away in embarrassment.[38]

The week after his Easter Sunday service, Kapaun fainted in the middle of a sermon. The American doctors discovered a blood clot in his leg and insisted that he rest and recover. Fellow prisoners gave Kapaun their medicine and extra food, carried him to the latrine, warmed bricks to help his swelling, and jerry-rigged a trapeze to support his leg. The special attention annoyed him, but after a couple of weeks Kapaun seemed to recover his old vigor. He even regained his mobility with the help of a makeshift cane. His dignified objections to Chinese propaganda, meanwhile, had made him a threat to the Chinese reeducation effort. Kapaun was the only chaplain at Pyoktong, and the camp officials seemed to fear his spiritual faith and his enormous influence on both the officers and the enlisted men. In late April, the Chinese summoned Kapaun and accused him of undermining camp discipline and slandering the Chinese Communist Forces. Their threats and accusations, however, had no effect on the priest, and the frustrated officials finally released him, perhaps fearing that any physical abuse would spark a riot.[39]

MacArthur Relieved

While the Chinese fought for control of their prisoners' minds, MacArthur waged a different battle. In December, critics had publicly blamed him for the UN reversals, and MacArthur refused to let such criticism go unanswered. In letters and interviews, he railed against "irresponsible correspondents at the front" and "unpatriotic elements at home" and argued that restrictions on air operations over Manchuria constituted a handicap "without precedent in military history." These statements frightened America's allies and embarrassed Truman, who had publicly supported his commander. In response, Truman issued a presidential directive to clear all public statements on foreign policy with the State Department. The so-called gag order was issued to all senior officials, but MacArthur was the obvious target.[40]

When it became clear that Ridgway could hold in Korea, Truman's advisors stopped discussing evacuation. MacArthur, however, continued to press his case in public and in private. On March 7, he issued a communiqué that praised the UN forces and observed that the Chinese "cannot hope to impose their will on Korea by military force." Noting the restrictions under which he labored, MacArthur added that without "major additions to our organizational strength," the two sides would soon reach "a point of theoretical military stalemate." Historian Clay Blair wrote that MacArthur's insulting words constituted "an indiscreet and wholly unnecessary public review of military strategy." Journalists dubbed it the "Die for a tie" speech.[41]

Truman ignored the jab, but MacArthur seemed determined to force a confrontation. On March 20, the Pentagon notified him that the president was preparing to pursue "diplomatic efforts toward settlement" before authorizing any major advance beyond the 38th Parallel. The new initiative would end MacArthur's opportunity to widen the war.[42]

On March 24, MacArthur issued another stunning communiqué. Declaring South Korea cleared of "organized Communist Forces," he proceeded to denigrate the lack of Chinese capabilities "essential to the conduct of modern war." MacArthur then delivered a clear threat: "[E]xpansion of our military operations . . . would doom Red China to the risk of imminent military collapse." In closing, he offered to meet with the opposing commander in chief in order to negotiate a settlement that met the UN's objectives "without further bloodshed."[43]

In essence, MacArthur was demanding a Chinese capitulation. His message violated the December gag order, sabotaged the administration's diplomatic initiative, and raised allied doubts about Washington's control over the general. Truman, meanwhile, had to shelve the diplomatic initiative and responded with "no comment" when asked to address MacArthur's ultimatum. MacArthur downplayed his message as a "routine communiqué." Acheson later described Truman's mood as combining "disbelief with controlled fury." Rather than relieve MacArthur on the spot, however, the president reviewed his options while measuring support within the Joint Chiefs for MacArthur's recall. In the meantime, he dictated a gentle reprimand through Bradley, reminding MacArthur of the December policy on public statements.[44]

On April 5, the confrontation escalated yet again. House minority leader Joe Martin, a staunch critic of Truman's Taiwan policy, read a letter from MacArthur that publicly criticized US policy. Martin had invited MacArthur to comment on Truman's "defeatist" policies and on the prospect of using Chinese Nationalist troops against the Communists. MacArthur's response—"There is no substitute for victory"—fully endorsed Martin's views. MacArthur would later protest that the congressman had publicized the contents of a personal letter without consulting him, but historian Michael Pearlman calls such claims "scarcely credible." MacArthur had not marked the letter "confidential," nor had he voiced any objections after its release.[45]

If MacArthur wanted to force a showdown with Truman, he succeeded. Upon reading the details of MacArthur's letter to Martin, the president moved carefully, first assembling his senior advisors to discuss the matter and then directing Marshall to review the issue with the Joint Chiefs. Absent their unanimous support, Truman could not remove MacArthur without inviting accusations that he had politicized the war. On April 8, the chiefs met to discuss alternatives, including the possibility of limiting MacArthur's responsibilities to the defense of Japan. These responsibilities, however, were too closely related to the ongoing war, and the idea was rejected. Admiral Sherman suggested that Marshall fly to Tokyo and deliver a final warning, an idea that Marshall flatly rejected. Sherman reluctantly agreed with the other chiefs to support MacArthur's dismissal.[46]

On April 9, Truman met again with his principal advisors. After receiving the Joint Chiefs' recommendation, the president announced his decision to relieve MacArthur. Mindful of the general's distinguished service, Truman insisted that MacArthur be informed of his relief in the most dignified, courteous manner possible.[47]

Unfortunately, this did not happen. Frank Pace, the secretary of the army, was visiting Japan and Korea, and Marshall decided to send him to Tokyo to deliver the message personally. Pace never received Marshall's instructions because a series of malfunctions had left him incommunicado. Unable to reach Pace, Bradley desperately tried to send word to MacArthur, but his message was also delayed. Meanwhile, rumors that the *Chicago Tribune* was about to publish the story spurred Truman to publicly announce his decision before MacArthur could submit his resignation. In Tokyo, one of MacArthur's aides heard the news broadcast over the radio and informed the general and his wife minutes before Bradley's cable arrived. For Truman, the botched delivery was a public relations disaster. "In typical fashion," Manchester later wrote, the president "had done the right thing, in this case avoiding the hazards of general war, in the wrong way."[48]

In Tokyo, Japanese citizens mourned MacArthur's departure as a national tragedy. When he and his retinue made their final drive to the airport, a quarter of a million Japanese lined the route to bid farewell. He received a hero's welcome upon his return to the United States, and enormous ticker-tape parades greeted him in San Francisco and New York. On April 19, he addressed a joint session of Congress, delivering one of the great speeches in US history. While thirty million Americans watched on television, MacArthur argued for total victory using "every available means," condemned would-be appeasers at home and abroad, and claimed, inaccurately, that the Joint Chiefs shared his views. He spoke for thirty-four minutes, was frequently interrupted by raucous ovations, and then concluded with his magnificent coda, a melodramatic and utterly disingenuous promise to "just fade away."[49]

In May, the Senate held closed hearings on the conduct of the war, and MacArthur appeared as the first witness. His appearance promised the Republicans another forum in which to denounced Truman's policies, but MacArthur's own testimony soon undermined his credibility. The general dismissed the Soviet threat to Japan, denied accusations of insubordination, and reiterated several proposals for widening the war. Meanwhile, he refused to admit any mistakes and backed away from his earlier confidence that attacks on mainland China would not provoke Soviet intervention. Most damaging of all, the general repeated his claim that the Joint Chiefs had supported his proposals. If MacArthur's own testimony damaged his reputation, subsequent testimony by Marshall and the Joint Chiefs destroyed it. First Marshall, then Bradley, then the rest of the Joint Chiefs appeared before the committee, expressed their admiration for MacArthur, and patiently explained that they had not, in fact, supported MacArthur's proposals, that they had endorsed his removal, and that various other claims the general had made were in error.[50]

The hearings lasted seven weeks, but the press and the public quickly lost interest. Truman's decision was vindicated, but his administration had been severely damaged in the court of public opinion and would not recover. MacArthur meanwhile embarked on a national speaking tour. His appearances initially drew curious throngs, but the more he talked, the more he sounded like just another political candidate. During his swing through Texas, the crowds began to dwindle, with more empty seats than spectators at the football stadiums where he had been booked. MacArthur's presidential hopes faded, and his political career ended sadly with an awkward keynote address to the 1952 Republican National Convention. Retreating with his family to their rooms at the Waldorf Astoria, the general became, as Joe Goulden later wrote, "a lonely old man in a Manhattan hotel suite."[51]

The Spring Offensives

In Tokyo, Ridgway assumed command of the UN forces, and LTG James Van Fleet replaced Ridgway in command of the Eighth Army. Van Fleet inherited a battle-hardened Eighth Army, its morale bolstered by its successful recapture of South Korea. In early April, UN intelligence reports indicated large Chinese troop concentrations near the Iron Triangle, but Ridgway had chosen to push farther north rather than simply wait for the expected Chinese counterattack. By mid-April, UN forces had advanced to the Kansas Line, which stretched 120 miles across the peninsula, most of it several miles above the 38th Parallel. The rapid seizure of Kansas persuaded Ridgway to conduct another limited advance, and Eighth Army forces moved forward toward Chorwon, on the southwestern corner of the Iron Triangle.[52]

As Ridgway had anticipated, the Chinese launched a massive offensive on April 22, hurling 350,000 troops against the UN defenses. The main effort again struck due south toward Seoul, while a secondary attack threatened the ROK 6th Division's sector in the central mountains. Following a grim pattern, the ROK units evaporated under overwhelming Chinese pressure, abandoning weapons and withdrawing twenty miles. Flanking units withdrew seven miles in response to the breakthrough, but the Chinese could not penetrate strong British and US blocking positions near the village of Kapyong. They did, however, cut the east-west highway linking Seoul and Chunchon, eventually forcing IX Corps to withdraw ten miles farther south.[53]

Farther west, Chinese forces penetrated the UN defenses in several places above Seoul, forcing the defenders back to positions four miles north of the city. The ROK 1st Division's withdrawal exposed the flank of a British unit, the 1st Battalion of the Gloucestershire Regiment, which had dug in along the Imjin River. The "Glosters" fought heroically for two days and two nights, inflicting thousands of casualties on the attacking Chinese. By dawn on April 25, however, the British were surrounded. Mounting losses and dwindling ammunition forced the commander, LTC James Carne, to order a retreat. Some of the British troops escaped, but more than three hundred were captured and subsequently marched north to the Yalu. Meanwhile, the Chinese offensive was losing its momentum as Van Fleet shuffled his reserves to consolidate his line. On April 29, UN aircraft caught a force of approximately six thousand enemy troops attempting to cross the Han River west of Seoul. Air attacks slaughtered the attacking force, and ROK marines captured most of those who survived the crossing. At month's end, Chinese forces again withdrew to replenish their battered divisions. At the cost of seventy thousand casualties, the Chinese spring offensive had achieved some local success but failed to recapture Seoul.[54]

Van Fleet refused to give the Chinese a respite. As May began, he sent patrols forward into ground abandoned by the communists and ordered a cautious advance along the entire Eighth Army front. Over the next few days, intelligence analysts detected a shift in enemy forces to the central and eastern mountains, opposite Almond's X Corps and the ROK III Corps. The Chinese struck again on the night of May 15, with twenty-one Chinese and nine North Korean divisions attacking through the mountains east of Chunchon. The rugged terrain limited the advantages of superior UN mobility and firepower, but Almond's divisions held excellent defensive positions along the steep ridgelines.

Communist forces concentrated their attacks on the 5th and 7th ROK divisions, pouring nine divisions into this sector. The ROKs held for a few hours, then fled in terror. Historian Clay Blair later described the South Korean bugout as "the largest and most disgraceful of the Korean War." Another six communist divisions slammed into the 2nd Infantry Division, which had already seen more than its share of fighting in Korea. The division's forward positions were strongly fortified and backed by a lethal assembly of artillery. On May 17, these batteries fired nearly thirty-eight thousand artillery rounds in the division's sector, while UN aircraft flew 172 sorties, including B-26 airstrikes. Napalm, white phosphorous, and high explosives shattered the closely packed enemy formations, and some rounds landed within a hundred yards of the American lines. The rain of fire slaughtered an estimated five thousand and stunned many of the survivors.[55]

Despite these deadly barrages, stubborn Chinese attacks threatened the division's position. Almond approved a withdrawal to the south, but both the 23rd and the 38th regiments lost several hundred men in the process, most of them captured by the Chinese. The 2nd Infantry Division's gallant stand inflicted an estimated twenty thousand casualties on the attacking enemy and stalled the offensive.[56]

On May 20, Van Fleet counterattacked. Heavy rains initially slowed the advance, which failed to cut off retreating communist units. The Eighth Army did, however, capture more than ten thousand prisoners, suggesting that repeated failures were finally beginning to wear down the enemy. By the end of May, Van Fleet's units had regained the Kansas Line and were pushing toward the Iron Triangle. In mid-June, however, these forces began encountering stiff resistance. Communist forces had carefully fortified the steep ridgelines of central Korea, thus discouraging any further Eighth Army advance. The two sides dug in, while diplomats sought to negotiate an end to the bloodshed.[57]

In Washington, the Eighth Army's success convinced Truman and his advisors that the time was finally ripe to explore a cease-fire. Acheson dispatched George Kennan to discuss the topic informally with the Soviet ambassador to the UN, Jacob Malik. On June 23, Malik broadcast a speech supporting a Korean settlement. Andrei Gromyko, the Soviet deputy foreign minister, confirmed Moscow's support of a military armistice and added that such a settlement should be negotiated by military representatives and without addressing political or territorial matters. The Soviet position dashed the North Koreans' hopes of conquest and undermined Mao's efforts to win UN recognition and gain control over Taiwan. On June 30, Ridgway broadcast a message, approved by Truman, offering to discuss an armistice. The Chinese responded on July 1, and the two sides held their first meeting at Kaesong on July 10. Once again, the war seemed almost over.[58]

In the Camps

Spring arrived late along the Yalu. Despite the boredom of the incessant political lectures, the warming weather was a tonic to the starving prisoners of war, who could now forage for weeds to eat. The Chinese, meanwhile, suddenly demonstrated much greater concern for the captives' health. Shipments of medicine and bandages began arriving at Pyoktong, and the prisoners began receiving vegetables in their rations, including cabbage, tomatoes, string beans, carrots, and daikons. The Yalu River finally warmed up enough for men to bathe in the still chilly water, and many were able to wash themselves for the first time in six months.[59]

In addition, a Chinese medical team arrived to deliver immunizations against typhoid and cholera. The Chinese used Russian vaccine, but they failed to refrigerate their vials, and they used the same syringe for multiple prisoners, merely wiping the needle with alcohol between injections. As a result, hepatitis epidemics broke out in both the officers' and the enlisted men's compounds. When the Chinese medical team returned for the second round of injections, American and British doctors complained loudly about the unsanitary procedures but to no avail.[60]

On July 8, Chinese guards confiscated the prisoners' tattered uniforms and boots and issued clean underwear, blue uniforms, and canvas sneakers. Armistice negotiations began two days later, and morale rose dramatically among the Camp Five prisoners, who expected an early agreement and their imminent release. Over the next few weeks, Chinese treatment improved steadily. The political indoctrination continued, but the prisoners received more food, and the guards seemed more civil. The death toll at Pyoktong fell to nearly zero during the summer of 1951, thanks to the improved diet and to the psychological impact of the armistice negotiations. As the deliberations wore on, Chinese treatment and prisoner morale fluctuated, depending on the progress of the talks. Nevertheless, those who had endured the winter of 1951 had good reason to believe they would survive the war.[61]

Father Kapaun's Death

Emil Kapaun did not survive to witness the improved conditions. In early May, the chaplain had recovered enough strength to move about the officers' compound on a pair of crutches. Shortly thereafter he was stricken by a severe case of diarrhea, for which the American doctors had insufficient medicine. The prison officials refused to issue any extra medicine to treat Kapaun, whose quiet opposition to their indoctrination had already branded him as a "reactionary" in their eyes. Sid Esensten and several other officers solved this problem by fabricating an epidemic in the officers' compound. Dozens of men reported to the Chinese medical team with complaints of diarrhea, and each received a small dose of medicine to treat the problem. The officers collected the medicine and provided it to Kapaun, whose diarrhea subsided after six days. A few days later, however, the priest collapsed in pain and sent for help. His friends found him slumped on the floor of his hut, breathing heavily.[62]

One of the Chinese political officers stumbled on the scene and announced that Kapaun would be transferred to the Chinese hospital in Pyok-tong, a half mile away from the officers' compound. The prisoners knew that this facility was a hospital in name only. No visitors were allowed, and the patients lay on the dirt floor in their own excrement, unfed and unattended, while maggots and lice multiplied on their bodies. Many victims did not survive the night in this building, which prisoners dubbed "the dying place." Burial parties evacuated the corpses each morning. The officers protested bitterly, but the Chinese officer left to summon reinforcements.[63]

Knowing that time was short, Kapaun spent his final minutes in quiet conversation with his friends, bravely reassuring them. Writing the words to the "Hail Mary" and the "Our Father" on a scrap of paper, he entrusted it to one of the Catholic prisoners and asked another to dedicate his life to the Virgin Mary. Felix McCool asked Kapaun to hear his confession, and the priest gave him absolution and a card containing the words to the Twenty-Third Psalm. The company of his friends seemed to revive Kapaun. Though still in pain, he sat upright and made a few wisecracks, but a squad of Chinese guards soon arrived with a makeshift stretcher. Again, the prisoners argued loudly, and the American doctors assured the officer in charge that they could cure Kapaun with the right medicine. The officer refused to listen, finally barking "He goes! He goes!"[64]

Kapaun's fellow prisoners gently lifted the gaunt chaplain onto the litter, and six of his friends carried him out of the officers' compound, escorted by the Chinese. The other officers fought back tears. Clutching his purple stole and his ciborium, Kapaun smiled and waved goodbye. He begged his friend Mike Dowe not to take his removal so hard: "I'm going where I want to go, and when I get up there, I'll say a prayer for all of you." When the procession reached the hospital, Kapaun looked up from his stretcher at Lt. Ralph Nardella and said "Ralph, when I do, and I know I am going to die, I will be up in heaven and I will say a prayer for your safe return." Once inside the hospital, the Chinese guards placed Kapaun by himself in an unlit room with a small bowl of food by the door, out of his reach. A Chinese doctor looked in periodically but made no effort to help the dying man. A fellow patient, Jack Stegall, slipped into Kapaun's room, but the priest was too weak to answer Stegall's greeting or eat the meager rations. Kapaun survived for two days on the dirt floor before he finally perished.[65]

His remains rest in an unmarked grave near Pyoktong, next to hundreds of other American prisoners who never made it home. A few weeks after his death, the Chinese plowed the field where he was buried and planted a garden above the mass grave. Despite their efforts to erase his influence, Kapaun's legacy of selfless heroism inspired countless other prisoners to endure hardship with honor, courage, and faith. After the war, the US Army awarded Kapaun the Distinguished Service Cross, its second highest medal for valor, in recognition of his courageous actions during the battle of Unsan. In 1993, the Catholic Archdiocese of the Military Services initiated an inquiry to determine whether Kapaun's actions merited canonization. In 2001, the diocese of Wichita assumed responsibility for that process. As of 2012, the church's inquiry is ongoing.[66]

9   The Pilots' War

> *The American imperialist aerial insurgents' mad bombardments*
> *neither destroyed our front line transportation capability nor did they*
> *weaken it . . . Thus, due to the heroic struggle of the Korean people, the*
> *American imperialist "air power" had come to nothing.*
> Official North Korean History of the Korean War, 1959

The air war over Korea differed radically from the ground campaign, and in many ways, so did the plight of the pilots and other aircrew members captured by the communist forces.[1] Throughout the war, UN aircraft controlled the Korean skies and destroyed enemy targets nearly at will.[2] This ability, however, proved inconclusive against enemies who were seemingly immune to the loss of men and matériel. The UN aircrews also suffered heavy losses, and their communist interrogators starved, beat, and tortured the captured aircrews to extract confessions of participating in germ warfare.[3]

From the very start of the war, air power seemed to be the United Nations' trump card. If the invading North Korean ground forces appeared more capable than either their South Korean opponents or the American units hastily deployed from Japan, Western leaders never doubted the superior ability of the American and allied air forces. In fact, this same confidence contributed significantly to MacArthur's dismissive attitude toward Chinese intervention prior to his fateful November offensive. During World War II, air power magnified MacArthur's ability to isolate and destroy Japanese strongholds, and the aerial delivery of two atomic bombs had proven decisive in ending the war. In fact, MacArthur felt that the threat of B-29s, which had devastated Japanese cities with fire and atomic bombs, would deter any Chinese thoughts of intervention. Moreover, he assumed that his aerial reconnaissance would detect any significant incursion and that his air forces would easily destroy the enemy's formations as they moved south. "If

The opening epigraph is from Mossman, *The Effectiveness of Air Interdiction.*

the Chinese tried to get down to Pyongyang," he promised Truman, "there would be the greatest slaughter."[4]

MacArthur was wrong. In Korea, the UN forces fought a different enemy on different terrain—and under very different constraints. Foreshadowing problems in Vietnam, American airpower could not force a resilient, technologically inferior enemy to capitulate. While early air attacks wreaked havoc on the North Koreans' supply lines, the Chinese proved exceptionally skilled at avoiding MacArthur's reconnaissance aircraft, enabling them to surprise and overwhelm UN formations during their offensives in November and December of 1950. Their primitive supply system, meanwhile, relied on human transport, dedicated repair crews, and the cover of night to keep supplies moving, facts that plagued UN air planners throughout the war.[5]

Attacks against roads, bridges, and rail lines, known doctrinally as "interdiction," proved especially frustrating. Communist labor battalions repaired the damage from airstrikes within hours of the attacks, and the supplies continued to reach their front lines. Truman's strategy of fighting a limited war on the Korean peninsula prevented MacArthur and his successors from attacking the Manchurian supply bases that were sustaining the communist war effort. Constrained to attacking targets below the Yalu, the UN airplanes eventually ran out of suitable targets, having destroyed most of North Korea's ports, airfields, factories, rail yards, and warehouses.[6]

At first, however, there were too many targets and not enough airplanes. By 1950, MacArthur's air forces were suffering from the same cost cutting that had crippled his ground-combat forces. Lieutenant General George Stratemeyer commanded a Far East Air Force (FEAF) of fewer than three dozen bombers and not even a hundred jet fighters. Prewar training focused on defending Japan against a Soviet air attack, and aircrews had done little training on ground-support missions. Moreover, North Korean troops soon overran most of the landing fields in South Korea capable of supporting U.S air operations. During the war's first weeks, most UN aircrews flew from Japan, limiting their time on station at the front lines. A shortage of cargo planes severely delayed MacArthur's efforts to resupply the withdrawing South Koreans and to rush his own forces to the peninsula. Stratemeyer immediately asked for reinforcements. Worried that North Korea's invasion might be part of a broad Soviet assault, the Pentagon refused to transfer aircrews from Europe. Instead, the air force scrambled to form combat squadrons and recalled thousands of reservists, World War II veterans who had since received little or no combat training.[7]

At least one of those reservists, Dan Oldewage, suspected he might be recalled when he heard about the war in Korea. Oldewage applied for pilot training during World War II, but the army air corps had enough pilots by the time he enlisted, and Oldewage became a nose gunner for B-24s. After completing his training, he flew missions in the Pacific. On August 9, 1945, Oldewage and his crew were flying over the Japanese coast when they saw the atomic mushroom cloud over Nagasaki. After the war, Oldewage joined the reserves and took a job selling appliances while attending college classes at night. He had mixed feelings when the air force notified him to report by September 1. Like other veterans, he felt that he had paid his dues, but he was still young, and selling appliances was dull.[8]

Another reservist, Capt. Harry Hedlund, had been flying nearly constantly since earning his wings as a flight cadet in World War II. Instead of shipping overseas with his classmates, however, Hedlund was assigned to instructor duties shortly after completing flight school. In 1943 and 1944, Hedlund taught other pilots at training bases in the southwest and learned to fly various fighters in the process. The army air corps eventually selected him for the new B-29 bomber program, but after qualification training in the B-17 and the B-29, Hedlund was again assigned to instructor duties. Finally, in the spring of 1945, he deployed to the Pacific, where he flew a handful of B-29 missions before the war ended. "They heard I was coming, so they called off the war," recalled Hedlund. "That's my story, anyhow."[9]

When the war ended, Hedlund had enough points to muster out, but his commander needed experienced B-29 pilots to fly an important new mission, so the young pilot agreed to stay in uniform. In an effort to measure the effects of radiation from an atomic weapon, the United States conducted tests at the Bikini Atoll during the summer of 1946. On July 1, Hedlund flew a B-29 camera plane overhead while another plane dropped an atomic bomb on the lagoon. "That was scary enough," said Hedlund. He finally left the service in 1947 and returned to his wife and family in Bakersfield, California.

He missed flying, however, and soon joined an air force reserve unit to make extra money. When his squadron converted to B-26 bombers, Hedlund became one of the first pilots checked out in the new aircraft and was assigned as an instructor. When the air force began scrambling for combat units to send to Korea, Hedlund's group commander volunteered the unit. He received a telegram recalling him to active duty on July 10, 1950. After several weeks of training, the squadron flew to Japan and immediately began conducting daylight bombing missions in support of Walker's hard-pressed forces along the Pusan perimeter.[10]

Like Oldewage and Hedlund, Jack Doerty enrolled in the army air corps' cadet flying program during World War II, but the program was canceled before he could gain a flying slot. The son of an army colonel, Doerty enlisted in the navy in hopes of qualifying for pilot training, but that hope ended abruptly with Japan's surrender. Doerty spent eighteen months as an able-bodied seaman, and his one adventure took place during a training cruise off the Oregon coast. Doerty was a novice sailor among a crew shepherding a decommissioned cargo ship to San Diego to join the mothball fleet when they ran into a major storm. Without adequate ballast, the empty ship threatened to sink. "I knew it was a really bad storm when I saw senior chiefs over at the rails because they were sick," recalled Doerty.[11]

In 1947, the air force became a separate branch of the armed forces and reinstated its flight cadet program. Doerty enrolled in one of the first classes. In 1950, Doerty was flying F-80s at a gunnery exercise when news of the war arrived. Worried that he might miss another chance to fly in combat, the aggressive young lieutenant bypassed his chain of command and asked the group commander to send him to Korea. To the irritation of his squadron commander, Doerty's stunt worked. En route to Korea, Doerty spent several weeks at Fighter Weapons School, where he finished first in his class. From there, he deployed to Korea and began flying F-80s with the 49th Air Wing.[12]

In the initial stages of the war, US fighter pilots rarely experienced the glamour or glory of aerial combat. Air force jets quickly chased North Korea's antiquated Yak fighters from the sky, then turned their attention to the far less glamorous missions of interdiction and close air support. The close air support missions helped fill a significant gap in firepower, as units in both the American and ROK armies fought early battles without adequate artillery or armor support. Air support proved especially critical in August, as the UN battle lines stabilized and coordination between air and ground units improved. The army's official historian, Roy Appleman, later credited the Far East Air Force with exercising "greater relative influence" on the outcome of battles in August 1950 than at any other time during the three-year war.[13]

Air interdiction missions, meanwhile, sought to destroy enemy troops, vehicles, and supplies before they reached the front lines. Fortunately for the UN forces, Soviet-equipped North Korean units were nearly as road bound as the US and ROK forces opposing them. To stem the movement of supplies, UN fighter bombers concentrated on rail and road bridges north of the 38th Parallel and on river crossings south of the 38th Parallel. On several occasions, UN aircraft caught and destroyed entire convoys on the open road. North Korean commanders quickly learned the value of camouflage and night movement. Nevertheless, when Eighth Army ground forces broke out of the Pusan perimeter in late September, they traveled north past the blackened remains of hundreds of enemy tanks and trucks destroyed by air power. After the Chinese intervention, priority for interdiction missions shifted to the Yalu River bridges.[14]

American bomber crews faced a different challenge during the first months of the war. Designed to conduct massive strategic bombing strikes against military and industrial targets, the bombers quickly ran out of strategic targets in Korea. Meanwhile, ground commanders fought to use the B-29s against tactical targets near the front lines, a mission usually allocated to fighter bombers. As North Korean pressure increased along the Pusan perimeter, MacArthur directed Stratemeyer's B-29s to carpet bomb several square miles of enemy territory opposite the Naktong Bulge. On August 16, bombers plastered suspected enemy positions west of the Naktong River. The high explosives produced enormous dust clouds, but captured NKPA prisoners later informed American interrogators that North Korean forces had already crossed the river before the bombers arrived. MacArthur considered a second air attack, but Stratemeyer persuaded him that, without better target information, such missions were a waste of resources.[15]

Stratemeyer faced other complications as well, including complaints about the accuracy and responsiveness of close air support from air force pilots. The first weeks of the war produced several embarrassing tragedies in which aircrews fired on ROK and UN troops or bombed friendly installations. Resentment increased after the marines arrived in late August with their own organic air squadron. As one officer complained, "Whenever we received air support from one of the Marine Air Wings, it was better than anything we got from the Air Force." Marine doctrine relied on aircraft to suppress enemy defenses during amphibious landings, so the marine pilots, unlike their air force counterparts, had trained extensively in ground-support missions before the war. In addition to the marines, the Fifth Air Force had to share the relatively confined airspace with other services, a problem that had not existed in the Second World War. Stratemeyer had no authority over the British and American aircraft carriers supporting the air war, which led to several problems. Like the air force bombers, the carrier strikes focused on targets north of the 38th Parallel, and deconfliction of air strikes became an ongoing challenge.[16]

The pilots were well aware of the chaos, both on the front lines in Korea and at higher headquarters in Tokyo. Harry Hedlund recalls that mission details would routinely change at the last minute:

> What they'd do, at midnight, an airplane would come in from Taegu and it would give you the bomb load. And about three o'clock in the morning, another plane would come in and give you the target. And then at four or five o'clock every morning, whichever it was, we'd get briefed on it, and then you'd go.

To Hedlund, planning at higher headquarters seemed casual at best. In Tokyo, MacArthur's staff included no senior air force officers, and targets were selected using outdated maps. Shortly before the Inchon landing, Hedlund and another officer flew to Taegu to coordinate mission support for the operation. While they waited, a junior staff officer asked for guidance on the bomb load for their mission. A colonel turned and said, "Oh, give 'em five-hundred pounders." The process was, said Hedlund sarcastically, "real scientific."

Stratemeyer's deputy commander, Maj. Gen. Otto Weyland, waged an ongoing battle with MacArthur's staff to improve the targeting process. Weyland later confessed to being flabbergasted by Far Eastern Command's incompetence:

> They knew nothing about it, so the results were just what you'd expect. . . . They would pick out a crossroad on a map, which was completely inaccurate, and would tell the B-29s to go bomb it. Well, they would probably go to bomb that crossroad, and maybe some of our troops would be there. The maps were so inaccurate. They didn't even know why they wanted to bomb it; they just thought crossroads ought to be bombed, I guess.

Despite this haphazard approach, the aircrews in Hedlund's squadron flew constantly, bombing empty crossroads and abandoned enemy airfields and searching for targets of opportunity.[17]

From the start, the American pilots dreaded the thought of being shot down behind the lines. Enemy units controlled much of the rugged countryside, and Western pilots had no way to blend in with the local population as the Allied pilots had done in Europe during World War II. Both the air force and the navy had seaplanes and helicopters available for rescue missions, but these became highly effective only in the spring of 1951, when the UN command implemented a sophisticated system to assist crews. In the first phase of the war, pilots shot down near the front lines might be saved by one of the

small H-5 rescue helicopters on strip alert in the forward area, and amphibious aircraft rescued several crews that crashed over water. Crews shot down
over North Korea, however, were on their own and faced the grim prospect
of making their way back to friendly lines on foot.[18]

Furthermore, the pilots well knew that North Korean troops often executed prisoners on sight. During the opening months of the war, airmen
who survived the initial moment of capture faced the exact same plight as
captured US soldiers and marines: long and often deadly marches to the rear,
starvation, torture, and deliberate brutality at the hands of their captors.
Marine Capt. Jesse Booker, for example, was shot down and captured on
August 7, 1950, and became the first marine prisoner captured in the war.[19]
He was sent to Pyongyang, where he joined the group of American prisoners
who survived the Tiger Death March in November.[20]

According to a postwar study by the air force, men captured during this
period had "the least chance of survival." To illustrate the hazards, the report
observed that:

> [A]lthough the period of June through December 1950 accounted for about
> twenty percent of all USAF personnel missing behind enemy lines in the Ko-
> rean [W]ar, less than seven percent of the repatriates were from the casualty lists
> of that period. Testimony from repatriates strongly suggests that no small part
> of this high mortality rate was due to atrocious living conditions, malnutrition,
> and to abuse and neglect on the part of the enemy.

Those who survived the journey to permanent camps on the Yalu River still
faced the challenge of surviving the deadly winter of 1951 and the probability
of brutal treatment at one of the interrogation centers established to extract
information from UN airmen.[21]

De Facto War

The air war changed dramatically on November 1, 1950, when UN pilots
spotted the first enemy MiG-15 jet fighter over North Korean airspace.
The appearance was so alarming that the Eighth Army relayed the news of
"enemy jet aircraft" down to regiment and battalion command posts. Able
to climb faster and fly higher than American jets, the MiG-15 was a more
capable fighter than any UN aircraft in theater, with a top speed that was
100 miles per hour faster than the air force F-80. Its presence immediately
threatened UN air superiority.[22]

In his study of the communist air war in Korea, Xiaoming Zhang observes that the November 1 incursion was not planned. The rapid advance of UN forces and MacArthur's subsequent decision to bomb the Yalu bridges increased the probability of a US-Soviet confrontation, and Zhang suggests that Soviet commanders may have felt the show of force supported their mission to defend Chinese airspace. Stalin had deployed MiGs and antiaircraft batteries to China in early 1950 to deter Chinese Nationalist air attacks. In the summer of 1950, he repositioned these forces to Manchuria with orders to train Chinese crews and defend Chinese airspace against potential UN attacks. Aircraft were stripped of all Soviet markings, Soviet personnel wore Chinese uniforms, and Soviet pilots were initially forbidden to fly south of the Yalu despite several American incursions into Chinese airspace.[23]

Their arrival did not go unnoticed by American pilots. On October 18, for example, an American reconnaissance plane counted seventy-five fighters parked on the ramp at Antung, just north of the border. When Mao began planning his winter offensive south of the Yalu, he asked Stalin to provide Soviet air support for the Chinese ground troops. Stalin declined, fearing American retaliation against Soviet and Chinese cities, a decision the Chinese viewed as a betrayal. In late October, the Chinese launched their Phase One Offensive without air cover, but Stalin did send several hundred more MiG fighters and thousands of antiaircraft troops to defend Chinese cities and accelerate the training of Chinese crews. American pilots dubbed the northwest corner of Korea "MiG Alley," and it was here that they faced the most serious challenge to their air superiority.[24]

Until this point, the US Air Force had sought to fight the war on the cheap, saving its best aircraft for a potential confrontation in Europe. The new threat, however, compelled the Pentagon to dispatch an aircraft carrier with seventy-five F-86 Sabre jet aircraft to Korea. The F-86 was America's best fighter, more maneuverable and with better visibility than the MiG-15. More important, American Sabre pilots were generally more experienced than their communist foes. Beginning in mid-December, they claimed a series of victories over their MiG opponents. For the duration of the war, the ongoing battle between Sabres and MiGs attracted enormous attention on both sides and enabled Soviet and American leaders to observe how their best aircraft would fare against each other. These duels also pitted the best Soviet and American pilots against each other, as Stalin gave tacit permission for his most skillful pilots to fly sorties against UN aircraft.[25]

Nicknamed "honchos" by their American opponents, the Soviet pilots were supposed to focus on B-29 bombers, but fighter pilots on both sides eagerly tested themselves against the enemy's best. The Soviet leaders wanted to focus on B-29s not only to protect North Korean and Chinese targets but also to gauge the MiGs' ability to protect Soviet airspace from any future attacks by B-29s, which played an essential role in America's nuclear deterrent. At the same time, Stalin wanted to avoid a wider confrontation with the United States. To maintain the secrecy of their involvement, Soviet pilots avoided flying south of Pyongyang or over open water, where they might be shot down and captured by UN forces.[26]

The presence of Soviet MiG pilots, however, was an open secret. American pilots heard Russian being spoken on enemy radio networks and observed men in enemy cockpits who were clearly not Chinese. In one memorable incident, Col. Robert Baldwin observed a MiG pilot bail out of a damaged aircraft and flew toward the pilot's parachute for a closer look. "There he was, hanging in the risers," recalled Baldwin, "red hair just shining in the sun. I don't think there were very many redheaded Chinese or North Koreans." A 1952 intelligence estimate by the Central Intelligence Agency reported "indications that Soviet participation in enemy air operations is so extensive that a de facto war exists over North Korea between the UN and the USSR." After the war, several American prisoners reported seeing European soldiers manning air defense sites and monitoring interrogations. Chinese and North Korean pilots gradually reinforced the Soviets, but according to a detailed study of Soviet archives by American scholar Mark O'Neill, "The Soviets bore the brunt of the air defense fighting throughout the war."[27]

Hazards in the Air

The dogfights over "MiG Alley" and the participation of Soviet pilots have attracted a great deal of attention from journalists and historians. The MiG threat was serious, but enemy ground fire proved far more dangerous, accounting for the majority of UN aircraft damaged or destroyed over North Korea. In fact, the establishment of a robust air defense network equipped with Soviet radar and antiaircraft guns posed the greatest threat to the UN aircrews, especially those involved in the less glamorous but more dangerous missions of interdiction and close air support. A Marine Corps study later noted that stabilization of the battle lines in 1951 "enabled the enemy to develop his anti-aircraft defense to peak efficiency . . . The number of aircraft losses increased, and with it, the number of Marine aviators who fell into enemy hands."[28]

By February of 1951, Harry Hedlund had already spent several months dodging enemy ground fire while flying low-level daylight interdiction missions against North Korean targets. On February 26, Hedlund led a three-ship mission that turned ugly. One of Hedlund's wingmen disappeared en route, perhaps the victim of ground fire, and when Hedlund reached the target, enemy fire damaged his bomb bay, and a thousand-pound bomb failed to release. Meanwhile, another of Hedlund's wingmen also suffered damage from ground fire. The two B-26s limped home to Japan, where the wingman landed safely on a single engine.[29]

Still carrying a live bomb, Hedlund made his approach, but the aircraft brakes failed on short final. On touchdown, Hedlund pulled the emergency air brakes and discovered that they had also been damaged by enemy fire. Hedlund's plane veered left on the runway, but he avoided a deadly collision at the last second by adding power to the left engine. Hedlund's brakeless aircraft barreled off the end of the runway at nearly 100 miles per hour. A raised railway embankment sheared off the landing gear, and the plane finally skidded to a halt near the front gate of the airbase. Fearing the impact with the embankment might activate their bomb, Hedlund and the other two crew members ran for their lives. An ordnance sergeant finally crawled into the wreckage and defused the bomb.[30]

Advancing communist ground forces posed a different threat to the aircrews. As Chinese pressure pushed the Eighth Army back below the 38th Parallel in the winter of 1950–1951, UN pilots faced greater risk of capture. Chinese combat and support units flooded into North Korea, making the task of escape and evasion nearly impossible for pilots who bailed out over enemy territory. Fortunately, Chinese troops were less likely than their North Korean allies to shoot pilots on sight. Furthermore, as the Chinese "lenient policy" began to take effect in the spring of 1951, airmen captured by the Chinese received food and medical treatment that prisoners seized earlier in the war had not.[31]

Chinese intervention coincided with another significant change in the communists' treatment of captured airmen: the implementation of a sophisticated, well-organized system for interrogating UN prisoners. Based on their experience with Chinese Nationalist prisoners, the Chinese military leaders believed that calculated leniency combined with exhaustive interrogation and indoctrination could extract useful information and modify the beliefs of captured enemy personnel. To begin this process as quickly as possible, the Chinese employed interrogation teams at several levels, all of the way down to regimental headquarters. A shortage of English-speaking interrogators, however, severely limited their ability to obtain immediately useful information from newly captured prisoners. To remedy this problem, the CCF issued interrogation booklets with pictures and simple instructions to small-unit leaders. The booklets were designed to allow the Chinese soldiers to acquire valuable information by asking prisoners to point to things such as rank, unit identification, and types of weapons.[32]

The NKPA also had a formal doctrine for the handling and interrogation of captured enemy personnel, but their forces generally ignored these procedures during the first months of the war. Most of the Americans captured by the North Koreans in this period underwent a brief interrogation shortly after capture but were not questioned again until they reached a permanent camp. After Chinese intervention, however, the Soviet advisors seem to have taken far greater interest in gathering technical information from prisoners, especially captured airmen. The North Koreans established several interrogation centers, and the Soviet advisors frequently monitored the questioning of captives.[33]

The Soviets' interest in technical information after November of 1950 might also explain the special interest given to UN pilots and crewmembers in communist custody.[34] Because of their unique technical knowledge and awareness of battlefield conditions, captured pilots have traditionally been considered valuable sources of intelligence. Perhaps because of disorganization, however, the NKPA initially made little effort to distinguish these prisoners from the rest of their captives. First Lieutenant Robert Layton, for example, was shot down and captured on July 12, 1950, and moved north through Pyongyang to Manpo with the group of prisoners that survived the Tiger Death March. Like many others in that group, however, Layton did not survive to be repatriated but perished in April of 1951.[35]

In early 1951, communist forces began segregating airmen (and later some US Army and Marine Corps ground officers) for prolonged interrogation sessions. These ordeals often lasted several weeks and took place at specially designated interrogation centers. The first and most notorious of these centers was dubbed "Pak's Palace" in recognition of the compound's senior interrogator, Major Pak.[36] Other interrogation centers included "Pike's Peak" (operated by the Chinese) and Camp Eight, but Pak's Palace, located in an abandoned brickyard north of Pyongyang, gained a reputation as "the worst camp endured by American POWs in Korea."[37]

Targets of Opportunity

Harry Hedlund had not heard of Pak's Palace when his luck ran out. On the morning of March 24, he and his crew—navigator/bombardier William Boswell and gunner William Ranes—took off on what Hedlund later described as "again, a mission that was screwed up." Flying low to avoid enemy radar, Hedlund and two other aircraft raced toward Sunan, a small city twenty miles north of Pyongyang, with orders to destroy a railroad bridge. "We got there," recalled Hedlund, "and there's smoke coming from the damned thing."[38]

Another flight had already destroyed their target, so Hedlund turned south, following railroad tracks toward Pyongyang in search of targets of opportunity (North Korean locomotives were a particularly valuable target). As the B-26 completed its turn, antiaircraft guns opened fire from a nearby hilltop. Hedlund's right engine caught on fire, and rounds also damaged his left engine and his flight controls. He was flying so low that enemy gunners were actually shooting down at the aircraft. Hedlund struggled to gain altitude and steer his plane toward the Korean coast, where the air force had established a rudimentary search-and-rescue network. Both ditching and bailing out over open water would have presented their own hazards. "I wasn't thinking about it," recalled Hedlund. "I just wanted to get out of North Korea."[39]

As the aircraft climbed, the engine fire spread to the ammunition storage areas in both wings. Rounds began to cook off because of the heat, and Hedlund realized they were not going to make it to the coast. The aircraft was too low for the crew to bail out, but Hedlund spotted a river bed and banked toward it. The plane belly flopped into the shallow stream and skidded several hundred yards, halting just short of a ninety-degree turn in the river bed. Hedlund and Boswell suffered head wounds during the crash but were able to crawl out of the plane. Sergeant Ranes, however, lay motionless in the back of the aircraft. Hedlund later concluded that Ranes must have been hit by the enemy fire that had shot down the aircraft. Hedlund and Boswell tried to pull the gunner's body from the wreckage but abandoned the effort when they saw an approaching North Korean patrol. The two officers started moving away from the patrol, which was now firing at them, only to discover that they were surrounded.[40]

Hedlund and Boswell raised their hands, but the patrol kept firing until a North Korean officer finally intervened. North Korean security police loaded the two prisoners into a truck and then drove them to a series of anti-aircraft sites. At each site, the officer would present the Americans to the gun crew and asked them whether they recognized the two prisoners. Finally, one of the soldiers identified Hedlund as the pilot they had shot down. "I figured that was a bunch of baloney," laughed Hedlund. "Like they'd recognize me, flying a plane—he wouldn't know who the hell I was from Santa Claus."[41]

Major Pak

After visiting several gun sites, the prisoners were placed in a hut. That night, a North Korean major arrived and identified himself as Pak. He offered them food, but they refused: "[N]either one us was in the mood to eat," said Hedlund. "Not that I thought we'd get anything." Pak promised that both officers would be taken to a doctor the following day, then announced that they were going to take a trip. Pak, the two Americans, and a dozen security guards began walking down the road. The group walked all night. The next morning, the sunrise was overcast, so the group kept walking, finally halting at another collection of huts. Pak separated the two Americans, and a short while later, a North Korean girl entered and offered food to Hedlund. By now, the tired pilot was happy to eat the bowl of vegetables she presented. Within minutes, Pak burst into the room, pointed his pistol at Hedlund, and demanded to know why he had tried "to rape our women."[42]

The exhausted prisoner replied, "You gotta be kidding." Hedlund's answer enraged Pak, who began yelling and waving his pistol. The North Korean officer began beating both Americans with the thick walking stick he carried. After the tirade, the two prisoners and their guards resumed marching. The next stop was a European interrogator, whom Hedlund assumed was a Soviet officer. The interrogator produced photos of different US airplanes and asked Hedlund to identify them, but the pilot feigned ignorance: "I said, 'I don't know. I'm a reserve officer. . . . I've only been in the Air Force for about six months. They took me from my job, put me in an airplane, sent me over here, and now, here I am.' And he didn't believe me, I'm sure."[43]

At dawn, Pak left the Americans in a crowded hut with a group of Chinese troops on their way to the front. The young soldiers tried to communicate with the two prisoners, but nobody spoke English. Using sign language, Hedlund asked where their weapons were, and they explained that they would retrieve rifles from fellow soldiers who had died in battle.

That evening, Pak returned and led his two prisoners on another trip. They walked for fifteen minutes and arrived back at the original crash site. Hedlund immediately noticed that Sergeant Ranes's body was gone. The

North Koreans forced their two prisoners to pose for pictures in front of the aircraft, and then Pak marched them south to a large supply point that contained other American prisoners. From them, Hedlund and Boswell learned that they had reached "Pak's Palace."[44]

Interrogation

Hedlund and Boswell were initially placed in solitary confinement and forbidden to speak to anyone. They could, however, see a few other American prisoners working in the compound, and the captives soon began communicating with each other by leaving notes in the latrine. Hedlund was interrogated nearly every day, sometimes by Major Pak and often by Colonel Lee, the compound commandant, who claimed to be an officer in the North Korean Air Force. Lee's questions were innocuous, but his temper was short. At his first interrogation, Hedlund was ordered to draw a map of his airfield in Japan. The pilot sketched a generic runway and two hangars. "That's not right!" barked the colonel and smacked Hedlund's ribs with a large stick. Lee then ordered Hedlund to draw a B-26 despite the fact, as Hedlund quickly pointed out, that an actual B-26 was sitting in the river bed two miles away. Colonel Lee insisted, so Hedlund sketched a pilot's console. Once more, his interrogator concluded that he was lying and again beat him in the ribs.[45]

One of Hedlund's fellow prisoners at the interrogation center, Air Force Maj. David MacGhee, reported a similar bizarre quality of the interrogations. After the war, an army intelligence report summarized MacGhee's interrogations:

> Pak would ask such questions as "What routes are followed by the B-29s?" MacGhee would spend four or five minutes giving evasive answers. Some abusive language, threats, or an occasional well-placed kick would follow, and then there would be the order to write out the answers. Pak would leave, return in a while, and would be satisfied if the sheets were filled with writing. He didn't care what was on the paper. He never gave any indication of having read any of it. It seemed to MacGhee that he was interested only in obtaining mounds of written material to show what a good job he was doing.

MacGhee, a B-29 radar operator, had been captured in November 1950 and was interrogated numerous times during his captivity. He thought the Chinese interrogators were more persistent and much harder to fool than their North Korean counterparts.[46]

In early April, the interrogators, a platoon of guards, and twenty prisoners, including Hedlund and Boswell, relocated to an abandoned brickyard near the supply point, perhaps to accommodate new arrivals. The prisoners were divided into groups and lived in three rooms with mud floors in an abandoned building. Each morning Chinese troops en route to the front crowded into the prisoners' rooms and spent the day with them, hiding from air attacks. Unfortunately, the brickyard included a large smokestack that attracted the attention of UN aircraft. Like other prisoner compounds, the brickyard had no marking to indicate that it held prisoners, and aircraft strafing posed a constant threat.[47]

Throughout 1951, Pak's Palace held both captured airmen and other prisoners of interest, including senior American and British ground officers captured during the Chinese April offensive. In April and May of 1951, UN aircrew losses mounted, and the brickyard took on more prisoners as the security forces sent captured airmen to the interrogation center. Meanwhile, the Americans who had been captured earlier were now moving north through Pyongyang toward the Yalu camps, and some were detained at Pak's for further interrogation. The communists also began identifying Camp Five prisoners with valuable technical information, and these men were also transferred to Pak's. The interrogation center grew overcrowded, and the North Koreans shipped men north to make way for new arrivals. In early May, Hedlund and Boswell finally left for the Yalu, having survived forty-five days at Pak's. During their stay, two fellow Americans died of dysentery and malnutrition.[48]

Unlike the Yalu camps, the Pyongyang brickyard was located less than a hundred miles from friendly lines and less than forty miles from Korea's western coast. Some of the prisoners at Pak's had barely survived several months of captivity and continued to suffer from the combined effects of dysentery, pneumonia, and malnutrition. However, the more recently captured soldiers still had sufficient strength to escape, and many of these were airmen shot down near Pyoktong. They were familiar with the city's proximity to the coast and with the expanding escape and evasion network being operated from islands in the Yellow Sea, where UN helicopters, boats, and amphibious airplanes waited to rescue aircrews shot down over water or behind enemy lines.[49]

Shortly before Hedlund's departure from Pak's Palace, three officers escaped with the assistance of a fourth prisoner, British Capt. Acton Henry Gordon "Spud" Gibbon. The escape enraged Pak, who marched Gibbon outside the camp. According to another prisoner, guards bound the British officer's wrists behind his back and suspended him from a tree limb until his toes barely reached the ground. Next, they kicked and beat him and twisted his genitals, hoping to extract information about the escape. Gibbon responded that he knew nothing and would not tell them if he did.[50]

The torture continued until Gibbon fainted. Guards lowered his body to the ground and threw water in his face. Shoving a pistol into Gibbon's neck, Pak threatened to shoot him if he did not talk, but Gibbon again refused. Finally, the guards bound his hands to a board and drove sharpened bamboo shoots under his fingernails until Gibbon fainted a second time from the pain. Pak concluded that Gibbon knew nothing and returned him to the prisoner barracks. The three fugitives were captured on May 12 and returned to the interrogation center, where they, too, were punished.[51]

Thirty-Day Rotation

As April turned to May, the Chinese military clung to the hope of driving their UN foes into the sea. In each of their previous major offensives, the Chinese had managed to achieve local breakthroughs. Each time, however, Ridgway's forces had employed superior mobility and firepower to block the enemy penetrations, while UN air power slaughtered enemy troop concentrations with napalm and high-explosive bombs. In Beijing, Mao dismissed the horrific casualties and ordered one more big push, aimed at the poorly equipped ROK divisions defending the Imjin River.

Near the small town of Inje, Jack Doerty had nearly finished his thirty-day tour as a forward air controller with the ROK 9th Division. Doerty had flown seventy interdiction missions as an F-80 pilot with the 49th Fighter Wing during the winter of 1951, bombing bridges, strafing troop concentrations, and attacking enemy trains. When his turn came in April, the lieutenant traded his jet for a jeep and joined the ROK 9th Division near the 38th Parallel. He was half of a two-man team whose job was to guide supporting aircraft toward attacking enemy forces, and doing it right required two things. First, Doerty needed to see where the enemy was, and second, he needed a radio that could talk to the aircraft.[52]

Unfortunately, his best radio was a heavy, ungainly apparatus bolted to his jeep, and Doerty had no way to get the jeep close enough to see the enemy. The team's other radio was a lighter contraption that Doerty and his enlisted radio operator faithfully humped up and down the hills along the Imjin River, hoping the weaker battery and the smaller antenna would provide enough strength to communicate with aircraft overhead. More often than not, they would lug the radio to the top of a hill, braving enemy fire, only to discover that they could not speak with the pilots trying to support his unit:

> We'd pack 'em up the hills, and pack 'em down the hills, and send 'em back, and they'd send us a new one. They'd never work: to include the final day, when we bugged out. I had one of those radios and could have had the champion air strike of the entire war with watching [a] Chinese corps coming our way.

On May 15, the Chinese launched their final major offensive, and Doerty's unit was in the way. True to form, the unreliable radio and overcast skies prevented the lieutenant from calling in air strikes.[53]

Instead, the two-man team followed the example of their ROK allies and withdrew on foot, still carrying the useless radio with them. They retreated for three days before Chinese infantry outflanked their column and captured them. The prisoners marched north and eventually joined several hundred other Americans at a temporary camp near Pyongyang. As at most temporary camps, the prisoners survived on a starvation diet of millet and cracked corn. One morning, Doerty spotted his reflection in a window and barely recognized the scarecrow looking back at him. He wisely concealed his identity as an air force pilot, but a fellow prisoner eventually betrayed him to the guards.[54]

Two North Korean officers took him away for interrogation, demanding details about his squadron and his home airfield. Doerty refused to answer. He had already seen other prisoners crumble in the face of the North Koreans' threats and promised himself that he would die on his feet:

> So, this guy whips out his pistol, put it to my temple, and cocks the gun. And that was a dark moment, I have to tell you. But—I didn't stutter at all—I just said, "I always knew that this was going to happen, because you're lying about the lenient policy." And when he heard those two words, that gun disappeared. And I remember, he didn't even put it in his holster. He put it in a drawer, in this room (laughs). I thought, "Aw, crud." And then they berated me and gave me all kinds of hassle and said, "The lenient policy doesn't apply to those who don't cooperate." But I had won. That game was over.

After the inconclusive interrogation, the North Koreans sent Doerty to Pak's Palace. Before he left, one of the North Korean officers warned him that he was going "to a very bad place."[55]

By the time Doerty arrived in August, the interrogation center's population had grown to more than forty prisoners of various ranks and services. By now, the prisoners were cooking for themselves and were careful to ensure that each man received the same amount. Prisoners warned the newcomers about interrogations, particularly the risk of trying to outsmart the North Koreans. As a postwar report by the air force noted:

[I]nterrogators . . . were not unusually intelligent or skillful, but they had a fund of accurate Air Force information against which to check the prisoners' statements. In addition, they were able to play one captive's statement against another's, to the confusion and sometimes the ultimate undoing of both.

Fellow prisoners warned Doerty to talk if necessary but to answer questions as briefly and ambiguously as possible.[56]

The lieutenant recalled one spectacular exception to this rule, when a fellow air force pilot finally agreed, in exchange for extra cigarettes and food, to explain how the Americans shot down MiG-15s. The pilot demanded a large sheet of paper, which the interrogators quickly provided:

And he said, "Now you guys have to leave me alone, because this is *detailed*." He had two pencils, and he put them together, the two pencils. And you know, he started here and ended up over there, going round and around and around [in a spiral]. And at the end, he showed one spinning in, labeled a MiG, and the other one going south, labeled an F-86. And he said, "That's the way we do it!"

I thought they'd beat the shit out of him! But, he got away with it.

In addition to Pak's relentless interrogations, the prisoners occasionally left the compound to work on details in the surrounding woods. Doerty was too weak at first to carry his weight on these details, but the other men helped him with his work, hiding his illness from the guards. Mainly Doerty recalled the sickness and despair and how the prisoners helped each other to survive. At one point, Doerty and some of the other prisoners found a bottle of fish oil. "I was one of about three or four people that every day had a spoonful of that, as long as it lasted," said Doerty. "The rest of the people didn't want it, you know, they wouldn't touch it—funny what people won't do." Later Doerty developed a boil on his neck, but a South African pilot lanced the boil twice a day for several days. "Probably saved my life," said Doerty.[57]

Several others were less fortunate. Pentagon analysts believe that at least a dozen Americans died at the brickyard, and Doerty vividly recalls burying several. In the fall of 1951, however, the population at Pak's Palace began to dwindle. With the beginning of cease-fire talks, both sides curtailed major offensive operations on the assumption that hostilities would soon end. Communist and UN lines stabilized, and the flow of new UN prisoners slowed to a trickle. In December of 1951, Doerty and a handful of the remaining survivors finally left the brickyard and headed north. For the time being, at least, Pak's Palace was closed. It reopened a few weeks later, and several dozen more UN airmen would endure Pak's interrogations.[58]

The B-29 Crew

With Soviet encouragement, the Chinese and North Korean interrogators spent a great deal of time and energy trying to learn more about UN aircraft. The B-29 Superfortress was a topic of particular interest. Five years after Hiroshima, the aging, propeller-driven B-29s remained the primary means of dropping atomic weapons on Soviet targets. In the summer of 1950, however, the air force was sending any aircraft that might slow down the North Korean columns descending upon Pusan. There were plenty of B-29s in storage, but the air force had a desperate shortage of experienced airmen available to fly. Until those shortages could be filled, reservists such as Dan Oldewage would have to take up the slack.[59]

Reporting for duty in September of 1950, Oldewage went to Tucson, Arizona, for training as a B-29 tail gunner. He and several other reservists were assigned to Capt. James Chenault's crew, and they eventually arrived at March Air Force Base in Riverside, California, to complete final training before deployment. In California, their instruction was delayed because they were short one "scanner," or waist gunner. Having recalled the entire crew on short notice, the air force now seemed in no hurry to send them overseas. After all, MacArthur's forces were approaching the Yalu, and the war seemed all but over.[60]

In November, Pfc. Marvin King arrived to fill the vacancy, and the crew began final preparations for deployment to Okinawa. Short and skinny, the eighteen-year-old gunner looked like a kid next to the older reservists, all of whom were sergeants. He had, in fact, enlisted only weeks after graduating from high school in Iowa but had earned his Pfc. stripe—and a flying spot—by finishing at the top of his basic-training class. During the few weeks before the crew's deployment, King met a young lady at a Riverside church. They became engaged on Valentine's Day, 1951, and King shipped out a couple of days later.[61]

Chenault's crew arrived at Okinawa's Kadena Air Base in late February and began flying missions almost immediately. Since late November, Chinese troops and supplies had encountered no trouble crossing the frozen Yalu, but with the spring thaw, the Fifth Air Force saw a chance to disrupt enemy logistics by destroying the Yalu bridges with its strategic bombers. Like many other aircraft flown in Korea, however, the B-29 fleet was left over from World War II, and the air force had retrieved many of these airframes from mothball status in the United States. Other, newer bombers were in short supply, and the air force held these in strategic reserve. The "Superfortresses" were old, slow, and vulnerable to attack from jet aircraft. They were also prone to mechanical and electrical problems, and the engines were particularly unreliable. Maintenance problems forced Chenault's crew to abort at least half of its missions before reaching the target. Each time the crew landed back at Okinawa with a mechanical problem, their ground crew chief accused them of "breaking his airplane again."[62]

Maximum Effort

Early on the morning of April 12, 1951, the crew took off on its eighth mission, a daylight bombing raid on Sinuiju, at the mouth of the Yalu. The city was heavily defended by antiaircraft batteries on both sides of the border, and the approach route would take the US bombers into the heart of MiG Alley. Chenault's aircraft was part of a "maximum effort" that morning to destroy the Sinuiju bridges, and Fifth Air Force had launched forty-eight bombers from all three of its B-29 squadrons, along with a squadron of F-86s and another of F-84s to screen the MiGs. The plan began to fall apart almost immediately. Nine B-29s had to abort before reaching the Korean peninsula, leaving only thirty-nine bombers in the strike package. Moreover, as the three groups of bombers approached the target at twenty thousand feet, their formation became strung out. Enemy flak exploded harmlessly below them, but more than seventy MiGs pounced on the overextended formation, concentrating on the weakest groups.[63]

For this mission, Chenault's aircraft flew in the trail position as part of a diamond formation of four aircraft and had the additional responsibility of dropping chaff (tin-foil strips designed to disrupt enemy radar). As part of standard procedure, Chenault also flew lower than the rest of the formation to avoid prop wash from the other aircraft. The flight of four was supposed to join formation with the rest of the squadron flying ahead of them, but the lead pilot inexplicably failed to close the two-minute gap between his flight and the rest of the bombers. The gap left the four bombers dangerously exposed as they turned toward their target. They were ordered to drop back and join the next group of bombers, a couple of minutes behind them.[64]

Sitting Ducks

From his tail-gunner position, Dan Oldewage had a good view of what happened next:

> We were kind of by ourselves. . . . When the MiGs saw that, why, we were dead meat . . . We spotted them on their first turn in, which was fortunate, because we were able to return a lot of fire. But they came in three abreast. I always contended one would be a Russian pilot, one would be a Chinese pilot, and one would be a Korean pilot, because they were no slouches.
>
> We got hit with the cannon. They had the 37mm cannon on the MiG; we got hit in the elevator initially. . . . My position was the tail, and there was a hole out there big enough to crawl through. That .37 made a good impact. At any rate, the pilot was having control problems. Of course, where I was sitting, I didn't know where else we had been hit. Apparently, we had been hit in the bomb bays as well.
>
> The pilot, when he saw that we were having control problems, he alerted us: "Prepare to bail out." So you get on the standby, ready to go, if your bell goes off. Well about that time, we were hit hard. You could feel the plane shudder, and the alarm bell went off. All of sudden, here comes these chutes—we were all alone, so they had to be from our plane. The guys in the waist were leaving the ship. When I saw those chutes, I pulled my window and went out and that was it. I was out of the plane.

Oldewage, King, and five other crewmembers made it safely to the ground.[65]

The damaged aircraft, however, kept flying. Enemy fire had caused a short in the electrical system, triggering the bell, and seven airmen had bailed out. The pilot and five remaining crew members coaxed the damaged aircraft south, away from the maelstrom over Sinuiju. Chenault was evidently trying to crash land the aircraft at Suwon, but the damage to the tail rudder was too severe. He and the others bailed out over friendly territory. Chenault's plane was one of three B-29s destroyed on the mission. Enemy fire damaged seven more. Bombs hit the target bridge at Sinuiju, but it survived the attack. The high loss rate prompted the suspension of B-29 missions over MiG Alley.[66]

Arrest and Interrogation

Oldewage hurt his back during his landing, but a North Korean farmer helped him to his house, where security police arrested him a short time later. Using the American's bootlaces to bind his hands, the police marched Oldewage to the nearest village, where an angry mob had gathered. While their captive stood in a ravine, the guards cocked their weapons. Oldewage assumed he would be executed. After the villagers shouted at the prisoner for several minutes, the police fired shots in the air to disperse the crowd and confined Oldewage in one of the village houses. He was soon joined by an American airman from another B-29 shot down that morning.

When night fell, guards herded the two Americans onto a charcoal-burning bus, which drove them toward Sinuiju. The bus stopped periodically, and Oldewage assumed the police were rounding up political prisoners: "[T]hey would come out with some guy and throw him on the bus." The Americans and the other captives were imprisoned at the Sinuiju jail, where Oldewage met still more captured Americans. From there, guards escorted them across the Yalu to an air base in Antung.

At the base, the Americans were isolated in a tiny cell and interrogated individually by Chinese officials and also by officers with European features. The Caucasian interrogators spoke excellent English and knew enough details about the bombing mission to convince the two Americans that they were MiG pilots who had attacked the formation. They asked Oldewage for equipment details about the B-29 and for names and units stationed at Okinawa. "We had just gotten there a few weeks earlier," said Oldewage, "so I couldn't tell them much." After the interrogation, Oldewage was confined in a schoolhouse in Antung and was eventually reunited with the other airmen who had bailed out of his B-29. One of them, SSGT Hank Metz, had spent time as a POW in Germany during the previous war.[67]

The two officers in the group were held for additional questioning and later joined the survivors of the Tiger Death March in the Apex camps.[68] The enlisted airmen returned to Sinuiju and, from there, went south toward Pyongyang. On one occasion, guards stopped their vehicle and marched them through a town, where angry townspeople cursed and beat them. Marv

King later recalled, "I thought to myself at the time, I can't really blame them for throwing rocks at me. After all, we just blew up their houses."[69]

By late April of 1951, UN bombers had flattened the North Korean capital. The city jail was one of the few surviving buildings, and the airmen were confined in its basement. The police locked their captives in individual cages, and Oldewage recalls guards jabbing him when he leaned against the bars. He learned to sit and sleep without leaning. After several days, the airmen marched in another parade through the city streets, and the civilian crowds again jeered and spat at them.[70]

The Caves

From Pyongyang, the North Koreans took the captured airmen to a farm west of the city, where they spent several nights in a barn. At night, they heard B-26 bombers flying low over the barn roof, while enemy rockets fired into the night sky. Finally, the prisoners marched to "the Caves." As the name suggests, this temporary camp consisted of a series of cold, damp caves and tunnels into which the North Koreans had herded hundreds of prisoners. An official British report after the war tersely summarized the camp's conditions: "[T]reatment was brutal, medical care non-existent, food inadequate, and the death rate high." The airmen arrived at night and were pushed into a crowded dark cave full of captured ROK troops. Unable to see their way, the Americans stepped on the bodies of other prisoners in search of a place to sit down and discovered that they had only eighteen inches of sleeping space per man.[71]

The B-29 crew spent several weeks at the Caves and later recalled it as the worst period of their captivity. They eventually transferred to a less crowded cave, but the roof dripped water onto the soggy floor. The men slept in several inches of mud and survived on a starvation diet of sorghum and millet. Once a day, the guards brought water to the mouth of the cave in a fifty-five-gallon drum. At first, the Americans literally had to fight their way to the drum for a drink of water because the South Koreans resented their intrusion. Later, the surviving South Koreans were marched away and replaced by a large group of American prisoners, mostly enlisted men from the army.[72]

Each morning, the strongest prisoners stumbled out into the sunshine to dry out and relieve themselves in a slit trench outside. Other prisoners, however, were too weak to move and died in their own filth. Details carried the corpses into the surrounding hills for burial. The airmen survived, encouraging each other to go out into the sun each morning. After a month in the Caves, Oldewage and his fellow airmen faced the prospect of imminent death by starvation or sickness. All of them had lost weight, and most suffered from diarrhea, dysentery, or pneumonia. One of the airmen, George Millward, had a severely wounded leg that had turned gangrenous. In early June, a North Korean officer offered the airmen a chance to transfer to a "peace camp." They had no idea what a peace camp was, but, as Millward later said, "I figured anything would be better than staying at the Caves and dying."[73]

En route to the new camp, Dan Oldewage stopped by a riverbank to wash his filthy body. Reaching down, he discovered that he could wrap his hand around his leg. He calculated that he weighed about eighty pounds at that time. Oldewage and the other airmen marched to nearby Camp Twelve, where they spent the rest of the summer.[74]

Camp Twelve

Organized along lines similar to those at Kanggye, the prisoners at Camp Twelve received relatively humane treatment while the North Koreans tried to convert them to communism. The first occupants were prisoners selected from Camp Five in February of 1951 and included Maj. Paul Liles, Maj. Henry Fleming, and Maj. David MacGhee, the three senior officers from the temporary camp at Sombakol. They and seventeen other prisoners, apparently selected at random, were marched back to Pyongyang, ostensibly to broadcast the names of the prisoners being held at Camp Five. An official army report later cast doubt on this explanation, suggesting that "most of them were aware of the propaganda aspects of the trip and had volunteered or willingly submitted to the suggestion in spite of this."[75]

In Pyongyang, they were paraded through the city streets and directed to record a peace appeal for later broadcast. The North Koreans shuttled this small group of prisoners between locations for the first few weeks, finally installing them in a compound several miles east of Pyongyang, near "the Caves." In an apparent effort to replicate the Chinese program at Kanggye, the North Korean officials subjected these prisoners to daily indoctrination classes and, after several weeks of "education," pressured them to form a "Central Committee for Peace." The North Koreans also asked them to record broadcasts condemning the war. Some of the prisoners found ways to avoid recording the broadcasts, while others simply refused. The North

Koreans punished the most recalcitrant prisoners, including MacGhee and Captain Bernie Gaeling, with several weeks in the Caves.

Other prisoners, most notably Majors Fleming and Liles, did record peace appeals, sign peace petitions, and form the prescribed committee. The population at Camp Twelve, meanwhile, increased to approximately one hundred captives. Like Oldewage and his crew mates, many of these were British and American soldiers facing certain death in the Caves. In exchange for better treatment, they agreed to transfer to the so-called Peace Fighters' Camp. Upon arrival there, they were subjected to daily indoctrination classes and expected to cooperate with propaganda efforts as part of the bargain. Chinese officials cited their example to encourage other prisoners to cooperate, and Camp Twelve became known as "Traitors' Row." In August, the North Koreans asked the group to broadcast a surrender appeal. When the Camp Twelve prisoners refused en masse, the North Koreans withdrew the request. The camp closed in November of 1951, and the prisoners were shipped north to permanent camps. Like most other captured airmen, Oldewage and his crew mates went to Camp Two, the officers' camp.[76]

Air Pressure

Beginning in the summer of 1951, the air war took center stage in Korea. Although the two sides had begun negotiations for a cease-fire on July 10, Washington ignored an offer from the Chinese to halt military operations. Instead, the Joint Chiefs reminded Ridgway that "there must be no relaxation in military effort on our part" until both sides agreed upon a mutually acceptable armistice. Recalling previous examples of Soviet perfidy, the American generals suspected a Chinese ploy, especially since the communist forces were capable of launching yet another large-scale offensive. Mindful that further UN ground assaults would be difficult and bloody among the steep ridgelines that both sides now occupied, Ridgway sought to maintain pressure on his communist foes through air attacks.[77]

Historian Bevin Alexander notes, however, that suspicion on both sides virtually guaranteed a continuation of hostilities. In Beijing, Mao directed his senior commanders in Korea to continue building up supplies and reinforcements for a sixth offensive. Meanwhile, the Pentagon's decision to continue military operations during the peace talks provided an opportunity for air force proponents to demonstrate the decisive influence of air power.[78]

In conjunction with the negotiations, Ridgway planned a major bombing raid against Pyongyang, the main transportation hub for communist troops and supplies headed for the front lines. Poor weather delayed and then disrupted a July 30 attack on the city, as well as a second strike on August 14, when some crews had to rely on radar to guide them to their targets. The results were disappointing, and Ridgway further postponed large airstrikes until the weather forecast improved.[79]

That same month, the Far Eastern Air Forces launched Operation Strangle, targeting North Korean cities, rail yards, roads, and bridges in a massive effort to cut off the frontline troops and thus force an enemy withdrawal. The aircrews were hampered by darkness, bad weather, and restrictive terrain, while the communist labor battalions, numbering several hundred thousand, worked doggedly to repair roads and rail lines, often building parallel segments to bypass damaged sections. In addition, communist planners rushed radar, spotlight, and antiaircraft batteries into North Korea to defend key targets. In October of 1951, attacks by MiG-15s forced American B-29s to shift from daylight bombing raids and resort to radar-guided night raids. Operation Strangle eventually cost the UN forces 343 aircraft destroyed and 290 aircraft damaged.[80] The air force defended this sacrifice by arguing that the communists had launched no major offensives. Ridgway, however, concluded that the effort to cut the enemy's supply lines was impossible "in a country as wild as Korea."[81]

Chemical and Biological Warfare

In early 1952, a Chinese general in North Korea reported that four enemy planes had flown over his headquarters and dropped "milky mucus" on his sleeve. In the following weeks, Beijing recorded other reports that suggested the employment of biological weapons. In late February, representatives of the North Korean, Chinese, and Soviet governments accused the United States of using biological weapons to break the Korean stalemate. In March, the Chinese expanded the accusation, claiming that the Americans were also using these weapons in northeastern China. Communist journalists had made such complaints since 1949 but offered scant proof for their accusations. In 1952, however, the Chinese government assembled a convincing case that UN airplanes had managed to spread deadly diseases across large areas of North Korea and Manchuria. The accusations peaked in October of

1952, when the Chinese delivered a lengthy scientific report to the United Nations that claimed to prove the United States was guilty of conducting biological warfare.[82]

The communists bolstered their accusations with a campaign to compel the captured American airmen to confess to having conducted secret germ-warfare missions. The first victims of this campaign were air force lieutenants John Quinn and Kenneth Enoch, captured on January 13, 1952, after their B-26 went down near Anju. The two officers were shipped to a small compound near Camp Two, the UN officers' camp at Pynchon-ni, where Chinese interrogators working in shifts questioned them about their participation in germ warfare. On May 4, 1952, Radio Peking and *Pravda* reported that both Americans had admitted their participation in a deliberate campaign to wage bacteriological warfare against the communist forces in Korea. Quinn's handwritten confession filled thirty-seven pages and blamed the bacteriological campaign on "the capitalistic wall street war monger [*sic*] in their greed, their ruthless greed."[83]

As further proof of American barbarism, the communists invited an international commission to investigate their allegations and to interview the airmen. At the United Nations, the US delegation had already proposed such investigations by the International Committee of the Red Cross (ICRC) and the World Health Organization (WHO). These resolutions were promptly vetoed by the Soviets, who had loudly echoed the Chinese and North Korean accusations in the general assembly. Instead, the Chinese invited a commission selected by the Committee for World Peace, a communist organization headquartered in Oslo, Norway. The commission of prominent leftist scientists visited several locations of alleged attacks and spoke with public-health officials and attack survivors. "Witnesses" described the aerial delivery of poisonous fleas, flies, mosquitoes, rats, and even cholera-infected clams, but the commissioners saw scant physical evidence of these weapons, as the villagers had subsequently destroyed the infected vermin during a massive public-health campaign.[84]

Even more damning than these witnesses was the self-incriminating testimony of the captured war criminals themselves. With Chinese officials present, the committee members met with the American airmen over a two-day period in July and determined that:

> no pressure, physical or mental, had been brought to bear upon these prisoners of war. . . . These declarations were made of their own free will, after long experience of the friendliness and kindness of their Chinese and Korean captors had

brought to them the realization that their duty to all races and peoples must outweigh their natural scruples.

The commission unanimously accepted both the prisoners' confessions and the communist allegations at face value.[85]

In September, the commission published its findings in a seven-hundred-page report. The authors conceded the absence of "perfect proof" in the form of a captured enemy aircraft laden with biological weapons. Nevertheless, they unanimously endorsed the communists' accusations that UN aircraft had, in fact, engaged in a covert biological-warfare campaign against military and civilian targets in North Korea and China. In October, the Soviet delegation presented the report to the UN general assembly, which responded by appointing a five-nation commission to further examine the allegations. Because both the Chinese and the North Koreans had refused to cooperate with the investigators, the commission eventually dismissed the Soviets' accusations as false.[86]

After the first American confessions, the communist interrogators intensified their efforts to produce corroborating evidence from newly captured airmen. In addition, airmen who had been seized in the previous months were reinterrogated. The Chinese focused on senior officers and experienced airmen, whose confessions carried greater weight among communist and third-world audiences. Those prisoners who were accused of conducting germ warfare were subsequently categorized as war criminals, placed in solitary confinement, often in cramped, unheated cells, and informed that they no longer enjoyed the protection of the Geneva Conventions. Their captors periodically withheld food and medical treatment, disrupted the prisoners' sleep patterns, and promised that questioning would continue until they confessed. Several forms of physical abuse were common, including slaps, kicks, and leg irons. The primary means of coercion, however, were psychological. The prisoners endured a variety of threats, including mock firing squads and life imprisonment, along with personal appeals that exploited their fears and anxieties. Married prisoners, for example, were repeatedly urged to think of their families, and the interrogators often tempted prisoners with the chance to send or receive mail.[87]

Throughout the interrogation process, Chinese officials attacked the war's legitimacy and depicted the prisoners as unwitting agents of imperialism, colonialism, or Wall Street profiteering, while extolling the blameless character of their communist victims. Once the exhausted and confused victims began to question their own role, a disturbing number rationalized the signing of a bogus confession. Whether because of fear, fatigue, or physical discomfort, thirty-eight Americans, including three colonels, eventually confessed to participating in germ-warfare missions. Of this group, Enoch and Quinn appeared to be the most cooperative. They recorded audio and video confessions, gave interviews, and described their war crimes for the benefit of other prisoners. Seven captives signed confessions after fewer than ten days of interrogation. Others held out for months, including one prisoner who endured nearly a year of isolation and psychological pressure before capitulating.[88]

American diplomats, meanwhile, vigorously denied the communists' accusations. In June, the US delegation at the United Nations adroitly exposed the Soviets' hypocrisy on the topic by forcing them to veto a resolution calling for ICRC and WHO investigations. The Americans then proposed a resolution condemning Soviet intransigence, which the Soviets also vetoed. The most persuasive renunciation, however, came from the prisoners themselves. Upon repatriation in 1953, they unanimously renounced their confessions and blamed them on communist torture. The declarations of guilt themselves often included deliberate inaccuracies and inconsistencies, and the Chinese withheld several from publication. Air force investigators later determined that most prisoners had deliberately withheld sensitive information. In one such case, a B-26 navigator provided the interrogators with a lengthy account of his involvement in the secret "G4Q" project.[89]

Despite their inconsistencies, the confessions bolstered a highly effective communist propaganda effort and placed US representatives on the defensive at Panmunjon and in the United Nations. The campaign gained significant credibility in the third world and among Westerners sympathetic to the communist cause. It also terrorized credulous Chinese and North Korean civilians and soldiers. To this day, Chinese scholars insist that US forces employed biological weapons in Korea. In 1998, a Japanese newspaper published Soviet records indicating that the campaign was a hoax designed to embarrass the United States. In 2000, military historian Conrad Crane argued persuasively that, although the Pentagon was working to develop biological weapons, researchers had not worked out an effective means of delivering such weapons by the end of the Korean War.[90]

Notably, however, at least forty captured US airmen successfully resisted all attempts by the Chinese to coerce such confessions. These prisoners endured mistreatment identical to that endured by the men who confessed, and yet they resisted every form of persuasion, from mock executions to threats of nonrepatriation. Air force Capt. Theodore Harris's extraordinary ordeal demonstrates the Chinese captors' capacity for brutality in their quest for more confessions.[91]

On the night of July 2, 1952, Harris bailed out of a damaged B-29 near Sinanju, suffering severe burns on much of his exposed skin in the process. Captured at dawn, the severely wounded pilot received no medical attention but was instead subjected to a week of interrogation by the local Chinese commander. Fortunately for Harris, the stench of his gangrenous wounds finally drove his interrogators from the room, and he received a three-week respite in a Korean hut, where his wounds healed. He was subsequently transferred to an interrogation center, where he spent several months shackled in a small, thatch-covered trench, enduring cold, filth, sleep deprivation, miserable food, isolation, and constant questioning.[92]

As the weather grew colder, Harris contracted frostbite on his hands and feet. After a mock firing squad failed to evoke a confession, Harris was shipped to Mukden, China, where he endured more interrogations and, later, a lengthy trial on charges of alleged war crimes. During the trial, guards repeatedly held the uncooperative American in a poorly ventilated box and beat on the lid until the prisoner's ears rang. The container was so cramped that the confinement temporarily paralyzed his limbs. The Chinese eventually transferred Harris to a larger, more comfortable prison and informed him that his trial had ended.[93]

Several weeks later, officials told Harris the war was over and offered to release him if he would write that he had been treated well. On a blank sheet, Harris jotted and signed a brief statement: "In my fourteen months of confinement, I have received more education than I have had in the previous twenty-nine years of my life." This satisfied the Chinese, and Harris rode a train south toward repatriation. The communists, however, had one more trick up their sleeve.[94]

At Kaesong, Harris's captors forced him and his fellow B-29 crew members in front of another court, photographed them, and read a statement declaring their innocence, adding that the Americans had admitted that other air force units had conducted biological warfare in Manchuria. "That's a God-damned lie!" barked Harris, who then refused repatriation until the falsehood was struck from the court verdict. After several hours, Chinese soldiers finally wrestled Harris into a cargo truck, where they sat on him until the truck arrived at Freedom Village to transfer him back to the UN. That evening, Captain Harris became the last American POW repatriated during Operation Big Switch.[95]

Prisoners in the permanent camps found other ways to resist the germ-warfare propaganda. Although the Chinese bombarded UN prisoners with "proof" of these war crimes, the cynical captives gave them no credence. Their prison guards, however, accepted germ-warfare propaganda as gospel, giving the prisoners an opening for their own form of mental torment. At Camp Four, American sergeants inspired panic among the guard force by secretly painting "US Mark 7" on the backs of several insects, then leaving them in the prison yard. Officers at Camp Two rigged a dead rat with a miniature parachute and hung it from a tree branch. The camp commandant responded by ordering all of the guards and prisoners to be disinfected with iodine. On another occasion, UN bombers dropped radar-scattering chaff onto the camp, and the Chinese ordered the prisoners to gather the "germ-warfare evidence" with tweezers. Several alarmed their captors by gathering the aluminum strips and chewing them.[96]

Escalation

In May of 1952, Gen. Mark Clark replaced Ridgway as commander of the UN forces and shifted the air campaign to attacks against North Korean hydroelectric plants, including the massive Suiho complex on the Yalu River. These air strikes caused a nationwide two-week blackout in North Korea and severely reduced power supplies on both sides of the Yalu but sparked an international protest, especially in Great Britain. In July and August, air force and navy fighter-bombers launched massive raids against Pyongyang, flattening most of the rest of the city. These attacks, however, had no impact on the progress of the truce talks. Throughout the summer of 1952, communist negotiators at Panmunjon enjoyed the upper hand due to the success of their germ-warfare accusations and the widely publicized riots at the Eighth Army's POW compound on Koje-Do Island. Negotiations stalled during the winter of 1952–1953, but raids continued against a diminishing list of suitable targets.[97]

In the spring of 1953, the White House implied that Eisenhower might use atomic weapons to break the deadlock. In May, General Clark ordered the bombing of previously undamaged irrigation dams in North Korea. Consequently, UN aircraft destroyed three dams, and the ensuing floods caused extensive damage downstream. Communist labor battalions made quick repairs, but further attacks against these dams posed a serious threat to the North Korean rice crop. In the final weeks before the truce, Clark directed strikes against enemy airfields across North Korea, thus preventing

the communists from seizing air superiority on the peninsula when hostilities ended.[98]

Lessons Learned?

When representatives finally signed the cease-fire agreement on July 27,
1953, senior US airmen congratulated themselves on bringing the enemy to
terms. During the war, UN aircraft had flown more than one million combat sorties and dropped nearly seven hundred thousand tons of ordnance on
enemy targets. Navy, marine, and allied aircraft had made significant contributions, but the Far Eastern Air Force had shouldered most of the load,
flying 69 percent of the sorties, delivering 68 percent of the ordnance, and
losing 74 percent of the aircraft shot down over Korea. In the process, the
air force developed important new capabilities, including aerial refueling,
electronic warfare, radar-guided bombing, and improved combat search and
rescue. Said one general after the war, "We are pretty sure now that the communists wanted peace, not because of a two-year stalemate on the ground,
but to get [US] air power off their back."[99]

Despite the tireless and often heroic efforts of the UN aircrews, however, the war did more to highlight air power's limitations than its advantages. Aerial reconnaissance did not, for example, detect the initial Chinese
deployment into North Korea, nor could air strikes stem the flow of troops
and supplies once Chinese intervention became obvious, failures that had
strategic consequences. For nearly the entire war, UN aircraft dominated the
Korean skies, but this control could not prevent the initial NKPA advance or
the later Chinese counteroffensives of 1950 and 1951. Finally, UN air strikes
destroyed nearly every target of significance in North Korea, often destroying them several times over, while inflicting an estimated 180,000 enemy
casualties. These efforts, however, failed to destroy the communists' supply
lines or isolate frontline troops. In July of 1953, communist forces stockpiled
sufficient supplies to launch a major assault that destroyed two ROK divisions. Air power contributed immensely to UN combat operations in Korea, but in the face of a ruthless, dedicated opponent, it proved incapable of
achieving victory by itself. A decade later, the Pentagon would relearn this
lesson against another ruthless, dedicated opponent in Vietnam.[100]

If military leaders failed to appreciate the limitations of air power in
Korea, they made no such mistake in studying the treatment and conduct
of the captured airmen. The air force took particular interest in the con-

duct of its personnel and carefully examined ways to improve their resistance to capture, interrogation, and indoctrination in future conflicts. Although frequently singled out for interrogation and mistreatment by their captors, most air force POWs (along with airmen from other services) had received little or no training in what to expect as prisoners. Noting this lack of preparation, a postwar study found it "reassuring that as many resisted as long and determinedly as they did" and concluded that the "general behavior of the USAF POW was very good."[101] Older and better educated than many other American prisoners, the captured airmen uniformly resisted communist indoctrination to such a degree that communist officials automatically categorized them, along with airmen from other services, as "reactionaries."[102]

Despite the coerced germ-warfare confessions, the air force concluded that nearly all of its 220 captured personnel had behaved honorably—and in many cases valiantly—during their imprisonment.[103] Meanwhile, the air force and the navy implemented rigorous survival-training programs to better prepare future aircrews for the possibility of capture, torture, and political manipulation at the hands of a communist foe, just in case history were to repeat itself.

10   **Mutual Suspicion**

When I've lost about 75 pounds, I don't roar very loud.
Maj. Harold Kaschko

In June of 1951, prisoner morale at Pyoktong hit rock bottom.[1] The days grew warmer, the snow disappeared, and after seven months of captivity, the filthy, malnourished prisoners were finally allowed to bathe in the Yalu. The survivors also began receiving clean clothes and more food. For many, however, these improvements came too late. Several hundred Americans had already perished, many of them teenage soldiers barely out of boot camp.[2]

The deaths continued, largely due to the lack of adequate medicine or treatment.[3] The Chinese blamed shortages on U.S. air attacks. They also restricted captured doctors from treating their fellow prisoners. The Chinese made an exception for Bill Shadish and a few enlisted medics, who were allowed to care for men in the enlisted compound. Without medicine, however, they had to rely on rudimentary solutions, such as soaking infected limbs in hot water. The gaunt, sickly prisoners spent most of their waking hours on work details or in political reeducation classes, where they heard distortions and outright lies about their own country. As May turned to June, the death rate among the enlisted soldiers finally began to diminish, but the survivors now faced the prospect of interminable imprisonment in the filthy mud huts along the Yalu.[4]

At random intervals, the prisoners were summoned for apparently meaningless interrogations. One day, for example, an interrogator presented Bill Funchess with a map and ordered him to indicate the locations of all Japanese military bases. The lieutenant had served there only briefly before the war and had spent most of that time on maneuvers. The interrogator deemed this explanation "uncooperative," so Funchess designed a map of Japan with imaginary military installations, making sure to fill in the available white space.[5]

The opening epigraph is from Lech, *Broken Soldiers*, 103.

Although these "talks" rarely involved physical coercion, the prisoners learned to detest them because of the suspicions they inspired in others. As Cdr. Ralph Bagwell later recalled, "Everyone who was taken out was under suspicion by the other men."[6] By the summer of 1951, many prisoners had already lost faith in their countrymen. The harsh winter conditions brought out the worst in some prisoners, and food was so scarce that any inequity, real or perceived, inspired harsh resentment. The Chinese segregation of prisoners by race, rank, and nationality further contributed to a corrosive spirit of "every man for himself." The interrogators shrewdly exploited this paranoia by publicly rewarding cooperative prisoners with food and tobacco while punishing groups en masse for the recalcitrant behavior of others. The Chinese also targeted the most outspoken prisoners, labeling them "reactionaries" and torturing them in various ways. When a man broke, the Chinese would pressure him into further cooperation by threatening to expose his earlier deeds.[7]

The Peace Appeal

In the officers' compound, a new Chinese commandant, Ding, had repeatedly demonstrated his impatience with officers who were foolish enough to defy him. Father Kapaun was dead, and so was Maj. Thomas Hume, the victim of a savage beating for speaking out during a propaganda speech. Other prisoners were simply beaten, tortured, or starved until their resistance faded. Meanwhile, the death rate spiked among the imprisoned officers. Most were older and had slower metabolisms, and their bodies had held out longer against the ravages of starvation. In the spring of 1951, however, the cumulative effects of malnutrition and disease finally began taking their toll. To survive, the Americans copied the Turkish prisoners, who were collecting grass and weeds in order to boil "weed tea." The foul-tasting liquid turned their urine green, but it also provided the desperate men with life-saving nutrients.[8]

The Chinese chose this moment to subject their sick and demoralized captives to yet another humiliation. First, they assembled the prisoners for a "peace rally" and pressured them to elect representatives to a "peace committee." When this effort proved dissatisfactory, the Chinese handpicked prisoners for the committee, including several recently tortured officers.[9] Like the earlier "committee" at Kanggye and a similar organization at Camp

Twelve, the committee at Pyoktong was then forced to draft a letter asking "the Five Great Powers" to peacefully resolve the current conflict. After rejecting several drafts, the Chinese finally procured a suitable document and assembled all of the officers and a few enlisted representatives in the mess area to conduct a "discussion." A few committee members spoke in favor of signing the appeal, and the Chinese forced the audience to divide into groups for or against. Convinced that signing was the only way to notify their families and the U.S. government of their survival, most of the officers agreed to cooperate. Some seemed too willing, however, and their enthusiastic denunciations of U.S. foreign policy both infuriated and embarrassed their colleagues. Led by Maj. John McLaughlin, who had already been subjected to the Chinese "peace appeal" gambit at Kanggye, a small group of officers refused. A third group initially declared themselves undecided.[10]

By the end of the day, few prisoners had changed their minds. The Chinese allowed debate to continue for two more days, but McLaughlin and other dissidents held firm. Finally, the Chinese intervened. They removed one of the dissidents, Lt. Joseph Magnant, and made him stand at attention for an entire day in the sun, then reminded the young officer of Major Hume's fate. Meanwhile, the camp commandant summoned McLaughlin to his office, accused him of leading opposition to both the peace appeal and the indoctrination program, and threatened him with a "people's trial" and a twenty-five-year sentence.[11]

Disappointed by the compliance of his fellow officers and facing the probability of never seeing his family again, McLaughlin finally consented: "We had no unity in opposition to this Peace Appeal and I just thought it was useless, futile to oppose this thing." McLaughlin directed the others to follow his lead, assuring them that he would take full responsibility. "We figured it was the only way to get our names out," recalled Bob Wood, an infantry lieutenant captured at Unsan and one of the holdouts. "But I always felt very badly about signing that damned thing."[12]

Having coerced the officers, the Chinese used their compliance as leverage to persuade prisoners in the enlisted companies to endorse the appeal, then added insult to injury by staging a "peace march." Prisoners were issued supplies and directed to paint signs proclaiming "We Want Peace." After two days of painting, the prisoners assembled with their banners at the front gates of the camp and marched through the streets of Pyoktong, while photographers snapped pictures. Intent on maintaining their captors' goodwill, a few prisoners shouted anti-American slogans with gusto.[13]

Others were less cooperative. Some groups carried their signs upside down, dragged their pennants in the dirt, and shouted "We Want Meat!" for the assembled cameramen. Another squad carried a banner with this slogan: "Labor is honor, when you get honor, keep honor." When the men returned to the compound, the peace appeal was waiting for their signature. A rain storm interrupted the signing process, so the Chinese guards carried the document from hut to hut, meticulously gathering 1,671 signatures from nearly every man in camp, including patients in the hospital. The last man to sign was Bill Shadish, the doctor who had witnessed so many tragedies at Death Valley. That night, the Chinese provided a "celebration" feast, complete with pork and corn fritters. With no end in sight, the Camp Five survivors faced a grim future at the mercy of their captors.[14]

Soon, however, the course of the war took yet another dramatic turn.

With their forces badly damaged and their Soviet sponsors losing enthusiasm, the Chinese were ready to talk. In fact, the only two parties unwilling to cease hostilities were the initial antagonists, Kim and Rhee. According to historian Callum MacDonald, the North Koreans were "stunned" by the Soviet call for a cease-fire. Heavily dependent on Chinese and Soviet aid, Kim's North Korean regime had little strategic input as the junior partner in the communist alliance. In Seoul, Rhee enjoyed more leverage over his Western allies, who were ostensibly fighting to maintain a free and democratic Republic of Korea. For the South Korean premier, however, any outcome short of reunification was "unacceptable." Dean Acheson later wrote that "Some rather plain telegrams restored better behavior but did not gain real acceptance of the policy." In the months to come, Rhee's displeasure would become a growing problem for both Truman and Eisenhower.[15]

Bargaining Chips

Cease-fire negotiations began at Kaesong on July 10, but the news was slow to reach the prisoners inside the Yalu camps. Earlier that month, rain showers had provided welcome relief from the summer heat, but these also washed away the topsoil on hundreds of hastily dug prisoner graves, enabling dogs and pigs to feed on the exposed corpses. Inside the wire, the prisoners continued to endure the seemingly interminable lectures about the injustice of "Wall Street's war" or were forced to discuss articles from the *London Daily Worker* or the writings of Mao and Stalin under the watchful eyes of Chinese monitors.[16]

Gradually, however, treatment improved. Men still lived in filthy mud huts, but these now received wooden doors and gauze sheeting to cover the windows and keep out the flies. The prisoners had been bathing in the river since May, but now the Chinese issued soap and towels and installed water spigots in the company areas at Camp Five. In addition, the patients at the Pyoktong hospital (which was still filthy) received combs and a ration of tobacco. Malnutrition and poor hygiene had contributed to an outbreak of dental diseases in May and June, but the Chinese began issuing toothbrushes and toothpaste, which seemed to resolve the crisis. More Chinese medical personnel arrived, and although they were no better trained than their predecessors, they brought with them medicine, vitamins, DDT, and bandages.[17]

Most important, the prisoners finally began receiving more and better food. They did their own cooking and served two meals a day. They used vegetables as the base for a watery soup, which they prepared daily. Twice a week, they also received rice, considered a delicacy after eight months of millet and cracked corn. The Chinese also began providing small rations of salt and flour, with which the prisoners made dumplings. On special occasions, they even received pork.[18]

In the permanent camps, prisoners stopped dying. They still suffered from various maladies, and they still had to endure the daily routine of communist lectures, monitored discussions, and written "cognitions." Still, with cease-fire talks under way, the men assumed they would be going home in the near future. Escape plans were scratched, and rumors spread of a hospital ship docking off Sinuiju to evacuate prisoners. The Chinese even began permitting prisoners to write home, adding that they could also receive mail from home, provided their families addressed the letters to Beijing in care of "the Committee for World Peace and Against American Aggression." En masse, the captives at Camp Five refused to include the last four words, and the Chinese relented. For the moment, at least, morale soared.[19]

Farther south, however, the situation remained grim for the hundreds of American prisoners held at interrogation centers and temporary camps across North Korea. Most of these men had been captured in April and May, during the Chinese fifth-phase offensive. As with earlier groups of prisoners, these men were initially marched to temporary camps, such as Pan's Camp, the Mining Camp, and the Bean Camp. The Chinese had belatedly recognized the propaganda value of keeping UN prisoners alive, but their North Korean allies continued to treat the men like cattle. None of these temporary camps offered adequate food, medicine, or shelter. To make matters worse, the communists temporarily halted the northern movement of captives that summer on the assumption that a prisoner exchange was imminent. This decision prolonged the ordeal of those who were stuck in the temporary camps.[20]

Prisoners on the Move

Not all American POWs were confined to a camp that summer. General Dean was held by the North Koreans in a small village eighteen miles northwest of Pyongyang, where a North Korean agent working for the CIA spotted him. The Eighth Army planned to insert a rescue team by parachute, but the raid, code-named "Mustang II," was cancelled at the last minute after enemy guns shot down the B-26 sent to reconnoiter the drop zone. The North Koreans promptly transferred their prize captive to a different safe house and moved him several more times during the next two years.[21]

Dean, at least, received adequate food and shelter. Other prisoners were less fortunate. Jack Chapman, Jim DeLong, and twenty-six other Kanggye prisoners, whom the Chinese had originally planned to release in May of 1951, now zigzagged back toward the Yalu under the watchful eye of Chinese guards. The small group gradually made their way north, moving at night while hauling food and supplies for their captors. [22]

Perhaps because of the hectic communist withdrawal in late May, the group followed a bizarre path. Starting near Chunchon, a few miles above the 38th Parallel, they marched northeast to the coast and then northwest to a mountain village, where they stopped for nearly a month. The local peasants secretly brought food, medicine, and tobacco to the sick and exhausted prisoners, who were battling dysentery, hepatitis, and malaria. Chapman and several other prisoners nearly died, but their fellow prisoners and the sympathetic Korean villagers helped them survive.[23]

In late September, the group marched southwest to the Mining Camp, where they joined a large group of American, British, and Korean prisoners that included most of the other men from Kanggye. A captured British chaplain noticed that Chapman's group seemed particularly cocky. To the disappointment of the Chinese, they also proved hopelessly reactionary. On their first night together, the Kanggye survivors celebrated their reunion with several loud verses of "God Bless America" until the guards finally ordered them to stop singing.[24] On October 11, Chapman and most of the other prisoners at the Mining Camp marched north to Sinuiju, finally arriving in late October at a newly established permanent compound at Camp One.[25]

Lieutenant Dixon's Odyssey

Army lieutenant Ralph Dixon endured a similar, circuitous path to the Yalu. The young artillery officer arrived as an individual replacement at Pusan in late August and spent ten days as a forward observer before he was wounded and evacuated to Japan. After recovering, Dixon returned to combat duty with the 2nd Infantry Division in November of 1950. On April 25, 1951, Chinese forces overran his position and captured him near Uijonbu. During the action, Dixon was wounded in both feet and could barely walk. At a prisoner-collection point, Chinese troops cut Dixon's blood-soaked boots from his feet and gave him a pair of oversized rubber galoshes instead. "With these galoshes," recalled Dixon, "I flopped around Korea for quite a while."[27]

It would have been tempting to abandon the tall, powerfully built officer on the battlefield, but the Chinese troops moved him to an assembly area in the rear, where he was left to recover from his wounds. After three weeks, his captors trucked him to the town of Yang Dok.[28] Dixon's wounded feet continued to bother him, but the bullet had passed cleanly through his ankles without breaking any bones. One night, a fellow prisoner accidentally stepped on Dixon's ankles in the dark. "And either he set the bones or he did something," recalled Dixon, "because the next morning, believe it or not, I could walk. Man, I don't know what happened. I do know that before that, it was very painful. After that, it was not."[29]

At Yang Dok, the Chinese turned Dixon over to a North Korean field hospital, where he and a small group of prisoners spent the next month as stretcher bearers, carrying wounded NKPA soldiers back and forth between the train station, the hospital, and an operating room. If they were carrying an officer, the Americans would manage to drop the stretcher "by accident." Several of the doctors spoke English, and one afternoon one of them warned the prisoners: "Don't be here tomorrow morning. You will be shot if you are. Get on the train tonight when it pulls out." On their next trip to the station, the six delivered their stretchers and hid in freight cars. The train left after dark, heading west toward Pyongyang. It halted in a tunnel before dawn, hidden from roving UN aircraft.[29]

Leaving the train, Dixon and the others followed a crowd of civilians trudging south. The Americans walked unmolested for several miles before the local police finally took notice and arrested them. After several days confined in a stable, the prisoners were marched to Sunchon, a major transportation hub north of Pyongyang. The men spent six weeks in a hut near the Sunchon rail yard, unguarded and ignored by their North Korean captors. To feed themselves, Dixon and the others scavenged for corn nightly in the fields and spent each morning begging for food in town. North Korean children would follow the Americans at a safe distance, giggling as the tall lieutenant and his ragged friends shuffled slowly from hut to hut.[30]

One morning, a Chinese officer found the prisoners. Using sign language, he indicated that he wanted them to inspect an unexploded bomb. Making their own gestures, Dixon and the others agreed to come if the Chinese would feed them and provide shoes to replace Dixon's galoshes. The Chinese agreed, and the hungry Americans followed him out of town, across a railroad trestle to the bomb crater. None of the others had ever seen a bomb, much less defused one. A fellow prisoner, Bill Keenan, admitted having once seen a bomb on an assembly line, which made him the resident expert. After a hearty breakfast, the prisoners inspected the bomb, which had a silver, three-inch fuse projecting toward the sky. While Keenan examined the fuse, another American lay down next to the bomb, and Dixon climbed up on top, announcing, "I'm going to sit on top of this sucker, because I'm going straight up with it." Keenan decided to twist the fuse counterclockwise and safely removed a twelve-inch cylinder.[31]

The Chinese were pleased that the bomb had been defused, and the Americans were pleased to be alive and momentarily well fed. The Chinese fed the prisoners a second time, but the mood darkened when the Americans "accidentally" dropped the fuse off the railroad trestle on their way back into town. A week later, the Chinese officer summoned the prisoners to defuse a second bomb, but it still had tail fins attached. Unable to remove the fins with their bare hands, the Americans told the Chinese they would need a crowbar. Unhappy with these results, the Chinese fed the men a few green peppers and sent them back to town. On September 28, Chinese troops marched Dixon and the others to a nearby prisoner-of-war camp, where they joined three hundred other prisoners, many of them from the 2nd Infantry Division. Together with these men, Dixon and his fellow survivors marched north toward Camp Three. Having lost half of his body weight during the previous months, the emaciated lieutenant became severely ill during the march. Placed with the sick and wounded, Dixon received a series of vitamin

B shots in a Chinese hospital and eventually arrived at the new prison camp for officers.[32]

Chinese Indoctrination Fails

While Ralph Dixon, Jack Chapman, and hundreds of other American prisoners marched north during the autumn of 1951, life in the permanent camps settled into a boring routine. In addition to Camp Five at Pyoktong, the Chinese had established two permanent camps a few miles to the southwest. Camp One, at Ch'ang-ni, eventually held approximately 1,400 American and British prisoners, most of them junior enlisted soldiers. Camp Three at Changsong was initially established in August of 1951 as a penal camp to hold approximately 160 reactionary prisoners from Camp Five, but the compound later expanded to hold 850 men.[33] At all three camps, political indoctrination continued to dominate the prisoners' daily lives. They rose before dawn, assembled for head count, performed calisthenics, and ate a meager breakfast, then left camp on work details or sat through political-indoctrination classes. They ate supper in the late afternoon and had some free time until lights out at 2100 hours.[34]

Expecting a cease-fire to be signed any day, most of the men paid little attention to the political lectures, which one prisoner described as "long, boring, and filled with lies, name-calling, and anti-American propaganda."[35] Guards would smack anyone who appeared inattentive or sleepy, so the men developed ways to appear interested while they daydreamed about home. The lectures were usually followed by mandatory group discussions back in the squad huts. The Chinese lacked sufficient personnel to monitor all of these discussions, and the prisoners invented a "bird-dog" system for avoiding the requirement. This system involved posting a lookout to watch for Chinese officials while the rest of the men napped, joked, or talked about cars, sports, women, or food.[36]

In fact, the entire, massive Chinese project to reeducate the prisoners about the virtues of communism would eventually prove a dismal failure. In the first place, brutal mistreatment at the hands of their captors had cost the lives of several thousand prisoners during the first half of 1951. Most of the survivors had endured death marches, starvation rations, filthy living conditions, and little or no medical care. Ignoring this deprivation, Chinese officials assured the prisoners that they were protected by the "lenient policy," which promised food, housing, medical care, and humane treatment to those who cooperated. Those who did not, recalled Bill Shadish, were threatened with execution as "war criminals."[37]

Second, despite the constant Chinese criticism of Truman, MacArthur, and Wall Street, the American prisoners were generally reluctant to blame their plight on their own country. Although the notion of appealing for peace probably found a sympathetic ear among the war-weary prisoners, the Chinese lectures often strained credulity by relying on naïve or false assumptions about American society, such as the assertion that Americans did not own their own cars.[38] Besides, World War II had made the United States the richest, most powerful nation on earth, with bustling cities, gleaming skyscrapers, supersonic jets, atomic bombs, and a surplus of more prosaic delights: clean sheets, movie theaters, hot rods, cute girls, cold beer, baseball, the Sunday comics, and the comforts of family and friends. For the lice-ridden prisoners living in mud huts, no Chinese workers' paradise could compete with these familiar American images of home. As one prisoner later recalled, "They had nothing and wanted to share it with the world."[39]

Third, the Chinese indoctrination model, parts of which resembled college seminars, had little effect on its intended audience. The Chinese inundated their captives with communist messages around the clock, but most American officers and noncommissioned officers proved too well educated to accept the communist claims at face value, and their inherent responsibilities as leaders exerted an additional, internal resistance to enemy propaganda.[40] The Chinese deliberately segregated these groups to minimize their influence on the junior enlisted prisoners, who were generally much younger and had less formal education. In addition, Chinese officials were quick to remove any "natural leaders" who emerged within these groups. Despite these measures, the American prisoners proved far more interested in disrupting class and avoiding work than in examining the inevitability of the proletarian class struggle. Efforts to exploit racial and national differences among the prisoners proved similarly unsuccessful.[41]

Finally, the Chinese lacked adequate time and leverage to achieve ideological conversion among their prisoners. Once cease-fire talks began, the prisoners assumed it would only be a matter of time before they were repatriated. Under these conditions, most American prisoners provided just enough compliance with the Chinese instructors to avoid punishment, but few took their lessons seriously, and even fewer took them to heart. Pentagon researcher Albert Biderman later observed that the "passive resistance of almost all the POWs to the Chinese attempts at group indoctrination was a noteworthy display of group organization and discipline." In early 1952, the Chinese quietly abandoned their compulsory indoctrination program.[42]

Divide and Conquer

If the Chinese failed to convert Americans to their political views, they achieved far greater success in establishing and maintaining nearly complete social control of their prisoners. This dominance minimized organized resistance and enabled the coercion and manipulation of the prisoners for propaganda purposes, such as the campwide "appeal for peace" orchestrated at Pyoktong in June of 1951. Chinese efforts at social control also disrupted most of the prisoners' efforts to organize escape committees, coordinate resistance efforts, or communicate with the outside world. Although Western journalists would portray such attempts as new and sinister, the Chinese, in fact, employed a wide variety of familiar techniques to isolate and alienate prisoners, thus dominating all aspects of daily life within their compounds. These techniques included the aforementioned segregation of prisoners by race, rank, and nationality, the strict regimentation of daily life, the employment of rewards and punishments to encourage cooperation, absolute control over news received and sent by prisoners (including the monitoring, withholding, and censorship of prisoners' mail), and the utilization of questionnaires, interrogations, and spies to gather detailed information about the prisoners.[43]

The most disturbing aspect of the Chinese strategy involved the exploitation of cooperative prisoners, who fell into two categories. "Progressives" generally followed camp rules and complied with their captors' demands. If they did not actually embrace communist ideology, they made little or no effort to oppose it. "Rats," on the other hand, seized every opportunity to gain an advantage, whether by informing the guards of an escape attempt or stealing a fellow prisoner's food. Sergeant Lloyd Pate, a well-known reactionary during his imprisonment at Camp Three, later described such men as "fence-sitters":

> They never participated in the discussions, but they were brown-nosers. They looked up to authority figures and always wanted a pat on the head. They had a weak character, and were more dangerous than the Progressives, who, for the most part, were not. The Progressives would stand up during the discussions and voice their opinions on how great Communism was. We knew who

they were. Hell, their articles were posted on the bulletin boards. But we didn't always know who the Rats were.

Although these two groups represented only a small percentage of American prisoners in Korea, the Chinese deliberately manipulated them in order to create dissension and mistrust among the prisoners' ranks.[44]

The "rats" were a problem from the very start. Within moments of their capture, most Americans were promised humane treatment by the Chinese if only they would cooperate and obey the rules, and this rudimentary system of reward and punishment persuaded the most selfish prisoners to do whatever it took to survive. Better fed and stronger than their fellow captives, those who curried favor with their captors became easy to recognize as the majority of prisoners slowly starved to death. During the first, deadly winter of captivity, some of the most reprehensible prisoners stole food, clothing, and valuables from the sick and the dying, thus further contributing to the barbaric atmosphere in the camps.[45]

After full-scale indoctrination began in the spring of 1951, the Chinese gained even more leverage over their prisoners. With men continuing to die at an alarming rate, the prisoners quickly learned to parrot the communist lessons in order to win their instructors' favor: The more enthusiastic the participation, the greater the reward. Those willing to write about world politics, for example, might receive tobacco, soap, or fresh fruit as a prize. The Chinese would then post the essays on a camp bulletin board, further undermining resistance to their indoctrination.[46]

In addition to attending and participating in daily classes, prisoners were required to serve as squad monitors and as delegates to Chinese-orchestrated "peace committees." Whether elected by fellow prisoners or appointed by the Chinese, many of these men simply did the minimum to satisfy their captors. Nevertheless, their apparent authority inspired resentment and suspicion among their fellow prisoners. Others, however, participated enthusiastically in the indoctrination program, either from curiosity, boredom, or a desire to curry favor, and some even volunteered to serve as lecturers. Their eagerness attracted similar resentment and suspicion. A significant number of "progressives" later tried to rehabilitate their reputations among their fellow prisoners, and some became active, outspoken "reactionaries."[47]

Meanwhile, the Chinese also developed a sophisticated network of informers. Some of these men had been blackmailed into service either through physical torture or because of earlier words and deeds. In one case, a field-grade officer who been severely tortured begged his fellow officers not to discuss plans for escape or resistance for fear that he would not be able to remain silent if tortured again.[48] Other prisoners legitimately endorsed communist ideas and may have agreed to inform on their colleagues to demonstrate their cooperative attitude. The most cynically opportunistic prisoners, the "rats," willingly informed on their buddies to gain small favors, such as letter-writing privileges, extra cigarettes, or a boiled egg. The Chinese, in turn, used this information to identify and quash most signs of resistance. Prisoners eventually developed small resistance groups, but these enjoyed relatively little success, as the Chinese were quick to punish the group members.[49]

In fact, Chinese officials seemed more interested in manipulation than effective intelligence, occasionally exposing their own informers in public. They also removed individual prisoners for extended interrogations and took them for long, apparently friendly discussions. These strategies created the exaggerated appearance of collaboration, often where none existed. The resulting atmosphere of mistrust between individual prisoners undermined their cohesion and ensured effective Chinese control within the camps for the duration of the war.[50]

11 The Pawns

There are two things which a democratic people will always find very difficult—to begin a war and to end it.
Alexis de Tocqueville, *Democracy in America*

By the autumn of 1951, conditions for prisoners in the Yalu camps had improved significantly. Chinese mistreatment and manipulation continued, but more food, better hygiene, and limited medical treatment dramatically reduced the death rate among prisoners, and the possibilities of a cease-fire and subsequent repatriation boosted morale considerably.[1]

At Ridgway's headquarters in Tokyo, however, the mood was far less optimistic. By October, negotiators had agreed on an agenda—and nothing else. Both sides began negotiations in July with the expectation of reaching a swift agreement, but mutual suspicion made this impossible.[2] While the fighting continued, the discussions themselves proved frustratingly slow. The negotiators, for example, spent the first sixteen days haggling over the wording of the agenda. Furthermore, communist officials undertook several early ploys at the negotiating site to intimidate the UN delegates and present them in a submissive role. These gambits infuriated Ridgway and his negotiators while causing further delays. In late July, the delegations finally agreed to discuss four major items: the establishment of a military line of demarcation; cease-fire arrangements, including the establishment of a supervisory commission; the exchange of prisoners; and recommendations to the governments of the countries on both sides.[3]

Mutual acrimony continued through August as both sides accused each other of neutral-zone violations. In discussions about a cease-fire line, the communists argued for the 38th Parallel as the line of demarcation, citing earlier statements by Secretary of State Dean Acheson. In response, the UN delegation initially argued for a line that extended well north of the existing battle lines. On August 23, the communist delegation suspended talks after accusing UN aircraft of violating the neutral zone at Kaesong.[4]

With the talks in recess, Ridgway approved a series of limited offensives to improve the UN positions and deter a potential communist offensive.

These assaults proved more difficult than expected—communist defenders occupied favorable terrain and had fortified their positions with bunkers and tunnels to reduce the effects of UN firepower. Despite heavy communist resistance, the UN attacks continued through September and October. The bloodiest fighting took place amid a series of hill masses, dubbed "Bloody Ridge" and "Heartbreak Ridge," where US, ROK, and French infantry struggled to dislodge the defending North Koreans. The operation cost 60,000 UN casualties, 22,000 of them American soldiers and marines. Intense combat would continue for the duration of the war, with each side trying to leverage battlefield gains at the negotiating table.[5]

When the communists offered to resume talks in September, Ridgway proposed relocating the negotiations to Panmunjom, a small village between the two battle lines. The communists initially rejected this offer, and the impasse continued. After more accusations of UN violations of the neutral zone, some of them legitimate, communist and UN liaison officers finally agreed to new procedural restrictions, and the talks resumed at Panmunjom on October 25.[6]

Consolidation and Segregation

As negotiations resumed, the Chinese relocated approximately 160 American, British, and Turkish officers, plus a small group of air force sergeants, from the three main Yalu prison camps to a newly established camp in the village of Pynchon-ni.[7] As more groups of UN prisoners trudged into the permanent camps during the final weeks of 1951, their officers were separated and transferred to the new camp, which soon held more than 300 prisoners. The Chinese may have transferred the officers in order to focus more attention on the political indoctrination of the remaining enlisted soldiers, or they may have simply needed more room for incoming prisoners.[8]

Located eight miles north of Pyoktong and dubbed Camp Two, the new compound was organized around an abandoned, vermin-infested schoolhouse that served as the prisoners' lodgings. As the weather turned colder, the prisoners received padded blue uniforms and wool blankets and were allowed the use of antiquated wood stoves in their cramped squad rooms. A barbed-wire fence surrounded the enclosure, which included a parade ground, a cook house, and a slit-trench latrine. The group would spend twenty-two months inhabiting these shabby quarters.[9]

New arrivals along the Yalu that autumn included 290 American prisoners from the so-called Apex camps in the northernmost corner of North Korea. These were the remaining survivors of the Tiger Death March a year earlier. More than half had died since then because of the North Koreans' brutality and negligence. A British officer described the group as "gaunt, silent men, afraid to raise their voices. . . . They felt grateful to the Chinese for food, fresh clothing, and material benefits which by comparison with North Korean prisoner of war standards seemed surprisingly good." The officers in the group were subsequently transferred to Camp Two, and the Chinese assigned the rest of the prisoners to Camp Three.[10]

Slow Progress at Panmunjom

At Panmunjom, the resumed talks focused on establishing a mutually acceptable line of demarcation, and the two delegations bartered for various positions along the existing front lines. The communists abandoned their insistence on the 38th Parallel but refused several UN proposals to relinquish Kaesong, an ancient Korean capital with great symbolic value in both Pyongyang and Seoul. On November 27, 1951, the two sides finally agreed on a mutually acceptable demarcation line and set a thirty-day time limit to resolve the remaining three issues. An armistice seemed imminent.[11]

In Seoul, however, an ill-considered press release threatened to dismantle the progress. Colonel James Hanley, chief of Eighth Army's War Crimes Division, issued a detailed report in mid-November that accused the communist forces of murdering 6,202 American prisoners.[12] Hanley had apparently gained prior approval to release his report, and its tone echoed earlier accusations by Ridgway's headquarters that charged the communist forces with committing war crimes against "approximately 8,000 US military personnel." The timing of the report, however, was disastrous because it threatened to disrupt the impending agreement on the line of demarcation. The report also provoked angry responses in the United States, where relatives of missing soldiers flooded the Pentagon with letters demanding information about their loved ones.[13]

In light of earlier accusations from Tokyo and Washington, Hanley's report seemed credible, but his numbers were poorly documented, and a delegation from Ridgway's headquarters soon arrived to investigate and clarify the accusation. Ridgway subsequently conceded the possibility that "6,000 American soldiers now listed as missing in action in Korea could have been captured and killed by Communist troops," but only 365 of these deaths could be confirmed.[14] The discrepancy raised suspicions that Hanley's report was merely a crude attempt at propaganda. *Time* magazine described the episode as "an Army blunder of appalling proportions," and there was talk of bringing charges against Hanley. Despite its flaws, the initial report focused significant attention on the plight of the UN prisoners and generated indirect pressure on the communists to return them safely.[15]

The communists responded with countercharges of mistreatment in UN prison camps, and Chinese officials launched a campaign to pressure the American prisoners into signing statements describing their good treatment. The campaign failed miserably, and some prisoners were severely punished for providing statements that accurately described the deadly conditions of communist captivity. As the prisoners' value as bargaining chips increased, the Chinese belatedly initiated a census to identify both living and dead prisoners, and conditions continued to improve for the survivors in the Yalu camps.[16]

With the issue of the cease-fire line apparently settled, the negotiators began discussions on the final three issues: withdrawal of foreign troops, prisoner exchange, and the establishment of a commission to inspect and ensure compliance with the cease-fire. In the meantime, negotiations at Panmunjom generated one more development that directly influenced life in the North Korean prison camps. As an initial step toward the exchange of prisoners of war, both sides agreed to identify all captives in their custody. On December 18, 1951, the communists provided the UN delegation with a list of 11,599 prisoners, of whom 3,198 were identified as Americans. Earlier communist broadcasts claimed to have captured 65,000 prisoners. Communist negotiators explained the discrepancy by claiming that most prisoners had been reeducated and "released at the front" and subsequently had volunteered to serve in the NKPA.[17] While the two delegates argued about the numbers, the prisoners in the Yalu camps rejoiced. With their status as prisoners now made public, the survivors could be reasonably confident that their captors would have to take steps to ensure their survival. As they had in July, rumors of imminent release again swept through the camps.[18]

Reeducation Fails

As 1951 turned to 1952, conditions in the Yalu camps continued to improve, and the major challenge for prisoners was overcoming boredom. Political classes remained mandatory for several months after the exchange of lists, but the "students" were growing increasingly disruptive and inattentive. In March of 1952, noncommissioned officers at Camp Five staged a two-day strike that forced the Chinese officials to suspend mandatory indoctrination classes and other propaganda efforts at the remaining permanent camps. Whether in response to the strike or because of the obvious failure to convert the British and American "students," the Chinese abandoned the mandatory indoctrination program. At several camps, "progressive" prisoners continued to attend voluntary classes, either out of curiosity or in order to maintain the goodwill and protection of their captors and to gain relief from work details.[19]

Although the Chinese abandoned their reeducation campaign, they continued their efforts to manipulate the prisoners for the sake of propaganda. In December of 1951, for example, Camp Two prisoners refused to sign a New Year's greeting to General Peng-Te Huai, commander of the Chinese forces in Korea. The senior officers in the compound had organized campwide resistance to the Chinese "signature" campaign. Betrayed by an informer, six senior officers in the compound were tried and given sentences ranging from three to six months of solitary confinement. Their example bolstered resistance within Camp Two and may have contributed to the early cancellation of the reeducation program.[20]

Prisoners at Camp One organized a similar protest a few months later when the Chinese ordered them to march in a May Day parade. The captives marked their new summer uniforms with the letters *P.O.W.* and staged a sit-down strike on the morning of the parade. Threatened at gunpoint, the men finally marched in the parade but refused to carry propaganda banners.[21] Although the Chinese constantly sought to identify and isolate the informal leaders, they were slow to realize the influence of the noncommissioned officers, who promoted resistance within the enlisted camps. In August of 1952, the Chinese finally relocated the sergeants to Camp Four, a new compound in the village of Wiwon, several miles north of Pyoktong.[22]

After the Chinese abandoned mandatory indoctrination, the prisoners spent most of their time participating in either various work details or recreational pursuits. Each camp depended heavily on manual labor to support daily operations, and the prisoners spent many of their waking hours fetching water and firewood, breaking down rations, clearing brush, repairing buildings, or digging latrines and ditches. Always looking for ways to manipulate their captives, the Chinese used labor as both a reward and a punishment. Cooperative prisoners, such as those who attended the voluntary study sessions and wrote articles for the camp newspapers, rarely participated in the work parties, which occupied so much of their fellow prisoners' time.[23]

Recalcitrant prisoners, meanwhile, could be sentenced to "hard labor," such as extra wood details. Occasionally, the Chinese would punish prisoners by sentencing them to perform meaningless tasks, as happened at Camp Two when a group of prisoners had to repeatedly dig and refill the same sixty-foot ditch over a period of several days. While hard work was routine in the camps, the communists rarely used prisoner labor for military projects. As the camps became more organized, the Chinese officials granted limited autonomy to the prisoners, permitting them to cook for themselves and to build amenities such as playing fields and bunk beds.[24]

The War against Boredom

As time passed, the Chinese also allowed—and later encouraged—prisoners to occupy their spare time with recreational pursuits. At first, these were limited to sedentary games that the men could make from scratch, such as chess, checkers, and cards, which they played in their squad rooms and in clubrooms established by their captors. The Chinese also set up libraries in each camp, and the shelves eventually filled with the works of politically acceptable authors, such as Jane Austen, Howard Fast, Charles Dickens, and John Steinbeck, along with periodic shipments of communist periodicals such as the *London Daily Worker*.[25]

The prisoners supplemented these pursuits with other activities, such as academic lessons and theatrical productions. At Camp Five, the prisoners gave each other lessons in French, swimming, and ballroom dancing. At Camp Two, the officers taught a variety of classes, ranging from Turkish to shorthand to mechanical engineering. Theatrical productions usually involved elaborate musical numbers, with the lyrics modified to suit conditions in the camps. Men also volunteered for work details, if only to relieve the boredom. "Curly" Reid, the marine captain captured at Hellfire Valley, became the Camp Two barber. As in many small towns, Reid's barbershop soon became a popular place for men to pass the time during the long, dull days of 1952.[26]

Humor provided one of the most effective ways to idle away the hours, especially after the exchange of prisoner lists, when treatment became more humane. Often the laughs came at the expense of the Chinese, whose language difficulties and ideological concepts left them open to ridicule. Caught in a minor violation of camp rules, for example, many prisoners "confessed" their regret at being caught and "promised" never to get caught again. Sometimes the prisoners deliberately taunted their captors. At Camp Three, a Chinese officer refused to cancel an outdoor class because of rain, informing Shorty Estabrook that "I will tell you when it is raining." When a thunderstorm inundated the camp a few days later, a rain-soaked Estabrook found the officer at his quarters and demanded to know whether it was raining yet. On another occasion, the prisoners spent hours digging a hole, placed a piece of paper at the bottom, and refilled the hole. The Chinese officials could not resist excavating the sheet of paper, which read "Mind Your Own Business." And there were simple pleasures. Jack Chapman and his friends in Camp One enjoyed throwing snowballs over their huts onto the heads of unsuspecting guards.[27]

Other gags required elaborate planning. When Camp Two prisoners grew tired of their guard kicking their boots during late-night inspections of their quarters, they nailed a boot to the floor and filled it with rocks. The guard's next kick produced a painful surprise and a chorus of laughter. Other gags were more involved. Another platoon at Camp Two responded to their guard's obnoxious midnight inspections by hiding from him one night. While he sounded the alarm, the prisoners sneaked back to their sleeping mats. The camp commandant and a phalanx of armed guards arrived to find all twenty-five men asleep in their places. Sometimes the gags backfired. Jim DeLong recalled that a fellow prisoner at Camp Four had feigned suicide. When guards discovered his "corpse" hanging from a beam, they alerted the guard force. By the time the Chinese returned, the prisoner had hidden the rope and the box on which he had balanced himself, but the guards kept the platoon awake all night while they searched the compound for "the body." In several camps, the prisoners deliberately acted crazy in order to puzzle their guards, as when the captives at Camp Five showed up for morning roll call carrying long sticks and barking like dogs.[28]

The most memorable act of feigned insanity, however, was the "crazy week" organized at Camp Two. For several days in early 1952, the Camp Two prisoners spoke gibberish, walked imaginary dogs, performed Native American rain dances, and flew about the yard like combat jets while "strafing" the guards. The most audacious performance, however, was delivered by Lt. John "Rotorhead" Thornton, a US Navy helicopter pilot. Thornton spent the entire week wearing a beanie cap outfitted with propellers and pretending to ride an imaginary motorcycle. He made such a pest of himself that the guards finally escorted him to the commandant's office, where he was ordered to abandon the bike. When Thornton demanded its return, the commandant responded that if Thornton were allowed to have a bike, the Chinese would have to give one to every prisoner. Therefore, the bike had been smashed and thrown into a ditch. Thornton, in turn, spent several days grieving over the ditch, his beanie cap held reverently over his heart, until the guards confiscated the cap as well.[29]

The easiest way to spend the hours, however, was simply to talk. Prisoners exchanged rumors, told jokes and stories, learned about each other's families and homes, and shared their fantasies about food, women, food, cars, and more food. Speculation about when they might be released was a popular topic, as was the question of how to spend one's back pay. Ray Mellin, the young medic from Task Force Smith who had survived the Tiger Death March and the Apex camps, recorded his plans after repatriation: "I was going to spend 2,000 dollars on a car, 500 dollars for clothes, and 2500 dollars for the bank, and I had 101 days of furlough coming." At Camp Two, Ralph Dixon and another prisoner spent several days designing an imaginary house. In Camp One, a former salesman entertained his squad mates every day with a new, dirty joke, while another prisoner recounted Zane Grey novels from memory to entertain his buddies.[30]

Escape and Reality

The most exciting way to relieve the boredom was to break out. In fact, US Army records listed 670 soldiers who managed to escape from captivity. As an official study later concluded, however:

> The men who escaped, without exception, had been prisoners for short periods of time and had not been evacuated to the permanent camps along the YALU [*sic*] River. They escaped from their immediate captors, from aid stations, and from front line holding areas. Some of these instances were probably not "escapes" in the usual sense because they involved no restraint by the enemy; the terms "abandonment" or "release" would be as applicable as "escape."

The study further noted that no American prisoner managed to escape from either a temporary or permanent camp and return to friendly territory because of the enormous obstacles involved.[31]

These obstacles included forbidding terrain, the widespread presence of enemy troops and checkpoints, and the racial, cultural, and linguistic barriers between the captives and the North Korean population. One prisoner later recalled that Americans were easy to spot from a distance simply by the way they walked. Another prisoner observed, "You could escape any time you wanted to, but you could not evade. . . . Every hill, every valley, there's a dog, and a Korean." North Korean villagers usually seemed ambivalent toward the Americans, and many conducted a brisk trade with the prisoners for goods such as food, clothing, watches, rings, and tobacco. In light of the constant presence of armed guards, however, very few were willing to risk their lives to help a prisoner escape.[32]

The distance from the Yalu camps to friendly territory also posed a major problem. Pyoktong, for example, was approximately 150 miles from the 38th Parallel and 125 miles from the eastern coast, and several mountain ranges lay in between. The west coast seemed to offer the best option. It was much closer, only fifty miles away, and offered the possibility of contacting UN air- and sea-rescue assets, including the network of guerilla bases established to rescue downed aircrews. Any prisoner using this route, however, would have to pass through one of the most heavily trafficked regions in North Korea, where he would have little chance of avoiding Chinese, Soviet, or North Korean troops and special police. Floating down the Yalu might bypass this traffic, but this route was complicated by the presence of the enormous Sup'ung dam and by the network of tributaries at the mouth of the river, which made it hard to locate the main channel to the sea.[33]

Despite these obstacles, men still tried to escape from the Yalu camps—some made multiple attempts—but always without success. Captain Anthony Farrar-Hockley, of the British Army, made at least five attempts and was brutally punished for his efforts. Few men tried to escape during the winter of 1950–1951, when malnutrition, sickness, and severe cold weather presented further impediments. Despite these desperate conditions, several groups made unsuccessful escape attempts from Sombakol (Kapaun's Valley) before their physical degeneration made such efforts impossible.[34]

On Christmas Eve, 1950, for example, Lt. Mike Dowe and five other officers headed south toward what they assumed were the American lines. After traveling several hours through the darkness, the group stopped at a farmhouse to warm up and beg for food. While the farmer's wife fed them, a daughter alerted neighbors, who flagged down a passing truckload of North Korean soldiers. While the unsuspecting refugees waited for their socks and boots to dry, the North Koreans took up positions outside the house and opened fire. As bullets punctured the walls, Capt. Ralph Nardella stepped on the hibachi and flew out the door, screaming in pain. When the North Korean troops paused to reload, the Americans quickly surrendered.[35]

Their captors ordered the prisoners to strip and then marched them to the road. The shivering Americans assumed they would be shot, but the farmer begged the soldiers to spare their lives. Instead of summary execution, the prisoners were given back their clothes and taken to a nearby village jail, where they were locked in an outdoor cell and inspected by gawking villagers. The local police seemed to be debating whether to kill the Americans, so Dowe offered his West Point class ring to the police chief in exchange for their safety. To the Americans' surprise, the Korean not only spared their lives but also fed them a hot meal before guards arrived to march them back to Sombakol.[36]

As the winter of 1950–1951 progressed, several thousand more American prisoners made their way toward the communists' ill-equipped temporary camps. While some of these prisoners managed daring escapes en route, lack of food, shelter, and medicine reduced most of them to haggard scare crows who were barely strong enough to feed themselves.[37] Nevertheless, when warmer weather finally returned, a few groups of prisoners felt strong enough to hazard escape attempts. In late April of 1951, for example, Air Force Maj. David MacGhee and several other prisoners fled from Pak's Palace and spent two weeks zigzagging toward the west coast before North Korean security police recaptured them.[38]

At Camp 12, Maj. Paul Liles and other officers developed a series of escape plans, including an elaborate helicopter rescue of the entire camp population. These plans depended on Liles's ability to persuade the North Koreans to repatriate two prisoners as a propaganda gesture. The North Koreans rejected this suggestion, and the plans collapsed. At the permanent camps along the Yalu, several groups of prisoners had begun thinking of escape, but news of the truce talks persuaded many to wait and see. In August of 1951, however, two prisoners broke out of the officers' compound at Camp Five and made their way southwest for three nights before a search party of Korean children armed with knives discovered them.[39]

By the spring of 1952, however, improvements in the weather and in their own physical strength inspired many prisoners to resume their efforts. At Camp Two, for example, the officers in the cookhouse began stockpiling food and equipment in a secret cache. Such preparations, however, were difficult to conceal from the Chinese and even more difficult to hide from informers. In early 1952, for example, a newly arrived officer was alarmed to discover fellow prisoners whispering to each other for fear of being overheard, and guards later disrupted an escape attempt by several British and American officers before the men left their barracks. At Camp Three, an attempt was foiled by waiting Chinese guards, who called the fugitives by name and stated that another prisoner had betrayed them. The presence of informers inspired widespread distrust among the prisoners and restricted the formation of well-organized escape committees. Many of those who fled did so alone or with a single partner.[40]

Like several officers at Camp Two, Jack Doerty attempted to escape a number of times. His first effort took place shortly after his capture in April of 1951, as he and a group of other prisoners waited by the side of the road while long columns of Chinese infantry passed by, heading south toward the front lines. When the prisoners finally took the road to head north, Doerty slipped in behind the southbound enemy troops. Several other prisoners had the same idea. The group had taken only a few steps, however, when they heard another American shouting at them, "Hey, you guys are going the wrong way!" The disturbance alerted the guards, who quickly apprehended Doerty and the others.[41]

After barely surviving several months at Pak's Palace, Doerty regained enough strength by the spring of 1952 to consider escaping from Camp Two. Doerty's partner in the scheme, a British special operations sergeant named Charlie Brock, spoke fluent Korean. The two assembled a small escape kit while volunteering for daily wood runs in order to reconnoiter the local area and develop their stamina. They escaped in August, heading northeast along the south bank of the Yalu to avoid the heavy troop concentrations to the southwest. Hiding by day and moving by night, the two relied on the cover of darkness and Brock's Korean-language skills to talk their way past several security checkpoints. "We thought we were invisible," said Doerty.[42]

On their fifth night, the two walked carefully through Manpo, wisely deciding not to sabotage the enemy vehicles parked in the center of town. "They probably would have shot us," remembered Doerty. "Besides, we thought we would need the sugar later." As they left town, however, they were arrested by North Korean security police. Doerty never knew what gave them away, but it might have simply been their distinctly Western gait.[43]

After the Chinese troops retrieved them, Doerty and Brock were sentenced to thirty days in "the hole," standard punishment for escape attempts from Camp Two. The hole was a root cellar measuring four feet wide and four feet deep. Guards allowed the two prisoners out of the hole twice a day, but both men suffered from dysentery, and the stench soon attracted the attention of the Korean seamstress who owned the shop above their cell. To pass the time, Brock translated her daily conversations with customers. These usually offered amusement, but one conversation proved tragic. At the local school, two Korean children had repeated their parents' anti-Chinese comments. North Korean security police subsequently arrested both parents, "and they took them right up the valley and shot them," recalled Doerty. "That was a bad moment."[44]

After release from "the hole," Doerty and Brock began planning another escape for the autumn of 1953.[45]

Stumbling Block

With escape seeming to be impossible, prisoners in the Yalu camps wondered how many years they would spend in captivity. In fact, the repatriation of prisoners had become the major obstacle to a cease-fire, and its resolution prolonged the war by at least seventeen months. When negotiations began, the communist delegates assumed that an "all-for-all" exchange would take place, as the Geneva Conventions of 1949 dictated.[46] Ridgway, however, was initially directed to agree to a one-for-one exchange until all UN prisoners had been returned and only then to repatriate the remaining Chinese and Korean prisoners.

For Truman's advisors, the issue was complicated by two factors. First, the UN held nearly 169,000 prisoners, far more than the communists, who would later acknowledge holding fewer than 12,000 men.[47] An all-for-all swap would dramatically strengthen the badly damaged NKPA. Second, among the prisoners in UN custody were several thousand South Koreans who had been impressed into the NKPA, presumably under duress, and several thousand former Chinese Nationalist troops impressed into the CCF under similar circumstances during the Chinese civil war. Recalling the Soviet Union's inhumane treatment of repatriated Soviet soldiers and refugees after World War II, a Pentagon staff officer proposed that former Nationalists be repatriated to Taiwan because it was technically part of China. Acheson initially opposed the idea, but Ridgway and the JCS believed the proposal had merit. During the fall of 1951, however, the JCS decided that a "voluntary repatriation" policy would be untenable if the communists insisted on an all-for-all prisoner exchange, as was likely. The Joint Chiefs and Robert Lovett, the new secretary of defense, reverted to the original position.[48]

In late October, however, President Truman expressed his opinion that any all-for-all exchange would be unfair, fearing that prisoners who had cooperated with the UN forces would be "done away with" if repatriated. Truman's personal interest in the matter sparked a renewed debate. Ridgway and his negotiators strongly preferred an all-for-all exchange immediately after a cease-fire, but Acheson now reversed his position and sided with Truman on the issue. In Washington, discussion on the issue continued through December, with several of the Joint Chiefs endorsing Ridgway's position. At the State Department, one official noted that senior policymakers had given inadequate consideration to the fate of the UN prisoners, who would now be left in enemy hands indefinitely. Torn between concern for the UN prisoners and their reluctance to forcibly repatriate the communist prisoners, the JCS left the matter undecided. At Panmunjom, negotiators discussed the exchange of prisoner lists and a UN proposal for the International Committee for the Red Cross (ICRC) to visit POW camps on both sides. The communists rejected the Red Cross proposal but agreed to exchange lists.[49]

The UN delegation made its opening bid on the repatriation issue on January 2, 1952. Citing the communists' claims that captured ROK soldiers had been allowed to choose release or voluntary service with the NKPA, the UN delegates argued that the communists had already embraced a form of voluntary repatriation. Based on this humanitarian precedent, the UN negotiators proposed that all prisoners be polled by a neutral commission such as the ICRC to determine their wishes and that those who chose nonrepatriation would be banned from service in the armed forces of the host nation. The communist negotiators labeled the proposal "absurd" and accused the UN delegation of treating the POWs like slaves.[50]

Over the next two months, subdelegates reached agreement on other details of a POW exchange, but the voluntary repatriation issue remained unresolved. In Washington, debate continued over the wisdom of this policy, while Ridgway complained about continuing press coverage of the disagreement and its impact at the negotiating table.[51] In February, the administration's support of voluntary repatriation hardened in conjunction with, and perhaps because of, renewed Chinese accusations that Americans had used biological weapons against their forces (see chapter 9). In late February, Truman and his advisors agreed to reject any cease-fire that did not include provisions for voluntary repatriation.[52]

While State Department officials embarked on a campaign to garner foreign and domestic support for the policy, the administration dispatched a team to inspect conditions at Koje-Do, the island where communist prisoners were being held. Upon their arrival, they discovered "the smell of mutiny in the air."[53]

Koje-Do

Conditions in the UN prison camps never descended to the depths of depravity found in most of the communist camps during the first year of the war, but neither did they meet the requirements specified in the Geneva Conventions, much less the idealized rhetoric of US officials. The US Army had assumed responsibility for all POWs in September of 1950, largely to prevent their mistreatment by ROK forces, whose capacity for brutality often matched that of their NKPA enemies.[54] Internment under US control was initially much safer; communist prisoners and civilian detainees received food, water, medical treatment, and fresh fatigues and were housed near Pusan under the hostile supervision of US and ROK guards. After Chinese forces entered the war, Eighth Army headquarters ordered the transfer of prisoners, now numbering more than 130,000, to the island of Koje-Do, a few miles southeast of Pusan.[55]

The island provided somewhat better security, but overcrowding, poor sanitation, and inadequate food contributed to a number of health problems, including tuberculosis, dysentery, malaria, and pneumonia. Prisoners hid food under sleeping mats, refused to wash their own clothes, and avoided delousing, which led to infestations of lice and vermin. The guard force was perpetually undermanned and afraid to enter the compounds, so US officials relied on prisoner trustees to run daily affairs within the camp. The guards were also poorly trained, inadequately disciplined, and prone to using deadly force at the slightest provocation. Finally, an increasingly violent rivalry existed between pro- and anticommunist prisoners. The anticommunists were aided and abetted by the ROK and Chinese Nationalist governments, often with American encouragement, while the Chinese and NKPA began infiltrating the prison camps with their own leaders in order to organize the pro-communist factions. By mid-1951, the two divisions were waging a bloody struggle for control inside the wire, as the US Army continued to rotate commanders, heedless of the problem. By February of 1952, more than six thousand prisoners had died in UN custody. After guards killed seventy-seven prisoners during a riot in mid-February, the probability of more bloodshed seemed inevitable.[56]

If agreement on the POWs remained elusive at Panmunjom, other issues proved less difficult. In March of 1952, the communists suddenly indicated a newfound flexibility on the remaining two issues: enforcement of the ceasefire and the establishment of a postwar commission to resolve outstanding issues. The communists had insisted that the Soviet Union serve on the post-war commission, while Ridgway and his representatives insisted on prohib-iting the reconstruction of damaged airfields in North Korea. By April, the communists seemed willing to trade concessions on these two issues, and the POW issue again became the focus of attention.[57]

To this point, the communist negotiators had repeatedly complained about the UN's failure to provide "a round figure" of communist POWs to be repatriated. The UN team finally responded with a number of 116,000 but would not commit to that figure until a thorough screening had taken place at Koje-Do.[58] When the communist delegation suggested a recess for this purpose, Ridgway ordered the screening conducted as soon as possible. Unfortunately, the operation was done under the same shoddy conditions that had previously characterized affairs at Koje-Do. During the process, the UN officials belatedly reassured the prisoners of their safe treatment upon repatriation and made no guarantees about the fate of the nonrepatriates.[59]

Nevertheless, 74,000 of the first 105,000 prisoners questioned insisted that they would resist repatriation. There was strong evidence to suggest that many who chose nonrepatriation did so under threats of recrimina-tion by anticommunist leaders in their compounds. In one case, the leaders among the prisoners conducted their own preemptive screening; those who chose repatriation were severely beaten or killed. Another 44,000 of the re-maining prisoners refused to submit to questioning, either individually or because their compound leaders organized resistance to the screening pro-cess. Ridgway's staff estimated that the negotiators could now promise only about 70,000 repatriates, a far cry from the earlier figure of 116,000. Ridg-way sent representatives to investigate the possibility of rescreening, but the probability of riots and the lack of personnel and facilities made such a plan impracticable.[60]

When a US delegate finally announced the screening results on April 19, his communist counterpart was so dumbfounded that he requested an im-mediate recess. When the talks resumed, the communists angrily accused the UN delegation of deliberate subterfuge and rejected its offer to invite rescreening by the ICRC. Meanwhile, Truman gained considerable support in both Congress and the press for his refusal to forcibly repatriate commu-nist prisoners, but these endorsements made it more difficult to find a mu-tually agreeable compromise with the enemy. Although the POW issue now stood as the only barrier to a cease-fire, the opportunity for peace had been bungled, and the delegations grew more intractable.[61]

As an embarrassing postscript to the screening debacle, the prisoners at Koje-Do kidnapped Brig. Gen. Francis Dodd, the US commandant, in early May. He was later released unharmed—but only after signing a statement endorsing the validity of the prisoners' concerns. The riot further damaged America's credibility on the POW issue, while giving the communists a major propaganda victory from the perception of UN mistreatment of its prisoners. General Mark Clark, Ridgway's replacement as UN commander, subsequently relieved Dodd, but trouble persisted on the island until June, when American infantrymen stormed the pro-communist compounds, killing 31 and wounding 139 while seizing an enormous cache of makeshift weapons.[62] Survivors were divided and relocated to smaller islands, but violence continued until the end of the war and was often deliberately provoked by communist cadres within the prison compounds.[63]

The Prisoner Olympics

Life in the Yalu camps that summer had its own dangers. Food, shelter, and medicine remained inadequate by Western standards, and many prisoners suffered night blindness due to vitamin deficiencies. Captured airmen were segregated from the rest of the prisoners and endured harsh interrogation and torture as part of the ongoing propaganda campaign to extract germ-warfare confessions. Other prisoners, including several senior officers at Camp Two, spent a large part of 1952 in solitary confinement. Most of the captives, however, passed the summer months engaged in all manner of sporting competitions, ranging from swimming and boxing to soccer, baseball, and basketball.

These competitions reached a climax in November of 1952, when the Chinese staged their last major effort to manipulate their captives for political gain. Capitalizing on the prisoners' enthusiasm for sports, the Chinese staged a "Prisoner Olympics" at Camp Five, inviting each permanent camp holding Western prisoners to send representatives. The invitation sparked fierce debate at Camp Two. Many felt that participation would strengthen an obvious propaganda effort by their captors and refused to participate. Others argued that this might be their only chance to check on the health and welfare of other prisoners.[64]

Although communication between the permanent camps was infrequent, the officers had heard rumors of collaboration and marijuana addiction among the enlisted prisoners.[65] The senior officers at Camp Two thus chose to send a group of forty participants. All of the other main prison camps also sent contingents. Upon arrival, individual officers were allowed to move about freely during the actual competitions, but the team was housed separately from other prisoners and gathered only limited information. They did, however, make a concerted effort to counteract Chinese propaganda efforts among the other prisoners. In addition, Maj. Tom Harrison gathered the names of captives being held outside the permanent camps because he feared that Chinese officials might try to withhold some of the prisoners once hostilities ended.[66]

Approximately five hundred prisoners competed in the games, which took place between November 15 and November 26, 1952. Each team received uniforms identifying its camp name, and the athletes dined on special rations that included meat, vegetables, bread, wine, and beer. The opening ceremony included a lighting of the Olympic torch and a parade of athletes past the grandstand, which was full of Camp Five prisoners. While the Chinese did not require the prisoners to carry any signs, a phalanx of communist photographers recorded the parade, the special meals for the athletes, and the competitions themselves. These included a wide variety of track and field events, as well as softball, soccer, football, basketball, volleyball, and boxing. The winners received small prizes, such as an extra ration of cigarettes.[67]

Prisoners at Camp Five contributed a series of short articles describing these events and the participants' cheerful demeanor. One article, for example, extolled Chinese benevolence in glowing terms: "At all times the cooperation, generosity, enthusiasm and selfless energy displayed by our captors was perfect and left nothing to be desired." The Chinese later published the photographs and accompanying articles in a series of propaganda booklets designed to illustrate the healthy, carefree environment within the prison camps.[68] After the war, a reporter asked Mike Dowe about the pamphlets. "I always think, when I see those Olympic pictures," answered Dowe, "that right in those hills they show are the graves of the men who died that first winter of cold and starvation and neglect."[69]

End Game

While the Chinese prepared for the POW Olympics at Pyoktong, three developments outside of Korea moved the war closer to its conclusion. The first of these was Dwight D. Eisenhower's victory in the 1952 presidential election. Korea was not the main campaign issue, but with talks at Panmunjom deadlocked and with US soldiers fighting and dying amid nameless hills, many voters had grown tired of the conflict. Some critics, frustrated by the image of a great superpower apparently stymied by its technologically primitive opponents, embraced MacArthur's proposal to use nuclear weapons and widen the war against China. European allies, meanwhile, feared that Eisenhower might embrace this drastic approach and pressed for a diplomatic solution at the United Nations. In Beijing, Mao Zedong also assumed that Eisenhower would escalate the conflict, most likely through amphibious assaults behind the lines. Chinese forces in Korea began preparations to resist such attacks.[70] On the campaign trail, Eisenhower had been vague about his Korean strategy, announcing only that he would "go to Korea" to assess the situation. His postelection visit lasted three days and involved no serious review of strategic options. Like Truman before him, Eisenhower resolved to negotiate a cease-fire as quickly as possible.[71]

The second important event that November was a proposal by the Indian delegation at the UN to establish a four-nation repatriation commission to assume custody of all POWs. The commission would repatriate all those who wished it and administer a ninety-day period during which the representatives could "explain" the right of repatriation to the remaining prisoners. The French, British, and Canadian delegates quickly endorsed the plan, and the General Assembly approved the Indian resolution on December 3. Although the Chinese and North Korean representatives quickly rejected the Indian proposal, it remained on the bargaining table as a viable path toward peace.[72]

In January of 1953, the new Eisenhower cabinet took several steps to pressure the communists into an agreement. These included expansion of the ROK Army, removal of the Seventh Fleet from the Straits of Taiwan (where it was supposedly protecting Communist China from the Nationalists), and the issuance of a veiled threat, conveyed through the Indian government, that Eisenhower would bomb targets in Manchuria and deploy tactical nuclear weapons if the stalemate continued. The efficacy of these measures remains a matter of debate. The nuclear threat has attracted the most attention, leading some scholars to credit Eisenhower with successfully bluffing the Soviets and the Chinese into an agreement.[73]

In fact, the most significant development of this period may have occurred in mid-December of 1952, when the League of Red Cross Societies met in Geneva, Switzerland, and resolved, over objections from the Soviets and the Chinese, to call for both sides in Korea to conduct a mutual exchange of sick and wounded prisoners. The proposal gained little attention in Washington, but State Department officials belatedly endorsed the concept in February 1953. In Tokyo, General Clark dispatched a letter to his communist counterparts repeating the Red Cross proposal.[74]

For once, the UN's timing seemed fortuitous. The communists did not respond immediately, but two weeks later Josef Stalin died unexpectedly in a Moscow suburb, signaling a shift in Soviet policy. The continuing war had devastated the Korean countryside and inflicted hundreds of thousands of casualties among the communist forces, but the Soviet leader had repeatedly urged his allies to stand firm in the face of America's threats. Eisenhower's bellicose gestures, the impending rearmament of West Germany, and the recent American testing of a hydrogen bomb may have convinced Stalin's successors that the risk of escalation with the West was becoming untenable. On March 19, the Soviet Council of Ministers voted to accept Clark's proposal and issued instructions to Kim and Mao, who were in Moscow for Stalin's funeral.[75]

That same month, the North Korean government began releasing Western detainees who had survived the Tiger Death March and the winter of 1950–1951. The civilians were transferred to Chinese control at the Manchurian border and traveled by train to Moscow, where the appropriate embassies took custody. Of the sixty civilians detained in 1950, only thirty-seven survived captivity. Father Philip Crosbie, Commissioner Herbert Lord, Larry Zellers, Nell Dyer, and journalist Philip Deane were among those who made it home.[76]

On March 28, Clark received a response from Kim Il Sung and General Peng agreeing to comply with this provision of the Geneva Convention and suggesting that agreement on this matter might "lead to the smooth settlement of the entire question of prisoners of war, thereby achieving an armistice in Korea for which people throughout the world are longing." Two days later, Chinese foreign minister Chou En Lai issued a lengthy statement that included his country's acceptance of the Indian proposal for a neutral state to take custody of prisoners who refused repatriation. On April 11, negotiators at Panmunjom signed the agreement for the initial prisoner exchange.[77]

Early Returns

That spring, prisoners along the Yalu knew that negotiations were going well because the quality of food and treatment improved dramatically. Kaoliang (sorghum) and cracked corn disappeared and were replaced by white bread, steamed rice, vegetables, and soup. As long as talks were proceeding amicably, the prisoners gained weight on the new and improved diet. When the talks stalled, both the quantity and the quality of food declined.[78] In late April, the two sides traded a select group of sick and wounded prisoners in what the UN Command referred to as Operation Little Switch. Over a period of two weeks, the UN returned 6,224 communist prisoners, most of them Koreans, along with 446 civilian internees. In a precursor of things to come, several groups of returning communist prisoners went on a hunger strike prior to repatriation, then chanted, shouted slogans, waved banners, and discarded portions of their POW uniforms for the benefit of neutral and communist media representatives covering the exchange.[79]

The communists, in turn, repatriated 684 prisoners to UN custody. Most of these were ROK prisoners, but the number also included 149 Americans. Most of the repatriated Americans suffered from legitimate wounds or illnesses, but the remaining prisoners believed the Chinese had excluded reactionaries from consideration. Moreover, it soon became clear to UN officials that the communists had withheld a significant number of severely wounded personnel, but Clark chose not to press the issue. Major Tom Harrison, who had lost his leg to an injury after bailing out of his plane, was among several prisoners with serious ailments who were left behind at Camp Two.[80]

Rhee's Bargain

While negotiators slowly worked out the final arrangements for the handling of nonrepatriates, Syngman Rhee worked energetically to derail the settlement. The ROK president had already seen his dream of reunification abandoned by his UN allies, who had ignored his subsequent demands for Chinese withdrawal and North Korean disarmament. Now, with the talks nearly concluded, he worried that his allies might bargain away his nation's future security. Rhee had proven a difficult ally early on, but the United States needed ROK consent to ensure the reliability of any cease-fire agreement with the communists. For the moment, at least, the junior partner in the alliance enjoyed a particularly good position from which to make demands.[81]

Beginning in April, Rhee and his agents had provoked a series of anti-armistice protests throughout South Korea, in which marchers carried banners that called for "Unification or Death."[82] In mid-May, Rhee announced that he would not permit a foreign power to assume custody of Korean nonrepatriates, nor would he allow Indian troops on South Korean soil. As India was a leading candidate to head any repatriation commission, Rhee's insistence presented a major stumbling block to the cease-fire arrangements. In response to Rhee's concerns, UN negotiators proposed the release of Korean nonrepatriates as soon as a cease-fire took effect. The communists quickly rejected this proposal, and Washington ordered Clark to abandon the idea. On June 10, the delegates at Panmunjom finally agreed on the terms of nonrepatriation; a vague stipulation regarding the neutral commission's obligation to assist the resettlement of nonrepatriates provided a face-saving compromise for the communists.[83]

That compromise nearly came undone on June 18, when Rhee defied his American allies by releasing more than twenty-five thousand Korean nonrepatriates from their holding camps. American forces managed to recapture a few hundred of the escapees and prevented any further release, but the damage had been done. The cease-fire talks recessed yet again, while the communist delegates demanded the recapture of all of the escapees and assurance of ROK compliance with the armistice. Clark declared recapture impossible but promised to expend every effort to achieve ROK cooperation. Meanwhile, a special delegation from Washington employed a series of carrots and sticks to bring about Rhee's compliance. On July 10, Rhee announced his support of an armistice, and Eisenhower's administration rewarded him with a mutual defense pact that committed US forces to the defense of South Korean sovereignty.[84]

On July 13, the Chinese hurled six divisions against the central sector of the UN line, pushing the defending ROK Army units back by six miles in some places before US units restored the line. The punishing offensive reinforced the image of communist military prowess while sending a clear warning to those South Koreans who advocated a unilateral ROK offensive after the armistice. On July 19, communist negotiators resumed serious deliberations at Panmunjom, and the cease-fire agreement was finally signed at midday on July 27. At Camp Two, Bill Shadish was unaware of these events, but he later recalled watching a blood-red sunset that evening and thinking something momentous had happened. It had. At 2200 hours that night, the guns on the Korean peninsula fell silent.

Freedom

When Chinese officials announced the war's end, some of the prisoners broke into tears, and others sank to their knees and gave prayers of thanks.

At Camp Three, Ray Mellin opened his Chinese-issue notebook and wrote the following:

> On the 27th of July, the Korean War was officially over, to the amazement of many who were pessimistic, and happily accepted by those who were optimistic. As if coming out of a dark room into the sunlight, radiant smiles crept across the many faces upon hearing the wonderful news, and now to wait patiently for repatriation and our loved ones once again, which will be the greatest moment of our lives. R. V. Mellin, July 27, 1953.

Many of his colleagues simply shouted for joy. At Camp One, recalled marine private Nick Flores, "Plenty of men were jumping around telling the world that the war was over and they would be going home."[85]

Other camps reacted differently. When the Chinese assembled all six hundred sergeants on the soccer field at Camp Four, the prisoners knew something was up. When a camp official announced the armistice, the prisoners stared back in a spontaneous demonstration of silence. "We all got up and marched back to our compound," recalled Jim DeLong. "It really hurt them that we didn't holler and hoop and hurray that the war was over. When we got back to our compound we celebrated, but we didn't let them know that we were happy."[86] The officers and airmen at Camp Two responded in similar fashion. Knowing a cease-fire was imminent, the senior prisoners put out the word: "No celebrations whatsoever." Chinese photographers were at the compound to film the festivities, but they went home disappointed. Like the sergeants at Camp Four, the Camp Two prisoners received the news in silence, saving their celebrations for the privacy of their quarters.[87]

Next came a delay, described by one American prisoner as "the most boring month I have ever lived through," while representatives from the neutral commission made their way to Korea. Arriving on UN helicopters, a contingent of Indian troops established a separate holding area for nonrepatriates inside the newly established demilitarized zone, thus complying with Rhee's prohibition against Indian forces on ROK soil. In the Yalu camps, the prisoners received more toiletries, cartons of cigarettes, fresh clothes, and generous meals, while the Chinese officials treated their "guests" with newfound cordiality.[88] Finally, trucks began arriving at the camps to ferry the prisoners to railheads in Manpo and Sinuiju. From there, the prisoners rode south in cattle cars to Kaesong, marveling along the way at the destruction wrought by the UN air attacks. For the Camp Two prisoners, the damage proved unnerving when their train stopped on a railroad bridge spanning a deep gorge. Initially, their locomotive had pushed the train from the rear.

The wooden structure swayed back and forth under the weight of the train, while the communist engineers attached the lead car to another locomotive. The train eventually crept forward, while the nervous prisoners stared down into the chasm.[89]

At Kaesong, the communists housed their prisoners in a heavily guarded tent city surrounded by barbed wire. Each night, the remaining UN prisoners could see the lights on the horizon from "Freedom Village," the UN reception station at Panmunjom. Each morning, the communist officials would call off a roster of names, and the prisoners would climb into Russian trucks for the short ride across the Imjin River to the reception station, where UN officials, medical teams, and scores of reporters and photographers were waiting.[90] From their trucks, the prisoners saw mounds of clothing and boots in the roadside ditches. In a final show of defiance, the repatriated communist prisoners again waved banners, shouted slogans, and discarded their POW uniforms. Between August 5 and September 6, UN forces returned more than 75,823 prisoners to communist control, a number relatively close to the figure of 70,000 determined in the Koje-Do survey conducted sixteen months earlier. The remaining 22,604 communist prisoners refused repatriation and were transferred to the Neutral Nations Repatriation Commission (NNRC) within the demilitarized zone.[91]

The communists, in turn, repatriated 12,773 UN prisoners during this period, including 3,597 Americans.[92] The reaction of Leonard Taft, a Marine Corps pilot who had survived Pak's Palace, was typical. Upon crossing into UN custody, Taft spotted the US flag and rendered a smart salute, then turned and saluted the Chinese in a very different manner, one involving his middle finger.[93] Like Taft, John "Rotorhead" Thornton had no love lost for his captors. When a despised interrogator from Camp Two joined Thornton's group for the final ride to the exchange point, Thornton planned to throttle the Chinese officer as soon as their vehicle crossed into UN territory. Anticipating such outbursts, the military police whisked the individual back into the truck before Thornton could take a swing at him.[94]

There was apparently some effort to hold back several groups of American reactionaries as punishment, but last-minute protests by the Red Cross and by the UN Command convinced the Chinese to release several dozen additional men in the final days of the exchange. At Camp One, for example, Jack Chapman was among sixty-five prisoners still imprisoned after the rest of the camp moved south, but Red Cross protests reportedly brought about the group's release in late August. At Kaesong, Mike Dowe was informed that he would not be released due to his "crimes against the people." On the night before the final day of the exchange, Dowe crept out through a latrine trench and later joined other prisoners on a truck leaving toward Panmunjom. At the last checkpoint, a Chinese soldier read their names from a list, and they crossed a bridge into UN custody. Dowe was still there when the guard finished his roster, but he strode forward and said his name, jabbed a finger at the clipboard, and walked across the bridge.[95]

Bill Funchess's final ordeal was equally bizarre. Like Dowe, Funchess was labeled a war criminal and told he would not be released. On the final morning of the exchange, guards forced him into the back of a truck and drove him to another compound, where he was greeted by several of the Americans who had refused repatriation. One of them invited Funchess to join them: "I emphatically shouted, 'No way!'" I told them they were American servicemen and expected to return home. They laughed and began taunting me. I told them they were making a mistake, and said no more. The truck pulled away." Funchess was taken to a wooded area and ordered out of the truck. A Chinese officer directed him to begin walking along a trail and warned him to stay on the path. Funchess expected a bullet in the back until he heard the truck leave. The lieutenant continued forward for several hundred yards and finally spotted an American ambulance. When he reached it, a major informed him how lucky he had been; the previous night, both sides had agreed to release all "war criminals."[96]

Twenty-three Americans, along with one British marine and several hundred Koreans, refused repatriation. Two of the Americans soon changed their minds and returned to the United States, but the remaining twenty-one "turncoats" resettled in China. Meanwhile, the news that any US soldier would choose communism over democracy sent shock waves through the American public. In the weeks after the prisoners returned from Korea, widespread media reports of misconduct and collaboration further influenced the public's misperceptions of the POWs, giving rise to the myth that devious communist jailers had somehow managed to brainwash their American prisoners.[97]

12 Freedom and Recrimination

*It is ironic that the major legend to have come out of this war should be
one that tarnishes the reputation of men who bore its brunt.*
Albert D. Biderman, "Dangers of Negative Patriotism"

As early as February 1953, Pentagon officials worried about the potential
impact of brainwashed American prisoners returning home. The men who
were repatriated at Freedom Village were greeted with genuine fanfare and
hospitality and were soon transported to Inchon. From there, those who
needed immediate medical attention flew to military hospitals in Japan for
additional treatment and recuperation. Jack Doerty, for example, had contracted malaria shortly before repatriation and came home from Korea by
way of Tokyo General Hospital. Most of the repatriated men boarded troop
ships for the two-week cruise back to the United States.[1]

If treatment at Freedom Village had been hospitable, the treatment on
board the troop ships was, at best, mixed. On some ships, returning prisoners were segregated from other military passengers, and some of the prisoners were called "communists." Lack of coordination between medical
teams and counterintelligence teams further complicated matters, causing
additional resentment among the repatriated men. On other ships, the crews
treated the repatriates with memorable hospitality. Captain Ernest "Curly"
Reid, captured at Hellfire Valley, initially resented having to take the slow
boat back to the States, but he never forgot his first meal on board—three
New York strip steaks and a strawberry sundae served in an enormous gravy
boat. "I missed all of the next three meals," recalled Reid, "but I've never
been hungry since."[2]

Regardless of their accommodations, most returning prisoners resented
the intrusive questions by military psychiatrists and counterintelligence
agents, who subjected them to numerous debriefings during the journey.
Psychiatrists asked questions designed to measure the former prisoners' mental health but also sought to determine whether any had, in fact, been brainwashed by their captors. Based partly on earlier information provided by the
149 Americans repatriated during Operation Little Switch, the counterintel-

ligence agents, meanwhile, sought to identify and gather evidence against those who had misbehaved during captivity. As Lloyd Pate later recalled, "They wanted to know everything from the day we were captured to the day the Chinese released us. It was at this time that they asked about the progressives, what they did and how they did it." Few investigators seemed concerned by the irony of the US government subjecting these men to further interrogations.[3]

Instead, the counterintelligence agents sought to obtain as much information as they could get. A Pentagon study would later characterize these interrogations as "an elaborate and highly effective system . . . established to produce a maximum of information from this valuable source."[4] Each investigator received a lengthy questionnaire that covered all aspects of imprisonment, with special focus on the extent to which prisoners embraced communist ideology. "I think we were all classified as communists until proven innocent," recalled one of the former prisoners. Another repatriate was dismayed by the fact that the interrogators seemed more interested in information about collaborators than in the former prisoners' health.[5]

The repatriated prisoners, meanwhile, proved to be their own worst enemies. One attorney later observed that they had been accompanied by "a great cargo of suspicion, conjecture, rumor, and ill-will." For a variety of reasons and with encouragement from their debriefers, many returnees accused their fellow captives of treasonous behavior. In his study of POW conduct, published in 1963, Albert Biderman argued that these accusations were largely the result of communist manipulation, which created among many prisoners the exaggerated perception of widespread misconduct. The former prisoners subsequently accused each other of every crime from assault and murder to receiving extra food, candy, and cigarettes from the Chinese. Some of these accusations were well documented and fully corroborated by multiple witnesses, but others merely repeated hearsay or unsubstantiated rumors and were, in some cases, fabrications. The internal strife extended beyond verbal accusations. On the USS *General Pope,* so many fistfights erupted between the former prisoners that the ship's captain segregated the so-called progressives from the other passengers.[6]

Docking in San Francisco, the repatriates received another heartfelt welcome. When the first ship arrived, local and national television crews broadcast the event live, and the Sixth Army Band boarded a ferryboat from which they serenaded the arriving ship as it passed under the Golden Gate Bridge.[7] Many former prisoners were greeted on the docks by loved ones who had driven across the country to meet them. When reporters in Dallas learned that Mary Louise Reid's husband was among the returning prisoners, the publisher of the *Dallas Morning Herald* paid her way to San Francisco to greet her husband, Captain Reid. Marv King, meanwhile, had sent several telegrams en route to ensure that his fiancée knew where to meet him. Because of a mix-up in the rosters, however, she was not allowed into the family waiting area when he disembarked. King was loaded onto a troop bus and driven to the military hospital. His fiancée followed, searching through several wards until she finally located the hospital bed containing her future husband.[8] For several weeks in September and October, American newspapers splashed pictures of these happy reunions across their front pages and ran feature stories detailing the former prisoners' ordeal.

These harrowing tales often included disturbing anecdotes of collaboration and betrayal by fellow Americans, and therein lay a problem. While the repatriated prisoners made their way home and tried to resume their normal lives, Pentagon officials reviewed the indications of widespread misconduct. These included radio broadcasts, peace appeals, surrender appeals, newspaper articles, propaganda pamphlets, and thousands of pages of bitter accusations from the former prisoners themselves. Mindful of the fierce anticommunist sentiment in Congress and among the public, senior military leaders could not simply ignore such evidence.[9]

The most embarrassing evidence was the collection of biological-warfare confessions made by forty-one air force and marine airmen. The air force leadership moved quickly to discredit these confessions, interviewing each "confessor" upon his arrival in San Francisco. The group unanimously denounced their earlier confessions and described the variations of physical and mental torture inflicted to extract these admissions. The air force subsequently provided audio and video footage of these interviews to newsreel services, which juxtaposed portions of them with earlier communist footage of the original germ-warfare confessions to illustrate the communist strategy of the "big lie." At the United Nations, US delegates presented this footage as part of a larger accusation of widespread communist mistreatment of prisoners during the war.[10]

Two of the most prominent biological-warfare confessions had been made by Marine Corps pilots, whose admissions drew significant and embarrassing publicity in the communist press.[11] One of these pilots, Col. Frank H. Schwable, was a Naval Academy graduate, the senior marine captured in Korea, and the senior officer to make a germ-warfare confession during his captivity. The recipient of four Distinguished Flying Crosses during World War II, Schwable attracted special attention from the Chinese interrogators, who learned of his identity from personal effects and documents found at his crash site. Because of his seniority, they kept him isolated in solitary confinement and subjected him to months of physical and psychological torture until his resistance collapsed. A Pentagon news release announcing his capture and a number of sensitive personal details provided interrogators with immeasurable leverage in destroying his resistance. Fortunately for Schwable, the Chinese remained ignorant of his detailed knowledge of US war plans. Like the air force pilots, Schwable renounced his confession upon arrival in San Francisco, where he was greeted warmly by colleagues. When he returned home to Washington, D.C., however, he was snubbed by the Marine Corps commandant, Gen. Lemuel C. Shepherd Jr.[12]

Schwable spent the weeks after repatriation at his home in northern Virginia, waiting for news of his fate. In January of 1954, the Marine Corps finally announced that a special board of inquiry would determine whether Schwable deserved a court martial. That same month, a public awards ceremony recognizing the heroic resistance of five marine POWs, including John McLaughlin, seemed to highlight the embarrassment of Schwable's confession. When the Naval Court of Inquiry convened, Schwable testified that after several months of torment, "I had lost my sense of judgment." Limiting answers under such conditions to one's name, rank, and serial number, he suggested, was an idea that sounded good to "some guy sitting behind a desk in Washington." After four weeks of testimony, including that of Maj. Gen. William F. Dean, who spoke on Schwable's behalf, the board recommended that no disciplinary action be taken.[13]

Having determined that Schwable "resisted this torture to the limits of his ability to resist," the board further recommended that the Pentagon establish a code of conduct to guide prisoners in future conflicts. General Shepherd upheld the board's finding but recommended limiting Schwable's future assignments to those that would make "minimum demands . . . upon the elements of unblemished personal example and leadership." The Secretary of the Navy and the Secretary of Defense endorsed Shepherd's recommendation, effectively ending Schwable's military career.[14] In addition to Schwable, the Marine Corps decided that forty-nine of the 194 marines who had survived captivity required further investigation, and one of these was administratively separated from the service.[15]

Like the Marine Corps, the US Air Force also faced a significant number of allegations against its former prisoners. Of the 224 air force personnel repatriated at the end of the war, 83 had been accused of collaboration, including 34 who made germ-warfare confessions. Rather than hold public trials by court martial, however, the air force chose to convene a board of senior officers to review each case and recommend disposition. After five weeks of deliberation in February and March of 1954, the board found that sixty-nine of the accused men were innocent of all charges and that fourteen merited further investigation. Of the latter group, six were honorably discharged at their own request, and the remaining eight appeared before a second "show cause" board. In July of 1954, the air force announced that four of these eight would remain on active duty, while the other four would receive honorable discharges.[16] An editorial in *Air Force* magazine concluded that the service had handled a delicate problem honorably and equitably.[17]

As a result of the hearings, air force leaders determined that pilots had been ill prepared for the rigors of communist interrogation and that captured pilots, in the absence of clear instructions, had revealed a great deal of personal and technical information. Some of this information, such as Harry Hedlund's bogus map and Aaron Shapiro's "GFQ bomb," had been fabricated on the spot, but other air force personnel had been more forthcoming. One pilot, for example, allegedly provided interrogators with instructions on how to build a B-29. Despite these embarrassing lapses, the air force declined to bring charges against its former POWs. Having failed to prepare them for the rigors of captivity, the air force thus felt no obligation to prosecute them. Moreover, the air force had moved swiftly to address the accusations against its personnel. The US Air Force, like the Marine Corps, had essentially resolved the matter by the summer of 1954.[18]

The US Army, however, took much longer to act. The overwhelming majority of repatriated American prisoners, 3,973 of the 4,435, were army personnel, as were the overwhelming majority of those accused.[19] Army policy, formulated during the summer of 1953, directed prosecution in cases "only where there appeared to be the most compelling and convincing evidence of the guilt of those accused of a serious offense."[20] Beginning immediately after Operation Big Switch, army intelligence officers sifted through mountains of evidence—radio broadcasts, communist publications, surrender leaflets, peace appeals, and the postrepatriation debriefings—to identify those army personnel suspected of collaboration. The screening itself took more than six months and produced a list of 425 army personnel worthy of further investigation. In the interval, many of the repatriated soldiers left the service, including 211 of the suspects on the list, complicating the army's efforts to interview witnesses and prosecute allegations of misconduct.[21]

At least one case proved relatively straightforward. The court martial of Pfc. Rothwell "Tiny" Floyd began at Fort Leavenworth, Kansas, on February 10, 1954. According to many of his fellow prisoners, the large, foul-mouthed soldier had bullied the weak and the sick and had stolen food, money, and other valuables from the dead and dying. His misconduct at the Bean Camp during the spring of 1951 had not gone unnoticed (see chapter 8). A few weeks after his return to the United States, Floyd was arrested and confined to the stockade at Fort Leavenworth, where military prosecutors accused him of thirteen counts of larceny, mistreatment of other prisoners, striking a superior officer, and premeditated murder.[22]

The government's case relied almost entirely on the testimony of other repatriated prisoners, and the prosecutors offered twenty-four witnesses in support of the allegations. Floyd's lawyers, meanwhile, produced sixteen witnesses in his defense, and much of the testimony focused on the relative credibility of various witnesses. Prior to the trial, Floyd made two decisions that may have damaged his hopes of acquittal. First, although himself an enlisted man, Floyd asked for a panel (the military version of a jury) composed of officers. As one of the charges involved striking an officer, this tactic may have backfired. Second, Floyd accepted the services of a prominent civilian lawyer, Elisha Scott, on the eve of his trial despite the fact that he had been provided military lawyers for his defense. Scott mounted a vigorous defense on Floyd's behalf, but his remarks often seemed more appropriate for a Sunday sermon than a military courtroom. After deliberations, the court found Floyd not guilty on the murder charge but guilty on six other specifications and sentenced him to forty years. A review board later upheld the court's verdict but reduced Floyd's sentence to ten years.[23]

Floyd's alleged crimes would have invited prosecution under most circumstances, but allegations against other army personnel were more complicated. First, as implied in the Schwable hearing, the communists had treated prisoners so brutally that many alleged acts of collaboration, such as making broadcasts and signing peace appeals, may have been committed under severe duress. Alternately, some social scientists speculated that the communist forces had used sinister oriental techniques to brainwash American prisoners into betraying their own nation. This hypothesis offered an apparently logical explanation for the condemnation of their own country by otherwise patriotic American service members. Although later rejected by other scientists and by the military itself, the brainwashing myth nevertheless gained widespread popular acceptance.[24]

The concept of brainwashing as a defense for collaboration faced its first test in the trials of Cpl. Edward S. Dickenson and Cpl. Claude J. Batchelor. Both men came from poor families in rural America, both had received lim-

ited education, both had been captured with the 8th Cavalry Regiment at
Unsan (see chapter 4), both had been active "progressives" during their cap-
tivity at Camp Five, and both had refused repatriation after the cease-fire.
During the agreed-upon "explaining period" that followed Operation Big
Switch, both subsequently changed their minds and abandoned the other
twenty-one American "turncoats" in the neutral zone.[25]

Dickenson left on the night of October 20, departing the Americans'
compound after his compatriots were asleep and asking representatives of
the Indian custodial force to send him home. He was quickly turned over to
US Army representatives, who flew him to Tokyo, where he provided investigators with the details of his captivity. During his debriefing, Dickenson
described an elaborate communist plot involving former "progressive" prisoners, who would help overthrow the US government. After three weeks of
interrogation, the twenty-three-year-old soldier traveled home to Cracker's
Neck, Virginia, where he received a hero's welcome, married, and departed
on a lengthy honeymoon. With his term of enlistment nearly complete,
Dickenson reported to Walter Reed Army Hospital in January 1954 for his
final physical examination. Instead, military police arrested him on charges
of collaborating with the enemy.[26]

On New Year's Day of 1954, Claude Batchelor also abandoned his
future as a peace fighter to come home. He had initially envisioned himself
as a leader among the group of American nonrepatriates, but he soon became disenchanted by his colleagues' lack of zeal and by the deceptive prac-
tices of the Chinese communists, who had secretly assigned all of the nonrepatriates to spy on each other.[27] As the former trumpet player wrote shortly
after his arrival in Tokyo, "Finally, I decided that I would go home and face
the music. I decided I had done wrong and hoped the American people
would forgive me."[28] During his debriefing in Tokyo, Batchelor provided
a 148-page narrative detailing his conduct during captivity. After returning
to Texas with his Japanese bride, Batchelor was arrested and confined in the
stockade at Fort Sam Houston, Texas.[29]

Dickenson's court martial began at Fort McNair, Virginia, in late April
1954, concurrent with the US Army–McCarthy hearings. Dickenson's defense attorney was a decorated war hero and distinguished former staff judge
advocate, retired Col. Guy Emery, who took the case for free because he
believed an injustice was being committed. Prior to the trial, Dickenson asserted that "explainers" in the neutral zone had promised him immunity if
he agreed to come home. True or false, the statement engendered a wave of
public support for Dickenson while undermining the perceived fairness of

the army's prosecution. In addition, some witnesses seemed intent on de-
monizing Dickenson in order to divert attention from their own misconduct. One of these, Cpl. Harold M. Dunn, would in turn be convicted by
an army court martial the following year. Perhaps believing the prosecution's
case was weak, the defense lawyers advised Dickenson not to testify. Instead,
the court returned a guilty verdict and sentenced Dickenson to ten years,
making him the first American ever convicted of collaboration.[30]

Meanwhile, army counterintelligence agents continued to sort through
the mountains of evidence. In February, perhaps in response to the sympathetic outcry regarding the news of Dickenson's prosecution, the secretary of
defense directed that no further trials would be conducted without his review and approval. The army subsequently established a Board on Prisoner
of War Collaboration to review and confirm the viability of all such prose-
cutions. Investigators eventually recommended further investigation of 72
of the 215 army personnel still on active duty, and the board endorsed 56 of
these recommendations. In turn, the secretary of defense approved further
action in 47 cases, and the army notified commanders in its various regional
headquarters to proceed with further investigations and, where appropriate,
trials by court martial.[31]

The delegation of court-martial authority to regional commanders was
an efficient, routine procedure and, in the case of the former POWs, a mistake. In recommending the establishment of the central review board, the
chief of the army's Military Justice Division warned that errors would be
inevitable:

> Another disturbing factor is the lack of uniformity in disposing of these cases.
> With witnesses scattered and difficult to obtain for verification of their initial
> stories, a certain lethargy is bound to develop in the people charged with ex-
> amination of the evidence for possible prosecution. To permit this to happen in
> cases deserving of punishment and to have zealous commanders in other areas
> prosecute individuals whose offenses, comparatively speaking, could be consid-
> ered as minor in nature could introduce numerous injustices and subject the
> Army to severe criticism.

The warning proved prophetic. Despite the establishment of the central review board, the responsibility for investigation and prosecution of the alleged collaborators remained decentralized among various regional commanders throughout the United States. The injustices happened, and the
severe criticism followed.[32]

While army investigators in each region gathered evidence throughout the spring and summer of 1954, more cases came to trial, albeit slowly. The US Army's third trial began on August 30, 1954, at Fort Sam Houston, Texas, where Corporal Batchelor faced a lengthy catalogue of accusations that included planning with the enemy to form subversive organizations in the United States, writing articles, circulating petitions, making speeches and broadcasts on behalf of the enemy, and informing on fellow prisoners. Perhaps the most damning accusation was the allegation that Batchelor had recommended the execution of a fellow prisoner, Pfc. Wilbur Watson, whom the Chinese had accused of espionage.[33]

Like Floyd before him, Batchelor retained the services of a civilian attorney, Joel Westbrook, who was unfamiliar with military law. During the month-long trial, Westbrook repeatedly tested the court's patience by asking witnesses to answer lengthy and complicated questions that often had to be repeated. Westbrook also submitted requests for thousands of classified government documents, most of which were denied on the court's opinion that they were irrelevant. Batchelor's case involved the testimony of several dozen former POWs and expert psychiatrists, including Leon Freedom, who testified that the defendant suffered from an extreme case of "induced political psychosis" and believed "he was a potential savior of humanity." These maneuvers, however, won little sympathy from the court, which found Batchelor guilty on multiple counts and gave him life in prison, a sentence later reduced to twenty years.[34] The harsh sentence further exacerbated public criticism of the army, although a military appeals court later found the evidence against Batchelor "overwhelming."[35]

While Batchelor's lawyers were trying to defend him as a victim of brainwashing, Lt. Col. Harry Fleming sat in a courtroom in Fort Sheridan, Illinois, facing accusations of collaboration and conduct unbecoming an officer. The forty-six-year-old reservist was the first officer tried by court martial for conduct during captivity. His trial began after the Marine Corps and the US Air Force had taken less punitive action against their officers, a fact that Fleming's lawyers noted in court. Prosecutors accused Fleming of signing peace appeals, writing articles, and recording broadcasts while serving as the senior officer at Camp Twelve in early 1951 and argued that he had acted in self-interest. Fleming's civilian attorney, Alfred A. LaFrance, made no effort to deny Fleming's cooperation with the enemy but presented his client as a hero whose conduct had saved the lives of every man at Camp Twelve. Fleming himself declared unapologetically that "the most futile thing in the world was a dead prisoner of war."[36]

Fleming's case presented the army's legal system with the same moral dilemma that had confronted so many American prisoners in Korea. Every man at Camp Twelve had, in fact, survived imprisonment during a period when other American prisoners were dying by the hundreds in the temporary and permanent camps scattered across North Korea. To save these lives, however, Fleming had committed embarrassing acts of collaboration and had encouraged others to do the same. At least some of the evidence from Korea, however, suggested that resistance to coercion had not proven fatal. This information, of course, was not available to Fleming, who had personally witnessed Chinese troops executing unarmed prisoners. Moreover, Fleming was only one of many prisoners who had committed acts of collaboration, yet he was one of only a handful who faced prosecution. After ten hours of deliberation, the court found Fleming guilty and sentenced him to dismissal from the service, with forfeiture of all pay and allowances. The absence of a jail sentence suggested at least some sympathy for Fleming's plight.[37]

Fleming became the fourth former POW convicted by court martial, but other cases were still pending. Of the original 215 cases warranting further investigation, the Pentagon initially approved 47 for further action, but only 13 went to trial (not counting Floyd). Regional commanders dismissed the other cases, although many of these men were administratively separated from the army.[38] The reluctance to prosecute sparked resentment within the army's counterintelligence section, which had reviewed the files in the first place.[39] In several cases, the assistant chief of staff, G-2 (intelligence) suggested that the secretary of the army should overrule the decisions of regional commanders. In response, the army's staff judge advocate reiterated the regional commanders' legal authority to exercise discretion and opined that there were insufficient grounds to overrule their decisions.[40]

If prosecuting former POWs still serving in the army was difficult, prosecuting those who had left the service proved even more frustrating. Perhaps fearing potential acts of espionage, the army's counterintelligence section forwarded files on the 210 former soldiers to the FBI for further investigation.[41] Meanwhile, US Army and Justice Department officials debated which agency had jurisdiction. Article 3(a) of the Uniform Code of Military Justice allowed the army to press charges against former service members if their alleged crimes were conducted on active duty. Senior military lawyers, however, felt that this "reassertion of jurisdiction" first required review by the Justice Department in order to determine whether the accused could be tried in federal court on charges of treason.[42]

The Justice Department responded that such reviews were unnecessary and that the army's evidence did not meet "the strict evidentiary requirements of the Constitution with respect to treason." Instead, suggested the assistant attorney general, the army should prosecute the alleged collaborators by court martial.[43] The army renewed its investigations, with the intention of filing charges where appropriate. In November 1955, however, the Supreme Court ruled that Article 3(a) of the Uniform Code was unconstitutional. In the case of *Toth v. Quarles,* the Court voted 6–3 to reject the military's jurisdiction over former service members.[44] Denied jurisdiction, the army sent the files back to the Justice Department. After two years of additional investigation and review, the attorney general determined there was "insufficient evidence to warrant prosecution of any of these individuals."[45]

While the former service members avoided prosecution, trials continued for those on active duty despite a growing public perception that the defendants were scapegoats being sacrificed to protect the army's reputation.[46] After the convictions of Fleming and Dickens in the autumn of 1954, the army tried nine more soldiers for alleged collaboration in 1955. The most notorious case was that of Sgt. James C. Gallagher of Brooklyn, New York, whose alleged crimes included collaborating with the enemy, informing on fellow prisoners, promoting disloyalty by signing a surrender appeal, and two counts of unpremeditated murder. Among other allegations, Gallagher had reportedly thrown two sick prisoners out of his hut at Camp Five during the winter of 1951, actions that resulted in their deaths. Gallagher denied these accusations, but the court disagreed and gave him a life sentence.[47]

The army eventually convicted ten of the thirteen former POWs accused of collaboration. The three men acquitted were Sgt. John Tyler, 1st Lt. Jeff Erwin, and Maj. Ambrose Nugent. Both Erwin and Nugent admitted to cooperating with the enemy by making broadcasts and signing documents during their incarceration at Camp Twelve, but the courts appeared willing to forgive these actions because of the appalling conditions under which they were committed. Prosecutors repeatedly argued that the concept of duress required the imminent threat of death, but attorneys for Nugent and Erwin managed to demonstrate that the communists were effective in using other means to coerce the desired behavior. In at least one instance, however, Erwin confirmed that he had cooperated because a gun was, in fact, pointed at his head. Nevertheless, a prosecutor challenged Erwin on the grounds that he could not be sure the gun was loaded.[48]

With the last court martial finished and the cases against the former soldiers transferred to the Justice Department, the army completed its legal actions regarding former Korean War POWs by the close of 1955. That same year, the Defense Advisory Committee on Prisoners of War, appointed by the secretary of defense to examine POW issues, produced a study recommending ways to better prepare service members to cope with the challenges of captivity. In preparation, the board had spent several weeks examining various aspects of captivity in communist hands. These examinations produced volumes of relevant information regarding the behavior of American prisoners of war in Korea and in previous wars.[49]

The board's final report, however, left several issues unresolved. It minimized, for example, the effect of brainwashing but added that "this time-consuming and coercive technique" obtained confessions through combinations of "mental and physical torture, psychiatric pressures or 'Pavlov Dogs' treatment." More often, argued the report, prisoners "were given a high-powered indoctrination for propaganda purposes."[50] The report also conveyed a mixed message regarding the behavior of American prisoners in Korea. Refusing to specify how many had collaborated, the board declared the record of POWs in Korea honorable, adding that the former prisoners had been victimized by "abundant" misconceptions among an uninformed public. On the other hand, the report seemed to condemn American conduct in captivity, closing with the ominous warning that "The Korean story must never be permitted to happen again."[51]

Acknowledging that the Americans had been ill prepared for captivity in Korea, the board proposed a code of conduct worthy of Sparta, which restricted captured American service members from providing the enemy with anything more than name, rank, serial number, and date of birth. The board's own research indicated that these restrictions, originally prescribed by the Geneva Conventions, did not reflect previous experience, particularly when prisoners were confronted by skilled interrogators. As the air force representative observed, "The complete breakdown of this limitation during the last war on the part of both German and Allied POWs resulted in the commanders of all three US Services recommending policy changes." The board reasoned that even if such a standard were unattainable, it was better to draw "a line of resistance . . . as far forward as possible."[52] On August 17, 1955, President Eisenhower issued an executive order prescribing the new Code of Conduct for all service members. Neither the report nor the recommended code addressed the moral dilemma of choosing between cooperation and death.[53]

From the Pentagon's perspective, the committee's report and the subsequent code seemed to resolve the matter of POW conduct once and for all.

In the court of public opinion, however, rumors of brainwashing, betrayal, and collaboration would slander the former POWs for at least another decade. The former prisoners would be excoriated for their alleged weakness, apathy, ill discipline, and treasonous behavior by disparate observers such as FBI director J. Edgar Hoover, feminist Betty Friedan, and *Scouting* magazine. Worst of all, the US Army itself would sponsor much of the criticism leveled against its own veterans.[54]

The defamation of American POWs began while they were still imprisoned. In April 1953, the *New York Times* cited "authoritative studies" claiming that communist "brainwashers" had warped the minds of some POWs so effectively that when the war ended, "they will publicly declare they do not want to come home." A week later, the Pentagon seemed to confirm the earlier report when it announced that some prisoners "appear to have succumbed to relentless Communist pressures" by accepting communist propaganda. When the prisoners who were released during Operation Little Switch held a press conference, reporters peppered them with questions about the alleged brainwashing. In an effort at damage control, the army announced that it would study the matter to determine what had actually happened to the prisoners during their captivity.[55] In the months to come, the army would decorate fifty-five prisoners for valorous conduct during their captivity, but these tales of individual heroism were soon overshadowed by a more disturbing theme.[56]

While the Pentagon seemed unsure what to make of the newly released Americans, Lt. Col. William E. Mayer, a US Army psychiatrist, had no doubts. After interviewing repatriated prisoners and conducting his own study of the matter, Mayer reached disturbing conclusions regarding the conduct of American prisoners and proceeded to broadcast them to audiences nationwide. For the first time in our nation's history, declared Mayer, too many soldiers had behaved in a manner that "fell far short of the historical American standards of honor, character, loyalty, courage, and personal integrity." Although this message contradicted the findings of several official studies, the army did not curtail Mayer's speaking engagements.[57]

While Americans read accounts of brainwashing and collaboration by POWs, Mayer toured the country giving presentations to military units and ROTC detachments, as well as schools, churches, civic and veterans' groups, and chapters of the John Birch Society. In 1956, *US News and World Report* published a lengthy interview with Mayer, titled "Why Did Many G.I. Captives Cave In?" In addition, half a million Americans bought printed transcripts of his speeches, and another hundred thousand bought audio recordings. At one point, Mayer was making two appearances a week. For those few groups that Mayer missed, an Arkansas Bible college sold kits with the text of Mayer's speech and exhibits, enabling individuals to spread the doctor's message in his absence.[58]

Mayer's primary claim was that 30 percent of POWs yielded to communist brainwashing and did so in the absence of torture or physical threats. According to Mayer's own research, emotionally weak American prisoners had simply lacked the willpower to resist. His figure did not correspond with the percentage of repatriated men initially suspected of possible misconduct (12 percent), much less the percentage actually convicted of collaboration (less than 0.25 percent), and he dismissed the starvation, sickness, filth, and torture that the communist captors had inflicted on their prisoners. Instead, Mayer questioned the manhood of these American soldiers, arguing that the POWs' weakness reflected the perilous decay of modern American society. Their failures, he argued, were the product of permissive, unpatriotic schools, overbearing mothers, and a military gone soft. Historian Lewis Carlson later noted that most of the POWs had grown up in poverty and joined the military to escape economic hardship. "As products of the Depression," observed Carlson, "they were arguably the least spoiled generation of the 20th century."[59]

Although both his evidence and logic were suspect, audiences welcomed Mayer's strident call for "old-fashioned, basic ideas" and a more disciplined, more authoritarian society. A Cincinnati newspaper, for example, described a 1961 broadcast by Mayer as "a scholarly, thoroughly responsible account of the brainwashing of American prisoners."[60] Large portions of the American public were dissatisfied with the outcome of the war and disturbed by Senator McCarthy's claims of widespread communist infiltration. To these listeners, the eloquent doctor's unflinching message of manly patriotism and firm resolve presented a clear solution to society's problems.[61]

While Mayer spread his gospel of guilt, the army continued to receive enormous criticism because of the perceived unfairness of the collaboration trials. In fact, the Pentagon Advisory Committee's published report took great pains to correct this perception by emphasizing the seriousness of the allegations and adding that the army had been "thorough and exacting in its research and investigation." To reach a wider audience, however, the army granted access to several writers, including William L. White, Rod Serling, and Eugene Kinkead.[62]

White's subsequent book, *The Captives of Korea,* painted a favorable picture of the American POWs, juxtaposing the inhumane treatment of Americans in communist hands with the plentiful food, clothing, and medical care provided to communist prisoners in UN camps. Although White labeled his work an "unofficial white paper," it clearly reflected the Pentagon's emphasis on the heroic behavior of American prisoners confined under barbaric circumstances.

Based largely on his research with the army's staff judge advocate, Rod Serling wrote *The Rack,* a televised play later produced as a motion picture with the same title. Serling's courtroom drama presented the trial of an officer accused of informing on his fellow prisoners. Seeking to "pose the problem dramatically," Serling's script provides sympathetic views of both the prosecutor and the defendant, whom Serling later described as a composite of the accused collaborators. Although his defendant endures brutal torture, Serling's central message firmly justifies the army's policy. "When it comes to its own," says Serling's prosecutor, "the Army walks tiptoe and in agony looking for justice."[63]

While these writers endorsed the Pentagon's official version of events, Eugene Kinkead took a different approach. Claiming that his research would complement the "hurriedly written" and "very sketchy" Pentagon study, Kinkead sought to "correct the incomplete and contradictory picture that had grown up in the public mind" regarding captivity in Korea.[64] Like Mayer before him, Kinkead based his arguments on the central claim of widespread collaboration among American POWs. As proof, Kinkead quoted Assistant Secretary of the Army Hugh M. Milton II:

> If we use as a standard the committing of some perhaps understandable act of "technical" collaboration, such as broadcasting Christmas greetings to relatives at home, the percentage might be as high as thirty per cent. One man in every seven, or more than thirteen percent, was guilty of serious collaboration—writing disloyal tracts, say, or agreeing to spy or organize for the Communists after the war.[65]

Milton did not define "technical" collaboration, and neither he nor Kinkead mentioned whether these figures included the US service members who died in captivity. Instead, Kinkead latched on to Milton's speculative 30 percent as proof that "almost one out of three prisoners in Korea was guilty of some sort of collaboration with the enemy."[66]

Based on this central assertion, Kinkead proceeded to catalogue other American shortcomings. These included the "fact" that no American prisoner successfully escaped from a permanent prison camp, a first in US history.[67] In addition, the captive Americans allegedly provided their interrogators with more and better information than they had ever before acquired. "There is no reason to suppose," concluded the author, "that the weaknesses and strengths, the gullibilities and insights, of United States military personnel are not at this minute being carefully studied in Peiping [*sic*] and Moscow."[68]

The alleged collapse of discipline represented another significant indictment against the quality of soldiers and leaders. As evidence, Kinkead quoted a lengthy monologue on the topic by Dr. Clarence Anderson, the 8th Cavalry Regiment surgeon captured at Unsan. Noting that the officers were segregated, Anderson blamed the noncommissioned officers for failing to organize and discipline the men in their squads and concluded that better discipline would have saved more lives.[69]

Perhaps the most damning observation in Kinkead's book was his analysis of the high mortality rate among American prisoners. Military casualty reports indicated that 2,730 American prisoners—38 percent of those officially recorded as captured—had perished in captivity. This figure represented the highest death rate among prisoners in US military history. In fact, the actual death rate in captivity was probably much higher. The Pentagon continues to list more than eight thousand American service members as missing in action during the Korean War, and analysts suspect that at least several hundred of these individuals are prisoners who died in captivity.[70]

Kinkead, however, showed little sympathy for the dead. Rather, he argued, their demise was their own fault. Citing unnamed Pentagon officials, Kinkead reported that "there was evidence that the high death rate was not due to Communist maltreatment—that it could be accounted for largely by the ignorance or the callousness of the prisoners themselves."[71] Based on his interview with Anderson, Kinkead wrote that the prisoners initially received first 1,200 grams and later 2,400 grams of food per day and that men refused to eat the soya beans, believing they caused diarrhea. Anderson had, in fact, commented earlier on the prisoners' refusal to eat certain foods, but the rest of the quotation contradicts the doctor's earlier statements. At a 1953 conference with the army's surgeon general, Anderson had estimated a daily ration of 400 grams between January and May 1951, with no meat or vegetables.[72]

Kinkead committed relatively little space to solutions to the "haunting and inescapable challenge" described in his book. Instead, the author devoted a lengthy chapter to the thoughts of an anonymous colonel, whose basic message was that discipline had gone to hell in a hand basket since the end of World War II. Kinkead presented these views as a sensible approach that the army had yet to embrace. Kinkead also endorsed the new Code of

Conduct as an important step in the right direction, and he relayed Assistant Secretary Milton's warning that defeating communism was not just an army problem but also one that confronted parents, teachers, and clergy. "By the time a young man enters the Army," warned Milton, "he should possess a set of sound moral values and the strength of character to live by them."[73]

Kinkead's book appeared in 1959, sold fifteen thousand copies, and was widely quoted by clergy, politicians, social critics, and other journalists. Several writers refuted Kinkead's "facts." Historian Peter Karsten, for example, dismissed the idea as nostalgia for a mythical past, and the *Harvard Business Review* published a statement from twenty-one prominent scholars repudiating their claims.[74] These rebuttals, however, drew little attention. The most detailed response was Albert Biderman's 1963 book, *March to Calumny,* which patiently dissected every dubious claim and distorted statistic in Kinkead's work. According to Biderman and others, misconduct by American prisoners was an unfortunate feature of every major conflict, most American prisoners in Korea did not collaborate with the enemy, and the appalling death toll among captured Americans resulted from neglect and mistreatment, not the social defects of the victims themselves.[75]

Still, the myth persisted. At a 1962 Senate hearing on military censorship, former president Eisenhower endorsed a program of political indoctrination for service members as a solution to "the sad record of Americans in Korea."[76] The 1963 movie *The Manchurian Candidate* portrayed former American POWs as brainwashed agents working for their communist spymasters. As late as 1995, columnist David Hackworth, a highly decorated veteran of Korea and Vietnam, referred to the "Korean War disgrace" during which "many American POWs ratted on and stole the food of their fellow inmates or allowed themselves to be used for propaganda purposes." Hackworth's column provoked several angry rebuttals from former POWs.[77]

While scholars debated the significance of the POW experience in Korea, another Asian war soon occupied America's attention. Like their Chinese predecessors, North Vietnamese officials deliberately manipulated the captured Americans to achieve propaganda victories. Declaring their prisoners "war criminals," interrogators employed isolation, starvation, and physical and psychological torture to coerce desired behaviors from their prisoners. Most of the seven hundred Americans captured in Vietnam, however, were US Air Force, Navy, and Marine Corps pilots who had received extensive training on survival, evasion, resistance, and escape (SERE) techniques prior to the war. This group proved far more effective in resisting the enemy's efforts at interrogation and indoctrination, and many later gave credit to the

Code of Conduct as a moral touchstone. In fact, there were significant problems for this group of prisoners as well. Their repatriation in 1973, however, seemed to provide a moral victory for Americans, who were tired of the long and demoralizing conflict in Vietnam, and the Nixon administration made a conscious decision to lionize the former prisoners as national heroes.[78]

The former Korean War prisoners, meanwhile, faded into obscurity. The majority of enlisted men left the service soon after repatriation and pursued civilian careers. Air force tail gunner Dan Oldewage, for example, bought a gas station in Orange, California. He and his wife still live in the same house where they raised their children. He has taken each of his grandchildren to Washington, D.C., to ensure that they appreciate the principles on which the nation was founded. Army medic Ray Mellin spent several months recuperating at the army hospital at Valley Forge, Pennsylvania, then enrolled at Rutgers University. He eventually became a chemical engineer with the Dow Chemical Corporation. Jack Chapman, the recoilless rifle gunner injured seven times at Hellfire Valley, went back home to Oklahoma. Feeling unwanted by the army, he left the service shortly after repatriation and enlisted in the air force, from which he retired in 1978. Several years after the war, an air force surgeon identified and removed a Chinese slug from Chapman's skull.

Most of the captured officers remained in the service, and many later served in combat during Vietnam. Paul Roach, for example, commanded an infantry battalion in the American Division, Ernest "Curly" Reid commanded a marine field artillery regiment, and Ralph Dixon served as a finance officer. Their experience as POWs seemed to have little impact on their career progression—three Marine Corps prisoners retired as general officers, and many of the army and air force officers retired at the rank of colonel. Not all of the officers stayed in. Bob Wood, the infantry lieutenant at Unsan, went back to Georgetown University for a master's degree in history and spent the next three decades as a college administrator. Hector Cordero, the lawyer tortured at Camp Five, became a prominent attorney and later a federal judge in Puerto Rico. Sid Esensten returned to his family and his medical practice in Minneapolis. He once tried to challenge Mayer's accusations at a public appearance, "but he knew who I was," recalled Esensten, "and he wouldn't let me speak."[79]

In the 1980s, Korean War POWs enjoyed something of a public rehabilitation, thanks to the 1979 establishment of a National POW/MIA Remembrance Day and the Reagan administration's avid interest in accounting for service members listed as missing in action in Southeast Asia. Although this renewed interest focused on Vietnam, Korean War veterans also gained a new appreciation. With POWs from three wars in attendance, Reagan acknowledged the heroic service and sacrifice of American prisoners at a 1984 White House ceremony.[80] As the war's fortieth anniversary approached, historians published several new accounts of the war, most notably a massive study by Clay Blair Jr., *The Forgotten War.*

In fact, the war has received a great deal of attention in the past two decades. Historians, journalists, and political scientists from several nations have written extensively about various aspects of the conflict, and some of the old issues still inspire disagreement. Some observers, for example, still criticize the restrictions against bombing Manchurian air bases and favor MacArthur's plan to widen the war. Others continue to debate whether the US military used biological weapons in Korea. Recent revelations about American interrogations of al-Qaeda fighters renewed discussion of communist brainwashing and torture techniques, while the prisoner-abuse scandal at Abu Ghraib reminded others of American incompetence at Koje-Do. In South Korea, journalists and scholars have reexamined the mistreatment of civilians during the war, and the government recently established a Truth and Reconciliation Commission to investigate atrocities allegedly committed by communist, UN, and ROK forces.

For the men who endured captivity in North Korea, these issues grow increasingly remote. Members of the Korean War Ex-POW Association still gather for an annual reunion, but as their ranks thin with each passing year, the attendees recall only the most humorous anecdotes. Names, dates, and locations have faded with time, but nearly every former prisoner can recount lively stories about stealing chickens or mocking Chinese officials. Perhaps this is just as well. These veterans have seen enough horror, endured enough pain, lost enough friends. They have earned their rightful place in history as courageous men who survived extraordinary times.

Appendix

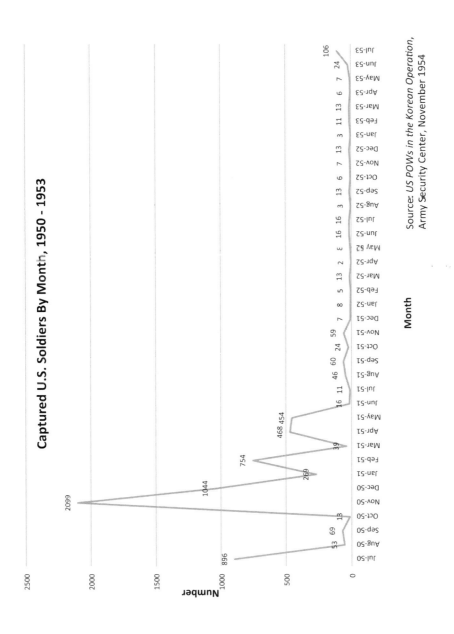

Captured U.S. Soldiers By Month, 1950 - 1953

Source: *US POWs in the Korean Operation,* Army Security Center, November 1954

List of Abbreviations

BAR	Browning automatic rifle
CCF	Communist Chinese Forces
CIA	Central Intelligence Agency
CO	commanding officer
CP	command post
DDT	dichlorodiphenyltrichloroethane (chemical pesticide)
GI	general issue (slang for US Army personnel and equipment)
JCS	Joint Chiefs of Staff
KATUSA	Korean Army Troops, United States Army
KMAG	Korean Military Advisors' Group
MiG-15	Soviet-manufactured jet fighter aircraft
M-26	American-manufactured main battle tank
MSR	main supply route
NKPA	North Korean People's Army
NSC	National Security Council
POW	prisoner of war
RCT	regimental combat team
ROK	Republic of Korea
SCR-300	Signal Corps radio set used by US infantry units in World War II and Korea
T-34	Soviet-manufactured main battle tank
UN	United Nations
US	United States

Notes

Prologue

1. Mellin interview.

2. Knox, *Korean War, an Oral History,* 8–9.

3. Fehrenback's polemic, *This Kind of War,* is perhaps the most outspoken critique of the US Army's readiness for war in 1950. See also Manchester, *American Caesar,* 555; Hastings, *Korean War,* 69. More recently, Thomas Hanson's *Combat Ready?* argues that the Eighth Army's poor performance in July 1950 was caused primarily by policy decisions in Washington rather than poor training and leadership in Japan.

4. Hanson, *Combat Ready?* 110; Manchester, *American Caesar,* 494–512.

5. Millett, *War for Korea, 1950–1951,* 66–67; Acheson, *Korean War,* 42.

6. Blair, *Forgotten War,* 49; Knox, *Korean War, an Oral History,* 18; Hanson, *Combat Ready?* 17–18.

Chapter 1

1. Zellers, *In Enemy Hands,* 13–20.

2. Alexander, *Korea,* 2; Ent, *Fighting on the Brink,* 26.

3. Zellers, *In Enemy Hands,* 13–20; Chinnery, *Korean Atrocity!* 45.

4. Condit, *History of the Office of the Secretary of Defense,* 47.

5. Alexander, *Korea,* 3–4; Toland, *In Mortal Combat,* 16–17; Hastings, *Korean War,* 27–28. For a detailed account of Korea between 1945 and 1950 see Millett, *War for Korea, 1945–1950.*

6. Ent, *Fighting on the Brink,* 19–24; Millett, *War for Korea, 1950–1951,* 29; Halberstam, *Coldest Winter,* 82–83.

7. Fehrenbach, *This Kind of War,* 66–67; Deane, *I Was a Captive in Korea,* 82–85; Zellers, *In Enemy Hands,* 50–56.

8. Millett, *War for Korea, 1950–1951,* 87–96, 104; Ent, *Fighting on the Brink,* 27–30; Fehrenbach, *This Kind of War,* 76.

9. Manchester, *American Caesar,* 548–49.

10. Acheson, *Korean War,* 16.

11. Ibid., 19.

12. Manchester, *American Caesar,* 549; James, *Refighting the Last War,* 15.

13. Fehrenbach, *This Kind of War,* 83.

14. Condit, *History of the Office of the Secretary of Defense,* 50.

15. Blair, *Forgotten War,* 77.

16. Fehrenbach, *This Kind of War,* 89.

17. Alexander, *Korea,* 55; Ent, *Fighting on the Brink,* 31. Smith and his soldiers were exhausted after serving on alert for an extended period.

18. Kennedy, "Force Protection Implications."

19. Knox, *Korean War, an Oral History,* 10.

20. Tomedi, *No Bugles, No Drums,* 2.

21. Knox, *Korean War, an Oral History,* 13–15; Mellin interview; Ent, *Fighting on the Brink,* 32.

22. Ent, *Fighting on the Brink,* 32; Alexander, *Korea,* 56.

23. Tomedi, *No Bugles, No Drums,* 3–4. Higgins was one of the few American war correspondents reporting from Korea during the war's first few weeks.

24. Kennedy, "Force Protection Implications," 89.

25. Ibid.; Fehrenbach, *This Kind of War,* 98.

26. Appleman, *South to the Naktong,* 61–68.

27. Alexander, *Korea,* 58.

28. Knox, *Korean War, an Oral History,* 20.

29. Alexander, *Korea,* 59.

30. Kennedy, "Force Protection Implications," 89–90; Alexander, *Korea,* 61.

31. Alexander, *Korea,* 61; Ent, *Fighting on the Brink,* 37.

32. Ent, *Fighting on the Brink,* 37.

33. Ent, *Fighting on the Brink,* 38–39; Fehrenbach, *This Kind of War,* 103–106.

34. Tomedi, *No Bugles, No Drums,* 7.

35. Mellin interview.

36. Maj. Ambrose Nugent, sworn affidavit (Record Group 153, Entry 183, Box 4), 1.

37. Lech, *Broken Soldiers,* 13.

38. Nugent, sworn affidavit, 1.

39. Blair, *Forgotten War,* 96–97. Blair has argued that a consolidated defense along the Kum River would have been more prudent.

40. Knox, *Korean War, an Oral History,* 33.

41. Ent, *Fighting on the Brink,* 44.

42. Ibid.; Alexander, *Korea,* 64. One of the reporters, Marguerite Higgins of the *New York Herald Tribune,* provides a detailed description of this engagement in her memoir, *War in Korea,* 59–64.

43. Fehrenbach, *This Kind of War,* 111–15.

44. Alexander, *Korea,* 64–65.

45. Knox, *Korean War, an Oral History,* 35.

46. Blair, *Forgotten War,* 106–107.

47. Ibid., 107–108; Fehrenbach, *This Kind of War,* 115–17.

48. Fehrenbach, *This Kind of War,* 118.

49. Blair, *Forgotten War,* 109.

50. Alexander, *Korea,* 66–67.

51. Blair, *Forgotten War,* 110.

52. Ibid.

53. Ibid., 111.

54. Lech, *Broken Soldiers,* 16.

55. Nugent, sworn affidavit, 2.

56. Lech, *Broken Soldiers,* 17.

57. Lt. Col. John J. Dunn, sworn affidavit (Record Group 153, Entry 183, Box 2), 2.

58. Nugent, sworn affidavit, 2.

59. Ibid.; Dunn, sworn affidavit, 2.

60. Dunn, sworn affidavit, 2.

61. Mellin interview.

62. Boysen, memorandum, Interrogation of Returned Prisoner of War, 8–9.

63. Nugent, sworn affidavit, 2.

64. Millett, *War for Korea, 1950–1951,* 138–40.

65. Charles Kinnard, testimony, Transcript of Hearings, US Senate Subcommittee on Korean War Atrocities, Dec. 3, 1953, 100–103.

66. Appleman, *South to the Naktong,* 347–50; Bowers, Hammond, and MacGarrigle, *Black Soldier, White Army,* 140.

67. Blair, *Forgotten War,* 114–15; Alexander, *Korea,* 70; Millett, *War for Korea, 1950–1951,* 140.

68. Appleman, *South to the Naktong,* 101–107; Millett, *War for Korea, 1950–1951,* 194–95, 199–200.

69. Appleman, *South to the Naktong,* 110–14; Condit, *History of the Office of the Secretary of Defense,* 56. See also Hanson's *Combat Ready?*

70. Condit, *History of the Office of the Secretary of Defense,* 60; Schnabel, *United States Army in the Korean War,* 118.

71. Schnabel, *United States Army in the Korean War,* 118; Blair, *Forgotten War,* 120.

72. Blair, *Forgotten War,* 126–27.

73. Ibid., 128–29; Ent, *Fighting on the Brink,* 65–66.

74. Alexander, *Korea,* 82.

75. Ent, *Fighting on the Brink,* 64–65.

76. Fehrenbach, *This Kind of War,* 136–39; Alexander, *Korea,* 85–91.

77. Ent, *Fighting on the Brink,* 66–67.

78. Appleman, *South to the Naktong,* 143, 150; Blair, *Forgotten War,* 132.

79. Appleman, *South to the Naktong,* 152–53; Ent, *Fighting on the Brink,* 69.

80. Ent, *Fighting on the Brink,* 77–78; Millett, *War for Korea, 1950–1951,* 193.

81. Millett, *War for Korea, 1950–1951,* 176–79. See also Dean, *General Dean's Story,* which provides a unique and valuable account of the war's first weeks and Dean's subsequent ordeal in captivity.

82. Millett, *War for Korea, 1950–1951,* 195–96.

83. Alexander, *Korea,* 109–11.

84. Millett, *War for Korea, 1950–1951,* 197–99.

85. Alexander, *Korea,* 123; Hastings, *Korean War,* 84–85.

86. Alexander, *Korea,* 134–35.

87. Ibid., 136–40.

88. Ibid., 141–47.

89. Ibid., 345–46.

90. Roy Paul Manring Jr., testimony, Transcript of Hearings, US Senate Subcommittee on Korean War Atrocities, 128–29.

91. Ibid., 130–31; Ent, *Fighting on the Brink,* 224–25.

92. Knox, *Korean War, an Oral History,* 98.

93. Chinnery, *Korean Atrocity!* 26.

94. Fehrenbach, *This Kind of War,* 199–200.

95. Col. Claudius Wolfe, testimony, Transcript of Hearings, US Senate Subcommittee on Korean War Atrocities, 9–10; Fehrenbach, *This Kind of War,* 200; Shen and Li, *After Leaning to One Side,* 72.

96. Hoyt, *Pusan Perimeter,* 190.

97. Ibid., 191.

98. Alexander, *Korea,* 181–82.

99. Ibid., 184–85.

100. Ibid., 186.

101. Appleman, *South to the Naktong,* 485–86; Blair, *Forgotten War,* 242–46. For a careful examination of the 24th Infantry Regiment's performance, see Bowers, Hammond, and MacGarrigle, *Black Soldier, White Army.*

102. Blair, *Forgotten War,* 254–58.

103. Ibid., 258–59.

104. Appleman, *South to the Naktong,* 433–35.

105. Ibid., 435.

106. "War Diary, 8th Cavalry Regiment" (Record Group 407, Sept. 13, 1950).

107. Blair, *Forgotten War,* 268–69; Alexander, *Korea,* 195.

Chapter 2

1. MacArthur, *Reminiscences,* 333–34.

2. Alexander, *Korea,* 160. See also Bradley, *General's Life,* 552–53.

3. Millett, *War for Korea, 1950–1951,* 207–12; see also Weintraub, *MacArthur's War,* 116–19.

4. Halberstam, *Coldest Winter,* 301.

5. Blair, *Forgotten War,* 270.

6. Ibid., 269; Halberstam, *Coldest Winter,* 304–305; Millett, *War for Korea, 1950–1951,* 249–50.

7. Headquarters, Department of the Army, *US Prisoners of War in the Korean Operation,* 101. The army's postwar study recorded 896 US service members captured in July and 53 in August.

8. Zellers, *In Enemy Hands,* 56.

9. Crosbie, *March till They Die,* 108.

10. Deane, *I Was a Captive in Korea,* 85–88.

11. Zellers, *In Enemy Hands,* 49.

12. Crosbie, *March till They Die,* 108.

13. Headquarters, Department of the Army, *US Prisoners of War in the Korean Operation,* 85–86.

14. Deane, *I Was a Captive in Korea,* 87.

15. Dunn, sworn affidavit (Record Group 153, Entry 183, Box 2), 3.

16. Boysen, memorandum, Interrogation of Returned Prisoner of War, 11–12.

17. Booker, sworn statement, undated (Record Group 153, Entry 183, Box 1), 2. Captured in August, Booker became the first Marine Corps POW of the war.

18. Nugent, sworn affidavit (Record Group 153), 2.

19. Boysen, memorandum, Interrogation of Returned Prisoner of War, 12; Zellers, *In Enemy Hands,* 68.

20. Booker, sworn statement, undated (Record Group 153, Entry 183, Box 1), 2.

21. Boysen, memorandum, Interrogation of Returned Prisoner of War, 12. Again, the number of reported deaths varies. Dunn later stated that twenty-five men died at Manpo, while Major Booker and others put the number at nineteen.

22. Zellers, *In Enemy Hands,* 67–68; Dean, *General Dean's Story,* 89.

23. Zellers, *In Enemy Hands,* 67–68; James Conley, sworn affidavit (Record Group 153, Entry 183, Box 1), 2.

24. Hastings, *Korean War,* 100.

25. Blair, *Forgotten War,* 280–81; Alexander, *Korea,* 219.

26. "Armed Forces: Renaissance in the Ranks"; Blair, *Forgotten War,* 259. See also Sorley's biography of Johnson, *Honorable Warrior.*

27. "War Diary, 8th Cavalry Regiment" (Record Group 407, Sept. 15–16, 1950).

28. McAbee interview.

29. "War Diary, 8th Cavalry Regiment" (Record Group 407, Sept. 17–18, 1950).

30. McAbee interview. See also Richardson, *Valleys of Death,* 94–96. Richardson served as the heavy-weapons platoon sergeant in Love Company until his capture in November 1950.

31. "War Diary, 8th Cavalry Regiment" (Record Group 407, Sept. 19, 1950).

32. Blair, *Forgotten War,* 305–308.

33. Alexander, *Korea,* 220–21.

34. Blair, *Forgotten War,* 305–306.

35. Alexander, *Korea,* 221.

36. Blair, *Forgotten War,* 312–16.

37. Ibid., 315; Appleman, *South to the Naktong,* 599; McAbee interview; "War Diary, 8th Cavalry Regiment" (Record Group 407, Sept. 26–28, 1950).

38. Chinnery, *Korean Atrocity!* 42–43.

39. Appleman, *South to the Naktong,* 587.

40. Chinnery, *Korean Atrocity!* 40–42.

41. Appleman, *South to the Naktong,* 587.

42. Ibid., 587–88.

43. Chinnery, *Korean Atrocity!* 46–47

44. M. Sgt. Casey H. Weinel, testimony, Transcript of Hearings, US Senate Subcommittee on Korean War Atrocities, Dec. 2, 1953, 21–23.

45. Chinnery, *Korean Atrocity!* 49.

46. Millett, *War for Korea, 1950–1951,* 273–74.

47. Dong-Choon, "Truth and Reconciliation Commission of Korea"; Cumings, "South Korean Massacre at Taejon"; Hanley and Chang, "US Okayed Korean War Massacres."

48. Alexander, *Korea,* 211 17.

49. Weintraub, *MacArthur's War,* 168; Alexander, *Korea,* 228–29.

50. Appleman, *South to the Naktong,* 326–27; Manchester, *American Caesar,* 584.

51. Millett, *War for Korea, 1950–1951,* 276–78; Foot, *Wrong War,* 68–70; Casey, *Selling the Korean War,* 100.

52. Appleman, *South to the Naktong,* 608.

53. Alexander, *Korea,* 233–37.

54. "War Diary, 8th Cavalry Regiment" (Record Group 407, Oct. 9, 1950).

55. Blair, *Forgotten War,* 350–51.

56. Alexander, *Korea,* 249–50.

57. Ibid., 250–51.

58. Pfc. John Martin, testimony, Transcript of Hearings, US Senate Subcommittee on Korean War Atrocities, Dec. 2, 1953, 34–37.

59. Ibid., 35.

60. Appleman, *South to the Naktong,* 652; Cpl. Lloyd Kreider, testimony, Transcript of Hearings, US Senate Subcommittee on Korean War Atrocities, Dec. 2, 1953, 49–50.

61. Cpl. Lloyd Kreider, testimony, Transcript of Hearings, US Senate Subcommittee on Korean War Atrocities, Dec. 2, 1953, 49–50.

62. Appleman, *South to the Naktong,* 646–47.

63. Kreider, testimony, 50, Chinnery, *Korean Atrocity!* 71.

64. Kreider, testimony, 51; Appleman, *South to the Naktong,* 663.

65. Kreider, testimony, 51.

66. Appleman, *South to the Naktong,* 655–57.

67. Sgt. Charles Robert Sharpe, testimony, Transcript of Hearings, US Senate Subcommittee on Korean War Atrocities, Dec. 3, 1953, 137.

68. Ibid., 138.

69. Appleman, *South to the Naktong,* 661–63.

Chapter 3

1. Zellers, *In Enemy Hands,* 74–75.

2. Deane, *I Was a Captive in Korea,* 90–91; Boysen, memorandum, Interrogation of Returned Prisoner of War, 12.

3. Boysen, memorandum, Interrogation of Returned Prisoner of War, 12; Zellers, *In Enemy Hands,* 80–81; Dunn, sworn affidavit (Record Group 153), 3; Crosbie, *March till They Die,* 122–24.

4. Boysen, memorandum, Interrogation of Returned Prisoner of War, 12; Dunn, sworn affidavit, 4; Crosbie, *March till They Die,* 126–33.

5. Crosbie, *March till They Die,* 135–37; Dunn, sworn affidavit, 4.

6. Crosbie, *March till They Die,* 138.

7. Nugent, sworn affidavit, 3. In his affidavit, Nugent notes that he learned about the cornfield executions from Korean officers several months later.

8. Dean, *General Dean's Story,* 187; Zellers, *In Enemy Hands,* 87. Several survivors later confirmed that Dean had seen the large group of prisoners on October 31, the night they left the cornfield.

9. Crosbie, *March till They Die,* 139–40.

10. Deane, *I Was a Captive in Korea,* 111.

11. Dunn, sworn affidavit, 3.

12. Boysen, memorandum, Interrogation of Returned Prisoner of War, 13; Zellers, *In Enemy Hands,* 89–90.

13. Zellers, *In Enemy Hands,* 90.

14. Deane, *I Was a Captive in Korea,* 113.

15. Zellers, *In Enemy Hands,* 91; Crosbie, *March till They Die,* 142.

16. Crosbie, *March till They Die,* 142.

17. Zellers, *In Enemy Hands,* 91–92.

18. Ibid., 92–97.

19. Crosbie, *March till They Die,* 144.

20. Zellers, *In Enemy Hands,* 97–99.

21. Mellin interview, 11.

22. Zellers, *In Enemy Hands,* 99–100; Deane, *I Was a Captive in Korea,* 114; Dunn, sworn affidavit, 4; Crosbie, *March till They Die,* 145. These sources cite various numbers of men who died in the night and those who had survived but could not continue. Zellers reports the Tiger's order to "bury the eighteen."

23. Zellers, *In Enemy Hands,* 100–102.

24. Ibid., 103.

25. Ibid.; Boysen, memorandum, Interrogation of Returned Prisoner of War, 14. Captain Boysen provided the estimated size of the larger room.

26. Crosbie, *March till They Die,* 147–48.

27. Zellers, *In Enemy Hands,* 103.

28. Ibid., 105–106.

29. Lech, *Broken Soldiers,* 23.

30. Crosbie, *March till They Die,* 148–49.

31. Ibid., 149–52.

32. Ibid., 152–53.

33. Zellers, *In Enemy Hands,* 107–109.

34. Ibid., 110.

35. Lech, *Broken Soldiers,* 23.

36. Zellers, *In Enemy Hands,* 110.

37. Ibid., 112–15. Lantron had been captured by the Germans during World War II (Newton William Lantron, RECAP-K Biographical Worksheet, Dec. 6, 1954 (Record Group 153, Box 2, "Case Files of Returned or Exchanged Captured American Personnel, 1053–58").

38. Zellers, *In Enemy Hands,* 118; Crosbie, *March till They Die,* 116; Boysen, memorandum, Interrogation of Returned Prisoner of War, 14.

39. Boysen, memorandum, Interrogation of Returned Prisoner of War, 15.

40. Ibid.; Lt. Col. Newton Lantron, sworn affidavit, 5.

41. Boysen, memorandum, Interrogation of Returned Prisoner of War, 15; Booker, sworn statement, undated (Record Group 153, Entry 183, Box 1), 3.

42. Zellers, *In Enemy Hands,* 168.

43. Ibid., 17–22.

44. Lech, *Broken Soldiers,* 26; see also Boysen, memorandum, Interrogation of Returned Prisoner of War, 22.

Chapter 4

1. Headquarters, Department of the Army, *US Prisoners of War in the Korean Operation,* 9.

2. Appleman, *South to the Naktong,* 663–68; Cumings, *Korean War,* 192–93; Millett, *War for Korea, 1950–1951,* 286–89.

3. Manchester, *American Caesar,* 599.

4. Alexander, *Korea,* 235.

5. Ibid., 256; Manchester, *American Caesar,* 599.

6. Alexander, *Korea,* 256; Manchester, *American Caesar,* 600; Toland, *In Mortal Combat,* 250. For a detailed analysis of MacArthur's relationship with the Pentagon and the Truman administration, see Pearlman, *Truman and MacArthur.*

7. Goulden, *Korea,* 262–71; Weintraub, *MacArthur's War,* 182–84.

8. Pearlman, *Truman and MacArthur,* 111–17; Manchester, *American Caesar,* 588–93. MacArthur's account of the conference appears in *Reminiscences,* 371–73, and makes no mention of the saluting incident.

9. Goulden, *Korea,* 104; Halberstam, *Coldest Winter,* 368–69; Acheson, *Korean War,* 28–29.

10. Chen Jian, *China's Road to the Korean War,* 129–37.

11. James, *Refighting the Last War,* 185; Alexander, *Korea,* 242–43. Because the United States had not recognized Communist China diplomatically, the two governments had no formal diplomatic relationship. Zhou utilized the Indian embassy as a neutral "trusted agent," a role the Indian government would play again in the war's final stages.

12. Alexander, *Korea,* 242–44; Fehrenbach, *This Kind of War,* 288.

13. Appleman, *South to the Naktong,* 666.

14. Ibid., 672–73.

15. Paik Sun Yup, *From Pusan to Panmunjom,* 85–90; Alexander, *Korea,* 263–67; Appleman, *South to the Naktong,* 676–77.

16. Appleman, *South to the Naktong,* 673–74.

17. Ibid., 674–76; Spurr, *Enter the Dragon,* 135–36; Paik, *From Pusan to Panmunjom,* 89–90.

18. Blair, *Forgotten War,* 377; Alexander, *Korea,* 265–66.

19. Blair, *Forgotten War,* 377; Halberstam, *Coldest Winter,* 377–78.

20. Alexander, *Korea,* 269.

21. Blair, *Forgotten War,* 380; Appleman, *South to the Naktong,* 690.

22. Capt. Jack Bolt, after-action interview with Capt. Edwin Williamson, in Eighth US Army, "Ambush of Battery C," June 1951, 1.

23. "War Diary, 8th Cavalry Regiment" (Record Group 407, entry at 301915, October 1950).

24. Eighth US Army, "Ambush of Battery C"; Appleman, *South to the Naktong,* 689; Blair, *Forgotten War,* 380; McAbee interview, 9.

25. Halberstam, *Coldest Winter,* 19–22; Lt. Col. Veale Moriarty, letter to Lt. Col. Roy Appleman, June 11, 1954 (Record Group 319, Box 738); Capt. Walter Mayo, "History of the 3rd Battalion, 8th Cavalry Regiment, 30 October–5 November 1950," undated (Record Group 319, Box 738).

26. McAbee interview, 9.

27. Spurr, *Enter the Dragon,* 135; "War Diary, 8th Cavalry Regiment" (Record Group 407, entry at 310616, October 1950); Appleman, *South to the Naktong,* 690.

28. "War Diary, 8th Cavalry Regiment" (Record Group 407, entry at 310616, October 1950).

29. Lt. Col. John Millikin, letter to Lt. Col. Roy Appleman, May 6, 1954 (Record Group 319, Box 738), 2.

30. "War Diary, 8th Cavalry Regiment" (Record Group 407, entry at 311415, October 1950). The Americans may have dismissed this report because it came from the ROK Army.

31. Appleman, *South to the Naktong,* 679; Maj. Gen. Hap Gay, letter to Lt. Col. Roy Appleman, Feb. 19, 1954 (Record Group 319, Box 738), 2.

32. Blair, *Forgotten War,* 381.

33. Ibid.; Halberstam, *Coldest Winter,* 20.

34. Halberstam, *Coldest Winter,* 20–21; Richardson, *Valleys of Death,* 140–41.

35. "War Diary, 8th Cavalry Regiment" (Record Group 407, entry at 312050, October 1950).

36. Millikin letter, 2.

37. Appleman, *South to the Naktong,* 689–90; Maher, *Shepherd in Combat Boots,* 13; Robert Wood, qtd. in Wenzl, "Miracle of Father Kapaun, Part 1"; Spurr, *Enter the Dragon,* 137.

38. Gay letter to Appleman, Feb. 19, 1954, 3.

39. Ibid.; Appleman, *South to the Naktong,* 690–91.

40. Appleman, *South to the Naktong,* 691; Gay letter, 3.

41. Millikin letter, 2.

42. "War Diary, 8th Cavalry Regiment" (Record Group 407, entry at 011440, November 1950, and entry at 011600, November 1950); Appleman, *South to the Naktong,* 691–93; Millikin letter, 2–3.

43. Richardson, *Valleys of Death,* 143–44.

44. "War Diary, 8th Cavalry Regiment" (Record Group 407, Nov. 1, 1950).

45. Appleman, *South to the Naktong,* 693; Spurr, *Enter the Dragon,* 136.

46. "War Diary, 8th Cavalry Regiment" (Record Group 407, Nov. 1, 1950).

47. Armstrong, *1st Cavalry Division and Their 8th Engineers in Korea,* 101–102.

48. Millikin letter; "War Diary, 8th Cavalry Regiment" (Record Group 407, Nov. 1, 1950).

49. Appleman, *South to the Naktong,* 694–96; "War Diary, 8th Cavalry Regiment" (Record Group 407, entry at 020100, November 1950).

50. Spurr, *Enter the Dragon,* 137; Maher, *Shepherd in Combat Boots,* 14; Lt. Col. Veale Moriarty, letter to Lt. Col. Roy Appleman, June 11, 1954 (Record Group 319, Box 738); 1st Sgt. Robert Hill, letter to Gene Paladina, Apr. 23, 2002 (copy furnished to the author by Rita Payne, Installation Chaplains' Office, Fort Campbell, Ky.); Capt. Edward Williamson, narrative report, in Eighth US Army, "Ambush of Battery C," 3.

51. Spurr, *Enter the Dragon,* 137–38; "War Diary, 8th Cavalry Regiment" (Record Group 407, Nov. 1, 1950).

52. Appleman, *South to the Naktong,* 696–99.

53. Williamson, narrative report, 4–5.

54. Ibid.; Appleman, *South to the Naktong,* 697.

55. Appleman, *South to the Naktong,* 698–99; Williamson, narrative report, 5–6; memorandum, "Operations of the 8th Cavalry Regiment, 1st Cavalry Division on 1–2 November 1950 in the vicinity of Unsan, Korea," Nov. 15, 1950 (Record Group 319, Box 738). In the memorandum, Edson describes the cargo truck following a tank and then jackknifing, while the tank made its way through the roadblock. Appleman's account relies on several sources, including correspondence with Edson after the war.

56. Appleman, *South to the Naktong,* 701; Armstrong, *1st Cavalry Division and Their 8th Engineers in Korea,* 102.

57. Spurr, *Enter the Dragon,* 143–44.

58. Halberstam, *Coldest Winter,* 28–29.

59. Maj. Filmore McAbee, letter to Lt. Col. Roy Appleman, Feb. 8, 1957 (Record Group 319, Box 738); McAbee interview, May 2002.

60. McAbee letter; McAbee interview; Moriarty letter.

61. Appleman, *South to the Naktong,* 701.

62. Moriarty letter. Although Moriarty's letter describes a series of heroic struggles, other versions are less charitable. McAbee later felt that Moriarty should have stayed with the battalion. In Frank Armstrong's oral history of the Eighth Engineers, Lt. George Skanske described meeting a major en route to Ipsok who "took command and also credit for leading us out."

63. Appleman, *South to the Naktong,* 703; Capt. Walter Mayo, letter to Lt. Col. Roy Appleman, Jan. 15, 1958 (Record Group 319, Box 746).

64. Maher, *Shepherd in Combat Boots,* 16.

65. Appleman, *South to the Naktong,* 703.

66. Peterson interview.

67. Appleman, *South to the Naktong,* 703.

68. Ibid, 703–705; Maher, *Shepherd in Combat Boots,* 17–18; McAbee interview; Tonne, *Story of Chaplain Kapaun,* 168–69. In a postwar letter to Father Tonne, Capt. Walt Mayo described Kapaun's exploits at Unsan and in captivity.

69. Appleman, *South to the Naktong,* 704.

70. Ibid.

71. Ibid., 705; Gay letter, 5.

72. Appleman, *South to the Naktong,* 705.

73. Ibid., 706; Armstrong, *1st Cavalry Division and Their 8th Engineers in Korea,* 102; Maher, *Shepherd in Combat Boots,* 18–19.

74. Appleman, *South to the Naktong,* 706; Maher, *Shepherd in Combat Boots,* 18–19; Wenzl, "Miracle of Father Kapaun."

75. Halberstam, *Coldest Winter,* 37–38.

76. Ibid., 38; Appleman, *South to the Naktong,* 706.

77. Halberstam, *Coldest Winter,* 39; Peterson interview.

78. Halberstam, *Coldest Winter,* 39; Mayo letter to Appleman, 2; Appleman, *South to the Naktong,* 706.

79. Appleman, *South to the Naktong,* 707; Richardson, *Valleys of Death,* 188–95.

80. Peterson interview.

81. Capt. Clarence Anderson, sworn affidavit, San Francisco, Calif., Dec. 7, 1953 (Record Group 153, Entry 183, Box 1), 1; Appleman, *South to the Naktong,* 707–708.

82. Millett, *War for Korea, 1950–1951,* 304.

83. Alexander, *Korea,* 283–86.

84. Ibid., 285–86.

Chapter 5

1. Biderman, *March to Calumny,* 115–18; Arias, sworn statement, Fort MacArthur, Calif., Jan. 8, 1954 (Record Group 153, Entry 183, Box 1), 1.

2. Knox, *Korean War, an Oral History,* 437.

3. Maher, *Shepherd in Combat Boots,* 113.

4. Dowe, summary of information, Arlington, Va., Mar. 16, 1954 (Record Group 153, Box 2), 4.

5. Lech, *Broken Soldiers,* 36. Lech cites the transcript of the court martial of Cpl. Claude Batchelor.

6. Funchess, *Korea P.O.W.,* 20–24.

7. Carlson, *Remembered Prisoners,* 184; Maher, *Shepherd in Combat Boots,* 110.

8. Headquarters, Department of the Army, *US Prisoners of War in the Korean Operation,* 27.

9. Capt. Clarence Anderson, sworn affidavit, San Francisco, Calif., Dec. 7, 1953 (Record Group 153, Entry 183, Box 1), 1; Appleman, *South to the Naktong,* 705–707. Ormond refused treatment until all of the other wounded men had been cared for. He was reportedly buried along the road north of Unsan.

10. Maher, *Shepherd in Combat Boots,* 111–15; Dowe, *Father Kapaun,* 7.

11. Maher, *Shepherd in Combat Boots,* 113; Anderson affidavit, 2; Mayo affidavit, 1; Maj. Filmore McAbee, sworn affidavit, Worcester, Mass., Nov. 18, 1953 (Record Group 153, Entry 183, Box 1), 2.

12. Lech, *Broken Soldiers,* 42–43.

13. Ibid.

14. Goulden, *Korea,* 297; Li, *History of the Modern Chinese Army,* 86. See also Whiting, *China Crosses the Yalu,* 118, and Stueck, *Rethinking the Korean War,* 112.

15. Appleman, *South to the Naktong,* 719; Halberstam, *Coldest Winter,* 363.

16. Millett, *War for Korea, 1950–1951,* 295.

17. Ibid.; Spurr, *Enter the Dragon,* 170–71.

18. Halberstam, *Coldest Winter,* 388.

19. Ibid., 381–82; Alexander, *Korea,* 287–88; Manchester, *American Caesar,* 601; Acheson, *Korean War,* 64.

20. Alexander, *Korea,* 289.

21. Acheson, *Korean War,* 64–65.

22. Manchester, *American Caesar,* 602–603.

23. Alexander, *Korea,* 290.

24. Halberstam, *Coldest Winter,* 384–86.

25. Acheson, *Korean War,* 65.

26. Blair, *Forgotten War,* 398; Alexander, *Korea,* 291.

27. Blair, *Forgotten War,* 398–89.

28. Goulden, *Korea,* 317.

29. Central Intelligence Agency, *National Intelligence Estimate Number 2,* i.

30. Goulden, *Korea,* 325–26.

31. Ibid., 335.

32. Appleman, *South to the Naktong,* 732.

33. Ibid., 735–38.

34. Appleman, *Disaster in Korea,* 37–40.

35. Ibid., 43.

36. Goulden, *Korea,* 329–30; Halberstam, *Coldest Winter,* 389.

37. Goulden, *Korea,* 329.

38. Armstrong, *1st Cavalry Division and Their 8th Engineers in Korea,* 107.

39. Halberstam, *Coldest Winter,* 401–402.

40. Appleman, *South to the Naktong,* 720.

41. Appleman, *Disaster in Korea,* 56; Goulden, *Korea,* 323.

42. Fehrenbach, *This Kind of War,* 300–301.

43. Knox, *Korean War, an Oral History,* 464.

44. Hastings, *Korean War,* 140.

45. Paul Roach, letter to the author, May 12, 2009.

46. Ibid.; Marshall, *River and the Gauntlet,* 54–55.

47. Appleman, *Disaster in Korea,* 50–55.

48. Li, Millett, and Yu, *Mao's Generals Remember Korea,* 16.

49. Roach letter; Marshall, *River and the Gauntlet,* 54; Blair, *Forgotten War,* 439.

50. Roach letter; Marshall, *River and the Gauntlet,* 54–55.

51. Roach letter; Marshall, *River and the Gauntlet,* 55.

52. Roach letter.

53. Marshall, *River and the Gauntlet,* 60–62.

54. Ibid., 78–79; Fehrenbach, *This Kind of War,* 308; Blair, *Forgotten War,* 440.

55. Alexander, *Korea,* 313.

56. Ibid.

57. Blair, *Forgotten War,* 442–43.

58. Esensten interview.

59. Ibid.; Appleman, *Disaster in Korea,* 122. After the war, Esensten spent several years trying to determine the fate of the other men in the convoy, with no success.

60. Blair, *Forgotten War,* 452; Alexander, *Korea,* 314–15.

61. Alexander, *Korea,* 314–16; Halberstam, *Coldest Winter,* 444–46.

62. Alexander, *Korea,* 316–17.

63. Ibid., 318.

64. Ibid.; Halberstam, *Coldest Winter,* 445–46.

Chapter 6

1. Appleman, *South to the Naktong,* 768; Crocker, "Chinese Intervention in the Korean War," 67.

2. Goulden, *Korea,* 345.

3. Appleman, *Escaping the Trap,* 3.

4. Millett, *War for Korea, 1950–1951,* 290, 302–303.

5. Halberstam, *Coldest Winter,* 435.

6. Montross and Canzona, *Chosin Reservoir Campaign,* 121; Appleman, *Escaping the Trap,* 7.

7. Montross and Canzona, *Chosin Reservoir Campaign,* 124, 131.

8. Ibid., 131, 136–37; Appleman, *Escaping the Trap,* 42, 209; Alexander, *Korea,* 308.

9. Montross and Canzona, *Chosin Reservoir Campaign,* 133–34. After the war, Almond politely acknowledged Smith's skepticism but emphasized the added logistical capability of aerial supply and evacuation created by the construction of the Hagaru airfield.

10. Ibid., 132–33.

11. Ibid.; Toland, *In Mortal Combat,* 273–74.

12. Halberstam, *Coldest Winter,* 437–38; Blair, *Forgotten War,* 456. Halberstam blames Almond for much of what went wrong during the campaign, and Blair argues that Almond failed in his duty to question MacArthur's orders. Historian T. R. Fehrenbach's assessment is more charitable: "Almond was neither a fool nor an ass—he had orders from Tokyo to move to the Yalu—and he intended to comply, whatever his own doubts" (*This Kind of War,* 361).

13. Fehrenbach, *This Kind of War,* 353–54; Appleman, *Escaping the Trap,* 10.

14. Blair, *Forgotten War,* 456–57.

15. Ibid., 458; Montross and Canzona, *Chosin Reservoir Campaign,* 154.

16. Montross and Canzona, *Chosin Reservoir Campaign,* 157. The authors note that had the marines achieved their second objective on November 27, these forces would have entered a "hopeless entrapment."

17. Fehrenbach, *This Kind of War,* 358–59; Blair, *Forgotten War,* 458; Appleman, *Escaping the Trap,* 156; Montross and Canzona, *Chosin Reservoir Campaign,* 197.

18. MacDonald, *Problems,* 25–30; Alexander, *Korea,* 346–47.

19. Alexander, *Korea,* 348; Knox, *Korean War, an Oral History,* 492–99.

20. MacDonald, *Problems,* 27–29; Knox, *Korean War, an Oral History,* 500–502.

21. Knox, *Korean War, an Oral History,* 504–13; Montross and Canzona, *Chosin Reservoir Campaign,* 201.

22. Montross and Canzona, *Chosin Reservoir Campaign,* 205; Appleman, *East of Chosin,* 106–107. MacLean's anticipated reinforcement was the 2nd Battalion, 31st Infantry, which was delayed en route by the Chinese interdiction of the MSR.

23. Montross and Canzona, *Chosin Reservoir Campaign,* 190–97; Appleman, *Escaping the Trap,* 161–62. An ROK lieutenant and a Korean agent, both attached to the 3rd Battalion, 1st Marine Regiment, conducted a remarkable reconnaissance of enemy positions on November 27 and 28 and accurately predicted the time and location of the Chinese attacks.

24. Montross and Canzona, *Chosin Reservoir Campaign,* 222; Camp, "Korea 1950," 15–16; Appleman, *Escaping the Trap,* 163.

25. Camp, "Korea 1950," 16.

26. Ibid.; Montross and Canzona, *Chosin Reservoir Campaign,* 226.

27. Camp, "Korea 1950," 17; Hastings, *Korean War,* 150.

28. Montross and Canzona, *Chosin Reservoir Campaign,* 229; Camp, "Korea 1950," 17.

29. Montross and Canzona, *Chosin Reservoir Campaign,* 229–35.

30. MacDonald, *Problems,* 37–38; Daugherty, *Train Wreckers and Ghost Killers,* 13–14.

31. Appleman, *Escaping the Trap,* 197–98; Montross and Canzona, *Chosin Reservoir Campaign,* 232; Mossman, *Ebb and Flow,* 102–103.

32. Reid interview; Appleman, *South to the Naktong,* 198; Montross and Canzona, *Chosin Reservoir Campaign,* 232–33.

33. MacDonald, *Problems,* 39. Nash later received the Silver Star for this action.

34. Reid interview; Montross and Canzona, *Chosin Reservoir Campaign,* 233.

35. Reid interview; Appleman, *Escaping the Trap,* 198–99.

36. Reid interview; MacDonald, *Problems,* 40.

37. Appleman, *Escaping the Trap,* 199.

38. Ibid., 199–200; Montross and Canzona, *Chosin Reservoir Campaign,* 234.

39. MacDonald, *Problems,* 40–41.

40. Reid interview; Messman, sworn affidavit (Record Group 153, Box 4); McLaughlin, statement (Record Group 153, Box 4).

41. Appleman, *Escaping the Trap,* 113–14; Appleman, *East of Chosin,* 132–42. According to fellow prisoners, McLean died a few days later while marching north to a prison camp. When Almond returned from the Tokyo conference, he placed Faith's task force under the control of the 1st Marine Division and ordered Smith to send a regiment from Yudam-ni to rescue it. This order proved impossible to execute and suggested Almond's continuing ignorance of the situation at the reservoir.

42. Millett, *War for Korea, 1950–1951,* 240; Alexander, *Korea,* 332; Blair, *Forgotten War,* 511–13; Appleman, *Escaping the Trap,* 127–28. The source of the withdrawal order to the 31st Tank Company would later inspire controversy and hard feelings. Quoting remarks by Lt. Col. William McCaffrey, Appleman suggests that the author was probably the 7th Division commander, Maj. Gen. Dave Barr.

43. Montross and Canzona, *Chosin Reservoir Campaign,* 204–208; Appleman, *East of Chosin,* 187.

44. Appleman, *Escaping the Trap,* 131; Blair, *Forgotten War,* 513.

45. Blair, *Forgotten War,* 517; Appleman, *East of Chosin,* 217–32.

46. Blair, *Forgotten War,* 517–21.

47. Ibid., 521; Appleman, *East of Chosin,* 278–92; Millett, *War for Korea, 1950–1951,* 240.

48. Alexander, *Korea,* 349–50; McCarthy, "Fox Hill," 20–23.

49. McCarthy, "Fox Hill;" Alexander, *Korea,* 350–52.

50. MacDonald, *Problems,* 51; Appleman, *Escaping the Trap,* 208–209.

51. Alexander, *Korea,* 355.

52. Ibid., 362–65.

53. Hastings, *Korean War,* 163–64; Stewart, *Staff Operations,* 30, 45–48.

54. Appleman, *Escaping the Trap,* 348–53.

55. Ibid., 347; MacDonald, *Problems,* 59.

56. Stewart, *Staff Operations,* 11.

Chapter 7

1. Hastings, *Korean War,* 166–67.

2. Blair, *Forgotten War,* 523–34; Goulden, *Korea,* 392–95.

3. Headquarters, Department of the Army, *US Prisoners of War in the Korean Operation,* 91–92, 101. According to US Army statistics, 2,099 American soldiers were captured in

November 1950, the highest monthly total of the war. An additional 1,044 soldiers were captured in December.

4. Carlson, *Remembered Prisoners,* 107–19; Lech, *Broken Soldiers,* 37–48.

5. British Ministry of Defence, *Treatment of British Prisoners,* 34.

6. Esensten interview.

7. Shadish, *When Hell Froze Over,* 27.

8. Carlson, *Remembered Prisoners,* 109–10; Richardson, *Valleys of Death,* 209–16; Headquarters, Department of the Army, *US Prisoners of War in the Korean Operation,* 441–44.

9. Pease, *Psywar,* 148–49; Department of the Army, Pamphlet 30–101, *Communist Interrogation, Indoctrination, and Exploitation of Prisoners of War,* 12–22.

10. Shadish, *When Hell Froze Over,* 26–28; Carlson, *Remembered Prisoners,* 110–16. In postwar debriefings by US Army investigators, several officers recalled this phenomenon of marching in circles. For example, Capt. Sidney Esensten reported marching back and forth "with no general direction" in the first days after his capture (Esensten affidavit, 1).

11. Lech, *Broken Soldiers,* 42; Maj. David MacGhee, USAF, testimony at the court martial of Lt. Col. Henry Fleming, Fort Sheridan, Ill., August 1954, 129.

12. Lech, *Broken Soldiers,* 42–43; Anderson affidavit, 2; McAbee affidavit, 1; Esensten interview. The estimated number of deaths varies according to different sources. Maj. Filmore McAbee reported 18 deaths at the Valley; Anderson estimated 20 deaths, and Esensten put the number at 26.

13. Lech, *Broken Soldiers,* 42–43; Carlson, *Remembered Prisoners,* 114–16; Esensten, address to the Korean War Conference, Smithsonian Institute, Washington, D.C., Oct. 30, 2000.

14. Maher, *Shepherd in Combat Boots,* 119–21.

15. Lech, *Broken Soldiers,* 43–45; Carlson, *Remembered Prisoners,* 114.

16. Capt. George Deakin, US Army, testimony at Fleming court martial, 870–80; Lt. Col. Paul Liles, US Army, testimony at Fleming court martial, 1218–36.

17. Lech, *Broken Soldiers,* 47; Deakin, testimony at Fleming court martial, 870–80; Liles, testimony at Fleming court martial, 1218–36. According to Maj. David McGhee, guards at Sombakol prohibited cooking before 1500 hours, ostensibly to prevent aerial detection of the wood smoke. The officers deliberately set one watch ahead by several hours to "kitchen time" in order to deceive the guards (Fleming court martial, 52–53).

18. Review of the staff judge advocate, trial by general court martial of Lt. Col. Harry Fleming, Headquarters, Fifth Army, Chicago, Ill., Nov. 15, 1954, 12–13.

19. MacGhee testimony at Fleming court martial, 50–51.

20. 1st Lt. Phil Peterson, sworn statement, court martial of Lt. Col. Henry Fleming, Fort Sheridan, Ill., August 1954; Dowe, summary of information (Record Group 153, Box 2), 6; Esensten interview.

21. O'Brien interview.

22. Headquarters, Department of the Army, *US Prisoners of War in the Korean Operation,* 93; Chinnery, *Korean Atrocity!* 105.

23. Roach affidavit, 1; Fedenets, sworn affidavit (Record Group 153, Box 3), 3.

24. Shadish, *When Hell Froze Over,* 25–29.

25. Ibid., 29–30; Lt. Col. Robert Abbott, US Army, testimony, Transcript of Hearings, US Senate Subcommittee on Korean War Atrocities, Dec. 4, 1953, 186.

26. Office of the Surgeon General, "Report of Conference," 13; Roach interview; Fedenets affidavit, 2–3.

27. Shadish, *When Hell Froze Over,* 31; Lech, *Broken Soldiers,* 40; Abbott testimony, 186;

Carlson, *Remembered Prisoners,* 110; Chinnery, *Korean Atrocity!* 109; Knox, *Korean War, Uncertain Victory,* 338.

28. Shadish, *When Hell Froze Over,* 32–33; Chinnery, *Korean Atrocity!* 108–10. In addition to Shadish and Lam, three other American doctors were imprisoned at Death Valley: Maj. Burt Coers, Capt. Peter Kubinek, and Capt. Edwin Ecklund. All three died of illnesses contracted while marching to the camp.

29. Liles testimony, Fleming court martial, 1227–28; O'Brien interview.

30. Shadish, *When Hell Froze Over,* 33–39.

31. Ibid.; Abbott testimony, 188.

32. Shadish, *When Hell Froze Over,* 39; Fehrenbach, *This Kind of War,* 469. Fehrenbach's account of Death Valley relies heavily on the narrative of Sgt. Charles Schlichter, a 9th Regiment medic. In an effort to embarrass the two doctors, the Chinese appointed Schlichter to run the hospital at Death Valley. After repatriation, both Shadish and Lam praised the efforts of Schlichter and other medics who cared for the sick and wounded.

33. Chapman interview; MacDonald, *Problems,* 62–63.

34. MacDonald, *Problems,* 62–63; Chapman, "Cherokee Warrior," 37. Prisoners at Kanggye were organized into two companies, each consisting of several squads of ten to fifteen prisoners.

35. MacDonald, *Problems,* 66–67; Chapman, "Cherokee Warrior," 38; Lech, *Broken Soldiers,* 81.

36. MacDonald, *Problems,* 66–67; McLaughlin, statement (Record Group 153, Box 4), 3; Sgt. Wendell Treffery, US Army, testimony, Transcript of Hearings, US Senate Subcommittee on Korean War Atrocities, Dec. 3, 1953, 87. Though suffering from multiple wounds, Jack Chapman recalled no medical personnel and received no medical aid at Camp Ten.

37. Lech, *Broken Soldiers,* 82; Carlson, *Remembered Prisoners,* 184.

38. Chapman, "Cherokee Warrior," 35; DeLong, personal memoir.

39. Chapman, "Cherokee Warrior," 35; Lech, *Broken Soldiers,* 82–83; Carlson, *Remembered Prisoners,* 184–45.

40. Harold G. Wolff, MD, testimony before the US Senate, 84th Congress, "Hearings on Communist Interrogation, Indoctrination, and Exploitation of American Military and Civilian Prisoners," 23.

41. Lech, *Broken Soldiers,* 84; Chapman, "Cherokee Warrior," 39; MacDonald, *Problems,* 66–67, 74–75.

42. MacDonald, *Problems,* 66.

43. Ibid., 37; Pettit, sworn statement (Record Group 153, Box 4), 3; Lech, *Broken Soldiers,* 84–85.

44. Lech, *Broken Soldiers,* 84–85; Chapman, "Cherokee Warrior," 40; MacDonald, *Problems,* 68–69. According to MacDonald, the Chinese published six issues and thirty articles: "By their own admission the Chinese were able to secure contributions of articles from only a small percentage of the prisoners, though any contributions represented a victory for the Communists."

45. MacDonald, *Problems,* 68–69; Messman, sworn affidavit (Record Group 153, Box 4), 2.

46. Carlson, *Remembered Prisoners,* 186–87. In his interview with Lewis Carlson, Hardage states that 279 prisoners signed the appeal, and only those too sick or wounded to attend the rally were exempt.

47. British Ministry of Defence, *Treatment of British Prisoners,* 11; MacDonald, *Problems,* 71–72; Chapman, "Cherokee Warrior," 49.

48. MacDonald, *Problems,* 75; Carlson, *Remembered Prisoners,* 187; Lech, *Broken Soldiers,* 86.

49. Headquarters, Department of the Army, *US Prisoners of War in the Korean Operation,* 95–97; Chinnery, *Korean Atrocity!* 112.

50. Esensten interview.

51. Capt. Sidney Esensten, US Army, summary of captivity, undated (copy furnished to the author by Doctor Esensten in 2001), 16–21; Lech, *Broken Soldiers,* 68; Abbott testimony, 189.

52. Funchess, *Korea P.O.W.,* 59–60; Hastings, *Korean War,* 292.

53. McAbee interview.

54. Esensten summary, 19.

55. Ibid.

56. Carlson, *Remembered Prisoners,* 139; Tonne, *Story of Chaplain Kapaun,* 188–89.

57. Tonne, *Story of Chaplain Kapaun,* 188–89; Funchess, *Korea P.O.W.,* 67; Lech, *Broken Soldiers,* 68.

58. Lech, *Broken Soldiers,* 68; Esensten summary, 19; Surgeon General's Conference, 24.

59. Esensten summary, 20.

60. Esensten interview; Doctor Sid Esensten, speech at the Smithsonian Institute Conference on the Korean War, Washington, D.C., Oct. 23, 2000 (copy provided to the author courtesy of Dr. Esensten); Funchess, *Korea P.O.W.,* 59–60; Segal, "Observations on Prisoners of War."

61. Esensten interview; Esensten speech, POW Reunion, Tucson, Ariz., Sept. 13, 2002 (copy furnished to the author courtesy of Doctor Esensten).

62. Esensten interview; Esensten affidavit, 3–4; Shadish, *When Hell Froze Over,* 44–45. In his affidavit, Doctor Esensten reported that "a fairly accurate census of death was kept during these first few months, and from January 18 until 8 March 1951 there were 375 deaths." When Shadish and Lam arrived, Doctor Ferrie was also exiled to the officers' compound, and Shadish assumed duties as the sole American doctor in the enlisted compound.

63. Shadish, *When Hell Froze Over,* 45; Headquarters, Department of the Army, *US Prisoners of War in the Korean Operation,* 221.

Chapter 8

1. Mossman, 149; "The Nation: Defeat"; MacDonald, *Korea,* 64–67.

2. Alexander, *Korea,* 375–76.

3. Toland, *In Mortal Combat,* 371–76.

4. Manchester, *American Caesar,* 619; Toland, *In Mortal Combat,* 380–81; Millett, *They Came from the North,* 360.

5. Alexander, *Korea,* 384–85; Toland, *In Mortal Combat,* 386.

6. Blair, *Forgotten War,* 624–26.

7. MacDonald, *Korea,* 90; Blair, *Forgotten War,* 580–87; Manchester, *American Caesar,* 625. Manchester argued that Truman's pursuit of a "limited war" was equally problematic, and cost him the White House in 1952.

8. Blair, *Forgotten War,* 688–89; Alexander, *Korea,* 392–93.

9. Millett, *They Came from the North,* 406–409; Blair, *Forgotten War,* 696–708. Crombez had insisted that an infantry company ride on his tanks but twice left groups of dismounted infantry behind. After reaching Chipyong-ni, he refused to go back and rescue these men.

10. Millett, *They Came from the North,* 411–13.

11. Ibid., 413–16; Alexander, *Korea,* 399–402.

12. Lech, *Broken Soldiers,* 49–50; Carlson, *Remembered Prisoners,* 116–17; O'Dowd, sworn affidavit (Record Group 153, Box 4), 6.

13. Carlson, *Remembered Prisoners,* 117–18; Lech, *Broken Soldiers,* 48–51; Memorandum, Review of the Staff Judge Advocate, trial by court martial of Pfc. Rothwell B. Floyd, Fort Leavenworth, Kans., May 27, 1954; O'Dowd affidavit, 6–7. The estimate of 150 deaths is based on Lieutenant O'Dowd's affidavit. Lech writes that 287 men died at the Bean Camp, based on testimony at Floyd's court martial.

14. Lech, *Broken Soldiers,* 51–57; Staff Judge Advocate review of Floyd court martial, 8–10, 26. In 1954, an army court martial convicted Floyd on several charges and sentenced him to forty years of hard labor. This sentence was later reduced to ten years.

15. O'Dowd, 7; Lech, *Broken Soldiers,* 56–57.

16. Lech, *Broken Soldiers,* 57–60.

17. Ibid., 60–61; Staff Judge Advocate Review of Floyd court martial, 8; Shirey, debriefing (Record Group 153, Box 5), 1–7; Hankey, sworn statement, undated (available at British National Archives, Kew, Richmond, UK, Defense Office 35/5848).

18. McLaughlin affidavit, 3; Lloyd, sworn statement (Record Group 153, Box 3); MacDonald, *Problems,* 75; Chapman, "Cherokee Warrior," 63.

19. MacDonald, *Problems,* 78; Chapman, "Cherokee Warrior," 51, 58.

20. MacDonald, *Problems,* 79–80; Chapman, "Cherokee Warrior," 49.

21. MacDonald, *Problems,* 82–85; Chapman, "Cherokee Warrior," 59; Lech, *Broken Soldiers,* 86; Headquarters, Department of the Army, *US Prisoners of War in the Korean Operation,* 217. The released US Army corporal, a Nisei translator named Sam Shimamura, had been attached to the 1st Marine Division at the Chosin Reservoir, and the Chinese thus assumed he was a US Marine.

22. MacDonald, *Problems,* 83; Chapman, "Cherokee Warrior," 53–68.

23. Esensten interview; Reid interview.

24. Esensten interview; Shadish, *When Hell Froze Over,* 43–44, 131–37; *Free Health Encyclopedia,* s.v. beriberi.

25. Shadish, *When Hell Froze Over,* 44–45.

26. Tonne, *Story of Chaplain Kapaun,* 187–88; Maher, *Shepherd in Combat Boots,* 128–31.

27. Tonne, *Story of Chaplain Kapaun,* 170–73; Maher, *Shepherd in Combat Boots,* 143–46; Dowe, *Father Kapaun,* 18–19; Carlson, *Remembered Prisoners,* 145–46.

28. Maher, *Shepherd in Combat Boots,* 143–47; Dowe, *Father Kapaun,* 18–19.

29. Lech, *Broken Soldiers,* 92–93; Funchess, *Korea P.O.W.,* 66.

30. Esensten interview; Edwards interview by Brown.

31. Lech, *Broken Soldiers,* 91–94; Funchess, *Korea P.O.W.,* 66.

32. Lech, *Broken Soldiers,* 91–96.

33. Paul Roach, email correspondence with the author, Aug. 25, 2009.

34. Bostwick affidavit, 3; O'Dowd affidavit, 9; Dowe, summary of information (Record Group 153, Box 2), 9; McLaughlin statement, 4. After repatriation, the debriefers typically asked the POWs to describe any atrocities they had seen or heard about. Many specifically mentioned Hume's brutal punishment.

35. Cordero affidavit, 3–4; Deakin statement, 5.

36. McAbee interview; McAbee affidavit, 4–5.

37. McLaughlin affidavit; McAbee affidavit; McAbee interview.

38. Tonne, *Story of Chaplain Kapaun,* 196–97; Maher, *Shepherd in Combat Boots,* 137, 148–50.

39. Tonne, *Story of Chaplain Kapaun,* 198–99.

40. Manchester, *American Caesar,* 613–15; Alexander, *Korea,* 374.

41. Blair, *Forgotten War,* 743–44.

42. Manchester, *American Caesar,* 634; Acheson, *Korean War,* 101; Halberstam, *Coldest Winter,* 595–99; MacDonald, *Korea,* 92. MacDonald further observed that the cease-fire initiative was "an attempt to fulfil (*sic*) the demands of both international and domestic politics."

43. Blair, *Forgotten War,* 767–69.

44. McCullough, "Truman Fires MacArthur," 92–93; Blair, *Forgotten War,* 769–70.

45. Pearlman, *Truman and MacArthur,* 178–80.

46. Blair, *Forgotten War,* 760, 786; Manchester, *American Caesar,* 641–42; Millett, *War for Korea, 1950–1951,* 421.

47. Blair, *Forgotten War,* 787.

48. Manchester, *American Caesar,* 643–44.

49. Ibid., 652–59; McCullough, "Truman Fires MacArthur," 98–99; Halberstam, *Coldest Winter,* 609.

50. Goulden, *Korea,* 513–40; Manchester, *American Caesar,* 664–75.

51. Halberstam, *Coldest Winter,* 617–22; McCullough, "Truman Fires MacArthur," 102; Goulden, *Korea,* 546–47.

52. Blair, *Forgotten War,* 804–807; Alexander, *Korea,* 402–404.

53. Alexander, *Korea,* 418–20; Blair, *Forgotten War,* 828.

54. Alexander, *Korea,* 420–22; Toland, *In Mortal Combat,* 440–47; Blair, *Forgotten War,* 823–25, 855.

55. Alexander, *Korea,* 423; Blair, *Forgotten War,* 874–78.

56. Blair, *Forgotten War,* 880–82.

57. Ibid., 888–91, 900n; Alexander, *Korea,* 423–25.

58. Alexander, *Korea,* 426–33.

59. Funchess, *Korea P.O.W.,* 69–70; Headquarters, Department of the Army, *US Prisoners of War in the Korean Operation,* 103; Esensten summary, 31.

60. Esensten summary, 32–33.

61. Funchess, *Korea P.O.W.,* 75; Esensten summary, 36.

62. Maher, *Shepherd in Combat Boots,* 149–50; Esensten interview; Dowe, *Father Kapaun,* 20–21.

63. Dowe, *Father Kapaun,* 20–21; Maher, *Shepherd in Combat Boots,* 151; Esensten interview.

64. Maher, *Shepherd in Combat Boots,* 151–53; Dowe, *Father Kapaun,* 21.

65. Dowe, *Father Kapaun,* 21–22; Maher, *Shepherd in Combat Boots,* 153–54.

66. Maher, *Shepherd in Combat Boots,* 154–55; Hotze interview. In September 2009, Secretary of the Army Peter Geren endorsed the nomination of Emil Kapaun for the Congressional Medal of Honor.

Chapter 9

1. Office of Special Investigations, *USAF Prisoners of War in Korea,* 1.

2. Chandler, *General Otto P. Weyland, USAF,* 27.

3. Showalter, "First Jet War," 124–36; Blair, *Beyond Courage,* 5.

4. Crane, *American Airpower Strategy,* 27; Manchester, *American Caesar,* 592.

5. Showalter, "First Jet War," 133–34; Crane, *American Airpower Strategy,* 112.

6. Hastings, *Korean War,* 267; Showalter, "First Jet War," 127; Evanhoe, *Dark Moon,* 48–

49. Evanhoe describes an early special-operations mission to destroy a rail tunnel near Wonsan. The mission succeeded, but within two days a temporary track had been built around the demolished tunnel.

7. Crane, *American Airpower Strategy,* 24–26; MacDonald, *Problems,* 229–30. Pentagon planners were primarily concerned about a possible Soviet attack in Europe, but Iran and Turkey were also potential hot spots.

8. Oldewage interview.

9. Hedlund interview.

10. Ibid.

11. Doerty interview.

12. Ibid.

13. Chandler, *General Otto P. Weyland, USAF,* 27–28; Appleman, *South to the Naktong,* 376. In August 1950 the Fifth Air Force sent more tactical air control parties to US Army and ROK Army units fighting along the Pusan Perimeter. These parties significantly improved the coordination of close air support by using jeep-mounted radios to speak directly with the pilots. The system was further improved by the deployment of airborne air controllers, or "Mosquitoes."

14. Mossman, *Effectiveness of Air Interdiction,* 1–8; Thompson, "Air War over Korea," 21.

15. Thompson, "Air War over Korea," 10–14.

16. Hastings, *Korean War,* 255; Thompson, "Air War over Korea," 18–20.

17. Hedlund interview; Chandler, *General Otto P. Weyland, USAF,* 38.

18. Blair, *Beyond Courage,* 4; Marion, *That Others May Live,* v, 51.

19. RG 153, Entry 183, Box 1, Statement of Maj. Jessee V. Booker, USMC, 1.

20. Ibid.; MacDonald, *Problems,* 1. Booker also survived the deadly winter of 1950–1951 and was eventually transferred to Camp Two, along with most of the other officers in captivity. He was repatriated in September 1953 as part of Operation Big Switch.

21. Office of Special Investigations, *USAF Prisoners of War in Korea,* 2–4.

22. Crane, *American Airpower Strategy,* 49; "War Diary, 8th Cavalry Regiment" (Record Group 407, entry at 011550, November 1950); Zhang, *Red Wings over the Yalu,* 78.

23. Zhang, *Red Wings over the Yalu,* 84–88; O'Neill, "Soviet Involvement."

24. O'Neill, "Soviet Involvement"; Futrell, *United States Air Force in Korea,* 217–19; Zhang, *Red Wings over the Yalu,* 84–85.

25. Thompson, "Air War over Korea," 29; Showalter, "First Jet War," 128–30.

26. O'Neill, "Soviet Involvement."

27. Knox, *Korean War, Uncertain Victory,* 237; Dixon interview; Central Intelligence Agency, National Intelligence Estimate, "Communist Capabilities," 4; O'Neill, "Soviet Involvement."

28. O'Neill, "Soviet Involvement"; *Steadfast and Courageous,* 30–31; MacDonald, *Problems,* 103.

29. Hedlund interview; Lindner, "Scotch and Soda II." Lindner was the navigator/bombardier on Hedlund's aircraft during this particular mission.

30. Lindner, "Scotch and Soda II."

31. Office of Special Investigations, *USAF Prisoners of War in Korea,* 8.

32. Headquarters, Department of the Army, *US Prisoners of War in the Korean Operation,* 164–76. The 1954 US Army report also speculates that the booklets might have been designed to impress prisoners with the amount of information the Chinese already possessed regarding the identity and disposition of the UN forces.

33. Ibid., 147–51.

34. Ibid., 198–99.

35. Tiger Survivor Roster, copy furnished to the author by Cms. (Ret.) Tim Casey, Tiger Survivor group historian, April 2009.

36. Lech, *Broken Soldiers,* 116.

37. MacDonald, *Problems,* 104.

38. Hedlund interview.

39. Ibid.

40. Ibid.

41. Ibid.

42. Ibid.

43. Ibid. Hedlund, sworn affidavit (Record Group 153, Entry 183, Box 3), 2.

44. Hedlund, sworn affidavit (Record Group 153, Entry 183, Box 3), 2.

45. Hedlund interview.

46. MacGhee, summary of debriefing (Record Group 153, Box 2). MacGhee was a crew member on the first B-29 shot down by a MiG over North Korea, which occurred on Nov. 10, 1950. He was interned at several camps and interrogation centers, including Sombakol, Camp Five, and later Camp Two.

47. Hedlund affidavit, 6.

48. Ibid., 7; O'Brien interview.

49. Marion, *That Others May Live,* 9–18, 51. During the course of the war, the USAF's 3rd Air Rescue Squadron saved 997 UN personnel from behind enemy lines, including 170 air force pilots.

50. Hedlund interview; Chinnery, *Korean Atrocity!* 151. Chinnery quotes the postwar testimony of US Air Force Capt. Zachary Dean, who was held with Gibbon at Pak's Palace.

51. Hedlund interview; British Ministry of Defence, *Treatment of British Prisoners,* 41; Chinnery, *Korean Atrocity!* 151–52. Chinnery's version is probably based on Eighth US Army war crimes files. After the war, Captain Gibbon was awarded the George Medal for bravery, based on his fearless resistance to enemy torture.

52. Doerty interview.

53. Ibid.

54. Ibid.

55. Ibid.

56. Ibid.; Office of Special Investigations, *USAF Prisoners of War in Korea,* 6. After the war, the US Air Force determined that a policy of limiting answers to name, rank, and serial number was impractical in the face of determined interrogators who disregarded the Geneva Conventions. During the Pentagon's formulation of the Code of Conduct, however, the US Air Force considerations were overruled by the concerns of other services.

57. Doerty interview.

58. Ibid.; O'Brien interview. Prisoners captured later in the war also reported being interrogated by a Major Pak at the brickyard.

59. Crane, *American Airpower Strategy,* 21, 27, 69, 94; Cantwell, *Citizen Airmen,* 87–92. By war's end, nearly 193,000 air force reservists and National Air Guardsmen would be recalled to active duty.

60. Oldewage interview; King interview.

61. King interview.

62. Ibid.; Oldewage interview; Futrell, *United States Air Force in Korea,* 296; *Steadfast and Courageous,* 9.

63. Futrell, *United States Air Force in Korea,* 298. The strung-out B-29 formations forced their F-84 escorts to spread their defensive screen across more airspace, and the faster MiGs

flew through those gaps with ease. The B-29s flew at high altitude to avoid the flak, which in turn diminished the accuracy of their bombing.

64. Ibid.; Oldewage interview.

65. Oldewage interview; King interview. The normal B-29 crew is eleven men, but Chenault's crew included two observers, or strap-hangers, that day. Both of them bailed out over Sinuiju and spent the rest of the war as POWs.

66. Ibid.; Oldewage interview; *Steadfast and Courageous,* 34.

67. King interview; Oldewage interview.

68. Tiger Survivor Roster, provided to the author by Csm. Tim Casey (US Army, Ret.), April 2009. Casey is an honorary member of the Tiger Survivors' group and is also their unofficial historian.

69. Ibid.; King interview.

70. Oldewage interview.

71. Ibid.; British Ministry of Defence, *Treatment of British Prisoners,* 13; SSGT George Millward, USAF, testimony at the court martial of Colonel Fleming, Fort Lewis, Wash., 1954, 1073. Transcripts for the postwar court martial trials of several former POWs are available at the US Army Military History Institute, at Carlisle, Penn. As of October 2009, these transcripts had not yet been catalogued.

72. Oldewage interview; Millward testimony, 1078–79, 1092.

73. Millward testimony, 1089.

74. Oldewage interview.

75. Lech, *Broken Soldiers,* 112–13; MacGhee debriefing.

76. Oldewage interview; British Ministry of Defence, *Treatment of British Prisoners,* 13–14.

77. Alexander, *Korea,* 431–33; Crane, *American Airpower Strategy,* 76. Alexander suggests that both sides would have fared better by embracing the cease-fire proposed by the Soviets in June of 1951, which merely called for a cessation of hostilities, with both sides remaining in place along the existing battle lines (435).

78. Alexander, *Korea,* 433–39.

79. Crane, *American Airpower Strategy,* 76–78.

80. Collins, *War in Peacetime,* 312–13. See Crane, *American Airpower Strategy in Korea,* and Futrell, *United States Air Force in Korea.*

81. Thompson and Nalty, *Within Limits,* 42–49; Hastings, *Korean War,* 265–66; *Steadfast and Courageous,* 41–42. In October of 1951, the US bomber command suffered twelve wounded B-29 crew members and another fifty-five dead or missing.

82. Crane, *American Airpower Strategy,* 143; Trembath, "Lie Based on a Delusion," 6–7; Headquarters, Department of the Army, *US Prisoners of War,* 246–47.

83. Bruning, *Crimson Sky,* 114; Endicott and Hagerman, *United States and Biological Warfare,* 156–57; Crane, *American Airpower Strategy,* 148; Needham et al., *Report of the International Scientific Commission,* 493–540.

84. Rogaski, "Nature, Annihilation, and Modernity," 173–76.

85. Needham et al., *Report of the International Scientific Commission,* 47–48. The ISC report includes a photostatic copy of both confessions, as well as those of two other USAF pilots. The commission's most prominent member, Dr. Joseph Needham, was a Cambridge professor and an avowed Marxist. White, *Captives of Korea,* 173–74.

86. Endicott and Hagerman, *United States and Biological Warfare,* 189; White, *Captives of Korea,* 174–78; Rosenthal, "Committee Ends Germ War Study."

87. Office of Special Investigations, *USAF Prisoners of War in Korea,* 15–18.

88. Ibid., 19–21; Crane, *American Airpower Strategy*, 148.

89. Crane, *American Airpower Strategy*, 146–48; Shapiro interview. Shapiro was captured in February of 1953 and endured several weeks of interrogation. He recalled his guards marching him barefoot across frozen cornfields and then forcing him to stand barefoot in a pool of icy water. When these measures failed, they broke the surface of a large, frozen puddle, ordered Shapiro to remove his flight jacket, and forced him to lie face down in the icy water. At this point, Shapiro agreed to write the bogus confession, which the interrogators accepted. After repatriation, he recounted his confession to the air force debriefers, who laughed and said, "That's great!" Shapiro retired from the air force in 1974.

90. Crane, *American Airpower Strategy*, 150–54.

91. White, *Captives of Korea*, 260–61.

92. Ibid., 178–80.

93. Ibid., 180–82, 256.

94. Ibid., 257.

95. Ibid., 257–59.

96. Crane, *American Airpower Strategy*, 146–47; Hedlund interview.

97. Crane, *American Airpower Strategy*, 266–67; Thompson and Nalty, *Within Limits* 51–52.

98. Thompson and Nalty, *Within Limits*, 54–56; Hastings, *Korean War*, 267; Futrell, *United States Air Force in Korea*, 679–84.

99. Boyne, *Beyond the Wild Blue*, 89; Futrell, *United States Air Force in Korea*, 688.

100. Futrell, *United States Air Force in Korea*, 691–92; Crane, *American Airpower Strategy*, 171–81. Crane quotes USAF Gen. Curtis LeMay, who believed that a concentrated bombing campaign against North Vietnamese cities would have won the war in two weeks.

101. *Interim Report for Commander, Air University on Communist Exploitation of USAF POWs in Korea* (Record Group 341, Box 440), 118.

102. Dr. Albert D. Biderman, "Briefing of the Defense Advisory Committee" (Record Group 341, Box 441), 9–13.

103. *Interim Report for Commander, Communist Exploitation of USAF POWs in Korea*, 120.

Chapter 10

1. White, *Captives of Korea*, 124. Throughout his book, White identifies specific American POWs by pseudonyms, here referring to "the Doctor," Capt. Clarence Anderson, MD, the battalion surgeon captured at Unsan.

2. Maj. Harold Kaschko, testimony at the court martial of Maj. Ronald Alley, Fort Meade, Md., September 1955, 922; Funchess, *Korea P.O.W.*, 69–75.

3. Kinne, *Wooden Boxes*, 59–63. Kinne recalls thirty-nine prisoner deaths in a single day shortly after his arrival at Camp One in May 1951. Kinne was a British infantryman captured with the Gloucesters at the battle of the Imjin River in April 1951. In general, the Chinese treated British and American prisoners identically.

4. White, *Captives of Korea*, 92; Funchess, *Korea P.O.W.*, 69, 75; Shadish, *When Hell Froze Over*, 56.

5. Funchess, *Korea P.O.W.*, 77–78.

6. Lech, *Broken Soldiers*, 103.

7. Ibid., 103–104; Shadish, *When Hell Froze Over*, 53; Schein, *Some Observations*, 21–22.

8. Shadish, *When Hell Froze Over,* 74; Funchess, *Korea P.O.W.,* 74–75; White, *Captives of Korea,* 93–95.

9. British Ministry of Defence, *Treatment of British Prisoners,* 13. The report quotes an officer who witnessed the Chinese pressure:

> Their timing, as usual, was excellent. Several officers had been returned to the compound who had undergone severe punishment for alleged and actual offences. The moral effect on their comrades was at its peak when a "petition for the cessation of hostilities" was produced for signature. Using the battered condition of those who had just returned to the compound as an example of what could happen to anyone who showed himself to be "an enemy of the people," and having encouraged some of these men to relate the horrors of "the treatment," they were able to get the signatures of all the officers.

10. Lt. Col. John MacLaughlin, testimony at the court martial of Maj. Ronald Alley, Fort Meade, Md., September 1955, 111–13; Capt. Raymond M. Dowe, testimony at the court martial of Maj. Ronald Alley, Fort Meade, Md., September 1955, 442, 467; Kaschko testimony, 925.

11. McLaughlin testimony, 115; Lech, *Broken Soldiers,* 99–101.

12. Lech, *Broken Soldiers,* 99–101; Wood interview.

13. Lech, *Broken Soldiers,* 101–102.

14. Ibid.; McLain, *My Country, My Family, My Life,* 75; Funchess, *Korea P.O.W.,* 79–80; White, *Captives of Korea,* 110; Kaschko testimony, 930. The Chinese staged a similar peace appeal at Camp One a few weeks later, again using the reward of extra rations to entice the starving prisoners into signing the appeal (Kinne, *Wooden Boxes,* 69).

15. MacDonald, *Korea,* 114; Acheson, *Korean War,* 122.

16. Thornton, *Believed to Be Alive,* 170; Kinne, *Wooden Boxes,* 63.

17. Shadish, *When Hell Froze Over,* 50; Edwards, *Korean War Educator;* White, *Captives of Korea,* 132; Office of the Surgeon General, "Report of Conference," 2–4; Headquarters, Department of the Army, *US Prisoners of War in the Korean Operation,* 368; Hedlund affidavit, 9.

18. Kinne, *Wooden Boxes,* 63; O'Dowd affidavit, 13; White, *Captives of Korea,* 125; Shadish, *When Hell Froze Over,* 49–50.

19. MacDonald, *Problems,* 150–51; Peterson interview; Roach interview; British Ministry of Defence, *Treatment of British Prisoners,* 21; Funchess, *Korea P.O.W.,* 82–83; White, *Captives of Korea,* 126–27. Both Funchess (*Korea P.O.W.*) and White (*Captives of Korea*) discuss the protest over the return address. See also Headquarters, Department of the Army, *US Prisoners of War in the Korean Operation,* which dedicates an entire chapter to the communists' exploitation of the prisoners' mail. This report notes that Chinese officials allowed some POWs to write letters in the spring of 1951, in conjunction with the newly implemented indoctrination program at Camp Five. Due to the continuing high death rate among prisoners during this period, however, the Chinese apparently had second thoughts and temporarily withdrew the letter-writing privilege.

20. Biderman, *March to Calumny,* 107; O'Brien interview; Headquarters, Department of the Army, *US Prisoners of War in the Korean Operation,* 94–95.

21. Evanhoe, *Dark Moon,* 117–23; Pelser and Pelser, *Freedom Bridge,* 25–26. Pelser was the navigator on the reconnaissance flight and spent the next twenty-five months in captivity.

22. DeLong memoir, 13; Chapman, "Cherokee Warrior," 60–68.

23. Chapman, "Cherokee Warrior," 60–68.

24. Ibid.; Davies, *In Spite of Dungeons,* 49–50.

25. Chapman, "Cherokee Warrior," 60–68. While marching through Sinuiju, recalled Chapman, the prisoners received bread from Russian troops who were manning antiaircraft batteries.

26. Dixon interview; Dixon, sworn affidavit (Record Group 153, Entry 183, Box 1), 1.

27. Dixon, sworn affidavit, 1–2.

28. Dixon interview.

29. Ibid.

30. Ibid.

31. Ibid.

32. Ibid.; Dixon, sworn affidavit, 2.

33. British Ministry of Defence, *Treatment of British Prisoners,* 25. "Reactionary" prisoners remained segregated from later prisoners and were eventually transferred to other camps.

34. Headquarters, Department of the Army, *US Prisoners of War in the Korean Operation,* 302–306, 625–30. A fourth group of several hundred American prisoners remained at the Apex Camps in the northernmost section of North Korea until late October 1951.

35. Shadish, *When Hell Froze Over,* 58.

36. White, *Captives of Korea,* 108; Carlson, *Remembered Prisoners,* 177, 187–91; Capt. Walter Mayo, US Army, testimony at the court martial of Maj. Ronald Alley, Fort Meade, Md., September 1955, 387; Schein, *Some Observations,* 83.

37. Davies, *In Spite of Dungeons,* 71–77; Shadish, *When Hell Froze Over,* 41–42.

38. Schein, *Some Observations,* 32–33, 81; Funchess, *Korea P.O.W.,* 104.

39. Gillespie, *Korean War Remembered,* 52; Schein, *Some Observations,* 82.

40. Schein, *Some Observations,* 26, 36, 68–71. Schein reports that noncommissioned officers were especially successful in helping others resist Chinese manipulation, "partly because of their strong identification with the Army, and partly because of a great deal of experience with a variety of situations" (*Some Observations,* 68).

41. MacDonald, *Problems,* 134; Schein, *Some Observations,* 26, 68–84; Biderman, *March to Calumny,* 26. The Chinese tactic of segregating black prisoners proved especially counterproductive since it replicated racial discrimination at home, while many Hispanic American prisoners avoided indoctrination classes by "forgetting" how to speak English.

42. Biderman, *March to Calumny,* 43; Shadish, *When Hell Froze Over,* 52, 64; Headquarters, Department of the Army, *US Prisoners of War in the Korean Operation,* 103.

43. Carlson, *Remembered Prisoners,* 179; Dunn, sworn affidavit, 6; Schein, *Some Observations,* 6–9. Schein reports that Chinese efforts at control extended to personal friendships: "Not only were formal and informal groups which might have supported resistance activity systematically broken up, but there was persistent emphasis on undermining all friendships, emotional bonds and such group expressions as religious services" (*Some Observations,* 26–27).

44. Schein, *Some Observations,* 6–9; Carlson, *Remembered Prisoners,* 200.

45. Lech, *Broken Soldiers,* 74–80; Carlson, *Remembered Prisoners,* 132; Grey, "Other Fronts," 3.

46. Schein, *Some Observations,* 20; British Ministry of Defence, *Treatment of British Prisoners,* 18.

47. British Ministry of Defence, *Treatment of British Prisoners,* 16–18; Schein, *Some Observations,* 20; Kinne, *Wooden Boxes,* 73; White, *Captives of Korea,* 103–106, 142–43. With the exception of twenty-one nonrepatriates, American prisoners universally renounced communism upon their release from captivity. See also Paisley, *21 Stayed;* Wang, *They Chose China;* and Adams, *An American Dream.*

48. Biderman, *March to Calumny,* 50; White, *Captives of Korea,* 107–108.

49. Schein, *Some Observations,* 8; British Ministry of Defence, *Treatment of British Prisoners,* 20.

50. Biderman, *March to Calumny,* 52.

Chapter 11

1. Office of Special Investigations, *USAF Prisoners of War in Korea,* 8; British Ministry of Defence, *Treatment of British Prisoners,* 2; Headquarters, Department of the Army, *US Prisoners of War in the Korean Operation,* 103.

2. Stueck, *Rethinking the Korean War,* 143–45.

3. Ibid., 147–52; Hermes, *Truce Tent,* 26–30.

4. Hermes, *Truce Tent,* 35–51; Acheson, *Korean War,* 118. At a congressional hearing in June of 1951, Acheson stated that the United States was willing to accept a cease-fire based on communist withdrawal above the 38th Parallel and "reliable assurances" of no further aggression.

5. Alexander, *Korea,* 438–48.

6. Hermes, *Truce Tent,* 112–13.

7. White, *Captives of Korea,* 134.

8. Pelser and Pelser, *Freedom Bridge,* 40–43; Headquarters, Department of the Army, *US Prisoners of War In the Korean Operation,* 119; Office of Special Investigations, *USAF Prisoners of War in Korea,* 9–10. The air force report cites accounts from repatriated officers indicating that the Chinese "exhibited great interest in the indoctrination of the young and of those with relatively little education or intelligence."

9. Lech, *Broken Soldiers,* 146; Shadish, *When Hell Froze Over,* 65–66; Davies, *In Spite of Dungeons,* 57–58; Thornton, *Believed to Be Alive,* 188–89; McClain, *My Country, My Family, My Life,* 80.

10. Davies, *In Spite of Dungeons,* 64–66; Dunn, sworn affidavit, 4–6; Headquarters, Department of the Army, *US Prisoners of War in the Korean Operation,* 91–92.

11. Hermes, *Truce Tent,* 113–16; Goulden, *Korea,* 575–82.

12. Stueck, *International History,* 245.

13. Biderman, *March to Calumny,* 107–108; White, *Captives of Korea,* 143; Blair, *Forgotten War,* 952; Casey, *Selling the Korean War,* 280–81.

14. Cole, *POW/MIA Issues,* 25.

15. "Armed Forces: Shocking Blunder"; Biderman, *March to Calumny,* 107–108; White, *Captives of Korea,* 143; Casey, *Selling the Korean War,* 281.

16. Biderman, *March to Calumny,* 107–108.

17. Stueck, *Rethinking the Korean War,* 162; Acheson, *Korean War,* 130; Hermes, *Truce Tent,* 141–43; MacDonald, *Problems,* 131–32. Most of those who were unaccounted for were South Koreans, but MacDonald notes that US negotiators also demanded further information on 1,058 Americans whom the communists had identified by name in previous broadcasts and newspaper articles. The communists responded that 570 had died, 153 had escaped, and 3 had been released. Their list also excluded prisoners at interrogation centers, such as Pak's Palace, and those still in transit to permanent camps.

18. Shadish, *When Hell Froze Over,* 68; Carlson, *Remembered Prisoners,* 213.

19. Headquarters, Department of the Army, *US Prisoners of War in the Korean Operation,* 222–23; Lech, *Broken Soldiers,* 150; Shadish, *When Hell Froze Over,* 74.

20. MacDonald, *Problems,* 137–38.

21. Chapman, "Cherokee Warrior," 79–80.

22. Headquarters, Department of the Army, *US Prisoners of War in the Korean Operation,* 116–20. Camp Four held approximately six hundred noncommissioned officers, most of them American. The remainder were British, Turkish, and French.

23. Ibid., 371–72.

24. Ibid.; Carlson, *Remembered Prisoners,* 137; Shadish, *When Hell Froze Over,* 66.

25. Headquarters, Department of the Army, *US Prisoners of War in the Korean Operation,* 373, 587–88.

26. Dixon interview; Reid interview.

27. Hastings, *Korean War,* 299; Chapman, "Cherokee Warrior," 87.

28. Thornton, *Believed to Be Alive,* 204–206; DeLong memoir; Carlson, *Remembered Prisoners,* 132–33.

29. Thornton, *Believed to Be Alive,* 207–14.

30. Mellin interview; Dixon interview; Carlson, *Remembered Prisoners,* 143.

31. Headquarters, Department of the Army, *US Prisoners of War in the Korean Operation,* 288.

32. Ibid., 289–293, 318–19; Carlson, *Remembered Prisoners,* 174; Dixon interview; Funchess, *Korea P.O.W.,* 94–95; Doyle, *Prisoner's Duty,* 179–80.

33. Headquarters, Department of the Army, *US Prisoners of War in the Korean Operation,* 289–93.

34. Ibid., 299; Dowe, summary of information (Record Group 153, Entry 183, Box 2), 7.

35. Dowe, summary of information (Record Group 153, Entry 183, Box 2), 7; McLain, *My Country, My Family, My Life,* 63–64.

36. Dowe, summary of information (Record Group 153, Entry 183, Box 2), 7; McClain, *My Country, My Family, My Life,* 63–64; Dowe interview.

37. Cole, *POW/MIA Issues,* 43. Cole's study observes that "rapid physical deterioration of US POWs was perhaps the most important factor that accounts for the lack of escapes."

38. MacGhee affidavit, 14.

39. Lech, *Broken Soldiers,* 138–40; Peterson interview; Chinnery, *Korean Atrocity!* 163–65. After the war, intelligence officers determined that Liles's escape plan, which relied on air attacks and a massive helicopter extraction, would probably have worked. Under the guise of presenting a peace appeal to the United Nations, a repatriated prisoner was supposed to sneak the plan out in the heel of his boot.

40. Headquarters, Department of the Army, *US Prisoners of War in the Korean Operation,* 321–22; MacDonald, *Problems,* 164–65; Farrar-Hockley, *Edge of the Sword,* 252; Doerty interview.

41. Doerty interview.

42. Doerty interview.

43. Doerty interview.

44. Doerty interview; Office of Special Investigations, *USAF Prisoners of War in Korea,* 10.

45. Doerty, "Freedom Is Not Free," 78.

46. Article 118 begins with the statement that "POWs shall be released and repatriated without delay after the cessation of hostilities."

47. Hermes, *Truce Tent,* 141.

48. Ibid., 135–38; Foot, *Wrong War,* 87–88.

49. Foot, *Wrong War,* 88–90.

50. Hermes, *Truce Tent,* 144–45.

51. Ibid., 145–51; Goulden, *Korea,* 590.

52. Foot, *Wrong War,* 91–92.

53. Stueck, *International History,* 261.

54. MacDonald, *Problems,* 134–35; Goulden, *Korea,* 181–82.

55. Hastings, *Korean War,* 306.

56. Foot, *Wrong War,* 109–19; Doyle, *Enemy in our Hands,* 255–56.

57. Stueck, *International History,* 265–66.

58. Hermes, *Truce Tent,* 168. The US Army's official history observed that the release of this figure "may have been a tactical error on the part of the UN Command, for it misled the enemy into thinking they would recover approximately that number of prisoners."

59. Stueck, *International History,* 266–68.

60. Ibid., 268–69; Foot, *Wrong War,* 116–17; White, *Captives of Korea,* 216–17. In his 1957 account of the POW saga, journalist William L. White observed that many of the Koreans who demanded repatriation were ROK turncoats whom the UN commander could have turned over to the ROK government as traitors and who would likely have been executed.

61. Hermes, *Truce Tent,* 171–74; Stueck, *International History,* 269–72.

62. Hastings, *Korean War,* 310–13; Hermes, *Truce Tent,* 259. The weapons cache included 4,500 knives, 3,000 spears, and 1,000 gasoline grenades. Guards also discovered the corpses of sixteen prisoners murdered by the communists.

63. Doyle, *Enemy in Our Hands,* 258–64; Alexander, *Korea,* 467–72. The deadliest riot took place on Dec. 14, 1952, when UN guards fired into a mob of prisoners at Pongam-do, killing 85 and seriously wounding 113.

64. Headquarters, Department of the Army, *US Prisoners of War in the Korean Operation,* 374–75; MacDonald, *Problems,* 190–91; Shadish, *When Hell Froze Over,* 75–76.

65. Esensten interview; Headquarters, Department of the Army, *US Prisoners of War in the Korean Operation,* 380–82; Carlson, *Remembered Prisoners,* 129; Shadish, *When Hell Froze Over,* 50; Chapman, 94–95. The US Army's 1954 report on treatment of POWs (cited earlier) and numerous memoirs report the POWs' use of marijuana.

66. MacDonald, *Problems,* 195–96; Headquarters, Department of the Army, *US Prisoners of War in the Korean Operation,* 375; Esensten interview.

67. Headquarters, Department of the Army, *US Prisoners of War in the Korean Operation,* 374–76; MacDonald, *Problems,* 194.

68. MacDonald, *Problems,* 194; Headquarters, Department of the Army, *US Prisoners of War in the Korean Operation,* 374–75.

69. Mike Dowe, correspondence with the author, Feb. 9, 2010.

70. Hastings, *Korean War,* 314–15; Stueck, *Rethinking the Korean War,* 171–72. In fact, American planners had presented just such a plan to the JCS during the autumn of 1952. According to Stueck, Eisenhower's visit to Korea and his subsequent meeting with MacArthur, the leading proponent of unrestricted warfare, reinforced Mao's expectations of escalation.

71. Hastings, *Korean War,* 315–18; Alexander, *Korea,* 472; Korda, *Ike,* 653–54. General Clark later observed that the issue of "how much it would take to win the war was never raised." Truman dismissed Eisenhower's trip as a political ploy. In his biography of Eisenhower, however, Michael Korda argues that Eisenhower realized a negotiated settlement would probably not occur without the threat of escalation and that such a threat would have more credence coming from a five-star general.

72. Alexander, *Korea,* 471.

73. Hastings, *Korean War,* 319; Matray, "Revisiting Korea."

74. Hermes, *Truce Tent,* 411–12.

75. Stueck, *Rethinking the Korean War,* 173–76; 180; Korda, *Ike,* 677–78. Stueck observes, "[I]ndications are that Kim Il Sung had wanted peace for over a year." Korda, on the

other hand, gives much of the credit to Eisenhower for bluffing the Chinese back to the negotiating table.

76. Zellers, *In Enemy Hands,* 203–14.

77. Hermes, *Truce Tent,* 412–15; White, *Captives of Korea,* 220.

78. Headquarters, Department of the Army, *US Prisoners in the Korean Operation,* 415.

79. Hermes, *Truce Tent,* 415–19.

80. Pelser and Pelser, *Freedom Bridge,* 75–76; Farrar-Hockley, *Edge of the Sword,* 261–62; Harrison, sworn affidavit (Record Group 153, Entry 183, Box 3), 8–9. Harrison was originally selected for early exchange, but the Chinese delayed his release because of alleged violations of the rules. He was eventually repatriated on Aug. 6, 1953, as part of Operation Big Switch.

81. Hermes, *Truce Tent,* 426–27, 436–45.

82. Ibid., 441–42.

83. Ibid., 426–29.

84. Doyle, *Enemy in Our Hands,* 266–67; Foot, *Wrong War,* 184–85.

85. Chapman, "Cherokee Warrior," 104; Mellin interview; Carlson, *Remembered Prisoners,* 216–17; Flores, *Confess, Confess, Confess,* 201.

86. DeLong memoir.

87. Shadish, *When Hell Froze Over,* 80.

88. White, *Captives of Korea,* 250–51.

89. Dixon interview; Clarke, *Journey through Shadow,* 409–11. Clarke's memoir provides a detailed account of this incident.

90. Pelser and Pelser, *Freedom Bridge,* 82–83; Funchess, *Korea P.O.W.,* 133.

91. Hermes, *Truce Tent and Fighting Front,* appendix B, "Prisoners of War," 514–55. *Time* magazine's correspondent described the communist defiance as "planned nonsense" (*Time* 62 [Aug. 17, 1953]: 7).

92. Hermes, *Truce Tent and Fighting Front,* appendix B, "Prisoners of War," 514–55.

93. Taft interview.

94. Thornton, *Believed to Be Alive,* 255–56.

95. Strait, *What Happened?* 176; Dowe interview.

96. Funchess, *Korea P.O.W.,* 133–35.

97. Carlson, *Remembered Prisoners,* 201–205; Shadish, *When Hell Froze Over,* 85–91.

Chapter 12

1. Lech, *Broken Soldiers,* 204–205; Doerty, "Freedom Is Not Free," 79.

2. Office of the Surgeon General, "Report of Conference," 11–12; Reid interview.

3. Pate, *Reactionary!* 124.

4. Defense Advisory Committee on Prisoners of War, Study Group II, Action Involving Repatriated Prisoners. This declassified six-page report is part of a much larger compilation that documents the committee's findings and recommendations, which eventually led to the establishment of the Code of Conduct.

5. Carlson, *Remembered Prisoners,* 219; Lech, *Broken Soldiers,* 206.

6. Lech, *Broken Soldiers,* 204–206; Biderman, *March to Calumny,* 207–208; MacDonald, *Problems,* 228.

7. "First POW Ship Arrives Tomorrow."

8. Reid interview; King interview.

9. See, for example, "Hostile Captives Had a Rough Time," 2; "In the Hills behind the Athletes the Men Who Died Were Buried," 5.

10. Crane, "Chemical and Biological Warfare," 71. The UN campaign included a blanket denial of the biological-warfare accusations.

11. Ibid., 69.

12. Lech, *Broken Soldiers,* 170–75, 208; Millett, *Their War for Korea,* 250. See also Lech, *Tortured into Fake Confession,* which provides a detailed account of Schwable's captivity and subsequent board of inquiry.

13. "Cracked under Mental Torture"; Severo and Milford, *Wages of War,* 332–33.

14. Millett, *Their War for Korea,* 254–55; MacDonald, *Problems,* 233–34; "Armed Forces: The Marines Decide." Schwable served until 1959 and was promoted to brigadier general upon his retirement.

15. MacDonald, *Problems,* 234.

16. Lech, *Broken Soldiers,* 222–24.

17. Loosbrock, "POWs: What Do We Owe Them?"

18. Ibid., 223–24. The US Navy had twenty-four service members repatriated at the end of the Korean War; none were accused of misconduct.

19. Kinkead, *In Every War but One,* 38–39. Of this number, 650 were categorized as having been released by the enemy or having escaped from captivity.

20. Prugh, "Justice for All RECAP-Ks," 16. As a member of the Staff Judge Advocate's staff, Prugh played a central role in executing army policy regarding alleged collaborators.

21. Kinkead, *In Every War but One,* 56; Prugh, "Justice for All RECAP-Ks," 17.

22. Lech, *Broken Soldiers,* 215–16; Floyd court martial, "Review of the Staff Judge Advocate, Headquarters, Fort Leavenworth, Kansas," May 27, 1954, from the *US Army Court Martial of Private First Class Rothwell B. Floyd,* 10–13.

23. Floyd court martial; Lech, *Broken Soldiers,* 235–37, 265.

24. Robin, *Making of the Cold War Enemy,* 162–68; Edwards, *To Acknowledge a War,* 33–36.

25. Hillman, *Defending America,* 49–50; Lech, *Broken Soldiers,* 210–11.

26. Lech, *Broken Soldiers,* 193–97, 201–11; "National Affairs: Handwashing."

27. Lech, *Broken Soldiers,* 196–97.

28. "Batchelor's Story," 1.

29. Lech, *Broken Soldiers,* 211–12, 218.

30. Ibid., 237–40; Hillman, *Defending America,* 50. Writing in the *Saturday Evening Post,* RAdm Dan Gallery argued that Dickenson's prosecution reinforced communist claims of American injustice. "How stupid can we get?" he asked.

31. Prugh, "Justice for All RECAP-Ks," 20; Kinkead, *In Every War but One,* 65.

32. Memorandum to the Staff Judge Advocate General, Subject: Disciplinary Action in Cases Involving Repatriated POW's [*sic*] (Record Group 153, Entry 60B, Box 1).

33. Prugh, "Justice for All RECAP-Ks," 20; Lech, *Broken Soldiers,* 191–92. Watson had been captured with papers identifying him as a deputy sheriff in Mississippi. The Chinese accused him of being a spy and tortured him until he confessed. Despite Batchelor's alleged recommendation, the Chinese released Watson during Operation Big Switch.

34. Lech, *Broken Soldiers,* 241–43; Prugh, "Justice for All RECAP-Ks," 20–21; Hillman, *Defending America,* 50–51.

35. Hillman, *Defending America,* 50–51; LeMay, "Collaboration or Self-Preservation."

36. Lech, *Broken Soldiers,* 243–45.

37. "Armed Forces: Drawing the Line"; Prugh, "Justice for All RECAP-Ks," 22; Montgomery, "Clemency OK'd for ex-POW in Area." Twenty-four years after Fleming's conviction, the secretary of the army granted him clemency and an honorable discharge, restoring his rank and his military benefits.

38. Memorandum for the Secretary of Defense, Attn: Assistant General Counsel, Subject: Summary of RECAP-K Actions, Office of the Assistant Secretary of the Army (Record Group 153).

39. Kinkead, *In Every War but One,* 73. Much of Kinkead's book relies on information gleaned from the army's counterintelligence section. In discussing the dismissal of thirty-five cases, the author noted that "In each instance, the field commander, as was his privilege, went on record as stating that basis for reasonable doubt in applying so stringent a measure existed, although it is hard for a detached observer to see why."

40. Message to Continental Army Commanders, Staff Communications Office, HQDA, October 23, 1954; comment no. 2, memorandum through AC of S, G-1, to AC of S, G-2 (Record Group 153, Entry 60B, Box 1).

41. Kinkead, *In Every War but One,* 65. Summarizing the army's rationale, the author notes that "all prisoners had been exposed to Communist propaganda" (64).

42. Letter from William F. Tompkins, assistant attorney general, to the secretary of the army, Nov. 29, 1954 (Record Group 153, Entry 60B, Box 2).

43. Ibid.

44. "Toth v. Quarles: A Death in Korea."

45. Letter from William F. Tompkins to the Honorable Hugh M. Milton II, assistant secretary of the army (Record Group 153, Entry 60B, Box 3).

46. Kinkead, *In Every War but One,* 74. The author suggests that by dismissing most cases without trial, army field commanders had "taken the easy way out" to avoid further adverse publicity.

47. Prugh, "Justice for All RECAP-Ks," 22; Lech, *Broken Soldiers,* 271–72. Gallagher's conviction was initially reversed by the Military Board of Review on the grounds that, after his repatriation, Gallagher had briefly separated from the army before reenlisting the following day. The Court of Military Appeals directed the board to reconsider this decision, and upon further review, the board subsequently upheld the original sentence. Gallagher ultimately spent a longer time in jail than any of the other convicted POWs. He was finally granted parole in 1966.

48. Prugh, "Justice for All RECAP-Ks," 20–22; Lech, *Broken Soldiers,* 249–51, 264.

49. Department of Defense, "Committee Documentation of the Secretary of Defense's Advisory Committee on Prisoners of War" (Record Group 341, Air Force Plans, Decimal File 1942–1954, Box 441).

50. Robin, *Making of the Cold War Enemy,* 180–81; Department of Defense, *POW,* 13–14.

51. Department of Defense, *POW,* 1–2, 32.

52. Department of Defense, *POW,* 18; Defense Advisory Committee on Prisoners of War, Study Group I, Problem I-1.

53. Ruhl, "Code of Conduct," 63. The code was subsequently modified in 1977, when the word "only" was removed from the phrase "I am bound to give only name, rank, service number, and date of birth" and the word "bound" was changed to "required."

54. Edwards, *To Acknowledge a War,* 33–35; Severo and Milford, *Wages of War,* 325–44; Wubben, "American Prisoners of War in Korea," 5. Citing conservative displeasure with the outcome of the Korean War, Severo and Milford argue that the army supported criticism of former POWs as a means of diverting attention from the mistakes of senior leaders in conducting the war. Their conspiracy theory, however, does not account for the studies underwritten by both the army and other services, which reached conclusions far less damning.

55. Severo and Milford, *Wages of War,* 321–33. The army published its seven-hundred-

page classified study, Headquarters, Department of the Army, *US Prisoners of War in the Korean Operation,* in 1954.

56. Biderman, *March to Calumny,* 298–306. Recipients included Lt. Col. John Dunn and several of the doctors who survived the first winter at Pyoktong, including Anderson, Esensten, and Shadish. Chaplain Kapaun was posthumously awarded the Distinguished Service Cross for his actions during the battle of Unsan. As of this writing, his nomination for the Medal of Honor is being reviewed by the Secretary of Defense. Kapaun has also been nominated for canonization by the Catholic diocese of Wichita, Kansas.

57. Carlson, *Remembered Prisoners,* 7.

58. Ibid.; Wubben, "American Prisoners of War in Korea," 6; Severo and Milford, *Wages of War,* 336. According to Severo and Milford, "Mayer quickly became the messiah of condemnation."

59. Severo and Milford, *Wages of War,* 335–36; Carlson, *Remembered Prisoners,* 14.

60. Lewis, "Mayer Case Slated for Muzzle Probe." In 1961, the army finally imposed restrictions on Mayer's public-speaking engagements.

61. Robin, *Making of the Cold War Enemy,* 164; Carlson, *Remembered Prisoners,* 7; Wubben, "American Prisoners of War in Korea," 6–7. Mayer later served as assistant surgeon general and assistant secretary of defense for health during the Reagan administration. His two-volume autobiography, *Beyond the Call: Memoirs of a Medical Visionary,* was published in 2009 by Mayer Publishing House International, University Place, Wash.

62. *POW,* 26; Carlson, *Remembered Prisoners,* 15; Kinkead, *In Every War but One,* 11; Serling, *Patterns,* 139.

63. Serling, *Patterns,* 136–42. In the 1957 film version of *The Rack,* Paul Newman offers a compelling performance as Captain Hall, the officer accused of misconduct. Unfortunately, the movie loses much of its dramatic focus during the final courtroom scene, in which Newman's defendant accepts responsibility for his crime and explains what he has learned. This "confession" unintentionally replicates the Chinese method of forcing prisoners to publicly confess their crimes against "the people."

64. Kinkead, *In Every War but One,* 23–24.

65. Ibid., 34.

66. Ibid., 16.

67. Ibid., 109.

68. Ibid., 116.

69. Ibid., 157.

70. "Korean War Casualties"; O'Brien interview.

71. Kinkead, *In Every War but One,* 17.

72. Ibid., 143; Office of the Surgeon General, "Report of Conference with Repatriated POW Personnel, Medical Corps," 21; Anderson affidavit, 2. Kinkead closed this chapter with an improbable quote from Anderson: "The nightmare of guilt that still haunts so many of those who returned would have been avoided, and, most important, more of us would have returned" (Kinkead, *In Every War but One,* 157).

73. Kinkead, *In Every War but One,* 170–210.

74. Karsten, "American Democratic Citizen Soldier"; Schein et al., "Statement: To Set Straight the Korean POW Episode," 94–95.

75. Wubben, "American Prisoners of War in Korea," 4–6; Biderman, *March to Calumny,* 16–30. Wubben's historical analysis further examines the misuse of history employed by Mayer and Kinkead in their claims that American misconduct in Korea was "something new in history."

76. Biderman, *March to Calumny,* 243. Conservative Republicans scheduled the hearing to investigate the alleged "muzzling" of Lieutenant Colonel Mayer.

77. Carlson, *Remembered Prisoners,* 13–14. See also Rowley, *US Korean War POWs.*

78. Gruner, *Prisoners of Culture,* 22–24.

79. Information based on subjects' interviews with the author.

80. "POW/MIA Recognition Day: Background."

Bibliography

Books

Acheson, Dean. *The Korean War.* New York: Norton, 1969.

Adams, Clarence. *An American Dream: The Life of an African American Soldier and POW Who Spent Twelve Years in Communist China,* ed. Della Adams and Lewis H. Carlson. Amherst: University of Massachusetts Press, 2007.

Alexander, Bevin. *Korea: The First War We Lost.* New York: Hippocrene, 1993.

Appleman, Roy E. *Disaster in Korea.* College Station: Texas A&M University Press, 1989.

———. *East of Chosin: Entrapment and Breakout in Korea, 1950.* College Station: Texas A&M University Press, 1987.

———. *Escaping the Trap: The US Army X Corps in Northeast Korea, 1950.* College Station: Texas A&M University Press, 1990.

———. *South to the Naktong, North to the Yalu.* Washington, DC: Center of Military History, US Army, 1961.

Armstrong, Frank, ed. *The 1st Cavalry Division and Their 8th Engineers in Korea: America's Silent Generation in the Hot Spot of the Cold War.* South Burlington, Vt.: Bull Run, 1997.

Biderman, Albert D. *March to Calumny.* New York: Macmillan, 1963.

Blair, Clay, Jr. *Beyond Courage: Escape Tales of Airmen in the Korean War.* New York: Van Rees, 1955.

———. *The Forgotten War: America in Korea, 1950–1953.* New York: Anchor, 1989.

———. *MacArthur.* New York: Pocket Books, 1977.

Bowers, William T., William M. Hammond, and George L. MacGarrigle. *Black Soldier, White Army: The 24th Infantry Regiment in Korea.* Washington, DC: Center of Military History, US Army, 1996.

Boyne, Walter J. *Beyond the Wild Blue: A History of the United States Air Force, 1947–2007,* 2nd ed. New York: St. Martin's, 2007.

Bruning, John R., Jr. *Crimson Sky: The Air Battle for Korea.* Dulles, Va.: Brassey's, 1999.

Cantwell, Gerald T. *Citizen Airmen: A History of the Air Force Reserve, 1946–1994.* Washington, DC: USGPO, 1997.

Carlson, Lewis H. *Remembered Prisoners of a Forgotten War: An Oral History of Korean War POWs.* New York: St. Martin's, 2001.

Casey, Steven. *Selling the Korean War: Propaganda, Politics, and Public Opinion in the United States, 1950–1953.* New York: Oxford University Press, 2008.

Chandler, Michael, Lt. Col., USAF. *General Otto P. Weyland, USAF: Close Air Support in the Korean War.* Maxwell Air Force Base, Ala.: Air University Press, 2003.

Chapman, Jack. "Cherokee Warrior: A Prisoner of the Korean War Who Served His Country with Honor and Dignity." Unpublished typescript; copy furnished by the author.

Chinnery, Philip. *Korean Atrocity! Forgotten War Crimes 1950–1953.* Annapolis, Md.: Naval Institute Press, 2000.

Clarke, Conley. *Journey through Shadow, 839 Days in Hell: A POW's Survival in North Korea.* Charlotte, N.C.: Heritage, 1988.

Cole, Paul M. *POW/MIA Issues.* Vol. 1, *The Korean War.* Prepared for the Office of the Undersecretary of Defense for Policy. Santa Monica, Calif.: RAND, 1994.

Collins, Lawton J. *War in Peacetime: The History and Lessons of Korea.* Boston: Houghton Mifflin, 1969.

Condit, Doris M. *History of the Office of the Secretary of Defense: The Test of War, 1950–1953.* Washington, DC: USGPO, 1988.

Crane, Conrad C. *American Airpower Strategy in Korea, 1950–1953.* Lawrence: University of Kansas Press, 2000.

Crosbie, Rev. Philip. *March till They Die.* Westminster, Md.: Newman, 1956.

Cumings, Bruce. *The Korean War: A History.* New York: Random House, 2010.

Daugherty, Leo J., III. *Train Wreckers and Ghost Killers: Allied Marines in the Korean War.* Washington, DC: US Marine Corps Historical Center, 2003.

Davies, Rev. Samuel. *In Spite of Dungeons: The Experiences as a Prisoner of War in North Korea of the Chaplain to the First Battalion, the Gloucester Regiment.* London: Hodder and Stoughton, 1964.

Dean, William F., as told to William F. Worden. *General Dean's Story.* New York: Viking, 1954.

Deane, Philip. *I Was a Captive in Korea.* New York: Norton, 1953.

Doerty, Walter J. "Freedom Is Not Free." Unpublished memoir, 2009.

Dowe, Ray M., Jr., , as told to Harold H. Martin. *Father Kapaun: The Ordeal of Chaplain Kapaun.* Notre Dame, Ind.: Ave Maria Press, 2001.

Doyle, Robert. *The Enemy in Our Hands: America's Treatment of Prisoners of War from the Revolution to the War on Terror.* Lexington: University Press of Kentucky, 2010.

———. *A Prisoner's Duty.* Annapolis, Md.: Naval Institute Press, 1997.

Drury, Bob, and Tom Clavin. *The Last Stand of Fox Company.* New York: Atlantic Monthly Press, 2009.

Edwards, Paul M. *To Acknowledge a War: The Korean War in American Memory.* Westport, Conn.: Greenwood, 2000.

Endicott, Stephen, and Edward Hagerman. *The United States and Biological Warfare: Secrets from the Early Cold War and Korea.* Bloomington: Indiana University Press, 1998.

Ent, Uzal W. *Fighting on the Brink: Defense of the Pusan Perimeter.* Paducah, Ky.: Turner, 1997.

Evanhoe, Ed. *Dark Moon: Eighth Army Special Operations in the Korean War.* Annapolis, Md.: Naval Institute Press, 1995.

Farrar-Hockley, Anthony. *Edge of the Sword.* London: Muller, 1955.

Fehrenbach, T. R. *This Kind of War: A Study in Unpreparedness.* New York: Macmillan, 1963.

Flores, Nick A. *Confess, Confess, Confess: The True Story of a Prisoner of War.* Paducah, Ky.: Turner, 2003.

Foot, Rosemary. *The Wrong War: American Policy and the Dimensions of the Korean Conflict, 1950–1953.* Ithaca, N.Y.: Cornell University Press, 1985.

Funchess, William H. *Korea P.O.W.: A Thousand Days of Torment, November 4, 1950–September 6, 1953.* Clemson, S.C.: Author, 1999.

Futrell, Robert. *The United States Air Force in Korea, 1950–1953,* vol. 2. Washington, DC: USGPO, 1983.

Gillespie, Bailey. *Korean War Remembered: 1013 Days of Hell.* Spindale, N.C.: POW Book, 1997.

Goulden, Joseph. *Korea: The Untold Story of the War.* New York: McGraw-Hill, 1983.

Grey, Jeffrey. "Other Fronts: Resistance, Collaboration, and Survival among UN Prisoners during the Korean War." In *The Korean War 1950–53: A 50 Year Retrospective,* ed. Peter Dennis and Jeffrey Grey, 136–49. Canberra, Australia: Army History Unit, 2000.

Gruner, Elliott. *Prisoners of Culture: Representing the Vietnam POW.* New Brunswick, N.J.: Rutgers University Press, 1993.

Halberstam, David. *The Coldest Winter.* New York: Hyperion, 2007.

Hanson, Thomas E. *Combat Ready? The Eighth US Army on the Eve of the Korean War.* College Station: Texas A&M University Press, 2010.

Hastings, Max. *The Korean War.* New York: Touchstone, 1988.

Hermes, Walter G. *Truce Tent and Fighting Front.* Washington, DC: USGPO, 1973.

Higgins, Marguerite. *War in Korea: The Diary of a Woman Combat Correspondent.* Garden City, N.Y.: Doubleday, 1951.

Hillman, Elizabeth. *Defending America: Military Culture and the Cold War Court Martial.* Princeton, N.J.: Princeton University Press, 2005.

Hoyt, Edwin P. *The Pusan Perimeter.* New York: Jove, 1992.

James, Clayton D., with Anne Sharp Wells. *Refighting the Last War: Command and Crisis in Korea, 1950–1953.* New York: Free Press, 1993.

Jian, Chen. *China's Road to the Korean War.* New York: Columbia University Press, 1994.

Kinkead, Eugene. *In Every War but One.* New York: Norton, 1959.

Kinne, Derek *The Wooden Boxes.* London: Muller, 1955.

Knox, Donald. *The Korean War, an Oral History: Pusan to Chosin.* New York: Harcourt, Brace, 1985.

———, with Alfred Coppel. *The Korean War, Uncertain Victory: The Concluding Volume of an Oral History.* New York: Harcourt Brace Jovanovich, 1988.

Korda, Michael. *Ike: An American Hero.* New York: Harper, 2007.

Lech, Raymond B. *Broken Soldiers.* Urbana: University of Illinois Press, 2000.

———. *Tortured into Fake Confession: The Dishonoring of Korean War Prisoner Col. Frank H. Schwable, USMC.* Jefferson, N.C.: McFarland, 2011.

LeMay, Rodney Ray. "Collaboration or Self-Preservation: The Military Code of Conduct." Master's thesis, Louisiana State University, December 2002, accessed March 8, 2010, http://etd.lsu.edu/docs/available/etd-0905102–114913/unrestricted/LeMay_thesis.pdf.

Li, Xiaobing. *A History of the Modern Chinese Army.* Lexington: University Press of Kentucky, 2007.

———, Allan R. Millett, and Bin Yu, eds. Trans. Xiaobing Li, Allan R. Millett, and Yu Bin. *Mao's Generals Remember Korea.* Lawrence: University Press of Kansas, 2001.

MacArthur, Douglas. *Reminiscences.* New York: McGraw Hill, 1964.

MacDonald, Callum A. *Korea: The War before Vietnam.* New York: Free Press, 1986.

MacDonald, James A., Jr., Maj., USMC. *The Problems of US Marine Corps Prisoners of War in Korea.* Washington, DC: Headquarters, USMC, 1988.

Maher, William L. *A Shepherd in Combat Boots: Chaplain Emil Kapaun of the 1st Cavalry Division.* Shippensburg, Penn.: Burd Street Press, 1997.

Manchester, William. *American Caesar: Douglas MacArthur 1880–1964.* New York: Back Bay Books, 2008.

Marion, Forrest. *That Others May Live: USAF Air Rescue in Korea.* Washington, DC: Air Force History and Museums Program, 2004, accessed September 19, 2009, http://www.airforcehistory.hq.af.mil/Publications/Annotations/MarionThat.htm.

Marshall, S. L. A. *The River and the Gauntlet.* New York: Time, 1963.

McCullough, David. "Truman Fires MacArthur." In *The Cold War: A Military History,* ed. Robert Cowley, 71–103. New York: Random House, 2005.

McLain, William A. "My Country, My Family, My Life." Self-published typescript; copy furnished to the author courtesy of Raymond M. Dowe Jr.

Millett, Allan R. *Their War for Korea: American, Asian, and European Combatants and Civilians, 1945–1953.* Washington, DC: Brassey's, 2002.

———. *The War for Korea, 1945–1950: A House Burning.* Lawrence: University Press of Kansas, 2005.

———. *The War for Korea, 1950–1951: They Came from the North.* Lawrence: University Press of Kansas, 2010.

Montross, Lynn, and Capt. Nicholas A. Canzona, USMC. *US Marine Operations in Korea.* Vol. 3, *The Chosin Reservoir Campaign.* Austin, Tex.: Brandy Able 1, 1987.

Mossman, Billy C. *Ebb and Flow, November 1950–July 1951.* Washington, DC: US Army Center of Military History, 1990.

———. *The Effectiveness of Air Interdiction during the Korean War.* Washington, DC: US Army Center of Military History, 1966. Also available at http://www.history.army.mil /documents/237ADH.htm (accessed Sept. 18, 2009).

Needham, Joseph, et. al. *Report of the International Scientific Commission for the Investigation of the Facts concerning Biological Warfare in Korea and China.* Peking, 1952.

Paik Sun Yup. *From Pusan to Panmunjom.* New York: Brassey's, 1992.

Paisley, Virginia. *21 Stayed: The Story of American GIs Who Chose Communist China—Who They Were and Why They Stayed.* New York: Farrar, Strauss, and Cudahay, 1955.

Pate, Lloyd W., as told to B. J. Cutler. *Reactionary!* New York: Harper, 1955.

Pearlman, Michael D. *Truman and MacArthur: Policy, Politics, and the Hunger for Honor and Renown.* Bloomington: Indiana University Press, 2008.

Pease, Stephen E. *Psywar: Psychological Warfare in Korea, 1950–1953.* Harrisburg, Penn.: Stackpole, 1992.

Pelser, Frederick, and Marcia Pelser. *Freedom Bridge.* Fairfield, Calif.: Fremar, 2003.

POW: The Fight Continues after the Battle: The Report of the Secretary of Defense's Advisory Committee on Prisoners of War. Washington, DC: USGPO, 1955.

Richardson, William, with Kevin Maurer. *Valleys of Death: A Memoir of the Korean War.* New York: Berkley, 2010.

Robin, Ron. *The Making of the Cold War Enemy: Culture and Politics in the Military Industrial Complex.* Princeton, N.J.: Princeton University Press, 2001.

Rowley, Arden A. "US Korean War POWs, from Calumny to Vindication." Self-published, 2002.

Schein, Edgar H. *Some Observations on the Chinese Indoctrination Program for POWs.* Washington, DC: US Army Medical Services Graduate School, October 1955.

Schnabel, James. *United States Army in the Korean War, Policy and Direction: The First Year.* Washington, DC: Office of the Chief of Military History, US Army, 1972.

Segal, Henry, Maj., US Army Medical Corps. "Observations on Prisoners of War Immediately following Their Release." Medical Science Publication 4, *Recent Advances in Medicine and Surgery Based on Professional Medical Experience in Japan and Korea, 1950–1953,* vol. 2. Walter Reed Army Medical Center, Washington, DC, April 19–30, 1954, http:// history.amedd.army.mil/booksdocs/korea/recad2/ch9–3.htm.

Serling, Rod. *Patterns.* New York: Simon and Schuster, 1957.

Severo, Richard, and Lewis Milford. *The Wages of War: When America's Soldiers Came Home— From Valley Forge to Vietnam.* New York: Simon and Schuster, 1989.

Shadish, William, with Lewis Carlson. *When Hell Froze Over: The Memoir of a Korean War Combat Physician Who Spent 1010 Days in a Communist Prison Camp.* New York: iUniverse, 2007.

Showalter, Dennis. "The First Jet War." In *The Cold War: A Military History,* ed. Robert Cowley, 120–37. New York: Random House, 2005.

Sorley, Lewis R. *Honorable Warrior: General Harold K. Johnson and the Ethics of Command.* Lawrence: University of Kansas Press, 1999.

Spurr, Russell. *Enter the Dragon: China's Undeclared War against the US in Korea, 1950–51.* New York: Newmarket, 1998.

Steadfast and Courageous: FEAF Bomber Command and the Air War in Korea, 1950–1953. Washington, DC: Air Force History and Museums Program, 2000.

Stewart, Richard. *Staff Operations: The X Corps in Korea, December 1950.* Fort Leavenworth, Kans.: USGPO, 1991.

Strait, Sandy. *What Happened to American Prisoners of War in Korea?* Unionville, N.Y.: Royal Fireworks, 1997.

Stueck, William W. *The Korean War: An International History.* Princeton, N.J.: Princeton University Press, 1995.

———. *Rethinking the Korean War: A New Diplomatic and Strategic History.* Princeton, N.J.: Princeton University Press, 2002.

Thompson, Wayne. "The Air War over Korea." In *Winged Shield, Winged Sword: A History of the United States Air Force.* Vol. 2, *1950–1997,* ed. Bernard Nalty, 3–52. Washington, DC: USGPO, 1999.

———, and Bernard C. Nalty. *Within Limits: The US Air Force and the Korean War.* Washington, DC: USGPO, 1996.

Thornton, John W., with John W. Thornton Jr. *Believed to Be Alive.* Middlebury, Vt.: Eriksson, 1981.

Toland, John. *In Mortal Combat: Korea, 1950–1953.* New York: Quill, 1991.

Tomedi, Rudy. *No Bugles, No Drums: An Oral History of the Korean War.* New York: Wiley, 1993.

Tonne, Arthur. *The Story of Chaplain Kapaun, Patriot Priest of the Korean Conflict.* Emporia, Kans.: Didde, 1954.

Weintraub, Stanley. *MacArthur's War: Korea and the Undoing of an American Hero.* New York: Free Press, 2000.

White, William Lindsay. *The Captives of Korea: An Unofficial White Paper on the Treatment of War Prisoners.* New York: Scribner's, 1957.

Whiting, Allen S. *China Crosses the Yalu: The Decision to Enter the Korean War.* Santa Monica, Calif.: RAND, 1960.

Zellers, Larry. *In Enemy Hands: A Prisoner in North Korea.* Lexington: University Press of Kentucky, 1991.

Zhang, Xiaoming. *Red Wings over the Yalu: China, the Soviet Union, and the Air War in Korea.* College Station: Texas A&M University Press, 2002.

Government Documents

British Ministry of Defence. *Treatment of British Prisoners of War in Korea.* London. Her Majesty's Stationery Office, 1955.

Central Intelligence Agency. *National Intelligence Estimate.* "Communist Capabilities and Probable Courses of Action in Korea." Washington, DC, July 30, 1952, accessed May 14, 2009, http://www.foia.cia.gov/docs/DOC_0001099167/DOC_0001099167.pdf.

———. *National Intelligence Estimate Number 2.* Washington, DC, November 8, 1950, accessed May 14, 2009, http://www.foia.cia.gov/browse_docs_full.asp.

Court Martial Transcripts (available at the US Army Military History Institute, Carlisle, Penn., uncatalogued):

Maj. Ronald Alley

Maj. Henry Fleming

Pfc. Rothwell B. Floyd

Maj. Ambrose Nugent

Defense Advisory Committee on Prisoners of War, Study Group I, Problem I-1, Consideration of a Uniform Code of Conduct: Course of Action, July 17, 1955 (available at NARA, College Park, Md., RG 341, Decimal File 1942–1954, Box 441), 2–3.

Eighth US Army. "Ambush of Battery C, 99th Field Artillery Battalion, 1st Cavalry Division," June 1951. Korea Command Report, Book 8. Available on microfiche at the Combined Arms Research Library, Fort Leavenworth, Kans.

Headquarters, Department of the Army. Pamphlet 30–101, *Communist Interrogation, Indoctrination, and Exploitation of Prisoners of War*. Washington, DC: HQDA, May 1956.

———. *US Prisoners of War in the Korean Operation: A Study of Their Treatment and Handling by the North Korean Army and the Communist Chinese Forces*. Fort Meade, Md.: Army Security Center, November 1954.

Office of Special Investigations. *USAF Prisoners of War in Korea*. Special Report. Washington, DC: Headquarters, USAF, July 1, 1954.

Office of the Surgeon General. "Report of Conference with Repatriated POW Personnel, Medical Corps, US Army." Department of the Army, Washington, DC, December 1, 1953.

National Archives and Records Administration, College Park, Maryland.

Record Group 153, Records of the Office of the Judge Advocate General (Army).

Record Group 319, Records of the Army Staff.

Record Group 341, Records of Headquarters, US Air Force (Air Staff).

Record Group 407, Records of the Office of the Adjutant General's Office.

Stalin, Joseph. Diplomatic ciphered telegram to Soviet ambassador in Pyongyang, North Korea, July 13, 1953 (Virtual Archive, Cold War International History Project), http://www.wilsoncenter.org/digital-archive.

Transcript, US Senate, 84th Congress, "Hearings on Communist Interrogation, Indoctrination, and Exploitation of American Military and Civilian Prisoners," June 19, 1956. Washington, DC: USGPO.

Transcript of Hearings, US Senate Subcommittee on Korean War Atrocities of the Permanent Subcommittee on Investigations of the Committee on Government Operations, 82nd Congress. Washington, DC: USGPO, December 1–3, 1953.

Periodicals

"Armed Forces: Drawing the Line." *Time* 64 (October 4, 1954): 14.

"Armed Forces: Renaissance in the Ranks." *Time* 86(24) (December 10, 1965). http://www.time.com/time/magazine/article/0,9171,898384,00.html.

"Armed Forces: Shocking Blunder." *Time* 58(22).

"Armed Forces: The Marines Decide." *Time* 63 (May 10, 1954): 19 (accessed February 25, 2010) http://www.time.com/time/magazine/article/0,9171,819821,00.html.

"Batchelor's Story: A Yank Tells How Reds Used Deceit to Woo Him." *San Francisco Chronicle* (January 10, 1954).

Biderman, Albert D. "Briefing of the Defense Advisory Committee on Prisoners of War by the Air Research and Development Command." Pentagon, Washington, DC, June 15, 1955. Available at the National Archives, RG 341, Box 441.

———. "Dangers of Negative Patriotism." *Harvard Business Review* 40(6) (November–December 1962): 93–99.

Camp, Dick. "Korea 1950: 41 Independent Commando, Royal Marines." *Leatherneck* 84(1) (January 2001): 14–21.

"Cracked under Mental Torture, Schwable Says." *Pittsburgh Post-Gazette* (March 12, 1954).

Crane, Conrad C. "Chemical and Biological Warfare during the Korean War: Rhetoric and Reality." *Asian Perspective* 25(3) 2001: 61–83.

Crocker, Harry. "Chinese Intervention in the Korean War." Master's thesis. Baton Rouge: Louisiana State University, 2002.

Cumings, Bruce. "The South Korean Massacre at Taejon: New Evidence on US Responsibility and Coverup." *Asia-Pacific Journal: JapanFocus,* http://japanfocus.org/-Bruce-Cumings /2826.

DeLong, James. Personal memoir, accessed August 3, 2009, http://www.koreanwar-educator .org/memoirs/delong_james/.

Dong-Choon, Kim. "The Truth and Reconciliation Commission of Korea: Uncovering the Hidden Korean War." *Asia-Pacific Journal: JapanFocus,* accessed March 14, 2010, http:// www.japanfocus.org/-Kim-Dong_choon/3314.

Edwards, Archie. Interview by Lynnita Brown, Douglas County Museum, Tuscola, Ill., November 6, 1996. *Korean War Educator: Memoirs,* accessed August 25, 2009, http://www .koreanwar-educator.org/memoirs/edwards_archie/index.htm.

Esensten, Sidney. Address to the Korean War Conference, Smithsonian Institute, Washington, DC, October 30, 2000 (copy of the text provided to the author by Dr. Esensten).

"First POW Ship Arrives Tomorrow." *San Francisco Call-Bulletin* (August 21, 1953). Available at the Army Heritage and Education Center, Carlisle, Penn., "Ralph Pearson Papers," Box 4.

Free Health Encyclopedia. S.v. beriberi. http://www.faqs.org/health/topics/40/Beriberi.html.

Gallery, Daniel V., RAdm. "We Can Battle the Brainwashers." *Saturday Evening Post* (January 22, 1955), 98; qtd. in Lech, *Broken Soldiers,* 238.

Hanley, Charles J., and Jae-Soon Chang. "US Okayed Korean War Massacres." *Associated Press* (July 5, 2008).

"Hostile Captives Had a Rough Time." *New York Times* (August 12, 1953).

"In the Hills behind the Athletes the Men Who Died Were Buried." *Washington Daily News* (November 10, 1953).

Interim Report for Commander, Air University on Communist Exploitation of USAF POWs in Korea. Submitted by the Intelligence Research Division, Officer Education Research Laboratory, Air Research and Development Command, Maxwell Air Force Base, Alabama, July 1954. Available at the National Archives, RG 341, Box 440.

Karsten, Peter. "The American Democratic Citizen Soldier: Triumph or Disaster?" *Military Affairs* 30(1) (Spring 1966): 34–40.

Kennedy, Edwin L. "Force Protection Implications: TF Smith and the 24th Infantry Division, Korea 1950." *Military Review* 81(3) (May–June 2001): 87 92.

"Korean War Casualties." Accessed March 6, 2011, http://www.abmc.gov/search/koreanwar .php.

Lewis, Fulton, Jr. "Mayer Case Slated for Muzzle Probe." *Saint Petersburg Independent* (October 3, 1961), 4A.

Lindner, Ernest A. "Scotch and Soda II." Accessed September 26, 2009, http://452ndbomb wing.org/articles/elindner.html.

Loosbrock, John F. "POWs: What Do We Owe Them?" *Air Force* (June 1954).

Matray, James I. "Revisiting Korea: Exposing Myths of the Forgotten War, Part 2." *Prologue Magazine* 34(2) (Summer 2002), accessed February 15, 2010, http://www.archives.gov /publications/prologue/2002/summer/korean-myths-2.html#f35.

McCarthy, Capt. Robert, USMC. "Fox Hill." *Marine Corps Gazette* 37(3) (March 1953).

Montgomery, Bruce. "Clemency OK'd for Ex-POW in Area." *Sarasota Herald Tribune* (August 30, 1978).

"The Nation: Defeat." *Time* 56(24) (December 11, 1950), accessed August 18, 2009http:// www.time.com/time/magazine/article/0,9171,814029,00.html.

"National Affairs: Handwashing." *Time* 63(5) (February 1, 1954).

O'Neill, Mark. "Soviet Involvement in the Korean War: A New View from the Soviet-Era Archives." *Organization of American Historians Magazine of History* 14(3) (Spring 2000): 20–24. http://magazine.oah.org/issues/143/#articles.

"POW/MIA Recognition Day: Background." *POW/MIA Freedom Fighters,* accessed March 6, 2011, http://www.powmiaff.org/recognitionday.html.

Prugh, Maj. George S., Jr. "Justice for All RECAP-Ks." *Army Combat Forces Journal* 6 (November 1955).

Rogaski, Ruth. "Nature, Annihilation, and Modernity: China's Korean War Germ-Warfare Experience Reconsidered." *Journal of Asian Studies* 61(2) (May 2002): 381–415.

Rosenthal, A. M. "Committee Ends Germ War Study." *New York Times* (November 1, 1953), 1:3 (available on microfiche).

Ruhl, Robert K. "The Code of Conduct." *Airman* 22(6) (May 1978): 63–66.

Schein, Edgar H., et al. "Statement: To Set Straight the Korean POW Episode." *Harvard Business Review* 40 (November 1962).

Shen, Zhihua, and Li, Danhui. *After Leaning to One Side: China and Its Allies in the Cold War.* Washington, DC: Woodrow Wilson Center Press, 2011.

Trembath, Richard. "A Lie Based on a Delusion: Australia's Role in the Korean War Germ Warfare Controversy." *Social Alternatives* 23(2) (3rd Quarter, 2004): 6–10.

"Toth v. Quarles: A Death in Korea." Accessed March 9, 2010, http://law.jrank.org/pages /25481/Toth-v-Quarles-Death-In-Korea.html.

Wenzl, Roy. "The Miracle of Father Kapaun, Part 1." *Wichita Eagle* (December 6, 2009), accessed February 20, 2011, http://www.kansas.com/2009/12/06/1085753/father-emil-ka paun-in-korea-kapaun.html#ixzz1EYd8drXU.

Wubben, H. H. "American Prisoners of War in Korea: A Second Look at the 'Something New in History' Theme." *American Quarterly* (Spring 1970): 3–19.

Interviews by the Author

Addington, Harold, Virginia, September 2008.

Chapman, Jack, Saint Louis, Mo., July 29, 2009; August 2009.

Dixon, Ralph, US Army (Ret.), Lawrenceville, Ind., July 20 and 25, 2001.

Dobbs, Barney, Riverside, Calif., August 2001.

Doerty, Walter J., Jr., USAF (Ret.), San Diego, Calif., Aug. 26, 2006, Denver, Colo., September 2008.

Dowe, Raymond Michael, La Jolla, Calif., August 2, 2001.

Esensten, Sidney, Minneapolis, Minn., July 31, 2001.

Estabrook, Shorty, Chicago, Ill., August 2010.

Hedlund, Harry, USAF (Ret.), Palm Springs, Calif., August 1, 2001.

Hotze, Rev. John, Denver, Colo., September 2008; October 2009.

King, Marvin, San Diego, Calif., September 2006.

McAbee, Filmore, East Yarmouth, Mass., May 2002.

Mellin, Raymond, West Point, N.Y., September 27, 2005.

O'Brien, Phillip, DPMO analyst, Alexandria, Va., March 2004; March 2005; September 2008; July 23, 2009; November 12, 2009; January 2010.

Oldewage, Daniel, Santa Ana, Calif., August 1, 2001.

Peterson, Phillip, Riverside, Calif., August 2001.

Reid, Brig., Gen. Ernest (USMC Rct.), Twentynine Palms, Calif., August 1, 2001.

Roach, Paul, San Diego, Calif., September 2006; Lawrence, Kans., October 2009; October 2010.

Shapiro, Aaron, telephone interview, November 7, 2001.

Taft, Lt. Col. Leonard, USMC (Ret.), Continental, Ohio, July 18, 2001.

Wood, Robert, Multiple phone interviews, Nov. 22, 2009; August 2009–March 2011.

Miscellaneous

Wang, Shui-Bo. *They Chose China*. Icarus Films, 2006.

Index